AN AMERICAN RACER

AN AMERICAN RACER

Bobby Marshman and the Indianapolis 500

By Michael Argetsinger

PHOTO EDITORS: JOE FREEMAN & GORDON KIRBY

RACEMAKER press

To Samuel Williams Argetsinger
With love to my remarkable brother, always

Published by Racemaker Press
39 Church Street
Boston, MA 02116
(617) 723-6533
www.racemaker.com

ISBN: 978-0-9998754-1-4

Library of Congress Control Number: 2019937767

Book design by Blue Design
(www.bluedes.com)

Printed in the USA

THIS PAGE: Bobby prepares to run Homeyer's Konstant
Hot midget in an ARDC race at Allentown Fairgrounds
in 1960. (EASTERN AUTO RACING MUSEUM)

Marshman Hopes to Take Early Lead And Stay in Front in 'Horne Race

By ED BROOMHEAD

Bobby Marshman, who sat in the middle of the first row in the recent Indianapolis '500, will be gunning for his first victory on a mile dirt track next Sunday when he competes in the 100-mile National championship race for Indianapolis cars and drivers at the Langhorne Speedway.

The 28-year-old driver from Pottstown, Pa., who led the Indianapolis race for 29 laps before his Lotus-Ford developed an oil leak in the late stages, forcing him to retire, turned in the second best time to win the front row with 156.867 clocking.

Marshman, who was co-rookie of the year in 1961, has made having remarkable success in the past several seasons against the nation's top drivers, and this year had an excellent chance of copping the "biggest" one of them all at Indy, only for the oil leak.

Got Start in 1955

He is the son of George Marshman, a midget car driver himself for 21 years, who now operates the Hatfield Speedway, where Bobby got his first taste of speed in 1955. Since then, driving practically every type racing machine, he has gained national prominence.

Marshman will be remembered by his followers for the ex-

BOBBY MARSHMAN

cellent display of driving in last year's race.

Piloting the Ecno-Car Special (Sunday he will be driving for Lindsey Hopkins) he led most of the race, but the terrific pace of the field forced him into the pits with complete exhaustion, and he relinquished his car to Don Branson, who failed to qualify for Agajanian-Willard Special. Branson lost valuable time in the pits, but managed to grab off fifth position at the finish. Bobby hopes to take the lead and hold it this year.

Marshman will be facing practically the same field he faced at Indianapolis, including A. J. Foyt, winner of the last three Nationals at the 'Horne, who will be driving the Ansted-Thompson Special in the United States Auto Club's sanctioned race.

Others will be Branson, former mile and 100-mile record holder Lloyd Ruby, third place finisher at Indy; Bobby Grim, Jud Larson, Chuck Hulse and Arnie Knepper.

• • •

The seventh running of the George Fonder Memorial race will be staged at the Hatfield Speedway Saturday with a 50-lap feature for midget cars on the ¼ mile clay track. A percentage of the profits will go to the Fonder estate.

• • •

Midget cars, which proved successful at the John F. Kennedy Stadium, two weeks ago, will return Friday night in a series of events, capped by a 25-lap feature. Tony Bonadies, who thrilled the 10,000 opening night fans, will be back, along with Ed Dutch Schaefer, Len Duncan, the defending champion, and Tony Romit. There will also be a 25-lap race for sports cars.

• • •

The Atco Drag Strip will again be in action today featur-

CONTENTS

PART 4: A REVOLUTIONARY ERA

MARSHMAN

Acknowledgments

Traditionally, the writer's spouse is given the final thank-you in the acknowledgments, but in this case, my wife, Lee Green, deserves to be front and center. She has been as active and vital a contributor to this book as anyone on these pages. She takes first place in my gratitude, for her commitment to the completion of my book, and for her positive, consistent encouragement in all of my research and writing.

Brian Brown has been essential to the creation of this book—in fact, it is fair to say that I could not have written it without his long-standing help, his vast knowledge of the subject, his generosity in sharing his expertise, his library, his time, and his unflagging enthusiasm. He has been an extraordinary colleague in this entire endeavor, and the final book is a tribute to his devotion to Bobby Marshman. He is a true friend. Many thanks as well to Brian's brother Bruce A. Brown II, his mother, Gerri Brown, and his father, Keith Brown.

I cannot say enough about the help and support I received from Kevin Hughey, International Motor Racing Research Center historian, who has gone out of his way to make this book possible. The Watkins Glen Research Center is an invaluable resource for any motor racing enthusiast, and Kevin is the man who makes it so. He should shine in any discussion of this book because he contributed so much. His input was consistently noteworthy, insightful, and central to my research and writing.

Bob Marshman's wife, Janet Marshman Woolley, has been key to the writing of this book. Janet provided the author with a deeper understanding of Bob, as well as an insider's view of the era when she and Bob were immersed in his racing career. I am indebted to Janet and her son, Andrew Woolley, for their time and their help.

Bobby Marshman's sisters, Elaine Marshman Heist and LaRone Marshman Innes, as well as Elaine's husband, Richard Heist, have been fully on board with this biography. They have been genuinely helpful, and diligent, in finding photos and other materials that would shed light on Bobby's life, a life very dear to this close family group.

Some of the greatest input for this book came from Bill Reiff and his wife, Florence Reiff, who shared their memories generously. Bill was one of Bobby's earliest friends, and a lifelong one.

Another important source in my research was Bill Marvel, also a longtime friend of Bobby's. Not only did Bill recognize Bobby's budding future early on, but he has remained one of the most faithful commentators on his career.

OPPOSITE: An exhausted Bobby shakes hands with relief driver Chuck Arnold in the victory circle after winning the 300-mile USAC/ARDC midget battle at Trenton. (RMA/ CHERNOKAL)

I was also privileged to talk to Bobby's good friend, Merit O'Neal, who greatly colored and described the early years of a youthful and teenage Bobby Marshman. Merit was a rich contributor to my research, sharing stories, photos, and other materials.

Bill Blatt, too, knew Bobby from his earliest years. My interview with Bill would have been memorable in any case, but it took on an added dimension when Bill told me that between the time we set up our interview and the day it took place, he officially (or medically) "died" from a cardiac event, but thankfully, was revived at the hospital. "I guess I was meant to talk to you about Bobby," he said. I'm grateful that he did.

The International Motor Racing Research Center at Watkins Glen has been the single most valuable institutional resource for this undertaking. In addition to Kevin Hughey's invaluable assistance, noted above, I am especially indebted to Glenda Gephart, director of communications for the Center. Glenda has done so much for the author and for this book. I am grateful for her professional acumen and enthusiastic support, qualities that she brings to her job at the Center every day.

I'm also grateful to other staff members at the Racing Research Center. I thank historian Bill Green for his indefatigable help and lifelong friendship, and I thank Samantha Baker and Kip Zeiter for their assistance.

My special thanks go to my brother, J. C. Argetsinger, president of the Center, who completed several interviews for this book.

At the Indianapolis Motor Speedway Museum, I benefited from the legendary knowledge of senior curator Donald Davidson, who provided invaluable information that would have been available nowhere else. Mary Ellen Loscar, director of the Museum's photo lab, was also a tremendous resource and help.

BELOW: Bobby and Lindsey Hopkins's team pose for their official 1963 Indy 500 qualifying shot. (RMA/IMS)

Another important institutional resource was the Eastern Museum of Motor Racing in York Springs, Pennsylvania, headed by the impressive Lynn Paxton. All present took an interest in Bobby's story.

My thanks also go to family members. I am grateful to my niece Sarah Smith for contributing her exceptional editing skills to this manuscript. Thanks also to my nephew, Arthur Smith, for his editorial comments. And my brother Philip "Duke" Argetsinger was an ongoing source of encouragement. In fact, my entire family was a tremendous support: my mother Jean Argetsinger; my sisters, Louise Kanaley and Getchie Argetsinger; my brothers, Peter Argetsinger and Sam Argetsinger;

ABOVE: Bobby finished second to Foyt at Sacramento at the end of October, 1964. Here he battles with Parnelli Jones and Rodger Ward as they lap Chuck Booth. (RMA/REEL)

my brother-in-law, Tom Kanaley; my niece, Amy Argetsinger; and my sisters-in-law, Joan Argetsinger and Sjoukje Scipstra.

Many more people deserve my thanks for their special help with this book. They include: Cary Agajanian, Auctions America, Hugh Baird, Ray Bell, Jacques Dresang, Rick Dresang, Don File, Jeff File, Bob Fleck, Dr. Gary "AJ" George, Walter Goodwin, Duke Henning, Ron Hills, Karl Kainhofer, Peter Luongo, Larry Neuzel, Rob Neuzel, Beth Nichols, Al Ribskis, Joe Scalzo, Bill Siegfriedt, Doug Stokes, and Mike Thomsen.

Finally, I would like to thank my sister, Marya Smith, who took on the task of bringing my book to completion when I was no longer able to do so. My gratitude also goes to my brother, Robert Argetsinger, for working closely with Marya to complete this book project.

—*Michael Reynolds Argetsinger*
Chicago, Illinois, July 2015

Publisher's Preface

Although not generally recognized in these days of diminished interest in open-wheel motor racing, America has produced some of the greatest racing drivers the world has ever seen. Dan Gurney, A. J. Foyt, Mario Andretti, Phil Hill, and Rick Mears come quickly to mind. These men and a host of others began racing when it was a truly lethal occupation. During the immediate post–World War II period, driver safety was not considered important enough to warrant taking even the simplest precautions. Racing fatalities were simply regarded as part of the game, and many drivers paid the ultimate price as a result.

It was within this world that young Bobby Marshman, the subject of Michael Argetsinger's excellent book, strove to reach the top rung of American motorsport, the United States Auto Club–sanctioned National Championship, and, above all else, the Indianapolis 500. After a few years in the "minor leagues" of local sprint car and midget racing, Bob joined the rarefied upper ranks of skilled professional drivers, proving that he possessed extraordinary talent and the competitive spirit necessary to be a winner.

Competing against such legendary greats as Rodger Ward, A. J. Foyt, Parnelli Jones, Jim Hurtubise, Len Sutton, Lloyd Ruby, and many others, Bobby Marshman raced stock cars, midgets, sprint cars, championship cars, and so-called Indy roadsters on the numerous famous dirt and paved ovals that made up the National Championship in the 1960s. Always in contention, he quickly earned a reputation as the potential winner in any car or race he entered.

Tragically, Bobby's brilliant career came to an early end following a practice accident at the close of the 1964 season. While testing his Lotus-built rear-engine champ racer at the one-mile track in Phoenix, Arizona, his car crashed heavily into the concrete barriers and burst into flames, becoming a gasoline-fed inferno. Marshman was able to exit the car, but not before he received lethal third-degree burns over most of his body.

Bobby died a few days later, and his passing shocked the entire racing community, all of whom knew that fire was one of the most dreaded potential risks that drivers faced. During his short career, Marshman, like others, had driven virtually unprotected by such modern safety devices as seat belts, strengthened cockpits, roll cages, self-sealing fuel tanks, and Nomex fire-resistant clothing. It was a lesson that took much too long to penetrate the thinking of racing officials, and even the drivers themselves, and the lack of these precautions cut short the career of one of America's greatest rising stars. Bobby Marshman's amazing story unfolds in this volume, which Racemaker Press is most proud to publish.

—*Joseph S. Freeman, May 2019*

OPPOSITE: Bobby proudly displays his pace-setting 160-plus-mph lap speeds at Indianapolis in 1964. (RMA/KNOX)

PART 1 / A RACING FAMILY

Prologue

He was a race car driver with an on-track competitive instinct that belied a gentle nature. On this famous day, the pure racer side of the man was in full evidence. Spotting a great rival on the track ahead, he was determined to not merely pass him, but to lap him.

Bobby Marshman was leading the 1964 Indianapolis 500 in spectacular fashion. Since taking the lead by passing Jim Clark on lap 7, Marshman had steadily—even relentlessly—opened a lead of nearly thirty seconds. Now, as he neared the fortieth lap, in his sight running in fourth place was A. J. Foyt. The prospect of lapping America's most successful race driver was irresistible. Despite a lead of nearly half a lap over Clark, his closest pursuer, and despite his chief mechanic Jack Beckley waving the pit board to implore him to slow down, Bobby continued to charge. He said later he could imagine Foyt "nearly jumping out of his seat" when he was lapped.

All the potential and promise of the young driver was being fully realized that day as he seemed to effortlessly drive away from the great drivers assembled for the forty-eighth running of the world's most famous auto race. He had been the fastest driver at the Speedway throughout the month of May, only to lose pole position at the last moment to Scotland's Jim Clark, the reigning World Champion and lead driver for Team Lotus. Marshman's Lindsey Hopkins–owned, Ford-powered, Pure Firebird Special Lotus 29 had been one of the Team Lotus cars the previous year.

Team Lotus represented the new technology that was revolutionizing the Indianapolis 500. Clark nearly won the race the previous year, and now the British team had returned with their newly designed Lotus 34 Ford. Rear-engine technology was the biggest—and most controversial—new development roiling the status quo. At the same time, Ford was mounting a challenge to the Offenhauser front engine that had dominated the 500 since 1934, and powered every winner since 1947. And new tire and lubricant manufacturers were giving longtime industry favorites a run for their money. It was a time of change and great excitement at the Speedway.

Most Indianapolis fans remained sentimentally loyal to the familiar roadsters that had dominated the Speedway for more than a decade. The roar of the crowd showed a clear preference for drivers who had come up through traditional American oval tracks—and an unmistakable coolness toward the Europeans and other drivers from road racing.

But Bobby Marshman was "one of theirs," and the 300,000-strong crowd loved him. He may have been driving one of the much-hated rear-engine "funny cars," but the Speedway was rocking with excitement as the greatly admired young man from Pennsylvania proved, lap by lap, that it didn't take a Formula One driver to make the rear-engine chassis fly.

Now Bobby paid the price for his determination to make a statement to A. J. Foyt. Johnny White in the Demler Special roadster was running in thirteenth position and Bobby closed in to lap him a second time. Bobby was carrying maximum momentum as he adjusted his speed and took his line down on the low side through turn one. Suddenly he was upon White, who had moved low on the track in front of him. To pass on the right promised disaster, as Bobby was carrying far too much speed in the Lotus to take the turn off-line. Braking hard was an equally poor option in the situation, and he was left with the sole alternative to move even lower in the turn, dipping below the white line to complete the safe pass.

In moments the calamity was clear. Below the white line the banked track joined the flat apron. The angle of entry was just sharp enough for the undercarriage of the Lotus to brush against the apron and tear out the oil and water plugs. Bobby Marshman rolled to a stop in the infield area inside turn four, out of the race. And he knew it was completely his fault.

In the heat of battle on the racetrack, the moment is everything: no time for reflection. Now, as he walked slowly away from the Pure Firebird Lotus, his race over, the full impact of the day fell upon him. But it wasn't the lost race that occupied his mind. Bobby Marshman's thoughts were with two friends who had died that morning in a calamitous multiple-car accident on the second lap that also injured several other drivers.

Eddie Sachs and Dave MacDonald had died in the crash that created the worst inferno the Speedway had ever experienced and stopped the race after the second lap. The veteran Sachs, a crowd favorite, had been an important mentor to Bobby Marshman. MacDonald, a rookie at the 500, was a new acquaintance. After the catastrophe, Bobby and the other remaining drivers had waited for an hour and fifty minutes, with great sadness and anxiety, for the race to restart.

Out of respect for the drivers who had perished, the enormous 500 crowd had remained largely subdued through the long wait. It had taken Bobby Marshman's dominating dash to the front to bring fans to their feet and to refocus the Speedway on the race at hand.

For Marshman to suddenly be sidelined was no doubt painful. He had earned great respect in his field: He was acknowledged as one of the sport's great rising talents, and acclaimed for his speed and finesse. This day's lapse seemed out of character with his reputation for judgment and coolness under pressure.

Having grown up in a racing family, Bobby Marshman understood the profession like few others. A preternatural maturity, developed by watching his father race and working at his father's racetracks as a young man, had marked him from the beginning of his own racing career. He was fast, dependable, with a practiced eye and craft beyond his years. He knew when to charge and he knew when to be patient.

The desire to lap Foyt was likely only part of the answer as to why, on this day, he ignored both the pit boards urging him to "cool it" and his own well-honed instincts. It is the rarest of days when a race driver finds himself in the right car, at the right moment, and in complete command. When it comes on Memorial Day, in the world's greatest race, the temptation to stay at that exalted level of performance may simply be far too great for any true competitor to ignore.

Bobby Marshman could now only watch from the sidelines as Jim Clark assumed the lead—and then fell out with a broken suspension. Next in the lead was his friend Parnelli Jones, with whom he had shared Rookie of the Year honors just three years earlier. Parnelli, winner the previous year, headed the field before a pit stop fire forced him out of the race as well.

And finally the 500, on the Speedway's most tragic day, was over. The winner: A. J. Foyt.

The race was fought by competitors Bobby Marshman liked and respected, and even after a day so clouded with tragedy, these drivers had every intention of returning to compete to the finish together in 1965.

Chapter 1
The Perky

Perkiomen Creek, known as the Perky to those within its valley, crosses the southeastern Pennsylvania counties of Berks, Lehigh, and Montgomery. Along some of its bends, it finds industrial backdrops that evoke the economic powerhouse that was once the greater Philadelphia area; along others, closer to historic Valley Forge, the landscape remains rustic. As the Perky flows briskly into the Schuylkill River, its breadth is sufficient to accommodate sizable islands.

It was on the banks of the Perky, in the tiny Montgomery County village of Yerkes, that George Robert "Bobby" Marshman was born into a close-knit extended family that made up much of the town's population.

ABOVE LEFT: George Marshman in his youth with younger brother Stanley, mother Julia, and father William. (MARSHMAN FAMILY COLLECTION)

ABOVE RIGHT: When George started racing he used some assumed names, including Kilroy, to keep his racing a secret from his parents. (MARSHMAN FAMILY COLLECTION)

Throughout Bobby Marshman's career, journalists consistently referred to his hometown as Pottstown. He was variously "the Pottstown Flyer," "the Pottstown Flash," and variations on the theme. In truth he never lived in Pottstown, a small city of roughly twenty thousand inhabitants located northeast of Philadelphia. Bobby grew up in the rustic village of Yerkes, some ten miles from Pottstown.

Outside of its major industrial cities, Pennsylvania was, well into the twentieth century, composed of strong clan-like regions. Yerkes, southeast of Pottstown, was just two miles south of Collegeville and a like distance north of the village of Graderford. Yerkes was populated almost exclusively by the Landes family, who had migrated there from Indian Valley in Lancaster County three generations earlier. Family patriarch Jacob Landes (Bobby Marshman's great-grandfather) had developed a novel method of processing grain, and came to Yerkes on the Perkiomen at the advent of the twentieth century. He built the mill and the Mill House, and brothers and cousins soon joined him and

developed businesses that supported the agriculture of Montgomery County. Jacob's sons Isaiah and Milton, based on a personal friendship with Henry Ford, established a Ford dealership: I. C. and I. M. Landes Motors in nearby Collegeville is recalled in family lore as the second Ford dealership established in America.

Bobby's mother, Evelyn Landes, was born into this prominent, and warmly cohesive, family on December 1, 1909. Evelyn, known to her friends as Evie, was the daughter of Isaiah Cassel Landes and Katherine Raudenbush Landes. Growing up in Yerkes, she enjoyed a loving and protected environment. She was close to her brother Floyd and her sisters, Cora and Miriam.

Bobby's father, George Marshman, was born on July 25, 1911, in Norristown, Pennsylvania, county seat of Montgomery County, to William Miller Marshman, a railroad conductor, and his wife, Julia Anderson Marshman. George had an older brother Phares, a younger brother Stanley, and a third brother James, who died in infancy.

Graduating from Norristown High School in 1930, George's determination to race cars quickly put an end to any thoughts of going to college (a life choice replicated by his only son twenty-four years later). When he began racing that year he initially used assumed names, including "Kilroy" and "Joe Riley," to deceive his parents.

Although they were both born in Montgomery County, Bobby's parents did not meet until they were young adults. The two were a study in contrasts: George Marshman ran on high octane, and Evelyn Landes maintained a calm presence throughout her life. Perhaps proving the proverbial notion that opposites attract, the two made a successful match.

Chapter 2
Evelyn and George

When George Marshman and Evelyn Landes met, there was a car involved. George had taken a job at I. C. and I. M. Landes Motors and one day Evie, the boss's daughter, drove up in a splashy new Ford convertible. George came out to pump gas with no idea who the customer was. When she said "Fill it up and charge it," he went inside to find out if it was okay if this woman charged her gas purchase. That was their first meeting, and a romance ensued.

Evelyn was taken with the handsome young man who had energy in abundance and more than a dash of charm. George was equally charmed by the gentle, lovely young woman, and they fell in love. George was already a race driver when the two met, and although racing was foreign to Evie's upbringing, she immediately embraced her future husband's passion, and soon became immersed in every aspect of the racing life.

After their wedding on June 20, 1933, George and Evelyn Marshman rented an apartment in nearby Collegeville, where they were living when their first child, Elaine, was born on October 1,

1934. Soon after, the young couple moved to the Mill House, built by Evelyn's grandfather when he first came to Yerkes, and they merged easily into the Landes family. The Mill House was on the east side of the Perkiomen, and it was there they brought home their second child, George Robert Marshman (called both Bob and Bobby from the outset), born September 24, 1936, at Montgomery Hospital in Norristown.

In 1942 George and Evelyn moved from the Mill House to take up residence next to her parents in the Landes double house just across the bridge on the west bank. The large, prominently located home easily accommodated two families, with the Marshmans occupying 109 Yerkes Road, the wing closest to the creek. The family was completed with the birth of daughter LaRone on January 15, 1944.

Elaine Marshman Heist, Bobby's older sister, remembered the warmth and security of the close family relationships: "One winter the village lost electricity in a storm and everyone in Yerkes came to our house because George, my father, had hooked up a generator. The women all cooked together, making spaghetti. It was great fun and all family. How wonderful it was to grow up in that atmosphere."

Along with this sense of safety and solidity, the young family was also immersed in an unpredictable world, thanks to George's vocation. Racing was a perilous undertaking in the 1930s, and, as in any era of the sport, demanded a commitment that often put a strain on family life. George was fortunate to be married to Evelyn, a woman both loyal and understanding.

"My mother was a sweetheart—she never got angry. I don't think she ever raised her voice," said Bobby's younger sister, LaRone Marshman Innes. "My dad was not the easiest man to live with, but she was just a very quiet, pleasant person. She was definitely the glue in the family; she kept everything together. I think Bobby had a lot of my mom's attributes."

The advent of World War II had a stabilizing effect on George and Evelyn's family life. Racing in America was banned, and, taking a position as a civilian machine designer for Welding Engineers, attached to the Army Signal Corps, George found himself in a steady, reliable job. He thrived in the position, and during that period was granted eleven US patents. He started a side business, Roto-Beam, from a design he patented privately, a rotating beacon light for school buses, which he maintained for many years. (He also shed blood for his country. His right thumb was lost when it slipped into a machine.)

Lack of a college education never intimidated George Marshman. His wartime achievements qualified him for membership in the Society of Automotive Engineers, and he took pride in being the only member of the Philadelphia chapter of the society without a college degree. When George moved his family into 109 Yerkes Road, he built his workshop between the house and the Perkiomen. The shop became the core of George Marshman Racing Enterprises. As racing reemerged after the war, there was a demand for new race cars, and George had the experience and talent to build—and drive—them.

OPPOSITE TOP LEFT: George's mechanical prowess was fully displayed by this two-man, Offy-powered Indy car that he built himself. (MARSHMAN FAMILY COLLECTION)

OPPOSITE TOP RIGHT: A delighted George at the wheel of his self-built Indy car. (MARSHMAN FAMILY COLLECTION)

OPPOSITE BOTTOM: George Marshman beams for the camera from the cockpit of his sprint car. (RMA / WALTER CHERNOKAL)

Personable and persuasive, George was involved in many ancillary activities related to automobile racing. He was a driver double in the racing movies *To Please a Lady* in 1950 and *Roar of the Crowd* in 1953. Later, he served as a consultant on *The Great Race*, in 1965.

"[Bobby's father] was an innovative person who could fix or build anything," remembered Bill Reiff, Bobby's closest boyhood friend. "He always had ideas for projects and patents on things he designed, including a supercharger for flathead Ford engines."

Bobby's sister Elaine also spoke of their father George: "He was almost like a sculptor when he was building midgets or sprint cars. The way he could form the sheet metal into the cowl—you would hear a bang, and a bang, and a bang as he made it fit."

The senior Marshman had numerous opportunities to race at Indianapolis, but later explained to Ed Broomhead of Philadelphia's *Evening Bulletin* that he was a "money driver." Spending the entire month of May at the Speedway meant missing many races where he could earn cash. "I wanted to

pick up money while the other drivers were sweating it out for positions," George said.

The magic of the 500 annually attracted top drivers from grassroots tracks around the country, many of whom roamed the pits and garages of the Speedway for the entire month of May, looking for a ride. The top teams already had their established drivers, and there were never enough cars to satisfy the hopes of all. George cannily chose not to be part of it.

After George drove his last race in 1950, he became a race promoter and track owner. His background enabled him to ease relationships between drivers and race management. When Eastern midget racing was on the wane in 1955, he brought the American Automobile Association (AAA) and the American Racing Drivers Club (ARDC) together to present jointly sponsored events. (The United States Auto Club [USAC] replaced the AAA in the arrangement in 1956.) George was an innovative and pragmatic promoter, willing to do what it took to bring a crowd through the gates, and his wife, Evelyn, remained an essential partner in his endeavors.

Chapter 3
"I Got to Run the Trains"

"I never saw him get angry," LaRone said of her big brother, Bobby. "He had a lot of patience with his little sister, and a great sense of humor."

LaRone was eight years younger than Bob and thought he walked on water. He had train tracks that he put up every Christmas season. "He was always willing to share anything he had. I never remember him being any other way," said LaRone. "The train was a big thing—and he would let his little sister run it. I got to run the trains."

Bob Marshman's fascination with trains was no surprise. His paternal grandfather had been a railroad conductor, and next door to the Marshman/Landes home was the Yerkes stop on the Perkiomen branch of the Reading Railroad.

"We had entertainment by watching the trains, and used them as an alarm clock," said Bob's boyhood pal, Bill Reiff. "The train went down at a quarter to seven in the morning and it went up again at eight-thirty; down again at four in the afternoon, and up at six-thirty."

Bobby started his education at H. K. Boyer Elementary School. When the family crossed the bridge to live on the west side of Yerkes, the move placed him in a different school district. Along with new best friend Bill Reiff, he attended Upper Providence Consolidated School from grades two through eight, until 1950.

Bob and Bill were among the only six boys living in Yerkes. Theirs was a youth of traditional rural pastimes. "We skipped stones and swam in the Perky in the summer, skated on it in the winter, and fished in it all year," said Reiff. "We also played a lot on the island in the middle of the creek."

When Bob was ten years old, a dog—just a pup—followed him home. The Marshmans tried to find the owners, but "Shep" quickly became part of the family and he and Bob became inseparable. Shep was, by all accounts, a remarkable dog. The stories are numerous of Shep's abilities, and Bob's older sister told one that was famous in Yerkes.

"There was a grocery store in a building that also housed the post office across the street from our house in Yerkes," said Elaine. "They kept the dog food down low in the back of the store. Shep would go in and get his own food—and it had to be Kennel Ration. The clerk would mark it down and Shep would head home with the food. He had his own account there."

As Boy Scouts between the ages of twelve and fourteen, Bill and Bob were in the Flying Eagle Patrol, Trappe Troop No. 1, which camped in northern Montgomery County at Camp Delmont. "There were about seven or eight of us in the patrol," Reiff recollected. "One year, Magnus Stender, who was the committee chairman for the Boy Scouts, organized a contest with a prize, sponsored by his company, of a trip to New York City for the patrol that got the most projects done. Our patrol got the most points. We went to the Statue of Liberty and from there to Jack Dempsey's restaurant for our afternoon lunch."

Other than participation in Boy Scouts, most diversions were self-generated. An unused chicken coop in the Marshmans' backyard gave Bobby and his friends an idea. "There were about six boys in the Yerkes area—we all hung out together," said Reiff. "We got the idea one day that we would have a carnival. We gutted the chicken house and cleaned it all up. We had half a dozen games, or more, that you would have in a carnival. On one wall, we had balloons that you could throw darts at. We didn't have any games of chance. People paid five cents to play the games; we had toys or gimmicks as prizes. It took us the whole summer to fix it up and do that. It was great."

Skating in the winter on the Perky was a favorite activity for the boys in Yerkes. "One year Bob wanted nothing else for Christmas but ice skates," recalled older sister Elaine. "Mom got him skates." Skating expeditions included erecting a tent for the occasion and roasting apples.

Elaine remembered the joy of sledding on the steep country roads. "Pop would drag us on our sleds behind his car up Hopwood Road when it had snowed, and we would then fly down the road on our sleds. He'd hook us up again and drag us back up the road. They didn't cinder or salt the roads in those days."

Bob was always a good student and received excellent grades. Along with his friend Bill he participated in the limited sports program available at the school. "In our seventh- and eighth-grade years we had a school basketball team organized by one of the teachers," Reiff recollected. "Although Bobby and I were not among the starters on those teams, we had fun and we got to play a lot."

After graduation from eighth grade, Bob went on to Collegeville Trappe High School where, as a freshman and sophomore, he played on the junior varsity football and baseball teams. "My best sport there was benchwarmer for the baseball team," Bob later told Red McCarthy of the *Norristown Times Herald*.

OPPOSITE: Bob looking good in his teen years. (MARSHMAN FAMILY COLLECTION)

By the time his junior year came around, the sixteen-year-old's priorities had changed. Saving money to buy a car took precedence over school sports. Bob, along with his friend Bill, worked at the Atlantic gas station in Collegeville. It was a local environment where the boys knew virtually every customer who came in. In addition to pumping gas and changing oil, they also greased cars and washed them.

"Girls were always after Bobby," said his sister Elaine. "He was good-looking, with good manners, and he treated everyone nicely."

Bob Fleck, a friend from Collegeville, was nearly two years older than Bobby and had a driver's license. "Bobby met a girl named Joan who lived in Broomall, Pennsylvania," recalled Fleck. "Broomall was a fair distance away, but Bobby's dad George would loan us his 1941 Ford sedan and I would drive Bobby to Broomall to see Joan. We had a lot of fun in that car. We would come up behind a car and Bobby would lean out the window with a megaphone he had and make a noise through it that sounded like a siren. The Ford was gray and looked the part, so people would pull over and we would drive by, laughing."

Bob was a junior in high school when he met Janet Fairlie, a pretty sophomore cheerleader at Schwenksville High School. Her friend Deanna Vogt was dating Donnie Heffentragger, a friend of Bob's. One evening Deanna and Donnie drove Janet to Collegeville and introduced her to Bob, who was driving his father's jet-black Lincoln Cosmopolitan.

"He was funny," said Janet. "He had his father's new Lincoln, and he thought it was so cool. He took me for a ride around Collegeville and back again."

Janet was the leading scorer on the Schwenksville girls' basketball team. Soon after meeting Bob, she spotted him at halftime at one of her games. Later he phoned to say that he couldn't understand why the newspaper said she was the high scorer in the game when she hadn't made a basket the entire time he was there. "His being there had rattled me," Janet remembered. "My coach kept me in the game because I was really hot in the first half. It was enough to make me high scorer."

Bob and Janet initially double-dated with Deanna and Donnie, and soon became inseparable. "He was always 'Bob' to me," said Janet. "His parents and his sisters always called him Bobby, but his friends mostly called him Bob. I was introduced to him as Bob, and always called him that.

"I soon became aware of Bob's values," continued Janet. "He was brought up primarily by his mother, who was raised in the Mennonite tradition. He didn't drink and he didn't smoke—not that he thought it made him any better, or any less. It just wasn't him; he didn't want to do it, and he didn't. He cared deeply for the welfare of others, and had fine qualities of loyalty and honesty when I met him, and he kept those values to the end of his life."

Chapter 4
Growing Up in a Racing Family

George Marshman remained active as a driver after the war, and early in 1949 he made his annual southern trip for the Tangerine Circuit midget series. On the drive south George and Evie brought the family along in their 1949 DeSoto sedan. As in previous years, for the six weeks or so they were in Tampa, Florida, Bob was enrolled in Woodrow Wilson Junior High School. Years later when Bob was making his first appearance at the Daytona 500, he made an informal side trip to visit the school on Swann Avenue.

Five-year-old LaRone was too young for school, and older sister Elaine had stayed home in Yerkes with her aunt Cora. "Elaine would not go to a race in those days," recalled family friend Merit O'Neal. "Bobby, if there was a race, he would be there; if he had to hold on to the bumper or ride in the trunk, he was going."

At the 1949 State Fair races on the half-mile dirt track at Plant Field in Tampa, George crashed

when fellow competitor Red Bowen spun in front of him. His injuries required surgery to his knee, the bones secured by several screws. It was a tough start to what would be his most successful season as a driver. He recovered sufficiently to win eight races, and captured the 1949 AAA Eastern Division Circuit Midget championship. A limp from the Plant Field accident remained with him the rest of his life.

"I remember the year when Dad had his wreck in Florida," said LaRone. "I must have been five. I remember a little tiny trailer with Dad, his leg in a cast."

For twelve-year-old Bob, seeing his father injured had a stronger emotional effect. Earlier in the week, before the accident, George had taken Bob out on the Plant Field racetrack in the family DeSoto. George had Bob steer for a while and then slowed the car enough to jump out, telling his son to "drive on." George was not a crasher and, up to that time, Bob had never seen his father seriously hurt. To now see his indestructible father, who could leap from moving cars, laid up, is remembered by family as a contemplative time for Bob.

The crash at Tampa was a potential setback for George in more ways than his status on the racetrack. An accomplished builder of race car chassis, bodies, engines, and running gear, George did a great deal of business on these Southern trips, building and delivering race cars and repairing others. He sent Evie to the local Railway Express Agency to pick up expected parts. It proved a crucial visit, as it brought into the family a young man who would make an important impression on young Bob Marshman.

Evie walked into the agency and explained that she was looking for parts arriving from Allentown, Pennsylvania. The man she talked to was Merit O'Neal, who promised he would keep an eye out for the parts, and asked for the family's phone number. When Evie returned for the parts, one of the crates would not fit in her car for the trip to Lakeland. Merit had a van and said, "I'll take them over there for you. I know where the place is."

Merit did deliver the crate that evening, and refused to take any money when Evie tried to pay him. The next day Evie returned to the agency and told him that her husband wanted to meet him. "I had seen George race and had heard that he was a pretty nice guy, but not to mess with him," said O'Neal, who was in his early twenties when he met the Marshmans.

When Merit arrived later that day he made enough of an impression that George invited him to come to Pennsylvania as a guest of the family and see what he termed "real race cars." It was the beginning of a close relationship. That year, and again in 1950, the young man from Florida spent the entire month of July living with the Marshmans and attending every race with the family.

"I knew Bobby Marshman when he was twelve or thirteen years old, and he was a nice, clean-living kid," remembered O'Neal. "He didn't curse or smoke or drink; in fact, he never did any of those things his entire life. He was a good person, and a kind one, and he stayed that way. I remember an instance years later when a fellow driver at a track had a bad day and didn't have the money to get

OPPOSITE: A brightly dressed starter waves the flag for a midget race at Sanatoga Speedway. (KEVIN HUGHEY COLLECTION)

home. Bob gave him [money] to get home and be able to come back the next week to race."

George gave up driving race cars at the end of 1950 and entered a new chapter of his life as a race promoter. He eventually owned Sanatoga Speedway and Hatfield Speedway, and held the promotional rights to racing at Municipal Stadium in Philadelphia.

Sanatoga, just a mile or two from Yerkes, was a good fit for George Marshman's vision. The fifth-of-a-mile paved track had first opened in 1939 and had primarily featured midget racing. Under George Marshman's leadership and the sanction of the Pottstown Stock Car Racing Club, the main show was his All-Star stock car series. Three-quarter midget races were also frequently on the schedule.

"Early in 1951 George called me and said he was retiring from active racing and was taking over Sanatoga Speedway and needed somebody to manage the track," said O'Neal. "He asked me to come up and spend the season from March to November. George wanted someone on the premises, so I lived in his trailer inside the track at no cost. I made more money in eight months than I would have made working for the railroad for two years. It worked out pretty good." Young, single, and open to a new adventure, O'Neal was also practical, and clearly valued in his Florida job. He was able to arrange to come back to the Railway Express Agency when he was ready, without losing his seniority there.

D. Kennard Smith of Philadelphia was George's silent partner at Sanatoga and looked after the office. He is remembered as personable and capable. Along with his wife, Patty, Smith would arrive on race day in his green MG TD. Jerry Hartenstein worked in the office and handled the money and the payouts to the drivers. "George surrounded himself with individuals who knew what they were doing," said O'Neal. "All of them were nice people."

The day O'Neal arrived by train in Philadelphia, he and the now-fourteen-year-old Bobby Marshman went to the track to put together a work crew. Bobby recruited his friend Bill Reiff to the team. Bill recalled that Merit was a natural leader. "He was a very neat person, he walked like a soldier, and everything he did had a purpose. He was organized and on time, and you did it now, the right way. He was just a wonderful boss."

RIGHT: A Hatfield Speedway program cover from 1950. (KEVIN HUGHEY COLLECTION)

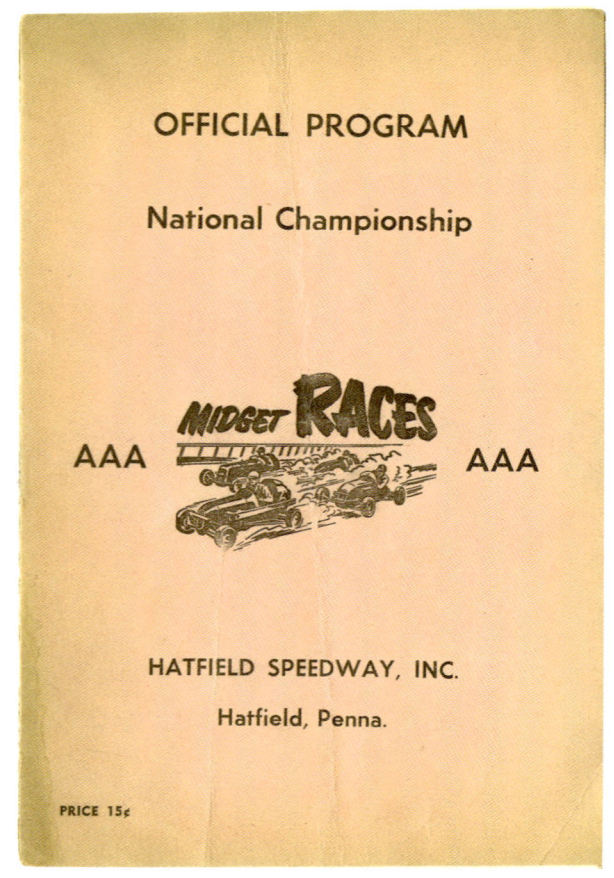

OFFICIAL PROGRAM

National Championship

MIDGET RACES

AAA   AAA

HATFIELD SPEEDWAY, INC.

Hatfield, Penna.

PRICE 15¢

ABOVE: George at the wheel of the Mohr midget at Williams Grove Speedway. (RMA/ CHERNOKAL)

Merit recollected an unexpected trip back to Tampa with Bobby Marshman as his traveling companion. "After I had been in Pennsylvania a few days, George decided I needed my car, which was in Florida. He gave me $200 for expenses and took Bobby and me to the train. He also bought us two pastrami sandwiches and sent us to Tampa. I think everyone on the train knew we had pastrami. The next day we got my car and Patches, my Welsh springer spaniel, and, with little sleep, headed for Sanatoga. This was a long trip with no interstate highways yet in operation."

George was a showman who knew the importance of creating excitement for the fans. Reiff revealed, "At Sanatoga the fences were put up with one nail per board, so if someone hit it, it was spectacular. We would then fix it up." O'Neal added that George understood the importance of making a strong presentation. "He would say, 'When everything is done and you're ready to run, I want you to whitewash that track barrier.'"

Lou Salamone, a friend of the Marshmans from the area, paid tribute to Sanatoga and Bobby Marshman in his Internet article on Sanatoga history. "My dad and I went there many, many times. Short, tight track with a lot of bumping, pushing, and shoving to pass. The epitome of 'rubbin' is racing.' At Sanatoga, if you did not rub, you did not pass. Bobby was my idol—as nice and down-to-earth a person as there ever was!"

George was pragmatic by nature, as described by daughter Elaine. "I played the records at the track, usually marches. Pop would look over the grandstands and if it was full of people, we wouldn't play the National Anthem. He was afraid that if everyone stood up at the same time the stands would collapse. It was a family secret."

Working with Merit O'Neal at the track during the week had an added benefit for Bob Marshman, who was too young for a driver's license, but eager to drive. "Most every day when we got through with our work Bobby would drive my 1950 Ford around," O'Neal recalled. "He would drive around the track eight or ten times, and up around the parking lot. I had told him: no spinning the tires and no sliding around the corner. He was always very respectful of my cars."

George, Bobby, and Merit would frequently attend other races that did not conflict with Sanatoga. They were standing together in turn one at Williams Grove on July 29, 1951, when Walt Brown was killed after rolling over in the No. 64 Jack Robbins Special champ car. That day came to be known in racing as Black Sunday. Cecil Green and Bill Mackey were killed the same day at

Winchester Speedway in Indiana.

O'Neal returned for the 1952 season. Impressed from the outset by the Northern girls, the handsome, well-mannered Southerner found himself popular with many of the young women of southeastern Pennsylvania. Bill Blatt, another friend of Bobby Marshman's who was on the work crew at the racetrack, had two attractive sisters. Bobby dated younger sister Iona at one time, but it was older sister Joanne Blatt who captured Merit O'Neal's heart. They were married on November 1 at the end of the season, and he took her home to Florida.

The O'Neals' first child was born on July 31, 1953. When Merit called George early in the year to say that Joanne was expecting, he was told that his job in Pennsylvania would be waiting for him the next year. When Merit, Joanne, and baby Linda returned in March 1954 there was a new challenge at hand. George had purchased Hatfield Speedway and obtained promotional rights to racing at Philadelphia's Municipal Stadium. Merit was now track manager at all three tracks run

under Marshman Enterprises—a job that came with a house for the O'Neals on the corner of the Hatfield property.

Hatfield, twenty-five miles from Sanatoga, had been a racetrack since 1922. It would take a great deal of work to remake Hatfield to suit George Marshman's plans. He renamed it Hatfield-Hi Speedway and started transforming the half-mile dirt track into a high-banked paved track, achieved by cutting ten feet out of the infield and bulldozing the dirt up. "We had a steamroller to pack the surface and a leaning wheel grader," O'Neal explained. "We also moved the grandstands back and added more seating in the fourth turn. George Hudick and Russ Bell, who were also race drivers, were the welders."

According to his daughter Elaine, George Marshman pursued an innovative method for raising the necessary capital for this project. "He approached the concession people and convinced them that he could bring a crowd and they could sell their products, but he needed a little front money," related Elaine. "That's the way he got his financing. Pop paid them back and they did good business. It was very successful, really a partnership."

The racing operation was a family business, and everyone was involved. Evelyn coordinated the refreshment sales. Elaine's husband, Dick Heist, handled much of the public address duties. Heist was well suited to the task as a popular local radio broadcaster renowned for his melodious and unmistakable voice. Bobby started his own snow-cone stand at age thirteen, buying an ice-making machine and enlisting Bill Reiff's help.

ABOVE: Evelyn and George Marshman raised Bobby in an environment fully immersed in racing. (MARSHMAN FAMILY COLLECTION)

"Bobby was entrepreneurial," remembered Reiff. "When he started out, he bought the cherry and lime and root beer, et cetera, to dump on the ice. That was getting expensive, so he bought concentrate from the grocery store, added sugar, and mixed his own flavors to put on the snow cones. But at twelve and thirteen years old, you're not necessarily too good at that kind of thing, and when we cooked the first batch, the sugary juice ran over the stove and we had pretty much of a mess. When his mother came home, she wasn't too happy, but we got better at it, and from then on, we cooked the syrups."

When Bob was fifteen, he opened a novelty stand at the track and Bill managed the snow-cone operation for him. Bob obtained the novelty items, such as pens, toys, and memorabilia, through the mail from Frank Smith of Patterson, New Jersey, who was also a well-known race photographer. "Bobby's novelty shop made money and his snow-cone operation made money," said Reiff. "Like George, whatever he did was done right, and he did a good job with it."

Bobby also sold his trinkets at Pitman Raceway in New Jersey, where Johnny Favinger was the flagger. A former race driver and contemporary of Bobby's father, Favinger was also the flagger at the three Marshman tracks. After school on Friday, Bill Reiff would rush to Favinger's home in Collegeville and sit on his doorstep to be certain of a ride to Pitman. On the way, Favinger would also pick up Bob and his boxes of novelties and folding tables for display. Bob and Bill would sit behind the Pitman grandstands and sell their goods.

When Bob obtained his driver's license, he bought a 1937 Ford two-door with a flat back trunk. George soon persuaded him to sell the vehicle and purchase a new 1953 Ford Courier. The Courier was billed as a sedan delivery car. It had no rear windows but was somewhat distinct from a delivery van.

"George was always big on 'doing the show,' and had to have something exciting," remembered Bill Reiff. "Bobby's blue Ford Courier was set up like an ambulance with a light on the top and a stretcher in the back. Whenever there was a crash, George wanted the light to go on in the ambulance—the whole bit. Rocky Ewing crashed one night at Sanatoga. They loaded Rocky in the ambulance, shut the door, and Bobby came out through the pits, came around the corner, and the door flew open—the stretcher wasn't fixed inside—and Rocky came flying out of the ambulance. He got more tore up sliding across the gravel road than he had crashing his car. They gathered him up, put him back in the ambulance, and took him to the Pottstown Hospital."

The Courier "ambulance" gave Bob a new role at the tracks. He turned his novelty business over to Bill and became the ambulance driver at all three tracks his father was promoting. Friday nights were at Philadelphia Municipal Stadium, Sanatoga ran on Saturday evenings, and Hatfield on Sunday. During the week, Bob and Bill still worked under Merit O'Neal, preparing the tracks for the next show. They also promoted the races, posting advertising signs up and down nearby highways. Any property owner who agreed to take a sign and display it received two tickets to the next race.

Chapter 5
"We Never Met Paul Whiteman"

The All-American Soap Box Derby has been beloved since 1934 when it was first run in Dayton, Ohio. It found a permanent home in Akron, Ohio, the following year where it has prospered and become an American institution. Qualifying races for the Derby are held in cities around America, and the local champions go forward to the finals in Akron.

Long before the sport became institutionalized at Akron, boys and girls made cars from whatever materials were available. There was a time when soap and other dry goods were shipped to retailers in wooden crates, generally described as "soap boxes." Once they were emptied, soap boxes were ready-at-hand structures to attach wheels to, and the name endured. On the simplest level, kids push one another around the backyard. A ride down the family driveway quickly progresses to finding a hill where gravity adds to the fun. Once a second soap box car appears in the neighborhood, a race becomes inevitable.

In 1949, at age thirteen, Bob Marshman decided to build a soap box racer to official specifications

and go for the big show in Akron. Friends Jackie Fitzcharles and Bob Strunk in nearby Grand View Park shared his ambition, and the boys together built three cars and entered the qualifying races at Phoenixville, Pennsylvania. Test runs were made on the hill in Yerkes near the Marshman home. Bob's car was white with green trim. The brake was a two-by-four with a spring attached, mounted in the center of the car and activated by the driver pushing it with his foot. The drag of the two-by-four on the road surface accomplished the stopping power.

Bob Marshman and friends Jackie and Bob competed at Phoenixville but did not qualify for the finals in Akron.

In 1951, when Bob was fifteen, he discovered that the Vaseys, garage- and gas station–owning brothers in nearby Eagleville, Pennsylvania, had a stock car they could be persuaded to sell—an orange 1934 Ford Victoria that had been built up for stock car racing. "It was pretty used up," recalled Bill Reiff. "I think Bobby paid about $25 for it. He never raced it; we used it as a toy."

The boys got the Ford running in George's garage, and Bob would drive it up and down the road. "There weren't many cops then, and Yerkes was kind of out of the way," recalled Reiff. "There was a place you could make a nice wide U-turn and come back again. He would drive it up and down the road until he broke it and then we had to go fix it. Bobby would take us all for rides."

George had purchased two Crosley coupes for a never-realized design idea. "Those Crosleys sat out for a while, so Bobby and I used to drive them around by the shop and up and down the hill in Yerkes," related Reiff. "There were cinders on top of the blacktop, and Bob would toss the car around and spin it out down at the bottom of the hill. One day, he got a better start up there than usual, and he tipped it over on its side." If they worried about the older Marshman's anger, they needn't have. "When George heard about it," Reiff added, "he had a laugh, and that was all there was to it."

It was in 1952 that Bob, frustrated at being too young to race, decided he would become a race-car owner. He was aware of a midget that George had repaired after driver Johnny Ackerman from Phoenixville had been killed in it. Bob purchased it from the current owner and launched a career in racing. Years later, when Bobby Marshman was an established star, he told the story to *Miami Herald* sports editor Tom McEwen. "At age sixteen, I was a midget owner. I hired drivers to race for me. I say 'hired,'" Bobby said, laughing. "I begged them. I only paid $50 for the car and had rain drains for exhausts. Anyway, I was in the business."

One prominent driver who raced Bob's midget was Mike San Felice, who did it as a favor to the young man. San Felice from Norristown, Pennsylvania, was a friend of the family, and later, as an influential sprint car driver in the United Racing Club (URC), became a mentor to Bobby in his earliest racing. Like George, San Felice had lost a thumb. When the men would meet they would greet one another as "thumbless bastards."

The boys first made money from the race car business in 1953—though it wasn't as car owners, or even as drivers in the traditional sense. Rather, Bob and Bill were hired to drive Paul Whiteman's cars to designated racetracks to be used for demos by older drivers. Band leader Whiteman, an important figure in American music before the war, had a passion for fast cars. The "King of Jazz" was well connected in the racing industry, and Bill France had appointed him national director of the sports-car division of the National Association for Stock Car Auto Racing (NASCAR). It was Whiteman's own Jaguar XK-120 coupe that Al Keller famously drove to victory in the NASCAR race at Linden Airport in New Jersey in 1954, still the only sports car to win a race in NASCAR's premier series.

The efforts of Paul Whiteman and Bill France to make inroads in sports-car racing resulted in the formation of the Sports Car Owners and Drivers Association (SCODA). SCODA sanctioned a sports-car series with races on both dirt and paved oval tracks in the Northeast and into the Carolinas, beginning in 1954, and continuing through the end of the decade.

Before SCODA was established, race promoter Red Crise, a close friend of George Marshman's, was working with Whiteman to popularize sports cars at oval tracks. It was through the connection with Crise that Bob and Bill put many miles on Whiteman's pair of Jaguar XK-120 coupes during the spring and summer of 1953.

"After school on Friday and again on Saturday, throughout the 1953 racing season, we would go in Bobby's car up to Walnutport, Pennsylvania, where Whiteman's cars were kept, and be told where we were to take them," related Reiff. "The cars were dull orange, and one had a number four [this was the car that Keller won in at Linden, New Jersey] on it, and the other was number six. Bobby would be sent to one racetrack and I would go to another. When we got there, we would take the muffler off and a local hotshot would run a bunch of hot laps in the car so the people in the stands could see the cars run. Most of the tracks were in Jersey or Pennsylvania. After the exhibition, we would replace the muffler, take the Jaguars back to Walnutport, and drive home together.

"We never met Paul Whiteman."

ABOVE: Reeding Speedway, a half-mile track, was a hotbed of midget and sprint car racing through the 1950s, '60s, and '70s. (KEVIN HUGHEY COLLECTION)

Chapter 6
Lure of the Brickyard

Bobby Marshman was sixteen the year he first saw the Indianapolis Speedway in person—albeit from the grandstands. That year, 1953, he and Bill decided they needed to witness the Indianapolis 500. They were completing their junior year in high school. Bob's grandmother, Katherine Landes, lived next door in the big house in Yerkes, and was happy to loan the boys her 1952 four-door sedan Ford. It was a 700-mile trip each way, and Bob and Bill shared the driving.

Bill Reiff remembered the adventure.

"We were advised to go into Indianapolis, park the car, get everything we needed, and then get on the train to the Speedway. It was good advice, because we never had to worry about parking. We bought some cheese and bread and, sure enough, the train dropped us right at the racetrack. Our tickets were in the first couple of chair seat rows right by the wall, in C Section. It turned out to be right across from the pit of Carl Scarborough, who died of heat exhaustion that day, although we

BELOW: Johnny Thomson at the wheel of Doug Stearley's sprint car. (RMA/CHERNOKAL)

didn't know it at the time. The heat was terrible.

"Then we took the train back to town and drove home, sharing the driving. We never did sleep anywhere except for catnaps here and there. I remember on the way back, I was driving and Bobby was sleeping in the back, and all of a sudden he woke up and said, 'Hey, you better pull over to the side of the road.' Here I was at two o'clock in the morning on the middle of the railroad tracks in Zanesville, Ohio, and I was asleep. The car was still running."

Bob and Bill's plans to return to Indianapolis for the 1954 500 were quashed by their parents because the travel days would have meant missing their own high school graduation. They stayed home for the ceremony. And as for Memorial Day, instead of Indiana, they were at Reading Fairgrounds to help George with a stock car race he was promoting. George, whose All-Star Drivers series ran primarily at his fifth-of-a-mile Sanatoga track, had rented the half-mile Reading Fairgrounds for a big holiday event. Emulating Indianapolis, George had the thirty-three cars lined up for the start in eleven rows of three cars each. Bob drove the ambulance and Bill ran the novelty stand in front of the grandstand.

"It was a fast racetrack," recalled Reiff. "After five or six laps, somebody blew a water hose going down the backstretch before the third turn, making the track slippery. Cars started spinning and crashing.

"A car went down the hill on the inside of the bank and stuck against the telephone pole and the next car went on top of him. Both cars burst into flames. One driver was halfway out through the windshield and there he burnt up, and the other fellow burned up in the seat. Bobby took one of them to the hospital, and I sat there at Reading Fairgrounds until seven or eight o'clock at night with this box of novelties, waiting for a ride home."

The drivers who died were brothers-in-law, Bobby Roland and Ringy Lloyd.

Bob's sister LaRone told race historian Brian Brown that the experience of transporting the burned driver to the hospital had a profound effect on her brother, making him very aware that fire is the driver's greatest enemy.

Long before Bobby Marshman climbed into his first race car, he had been exposed to the harsh realities of the sport. Like most drivers, he seldom lingered on the potential for injury in a race car. He did, however, fear the thing most drivers did, though they rarely spoke of it: fire. George Maxwell, chief of the Speedway police at Sanatoga, remembered Bobby as "a very nice fellow. As good a driver as he was, he was likable. You could talk to him. I remember him telling me that his great fear was

burning up in a race car. He used to wear asbestos underclothes and everything."

Although Bobby saw the dark side of racing from early in his life, the family business also gave him a real connection to his race heroes. In the summer of 1954, Merit O'Neal and his crew were busy preparing the Hatfield-Hi Speedway track for the July 11 AAA sprint car race when George announced they were opening the track early that day for a private test for Sam Traylor's team. Traylor, from Allentown, Pennsylvania, where his father was a prominent hotel owner, was a well-known race car owner and entrant. Traylor and his crew arrived early with three sprint cars for drivers Al Keller, Johnny Thomson, and Wally Campbell, plus a midget for Charlie Musselman to try. The track was closed to anyone else until the normal opening time late that afternoon.

After the long day at the track, the team went off together for dinner and took Bobby along as a special treat. Johnny Thomson was a great hero to Bob. In fact, when Bobby started his own racing career, he sought to emulate Thomson's style and approach to the profession. Al Keller, who also became an influential figure in Bob's life, rented an airplane at a local airport for the sole purpose of giving Bobby a ride. Keller, an excellent pilot, showed off some special moves. While Bobby was likely appreciative of the interest taken by Keller, he never developed a taste for small airplanes.

Chapter 7
"Laverne Just Happened to Have a Hitch on His Truck"

The desire to drive race cars is powerful for those who feel the call. For Bobby Marshman, it was irresistible. Racing demands a commitment that can require tough choices and personal sacrifice. The willingness to set aside virtually everything to make one's racing possible was something Bob understood and embraced without question.

Ten years into his racing career, Bob shared an insight on his beginnings as a race driver with Jep Cadou Jr. of the *Indianapolis Star*. "My dad didn't actually say he wanted me to be a race driver, but he did tell me where to buy a race car."

After high school graduation, Bobby sold the Ford "ambulance" to his father. Combining those funds with money earned working at the racetrack and at a job washing trucks for the Jones Motor Company in nearby Spring City, he purchased a new 1954 Ford Club Coupe. It was a handsome automobile—dark blue on the bottom, white on top, and powered by Ford's just-introduced overhead-valve V8—and he added a Belond dual exhaust. Bob loved the car.

So did Janet, still his girlfriend. "I drove it a lot because Bob was always working," she recalled. "I loved that sound. When Bob would drive by, my father thought the house was going to fall in."

The romance between Bob and Janet remained strong. The Marshmans had been quick to take Janet into the bosom of the family. "I was fifteen when I started to date Bob," said Janet. "I would be at the house for dinners, for Christmas, and other family events. His cousins became my cousins—his aunts became my aunts. Bob's mother and others belonged to the same women's social club that my mother belonged to."

Bob had graduated from Collegeville Trappe in June of 1954 and turned eighteen in September. Determined to be a racing driver as soon as possible, Bob resisted all suggestions that he consider entering college in favor of working and saving money to launch his career.

"Bob was frugal, but not quite tight," said Janet.

By the spring of 1955, Bobby Marshman had a plan.

"One day Bob said we were going to drive up to the weekly Gilbertsville Sale. The Sale was a huge outdoor market, a local institution. We were in that gorgeous '54 Ford that I loved," recalled Janet. "I couldn't imagine why Bob's friend Laverne 'Jake' Miller was following behind us in his truck. Bob gave some excuse that Laverne was going to do this or that."

When revealed, the purpose of the trip came as more than a surprise to Janet. Once in Gilbertsville, Bob sought out Les Weidner, whose meat market was a prominent feature of the weekly event. The butcher Weidner owned a sprint car that George Marshman had built in 1950. An even-up swap of Bob's Ford for the white No. 99 sprint car was quickly completed. The No. 99 car had won a URC championship, and, more recently, had been raced by Les's brother Mel, also known as Schnick.

The swap of the new Ford coupe for the race car included the throw-in of a historic trailer, originally owned by Indianapolis legend Ted Horn. Horn's death on October 10, 1948, at Du Quoin, Illinois, was national news. The AAA National Champion in 1946, 1947, and 1948, Horn was praised by Frank "Jim" Lunt in *National Speed Sport News* (*NSSN*) as a man "who will live on in the annals of all-time racing greats."

"I was mad," Janet recalled, still expressing shock nearly sixty years after the transaction. "He traded his beautiful new Ford for this race car. He kept saying to me, 'It has my dad's chassis.' And Laverne, of course, just happened to have a hitch on his truck."

Bob approached his friend Bill Blatt to ask if he would help him look after the race car. Blatt had recently started an auto repair business in the basement of his home in Mont Clare, just three miles from Yerkes. He had become part of the track crew at Hatfield by invitation of his brother-in-law, Merit O'Neal, and he and Bob had quickly become friends. Stationed at the fourth turn, Blatt often would ride along with Bob in the ambulance, taking injured drivers to the hospital. Before meeting the Marshmans, Bill Blatt had become hooked on racing when he attended a race at Williams Grove Speedway near Mechanicsburg, Pennsylvania, right after the war. He briefly raced stock cars at Sanatoga and Municipal Stadium.

Blatt had a Cessna 150. The first time he took Bob up in the plane he did some fancy maneuvers, including a power stall. "That was the only time I ever saw Bobby shaken up," Blatt recalled. "We had a good laugh about it when we landed.

"Of course Bobby didn't have a car to tow with because he had sold his street car," said Blatt. "I had a '39 Ford two-door sedan that we towed with. We would work on the car in my basement garage, and sometimes we would work on it over at his dad's shop in Yerkes. Most of the time, though, I kept it at my house."

The red-accented white No. 99 sprint car, with its flathead six-cylinder Ford motor, was not the latest or most competitive car in the URC field, but it was good enough for Bobby to learn his craft and gain valuable seat time in a very competitive sprint car series.

"I was a little sad when Bobby went into racing because, growing up, we had seen a lot of people who didn't make it," said his sister Elaine. "I felt he had so much potential to do other things, and I hoped he would go to college to get away from the racing.

"I wasn't surprised, though. He knew a lot about it, having grown up around it, so it didn't seem unusual. To me though, it was sad. But he loved it."

Charlie Franks was a friend of Bob's who also had the bug to go racing. Charlie bought a red, Dodge-powered sprint car which Bill Blatt painted white and added a No. 66. Bob and Charlie would tow to the races together and would park the two white cars, with numbers 99 and 66 in red, together and help each other out. Although Charlie raced his car occasionally, it was often piloted by veteran race driver Mike San Felice.

Charlie's father owned and ran Franks Funeral Home in Collegeville. Charlie had a small workshop behind the funeral home where the group of friends would gather to help work on the race car. On more than one occasion, someone had to come out during a funeral service and tell the guys to turn the radio down or stop revving an engine.

Bob purchased a 1936 Packard 7-Passenger sedan, well remembered as the source of a great deal of fun. Although the Packard was not used as a tow car, Bill Reiff explained how the elegant but massive vehicle contributed to the racing effort.

"URC guys had to haul their own fuel to the races; there were no fuel trucks at the races. Tommy Hinnershitz sold fuel, and we would go up to his place in Oley and buy a barrel of fuel and put it in the back seat of that Packard to bring back and then transfer the fuel to five-gallon cans. Bobby would drive up Route 73 on our way back from Oley, and if we had ever hit anything, we'd have been in orbit."

Janet spoke of the Packard with little reverence. "I had to go to my senior prom in high school in that limousine, and it looked like a hearse to me. Oh, I hated it. But that was just the way it was.

"He [Bobby] was so intent on the racing, and this was what he wanted to do, and I know he wanted me to be on the same page," said Janet. "And even though I was, I didn't like the feeling of being taken for granted, although I seldom did feel that way. He was a considerate man."

PART 2 / LAUNCHING A CAREER

Chapter 8
"The Best of Good Luck to You"

Joining the URC at age eighteen, Bobby Marshman launched his career as a race driver. The URC was a well-regarded, second-tier sprint car series, founded in 1947. It was fiercely independent of oval racing's major sanctioning body, the AAA. In fact, the URC prohibited its members from competing without permission in any other series. The club raced primarily at tracks in the Northeast, with occasional end-of-season visits to Southern venues on the Eastern Seaboard.

URC rules did not permit pure race engines, and that largely meant it was a non-Offenhauser series. Engines powering the URC sprint cars were conversions of standard American motors from Ford, Chevrolet, Dodge, Mercury, Cadillac, GMC, and others.

Bobby's first chance to run his race car seriously came in late April 1955 at Lancaster Speedway outside of Landisville, Pennsylvania. It was at a test day where he was able to get laps under his belt and gain a feel for the car—the beginning of a learning curve. Along for the occasion were Bill Blatt, Bill Reiff, Jake Miller, and Bill Pengally. Well remembered is the Chinese restaurant where they consumed Chinese waffles at 60 cents a plate. It was also on this trip that the team first observed Bill Blatt's affection for shoofly pie. This standard of Amish and Mennonite cooking was loved by all, but apparently Blatt had a special attraction to the tasty dessert. "I would always order shoofly pie whenever we were in central Pennsylvania, and Bobby started calling me Shooey, and it just stuck," said Blatt.

The URC attempted to launch its season at Shangri-La Speedway in Owego, New York, on April 1, but the twenty-seven drivers on hand were disappointed when rain washed out the event in the middle of the third heat. Bobby wasn't ready for that race, but he and his team were in Owego on the rain date of May 8, hoping to field a car in the race. Once again, the weather spoiled the competition. His debut race, and that of the URC season, was delayed another week.

The Reading Fairgrounds' fast half-mile dirt track became the first outing for the No. 99 car on May 15. The Pennsylvania track had opened in 1924 and was one of the most prominent race venues in the East, with a rich history and tradition. The URC was proud to have a show there, as for many years, Reading had been an AAA-only track. The race produced the largest field of sprint cars ever seen at Reading, bolstering URC officials' hopes that their appearance, in front of the entire Eastern motor racing media, and with Chris Economaki as public address announcer, would open the doors

to run at other major fairground tracks. H. W. Luther in *NSSN* called it "the greatest day in the history of the URC," and in the same paper, Jim Lunt wrote that "URC stands on the threshold of becoming the mightiest independent big car group in the history of Eastern racing."

Media described the Reading track condition as "very greasy," and many drivers spun. Bobby was one of them. As Bob later told journalist Red McCarthy for the *Norristown Times Herald*, "That put me in the racing game. In my first race at Reading I set some kind of a record. I spun out—only going about twenty miles an hour. And that's hard to do."

He later elaborated to the Associated Press (AP): "My first race was spectacular," laughed Bobby. "It was in Reading, twenty miles from my home—it was a big deal—they made a big promo fuss that Marshman was going to make his debut. I beat one guy qualifying—I think he was running on only three cylinders. Since I was a new driver I had to start last, even if I did beat the man. We came down for the green flag—I was forty yards behind the last car. I charged into the first turn at twenty miles per hour and spun out on the fourth turn."

Bobby made it a little farther than he modestly claimed later: It was on the third lap of the ten-lap third heat that Bobby spun coming off the fourth turn, without damage. The race was not halted. Bobby jumped out of the race car, ran to the top of the track, and climbed on top of the fence to get out of harm's way.

As a result of the spin, Bobby was not placed in the heat and ran in the semi, where again he failed to finish. Not qualifying for the seventeen-car feature, Bob ran in the consolation race (the consi), and, for the third time that day, was out of the race before the finish. "Leadfoot" Lou Johnson of Wilmington, Delaware, won the feature, in the Anfuso-Campbell-entered Highway Auto Body car. It was the first of Johnson's four victories on his way to becoming the 1955 URC champion.

Despite a less-than-stellar debut, Bobby had caught the eye of the motoring press. In his *NSSN* column, H. W. Luther wrote, "Young Bobby Marshman, son of the Hatfield Speedway owner, cut his eyeteeth in a sprinter on Sunday, and under Daddy George's teaching may well become as expert a wheel twister as his famous father. The best of good luck to you, Bobby."

Chapter 9
"We Were Greenhorn Kids" (1955)

Although the URC held two events over Memorial Day weekend, with a race on May 29 at Canandaigua, New York, and one on May 30 at Pitman, New Jersey, Bob gave them both a pass in favor of a second trip to Indianapolis. With friends Laverne Miller, Bill Reiff, and Bailey Hunsburger sharing the driving in Hunsburger's 1955 Plymouth, they made the pilgrimage to the 500.

The race Bob and friends saw in 1955 is remembered for the death of the incomparable Bill Vukovich. Vukovich had demonstrated his mastery of the Speedway by winning the 500 in 1953 and 1954—after losing what seemed a certain win in 1952, when his steering failed with eight laps to go—and was well in the lead in 1955 when he became involved in a multiple-car wreck on lap 57. Vukovich, in his car, somersaulted out of the Speedway. The burning wreckage was quickly put out, but Vuky never knew it. He died instantly of a skull fracture and other injuries. Bob Sweikert drove on to win the race.

It was a terrible time for automobile racing, as just a week later, Alberto Ascari, World Champion in 1952 and 1953, was killed at Monza, Italy, on a test day. On June 11, the racing world was further shaken by a horrendous crash at Le Mans, France, in the famous twenty-four-hour race of endurance. The incident claimed the lives of eighty-two spectators and Mercedes-Benz driver Pierre Levegh, injuring hundreds more.

The tragedy at Le Mans had profound effects on racing around the world, with many events canceled and racing banned entirely in some countries. In America, the AAA quickly departed the racing scene. The AAA had long been the recognized arbiter of the sport in the United States, and was the American delegate to the world governing body in Paris, France, the Fédération Internationale de l'Automobile (FIA). The AAA had for several years been in the process of redefining itself and its mission to become an insurance and travel organization, but it was the calamitous crash at Le Mans, on the heels of the deaths of Vukovich and Ascari, that solidified the decision for the prestigious sanctioning body to leave motorsport.

In July, the organization stated its intent to ". . . disassociate completely from all types of auto-mobile racing." By the end of the year, the AAA was no longer a leader in—or even affiliated with—motorsport.

The news had an enormous impact on automobile racing in America, resulting in leadership changes for the sport. The United States Auto Club (USAC) was formed shortly after to fill the void as the premier sanctioning body in oval track racing, and briefly assumed the position as American representative to the FIA. This was considered preemptory by other sanctioning bodies, and led to the creation of the Automobile Competition Club of the United States (ACCUS); its directors were representatives of each of the major sanctioning bodies at that time: USAC, NASCAR, the Sports Car Club of America (SCCA), and the National Hot Rod Association (NHRA).

While these developments in his sport were underway, Bobby continued racing. After his visit to Indianapolis, Bobby's next outing was on June 18 at the Orange County Fair Speedway in Middletown, New York, in the Central Hudson Valley. It was a night race, and Bobby, in the No. 99 sprint car, scored a fourth-place finish in the second heat.

Bill Blatt described the fledgling team's challenges: "I didn't know much about setting up a race car, and neither did Bobby. His dad would help us out a little. George taught me how to weld and showed me a lot about different race cars. We didn't have quick-change rears. The shocks were adjustable, but they were nothing but stock Ford shocks. I would set the timing on it with the magneto, but, really, we were greenhorn kids, and went out there for the fun—we just grew up together and learned things together."

On the fourth of July, the No. 99 team was in Altamont, New York, for a URC event on the half-mile dirt Altamont Speedway. Although Bobby did not figure in the final results, he impressed a reporter sufficiently in qualifying to enthuse that Bobby "lashed around the oval in amazing style to come up with third best."

Between qualifying and the race, the Altamont crowd was treated to an appearance by a legend. Frances Helen "Fay" Taylour turned exhibition laps in Bob's No. 99 car and was reported in *NSSN* to have "impressed all present with her speed."

When Fay Taylour drove Bobby Marshman's sprint car, she was, at age fifty-one, in the final years of a colorful career in motorsports. "Flying Fay," as she was dubbed by the press in her native Ireland, had learned to drive at the age of twelve; by the late 1920s, she was a leading competitor in Speedway motorcycle races on dirt ovals. When she competed in international road races in the 1930s, she would race anything, proving as fast on four wheels as two. Fay Taylour was immensely popular around the world for her personality and flair as much as for her undeniable talent.

After the war she came to America and sold sports cars at International Motors in Hollywood, California, where she became a favorite of the movie set. "Lady Leadfoot," as she was often referred to in America, raced midgets in the United States and Formula 3 cars in England. On world tours that saw her visit India, South Africa, New Zealand, Australia, Italy, and Sweden, she would participate in match races against local stars.

Next up for Bobby was racing in front of a record crowd at the Erie County Fairgrounds in Hamburg, New York, on August 20. Thirty-eight URC sprint cars participated in qualifying. Bobby acquitted himself well with a seventh-place finish in the first heat. Moving on to the eighteen-car semi, he was eleventh, which did not advance him to the feature.

URC races had minimal bureaucracy. At whatever time Bobby and the crew would roll into a racetrack, they would head for the pit area, where they would find a place to park their rig. They likely would then take a nap, as, in most cases, they would have driven through the night. Later they would sign in and execute a waiver.

When the track opened, Bobby would run hot laps to warm the car and check that everything was working. Heat races were important to move forward. If you failed to finish high enough, you had a shot again in the semi. If you still hadn't made the feature, you ran the consi.

On the Sunday of Labor Day weekend, September 4, Bob finally had a performance that qualified him for a feature: He ran in the sixteen-car feature at Nazareth, Pennsylvania. On the fifth lap he had a big spin coming out of the third turn, blocking the track and bringing out a red flag. The sprint car race winner was Pennsylvanian Buddy Powers, one of the early stars of the URC.

On September 7 the URC published the up-to-date point standings. Bob was not listed in the top twenty. Veteran driver Charlie Miller—another fellow Pennsylvanian, and a friend of Bobby's—had the points lead.

Chapter 10
URC's Rookie of the Year (1955)

Janet Fairlie attended as many of Bob's races during the spring and summer as she could. "But my dad put the kibosh on many planned race trips," Janet recalled. "I was at close-by races, like Flemington and Reading.

"It was the 1950s, and our family was so remote from racing. I never would have chosen racing—I was into horses, sports, tennis. I never thought about racing until I met Bob."

When Janet went off to her freshman year of college in the autumn of 1955, she and Bob continued dating. His involvement in the college decision demonstrates the seriousness of the relationship. Her parents wanted her to go to Colby College in Maine, but, "Bob had a fit; it was so far," Janet recalled. "My parents wanted me at an all-girl school, but I would not consider it." East Stroudsburg State Teachers College in the Poconos became the compromise choice.

The first stop on the URC's Southern tour of fair dates, organized by legendary promoter Sam Nunis, was at Shelby Speedway at the Shelby, North Carolina fairgrounds on September 24, Bobby's nineteenth birthday. Shelby was the first race in the "series within the series," comprising seven races on five consecutive weekends in Virginia and North Carolina, plus one back in Pennsylvania. It was in these crucial five weeks, closing out the URC season, that Bobby Marshman's talent and potential came to public attention.

The fastest qualifier at Shelby was Charlie Miller, remembered by *NSSN* as "one of auto racing's most beloved figures." On the third lap of the first heat Miller was squeezed tight on the inside of the first turn by Jimmy Packard. Miller went through the inside fence and suffered fatal injuries. "The Old Fox," as Miller was called by his host of fans, was forty-three years old, and left a wife and a six-year-old son. Miller was the URC points leader at the time of his death.

The scheduled heats went on, with Bobby Marshman achieving a breakthrough win as he led

the field home in the third heat. The feature was ultimately a disappointment: Though he was well placed, engine trouble put him out of the race. Bobby and his team headed home with heavy hearts for the loss of their friend, Charlie Miller.

A long trip the next weekend to Richmond, Virginia, for the Atlantic Rural Fair, was not rewarded, as the race was rained out. Upon confirmation of the rainout, they immediately turned around and drove home. It was a rare day when they would stop at a hotel; more often they would drive straight through when the race was over.

Rain was again the disappointing result the following weekend when the team ventured even farther south, to Charlotte, North Carolina, for the fair race at Metrolina Speedway on October 8. An unexpected encounter on the drive to Charlotte remains an important event in Bob's personal history.

•   •   •

The route of choice to the Southern races was US 301, and a favorite stop on the way was Bruce's Truck Stop in La Plata, Maryland. Bill Reiff remembered the day.

"Bruce's was the only place you could play the one-armed bandits. We didn't have any money, so we would take a dollar and get twenty nickels; Bobby would take ten, and I'd take ten. So we're sitting in there, drinking our cups of coffee in the middle of the night, on our way to Charlotte, no one around. Truck stops weren't like they are now—it was a big dirt parking lot. This guy comes in the door, sat down alongside us, and said 'Hi.'

"We were two teenage kids. We didn't know if we should talk to this guy or not. 'You guys on your way to Charlotte?'—'Yeah, we are.'—'You're Bobby Marshman, aren't you?'—'Yeah.' The man was Jay Miller, and he became a major figure in Bobby's career, and his best friend. He left his 1953 Pontiac in the parking lot, climbed in with us, and we went to Charlotte. And that's how Jay and Bobby got hooked up.

"Jay was a race car-oriented person, and he was one of the originators of the Checkered Flag Fan Club," continued Reiff. "He went to a lot of races and knew a lot of people. He could go to the races all summer long because his dad had a bowling alley in York, Pennsylvania, and Jay ran the maintenance of the alleys and looked after the pin setters, and he also sold bowling pins on his own. He could get away in the summer because the bowling alleys don't do much business then. Jay had already gone to Indy and he knew his way around out there. And he was a nice guy and could express himself very well. [He] and Bobby became the best of friends, and they traveled together a lot."

Undeterred by consecutive weekends of rainouts after long trips south, the team immediately turned back north from Charlotte to make the October 9 show at the legendarily challenging Langhorne Speedway, Pennsylvania. The 'Horne, as the racing fraternity knew it, was a one-mile dirt track with a remarkable difference. Unlike virtually every oval racetrack—be it a one-mile, half-mile, or quarter-mile—Langhorne was a near-perfect circle. The 'Horne had a well-earned reputation as the most physically demanding track in America. With no straightaways, a driver was constantly turning and sliding his car, with no opportunity to rest his neck and other body parts that were under a constant state of stress.

Bob finished sixth in the first heat, and along with race winner Jack McLaughlin of Paulsboro, New Jersey, and every other driver in the race, accepted no money for his efforts at Langhorne. Every man in the URC had agreed in advance to donate the entire purse to the widow of Charles Miller. A racing fatality always has its greatest impact on the surviving family. It was rare for a race driver to leave an estate sufficient to take care of his family for any significant period of time. Irrespective of any personal insurance policy a driver might have had, URC drivers were party to a blanket insurance policy that at the time paid a death benefit of $3,000. As Bobby Marshman's career matured, he became a tireless leader in organizing benefits for drivers fatally or severely injured.

·   ·   ·

The Winston-Salem, North Carolina, fairground track featured races on both Saturday and Sunday, October 14 and 15, each carrying full points. Although Bobby spun out of the Saturday race and gained minimal points both days, he rebounded dramatically the following week at the Raleigh, North Carolina, State Fair races on October 22. Raleigh was the last race of the URC season, and George Marshman made a rare appearance, working the pits alongside Bill Reiff and Jay Miller as Bobby made his best showing of the year, winning the third heat and finishing third in the feature. Buddy Powers of Philadelphia was the race winner, and Lou Johnson finished second. Johnson's finish was sufficient to clinch the 1955 URC championship for himself and his car owners, "Scats" Anfuso and Sam Campbell.

The last five weeks had meant five separate drives down US 301 to a Southern tour fair track. Although two of those trips were spoiled by rainouts, in the other three Bobby had come into his own. The excellent end-of-the-season results left Bobby and his team with positive thoughts to carry into the new year. His strong finish in the Southern tour catapulted him into the top ten in points, and he was named URC Rookie of the Year. The award was well justified, as Bobby Marshman was the first rookie in URC history to ever finish in the top ten in seasonal points.

The annual URC banquet, celebrated at the Stacy-Trent Hotel in Trenton, New Jersey, on January 6, 1956, was a gala event, with Chris Economaki as toastmaster. Club president Harry Johnson personally presented the championship trophy to Lou Johnson (no relation) of Wilmington, Delaware. On his way to the title Johnson had won four races in the Mercury-powered Anfuso-Campbell car. Each of the drivers finishing in the top ten was personally introduced and brought to the podium. Harry Johnson announced that eighty-seven individual drivers had scored points in the 1955 series.

Among the honored guests was George Marshman, who was invited to personally present his son Bobby the trophy for finishing ninth in championship points. He praised Bob for his achievements and said how very proud he was of him. George took the opportunity to announce that in addition to continuing operations at his Hatfield and Sanatoga race tracks, he had also reached an agreement to promote seven races in 1956 at Lakewood Park in Atlanta, Georgia.

When promoter Sam Nunis took the podium, he praised the URC series, saying he hoped to double the number of events he presented for the club. He lauded the professionalism of the drivers, "who run a race the way it should be run—no stalling or prima donna tactics."

Bob was brought to the podium again to receive the Rookie of the Year award, presented by Joe Barzda. Featured speaker, race promoter Al Gerber, brought down the house when he said, "Bobby has received more tributes in one year than his dad George did in a lifetime, and he is a better driver today than his dad was in his lifetime."

While this was presented in the spirit of fun, Jim Lunt in his *NSSN* column the following week, while reporting Gerber's comments, made a point of lauding George for his personal modesty, concluding, "Don't let this fool you, folks; George was a good driver, and won the Eastern AAA midget title in 1949."

Chapter 11
Racing Friends (1956)

To escape a typically rugged Pennsylvania winter, and gain more race experience, Bobby and Jay Miller drove the '53 Ford ambulance south to Florida in late January, hauling the No. 99 racer with its flathead straight six Ford engine.

Their first stop was Southland Raceway in West Palm Beach. The track's February 5, 1956, event marked an important debut: The program was the initial sprint car meet sanctioned by the newly formed United States Auto Club (USAC). Bobby qualified in No. 99—quite a feat, since he was piloting a strikingly less competitive car amid the high-level lineup. Despite the odds, Bobby started thirteenth in a field of sixteen on the half-mile paved oval. However, at the end of the first lap of the feature, he and twelfth-place starter Bobby Wright spun together into the infield, putting them out for the day. Indy champ Bob Sweikert was the race victor in the D. A. Lubricant Special, with Don Branson second in the Willis Special. Bobby's father George Marshman was not only on hand, but was the race manager/promoter, along with Jim Van Cise.

Bobby and Jay went on to Florida's Jacksonville Speedway where Bobby took part in another USAC debut on February 12, this time USAC's first dirt track sprint car event, on the Speedway's half-mile oval. George Marshman and Van Cise were again the race managers. The race was notable for the high number of Florida regulars in their International Motor Contest Association (IMCA) cars. Driving his own No. 99, Bobby qualified deep in the field and he did not figure in the results. Chuck Weyant claimed first place in the Rosemont Special, with Branson second in the Hoover Motor Express.

Plant Field and other tracks in the Tampa area were familiar ground to Bob. He had grown up with a tradition of January family trips south for George's racing calendar. On their 1956 trip, Bob and Jay slept in the ambulance in a campground owned by Ralph Liguori. Liguori, who became a driver of note in both the USAC and NASCAR, was known to Bob from his occasional appearances in URC races. Jay and Bobby were soon joined by Bill Reiff and Jay Fenstermacher, who had driven down from Pennsylvania in Bill's new '56 Ford.

One evening the friends went out to Davis Island to watch the roller-skating at a popular rink there, where they happened to encounter Will Cagle, whom Bob knew from his days at Woodrow Wilson Junior High School. Cagle was racing his stock car the following evening at Plant Field, and he invited the guys to come out to see him run. Although Cagle put the car in the fence that day, he went on to become a champion dirt-modified driver in New York State and throughout the East Coast, with more than four hundred wins.

Bob was home in time to attend the URC organizational meeting on February 19 in Trenton, New Jersey. The club announced a twenty-six-race series for 1956 with increased purses. Although Bob eagerly anticipated the start of a new season, he knew his competitive situation would be little improved, as he was still driving the reliable, but not ultra-competitive, No. 99.

•   •   •

The opening race of the season at Nazareth on May 20 featured a strong showing for Bobby, with a fourth place in the second heat and a drive in the feature where he advanced from mid-pack to a fifth-place finish. The race featured a number of spins and crashes and Bobby drove through them with élan. Bobby Courtwright from Butler, New Jersey, now driving the Anfuso-Campbell car, was the race winner.

Courtwright won again at Williams Grove on June 3, but it was not a happy day for Bobby Marshman or the URC. Bill Dixon was seriously injured in a crash in the third turn of the second heat when he drove over the rear wheels of Bobby's No. 99. Bob was not injured, but Dixon's safety belt broke and he was thrown from his car. In a separate incident, Bob's friend Mike San Felice, driving Charlie Frank's No. 66 car (which was powered by the popular Dodge Red Ram overhead valve engine), tangled with another car. Both cars rolled and the drivers were briefly unconscious, San Felice suffering facial lacerations and other injuries. The drivers were taken to Carlisle Hospital.

An indication of the sadly missed social mores and standards of the time is reflected in Jim Lunt's column in *NSSN*. Lunt noted that a photographer at Williams Grove was moving about taking pictures during the playing of the National Anthem. Lunt concluded with the comment, "Now, really!!!"

In a race at Middletown, New York, on June 30, Bob's bad luck persisted. He hit the wall a glancing blow and never figured in the results. Defending URC champion Lou Johnson won in his Ram-powered car. With races on three consecutive weekends, the URC moved to the Flemington Fair Speedway in Flemington, New Jersey, on July 7. Points leaders Bobby Courtwright and Lou Johnson touched while battling for first place. Johnson went on to win the race, but Courtwright crashed heavily. He suffered a facial fracture and broken nose and was confined to a hospital for ten days. Bobby Marshman managed a third-place finish in the ten-lap second heat. The three-week run was completed on July 14 at Fonda Speedway in Fonda, New York, with a victory by Bert Brooks. Bob was fourth in his heat.

The accident between Johnson and Courtwright was particularly unfortunate, as they were friends. Along with Bert Books they were among some half-dozen leading URC drivers remembered for sitting in the pits long after events talking motors, cars, and racing. These relationships are a staple of all forms of racing, and his warm personality and readily apparent goodwill brought Bobby Marshman many such racing friendships. One of the closest of such relationships was with Lucky Lux, a veteran URC driver.

Bobby and his crew would often trailer to races with two URC teams from Riverside, New Jersey—the Ellis Brothers and the Pappy Hankins–Johnny Wilkins team. Lucky Lux was the driver for the Ellis Brothers in the No. 8 Dodge Ram–powered car, and Richard "Toby" Tobias drove the No. 11 car for the Hankins/Wilkins team. If they didn't connect on the way to the race, they would invariably leave the track in tandem and stop together at a favorite restaurant before driving home.

Harold "Lucky" Lux lived in Lebanon, Pennsylvania, and frequently rode with Bobby and Bill to and from the races. His moniker stemmed from his first-ever race in 1941 when he escaped serious injury despite flipping Buster Warke's midget at the Golden Speedway in Savannah, Georgia. He became a driver of the first rank, winning the URC championship in 1950, and, as a racing veteran, remained one of the leading drivers on the circuit. Lucky is remembered as a great companion, keeping the guys in stitches with his humorous comments on the passing scenery. On the Ellis Brothers team, Paul—usually called Peck—Ellis was the younger of the two, but was the principal. His older brother Harry, both men's wives, and their sister Marie were all part of the team. The family was well thought of and had a reputation for fielding a first-rate race car.

In the URC mid-season point standings, Bobby Marshman was in a respectable tenth place and Bobby Courtwright was leading, although just out of the hospital. The No. 99 car and its flathead Ford six-cylinder engine did not have the power or the handling of the top cars, as remembered by Bill Blatt.

"It's amazing how well he did in the car. We didn't even have money to buy tires. We used to go up to Allentown to a race car owner by the name of Sam Traylor whose father owned hotels. We would go up there and buy used tires off of Sam.

"Bobby was a natural-born race driver and could run any kind of race car with good results."

Chapter 12
"Lucky Was a Racer—That's One Step Above a Driver" (1956)

Marlboro, Maryland, within fifteen miles of the nation's capital, was the next stop on the circuit on July 29. Bobby showed well in his heat with a third, but again failed to crack the top six in the feature.

Sam Nunis was promoting "Racing's First Spectacular" at Flemington, New Jersey, on August 18, and the URC was part of it. The sixteen-event program featured NASCAR, the ARDC, and the URC all running full heats and features. It was a ten-hour grind for competitors and fans alike in intense 105-degree heat. A flash thunderstorm hit at 7:00 p.m., delaying racing for an hour and a half. The program finished at 1:30 a.m. Monday morning. Bobby Marshman did not appear in the top ten in the URC feature.

The URC show in Hamburg, New York, on August 25 marked the conclusion of the Erie County Fair and drew an excellent crowd. Bobby Courtwright, returning to racing for the first time since his early July injuries, made the most of it with a victory in the thirty-two-lap Erie County Sweepstakes. Bobby Marshman had a competitive day with a fourth in his heat. He made an excellent start in the feature, taking the lead and holding the position for two laps. Charging hard to stay with the leaders, Bobby had a big spin on lap four. Another driver went into the wall, bringing out the red flag to stop the race. Bobby recovered to finish seventh.

In late August, Mike San Felice announced his retirement from racing shortly after being released from the hospital following his June 3 crash at Williams Grove. Known as "Mighty Mouse" by his fans, San Felice was one of the most admired drivers in the URC and considered a promoter's dream. Although short of stature, he was handsome, well-spoken, and charismatic. In retirement he remained a friend and mentor to Bobby Marshman.

There were two URC races on Labor Day weekend, with a show on Saturday afternoon at Essex Junction, Vermont, for the Champlain Valley Fair. Although Bobby failed to feature in Vermont, he returned to his recent competitiveness with a fifth place in the feature at Flemington on Monday, September 3, for the Labor Day race. With Toby Tobias third in the Pappy Hankins car, it was a day for the three teams to celebrate on the drive home. It was not a happy day for Earl Halaquist of Sidney, New York, who was taken to Hunterdon Medical Center with face lacerations and loss of teeth after crashing.

With Lucky Lux unavailable on September 22 for the first round of Sam Nunis's Southern tour at Shelby, North Carolina, for the Cleveland County Fair, the Ellis Brothers offered their friend Bobby Marshman the drive in their Red Ram Dodge–powered No. 8. It must have seemed like the best possible present to Bob, who would celebrate his twentieth birthday in two days. Bobby, "in a red hot Red Ram," as described by *NSSN*, immediately displayed his pace with a second place in the first heat and a sixth in the feature. New England's Ted Blair suffered a severe concussion and facial lacerations when he flipped four times in the second heat.

On Saturday, September 29, Lucky Lux returned to his familiar seat in the Ellis Brothers' Red Ram No. 8, and won the first heat at Richmond, Virginia, the race marking the conclusion of the Atlantic Rural Exposition. Bobby, back in No. 99, was fourth in the second heat. With Chris Economaki calling the action, both men shone in the feature, with Lucky finishing a strong third, running in a tight group of four cars that included race winner Lou Johnson. In another four-car battle just behind the lead pack was Bobby Marshman, who drove a good race to finish eighth.

Lucky Lux made his living away from the racetrack driving a Mack truck hauling hot tar. On Monday after the race at Richmond he drove his truck and trailer to the tar plant at Marcus Hook, Pennsylvania, and went to bed. Another driver, running in tandem with Lux, said that Lucky told him that he had suffered a bad night. On the morning of October 2, 1956, the two men went to the plant where they loaded hot tar. Once loaded, they headed south together out of Philadelphia on Route 1, toward Delaware. For unknown reasons, Lucky's truck left the road, went straight up a bank, and hit a tree. The entire rig flipped over and Lucky Lux died in the fiery accident.

In a tribute in *NSSN*, John Heisler Jr. said, "Lucky was a racer—that's one step above a driver." Lux had been considered an up-and-coming driver in the AAA in the 1940s. At the time of his death he was placed fourth in URC season points.

Bill Reiff and Bobby Marshman were among the enormous group of racing friends who crowded the church in Avon, Pennsylvania, for Lucky's funeral service. Bobby and Bill, on their way to Charlotte, North Carolina, for the URC race, parked their tow vehicle with No. 99 on the trailer outside the church. It proved another trip without reward when Charlotte was rained out.

After the race Bob and Bill Reiff towed the race car to Langhorne for a Sunday-afternoon show. "We got up there just in time to run," remembered Bill. "Bobby ran well until the engine failed. It didn't explode—it just wore out."

It was Bobby's last race in the white No. 99 that had served him so well. Bill Blatt recalled what became of the race car. "He sold the body and frame to somebody—they didn't want the Ford engine—so I bought that from Bobby for $125, including the rear and front end. At that time I was building hot rods, so I took a 1930 Ford Model A coupe, cut the top off it, and made a roadster out of it, and I put Bobby's race motor in it. It was fun. In those days a six-cylinder Ford was a good runner; it had triple carburetors on it."

For the last race of the 1956 URC season at Raleigh, North Carolina, on October 20, the Ellis Brothers invited Bobby Marshman to again drive their No. 8 car. Although Bobby had distinguished himself in his first drive in the car when Lucky was unavailable for the Shelby race, this was different for all parties. Bob was stepping into the seat of his recently departed friend. For Paul and Harry Ellis, it was a decision to finish out the season, albeit with heavy hearts.

At Raleigh Bobby proved again that all he needed to move forward was a competitive race car. Heavy rains for days prior to the race had left the half-mile dirt Raleigh Fairgrounds a mess. Work on the track continued right up to the first heat, which didn't start until three p.m., and qualifying was eliminated. The feature started under heavy skies with Bobby in ninth position. *NSSN* reported enthusiastically on his race progress. "Marshman from ninth spot started flying at the halfway point of the race and the Ellis Brothers' Dodge clicked forward in brilliant style, riding high in the corners and low through the chutes in an amazing ground-gaining, car-passing exhibition." Bobby finished fifth behind race winner Lou Johnson, Bert Brooks, Bobby Courtwright, and Ed Gallione—the cream of the URC veterans. Despite Johnson's win, Brooks's second-place finish was enough to clinch the 1956 URC championship.

In *NSSN's* season recap Bobby was profiled as "having proven himself as a very competitive and front-running driver—especially after taking over the Ellis car." An unexpected honor came at the URC annual business meeting in November when Bob was elected a member of the board of directors. This was singular recognition of the respect enjoyed in the racing community for a young man barely turned twenty.

BELOW: Aboard the Ellis Brothers sprinter at Flemington, New Jersey. (RMA/CHERNOKAL)

Chapter 13
"How About This Youngster, Bob Marshman?" (1957)

On January 12, 1957, the URC banquet was held at the Stacy-Trent Hotel in Trenton, New Jersey. Bert Brooks, the "Garfield Gunner," was honored as 1956 URC champion. Brooks graciously acknowledged that had Courtwright not had his crash and time in the hospital, he might not have beaten him. The difference was only 54 points at the end. Bobby Marshman was awarded a trophy for placing eighth in season points of the seventy-six drivers who had participated in the series. It was an emotional moment when Marie Ellis presented a special trophy to Lucky Lux's brother Herbie, inscribed "In Memory of Lucky Lux, Sportsman, Driver, Friend." Additionally, a Lucky Lux Award was inaugurated to honor the driver displaying the best characteristics of sportsmanship on and off

the track. It was presented to Mike San Felice by the New Jersey Speedway Club.

Bob remained devoted to Janet Fairlie, now a sophomore at East Stroudsburg College, and though the commitment was returned, it was not without continued parental pressure. "My father wanted me to marry someone who was a college boy; my mom wasn't like that," recalled Janet. "There were a lot of nice guys in school, but I knew Bob's special qualities, and that made me extremely critical of other guys."

The Ellis Brothers made a public announcement on March 13 that Bobby Marshman would be the driver of their Dodge-powered No. 8. This represented the first full-time professional drive for Bobby, and presented him a car with the potential to compete at the front of the pack.

Driving in a professional series, and even driving for a team other than your own, does not mean that you are making a living driving race cars. Bob continued to live at home and earned most of his income working for George, helping to maintain the racetracks. He also worked for his friend Bill Blatt in Bill's auto repair business in Mont Clare. "Sometimes over the winter, even when he was already successful, he would work with me at my shop," Blatt recalled. "I still have the stubs of what I paid him for working for me."

The All-American Racing Club (AARC) was a Midwest-based sanctioning body with ideals and rules—no Offenhausers welcome—similar to the URC. To open the 1957 season, the two groups combined to honor Lucky Lux in a race at Williams Grove, Pennsylvania. The fastest twelve cars in qualifying from each club would square off in a fifty-lap, East versus West challenge. On May 19 Bobby and the Ellis Brothers were on hand, along with sixty other entrants. But a steady rain sent everyone home.

Just a week later the teams were all back at Williams Grove to contest the Lucky Lux Memorial Sweepstakes. Bobby was impressive in winning his heat, prompting *NSSN* to remark, "How about this youngster, Bob Marshman? The guy is a real comer with plenty of savvy." Bobby, however, did not place well in the feature. Easterner Bobby Courtwright in Scats Anfuso's car won the race overall.

In three races on consecutive days over Memorial Day weekend, Bobby displayed the form he would maintain throughout the season. On the holiday itself, Thursday, May 30, he was on home ground at Hatfield, where he was second in his heat to Lou Johnson. He followed up with a competitive run to fourth place in the feature. On Friday night at Nazareth, Bob was fifth in the feature. At Manassas, Virginia's Old Dominion Speedway on Saturday, June 1, Bob looked like he would follow up his heat win with a win in the feature. From his starting position in second place Bob had taken an immediate lead until lap 11, when his handling went sour and he was passed by race winner Bob Cleberg of Rio, Wisconsin. Ultimately Bobby Courtwright took second, but Bob remained in contention throughout, and earned his third-place finish.

The undoubted high-water mark for Bobby with the Ellis Brothers came on the half-mile asphalt track at Old Bridge Speedway in New Jersey on the evening of Friday, June 21. Bobby won his heat and completely dominated the feature for his first major victory. Despite being chased hard all the way by veteran URC champions Bert Brooks and Bobby Courtwright, Bobby took the lead at the start and was never headed. *NSSN* reported that Bob "stood the field on its head in the pretty Ellis Dodge," with Brooks "unloading his full bag of tricks in attempted passing moves." The next day at Victory Stadium in Middletown, New York, Bobby won his heat but did not place in the feature, won by Lou Johnson. Mike San Felice came out of retirement for the race.

The Fourth of July holiday fell on a Friday, and the URC raced at Fonda Speedway that evening. Bobby finished second to Lou Johnson in the first heat, and it was Johnson who took an early lead in the feature. On the thirteenth of thirty laps Bobby Courtwright went by Johnson for the win, with Bobby Marshman finishing fourth. The next day, for a race won by Bert Brooks, the teams traveled to Nazareth. Bobby was again fourth in the feature after finishing third in his heat.

Races came fast and furious in the summer, with two more scheduled the following weekend. On the half-mile dirt Monroe County Fairgrounds in Rochester, New York, on Saturday, July 12, Bobby was third in the heat and the feature. A serious accident sent URC points leader Bobby Courtwright to Rochester's Strong Memorial Hospital for a lengthy recovery. An exhaust pipe came off a competitor's car and lodged in Courtwright's front wheels before being launched into his face. The car vaulted the rail and turned over repeatedly. Courtwright's serious injuries included a broken jaw, a broken frontal bone above the eye, and a punctured lung. The same pipe slammed into the steering linkage of Ed Gallione's car, sending him over the fence and upside down. Gallione escaped without serious injuries.

The next day the URC teams moved west to Buffalo, New York, to again join the AARC in a jointly sanctioned race on the Buffalo Civic Stadium's quarter-mile asphalt track. Johnny White from Warren, Michigan, who would later play a pivotal role in Bobby Marshman's career, continued his near domination of the AARC season. He took first over URC drivers Bert Brooks in second, Don Allison in third, and Bobby in fourth.

On July 15 the URC announced its current points table, and Bobby Marshman was in second place, behind only the now-hospitalized Bobby Courtwright. Bobby was trailed in third, fourth, and fifth positions by Bob Cleberg, Lou Johnson, and Ed Gallione. Then, on July 20, Bobby catapulted into the points lead at Old Dominion Speedway in Manassas, Virginia. Bert Brooks won the race, but Bobby's third-place finish—and a win in his heat—put him out front in the URC championship contest.

Chapter 14
Battling for the Championship (1957)

The move to the Ellis Brothers' No. 8 Dodge Ram–powered car had changed Bobby Marshman's status from that of a promising up-and-comer to the man everyone else was chasing. The move had also changed the character of his racing experience. Bill Reiff and Bill Blatt remained close friends and attended races as spectators when they could, but the Ellis Brothers were a well-established team with their own race preparation and procedures. Bill Reiff had taken a full-time job with the Collegeville-based Doug Stearly Motor Freight business. Bill "Shooey" Blatt was now spending more time on his growing auto repair business. Bobby and his close friend Jay Miller usually drove to the races together.

Defending URC champion driver Bert Brooks, now driving a new Corvette-powered sprinter of his own construction, was Bobby's closest pursuer in the points battle. Back at Rochester on August 2 for a Friday night show on Monroe County's half-mile dirt fairground track, Bobby beat Brooks to

the win in the first heat. Brooks turned the tables in the feature when he took the lead from Bobby on the eighth lap, and they finished 1-2. Another Brooks-Marshman 1-2 was the result on Sunday afternoon, the fourth of August, at Shangri-La Speedway's third-of-a-mile asphalt track in Owego, New York. Brooks continued to make inroads on Bobby's points lead.

At the Bedford County Sweepstakes in Bedford, Pennsylvania, on August 10, Dick Spaulding's sprinter catapulted over Fran Hagele's wheel, went through the guardrail, and up a ten-foot embankment before coming to a stop in the crowd. Spaulding was not injured, but seven spectators were taken to the hospital. All were released that day except for a ten-year-old boy who suffered facial lacerations and a broken leg. Bobby was second in his heat and fourth in the hotly contested feature won by Hal Rettberg of Albany, New York.

Over Labor Day weekend the URC scheduled four races in three days. On Saturday, August 31, before a reported crowd of 25,000, the feature race at the Champlain County Fair in Essex Junction, Vermont, was won by Hal Rettberg, with Bert Brooks and Bobby Marshman a close second and third. Bobby also scored points for winning his heat. The following day at the Flemington Fair, Bobby again won his heat but was sixth in the feature, dropping him behind Brooks for the points lead. That evening the teams moved to Nazareth where Bobby was third in his heat. In the feature he was running third and contesting for the lead when on the eighth lap a frozen front brake on the Ellis Brothers' machine threw him into a wide slide, costing him many positions. He rallied at the end of the race, but because of the incident, he finished in seventh place. On Labor Day, September 2, the URC returned to New Jersey for a second race at Flemington, where Brooks won, with Bobby fourth.

Bert Brooks had been surging in recent weeks, and his performances over Labor Day weekend were strong enough for him to overcome Bobby for the points lead. Though Bobby Courtwright continued to convalesce from his injuries, Lou Johnson returned to the seat of the Scats Anfuso car, and competition at the front of the URC pack was intense. Brooks began to extend his lead by winning the Eastern States Exposition race at West Springfield, Massachusetts, on September 20; Bobby did not place there. Bobby's championship bid continued to diminish at the September 28 event in Richmond, Virginia, when his Ram engine seized and the wheels locked up, and the No. 8 car spun broadside in front of other competitors. No damage was done, but Bobby could not restart the Ellis Brothers' car.

Brooks clinched the 1957 URC championship by winning at Raleigh, North Carolina, on November 19. Bobby ran poorly in his heat and had to enter the consi in order to qualify for the feature. He did so in dramatic fashion, starting dead last and driving through the entire field to win. He was then sixth in the feature. The following day, the long URC season ended at Waynesboro, Virginia's, East Side Speedway, with a win for Lou Johnson in the Scats Anfuso Thunderbird-powered car, with Brooks second. Bobby had a dramatic slide on the twenty-fourth lap that blocked the track and brought the race, and the season, to a finish.

OPPOSITE: The 1957 season with the Ellis Brothers' sprint car established him as a fast-rising new star. (RMA/KING)

The URC announced that they had completed a season of twenty-five races in nine states, with 96 drivers and 102 car owners participating. Bert Brooks won twelve races, as he added the 1957 championship to his two previous URC crowns earned in 1954 and 1956. While the highlight of Bobby Marshman's season was his victory at Old Bridge, he impressed with remarkable consistency, demonstrated by his runner-up position in the series despite only one feature win. His season was impressive by any measure. In only his third year of racing he had matured to a front-runner, finishing second in URC points, with 1,214 to champion Bert Brooks's 1,515. Lou Johnson was third, with 1,197 points.

At the URC annual meeting Bobby declined a nomination to serve a second year as a director of the organization. Close observers read this to mean that Bobby was looking in new directions for the year ahead.

Chapter 15
"Easy on the Down Stroke, Daddy-O" (1957)

With the 1957 season over, Bill Reiff offered Bobby a part in an adventure. Bill's employer Doug Stearly had secured an entry in the Bahamas Speed Weeks in Nassau, and asked Bill to transport and look after his new red Mercedes-Benz 300SL Gullwing. Doug was not an experienced competition driver, and entries for Nassau were notoriously difficult to come by. The Marshman family and the Stearlys were friends, and George was closely allied with Nassau race originator and promoter, Captain Sherman "Red" Crise. The races were sponsored by the Bahamas Tourist Board, sanctioned by the Royal Automobile Club of England, and listed on the FIA international calendar. Since the inaugural Nassau races in 1954, George and Evie had been flown to the island and provided a room for the week in return for being part of the organizational team. George was one of the public address announcers. The family connection no doubt secured Doug Stearly the much-sought-after entry.

Each race entrant was provided a room in Nassau along with shipment of their race car from Miami to the island. Bill Reiff, accompanied by Bobby Marshman, transported the 300SL to the port of Miami to arrive in time for their scheduled passage. "We had a '53 International—a furniture truck—with a wooden roof on it and open sides where the tarp rolled down, and it had a tailgate. We loaded the Mercedes at a gas station where we put it up on a lift, backed the truck up to that, and put it on. Bobby rode with me in that truck, and in Miami we did the same thing to unload it. We stayed with friends of mine in Miami. In the morning we drove the 300SL down to the docks where it was loaded on the SS *Florida*, and we sailed with it to Nassau."

Nassau attracted the great road-racing drivers from Europe and America, including Stirling Moss, Ricardo Rodríguez, Carroll Shelby, Phil Hill, John Fitch, Masten Gregory, Joakim Bonnier, and Richie Ginther. These greats were among the 120 competitors who managed an entry from the

217 who applied. Lance Reventlow, only beginning to become prominent in racing, impressed Bill and Bobby mostly because of his wife, actress Jill St. John. Although the racing itself was serious, the Bahamas was largely an end-of-season social scene. The most prominent resorts hosted gala cocktail parties each evening during the week—events that remain legend. Although Bobby and Bill (as well as Bobby's parents and the Stearlys) did not drink, their time on the island is well-remembered.

The Bahamas experience was unique within the racing world. There were other races around the world that combined amateurs and professionals, but nowhere was it experienced in such a casual and "fun-first" environment. Author Terry O'Neal in his wonderful book, *The Bahamas Speed Weeks*, summed up the prevailing spirit of the event when he quoted Captain Crise: "In the Bahamas no cocktail party ever gets held up by a late race."

It was a memorable trip for all involved. Doug Stearly, despite little racing experience—he borrowed Bobby's helmet for the race—acquitted himself well in the red 300SL Gullwing, with finishes well up among notable names. Bill Reiff, as always, was operating at a high level of energy. One morning he awoke hours before anyone else to do preparation on the race car. The car was parked under a fifty-foot-high palm tree, and as he worked, a branch fell from the tree and knocked him unconscious. Another night while Bob and Bill slept, an intruder entered their room and made away with Bill's billfold and money. Bob's was spared because he had taken the precaution of placing his wallet under his pillow.

Races on the fast five-mile Oakes Field circuit were held for a wide range of cars and categories throughout the week, culminating on Sunday, December 8, with the 100-mile Nassau Memorial Trophy and, starting just a half-hour later, the 250-mile Nassau Trophy. Stirling Moss in a works-entered Aston Martin DBR2 and Carroll Shelby in the John Edgar–entered Maserati 450S were among the drivers favored for victory. On Saturday, the day before the feature races, a Ladies' Race was held in two five-lap heats. Some of the best American women drivers were entered, including New Yorker Denise McCluggage in her Porsche 550RS and Ruth Levy of Minnesota and California. Stirling Moss invited Levy to race the Aston Martin, and the result was a tremendous and exciting battle for the lead in the first heat, won by McCluggage by the narrowest margin at an average speed of 96.292 mph over the seventeen-turn circuit. Either of these exceptionally talented women was on a par with most male drivers, and a great race was expected in the final heat.

Bobby and Bill were watching with great interest and found themselves in the middle of the action that followed. "Bobby and I would go around to different parts of the circuit. Before the start/finish was a hard left-hand turn," said Reiff, who recalled a "wheel-to-wheel battle" there between the two women drivers. "On the last lap they got into that corner hot, and [Levy] flipped that Aston Martin right in front of us. It was the car that Moss was supposed to run in the big race the next day. The car could not be repaired in time for Sunday's feature races, but Moss was still the victor in a borrowed Ferrari.

"[Levy] wound up on the other side of the racetrack from where Bobby and I were standing with one or two track workers. Safety wasn't a big thing back then. We ran over there with the track workers and they put her on a stretcher. Bobby goes in his pocket and gets his handkerchief out because she had junk all over her and he's wiping the cinders out of her eyes. We followed the guys carrying the stretcher to help put her in the ambulance—she was shook up. They got her over to the ambulance and they dropped her—they dropped the stretcher! I'll never forget, I can hear her saying it today, 'Easy on the down stroke, daddy-o.'"

Bobby had to be back in Pennsylvania for the December 14 Checkered Flag Fan Club dinner, where he was a finalist for an important award. He caught a flight home and Bill came home in the truck with the 300SL by himself.

At the Checkered Flag Fan Club annual banquet in Pottstown, one of the Club's prestigious awards was given out. It was the "Most Improved Eastern Driver" award, and finalists in 1957 were Ralph Liguori, Jim Packard, and Red Riegel from the USAC, and Bobby Marshman and Don Allison from the URC. At the Club's December meeting, Bobby was announced as the winner. It was a meaningful honor. The Club—whose slogan was "For better and safer auto racing"—was far more influential than its name implied. Originally a southeastern Pennsylvania organization, by the late 1950s it was composed of fans, promoters, drivers, owners, pitmen, and officers of various tracks and sanctioning bodies throughout the Northeast.

Although his trip to Nassau had happened almost by accident, Bobby likely spent some time there looking for a ride. With the advice and support of George and Red Crise—neither man ever known to be shy—it is probable that inquiries were made. Bobby told Chris Economaki that he was disappointed not to have been offered a "sporty-car" ride. Economaki attributed this, along with Bob's decision to not accept an additional year as a URC director, as an indication of a move to accept a ride with a USAC team.

Chapter 16
"Bobby's Sights Are on the Brickyard" (1958)

The news came in March of 1958 that Bobby Marshman would join the four-car Harry Hespell team to contest the ARDC midget championship for 1958. The ARDC, closely associated with the USAC, was considered a top-level Eastern midget series. Bobby's friends at the URC took the news as gentlemen as they bid farewell to a star-quality driver who enjoyed tremendous fan support. In an official statement, URC press director Louis Kunz said, "Bobby's sights are on the Brickyard, and in order to accomplish this, he must forsake URC. Our best wishes go along with this fine driver."

Theoretically, sprint cars superceded midgets in importance, but in the real politik of racing, it is all about the prestige and recognition of a given series. Although the URC sprint car series carried respect and featured some of the hardest-nosed veteran drivers to be found anywhere, the ARDC was where the real action lay for ambitious drivers. The hungry young talents found themselves battling for position alongside the many established stars already populating the midget ranks.

When midgets began making their appearance in the mid- to late 1930s on quarter-mile and fifth-of-a-mile tracks, they were initially dismissed as a passing fancy by sprint car owners and drivers. It was widely postulated that midgets would not maintain fan interest. In fact, they quickly became a fan pleaser with their short wheelbases, narrow track, and light weight that made them better handlers than big cars (as sprinters were commonly referred to at that time). The midgets put on a show that the fans could see and enjoy up close. After the war they established a strong fan base and, despite a brief decline in the early 1950s, soon became a favorite of fans and promoters, drawing excellent crowds to their own feature races.

As suggested in Lou Kunz's statement, ARDC midgets were an important step on the path to Indianapolis. It was also true that one had to be twenty-one years old to race in a USAC-associated series. Bobby's three years in the URC had not been wasted, and, with the benefit of perspective, proved to be a wise career step.

Bobby spent time in Pennsylvania's state capital the last week of March as one of several drivers manning a booth at the Sportsmen's Show and Exposition held at the Farm Show Building. One of the drivers helping Bob at the booth, co-sponsored by Williams Grove Speedway and the Checkered Flag Fan Club, was Al Herman, one of his new teammates on the Hespell midget team. Others helping at the booth included Charlie Musselman, Toby Tobias, and Bill Miller.

It was in the off-season that Bob was able to spend time with Janet, now in her junior year, for college social activities. "He would come to all the balls and things like that when he could," recalled Janet. "Everybody at college loved him; he had this quiet strength, and was absolutely outgoing and welcoming to new people, and treated everybody the same. This was true whether in a social situation at college or with people we encountered at the racetracks. At the same time, though, he was very loyal; you always knew who his real friends were."

Harry Hespell ran a well-regarded team of four midgets out of Montgomeryville, Pennsylvania, and was the ARDC owner-champion four times. Hespell, a successful quarry operator, fielded beautifully prepared cars and recruited top drivers. It was a mark of respect that Bob was included with the team's established stars Len Duncan, Wayne Doerstler, and Al Herman. Herman had been Rookie of the Year at the Indianapolis 500 in 1955. Ed "Dutch" Schaefer, who had won the championship for Hespell in 1956, was not part of the team in 1958, but later returned to the Hespell stable and won the 1960 championship. In the eleven-season span from 1955 through 1965, Duncan and Schaefer had a complete lock on the top spot of the year-end ARDC points tally, with Duncan winning six championships in that period, and Schaefer, four. (Duncan added a seventh and final ARDC championship in 1967.) Len Duncan, a Brooklyn, New York, native residing in Philadelphia was, at age forty-seven, in his prime, and acknowledged as one of the smoothest and fastest drivers in any type of racing. Along with the other veteran drivers on the team, Duncan was a great mentor to twenty-one-year-old Bobby Marshman.

"On the Hespell midget team each guy had their own helpers," recalled Bill Reiff. "Hespell had a big open trailer that he towed all four cars on, and there may have been five guys he would bring to help. Really, everyone on the team helped everybody, but Bud Tyson was the crew member most responsible for Bob's car. He and Bobby were pretty tight."

Saturday, May 3, was a scheduled ARDC event at Hatfield, and George promoted Bobby's presence in the race. Rain came to the entire Eastern Seaboard, and races, including Hatfield, were rained out as far south as the Carolinas. The rain date on May 17 did not bring a good result for Bobby, but his teammate Len Duncan won the race. Popular Al Graeber was thrown from his car in a multicar crash, suffering a broken leg and other injuries. Midgets were running virtually flat out at the very fast paved and banked Hatfield track, and the venue was considered dangerous by many.

On Memorial Day weekend the big ARDC show was on Friday, May 30, at Williams Grove, Pennsylvania, a 100-lap feature on the half-mile dirt track. After a fourth-place finish in his heat, Bobby made the best of his start in the feature, and led the race for eleven laps before being passed by Jiggs Peters, who went on to win the race. Teammate Len Duncan demoted Bob a position on the twelfth lap. Despite his likely disappointment with an eventual eighth-place finish, Bob could count this as a good result in a strong and large field. George Fonder of Lansdale, Pennsylvania, finished second to Peters, and Bob's teammates Duncan and Wayne Doerstler were third and fourth.

That evening, after the Williams Grove afternoon races, Bobby competed at Sanatoga Speedway. There he took the three-quarter midget feature, with Duncan, second; Ben Landis, third; and Carl Miller, fourth. The next day, Saturday, May 31, Bobby was at Hatfield. He claimed a strong third-place finish on his "home track," with teammate Duncan winning the race ahead of Tony Bonadies.

The fast learning curve continued on June 6 at the Victory Speedway on the Orange County Fairgrounds in Middletown, New York. There, Bob was fourteenth of twenty starters in the feature after finishing third in his heat behind Chuck Arnold and Ernie McCoy. Arnold won the feature, with Duncan second.

On the evening of June 8, Sanatoga Speedway's three-quarter midget race ran despite the threat of rain. Bobby captured second place in the twenty-five-lap race behind winner Len Duncan. Ben Landis was third. A scheduled race the following day at Langhorne was postponed by rain.

Just two weeks after his second place at Williams Grove, veteran driver George Fonder, thirty-nine, crashed to his death on June 14 in the feature race at Hatfield-Hi Speedway. Fonder's

incident occurred on the sixth lap when he ran wide, hitting a fence post and dying instantly. An Indianapolis 500 veteran, Fonder had been racing since 1937 and had a 1941 AAA Eastern midget championship to his credit. Jim Packard of Indianapolis won the race, driving for Ken Brenn. Bobby Marshman made the feature by finishing third in the consi. He did not figure in the feature results.

Tragedy continued to follow the midget runners at Langhorne Speedway. The June 29 race, already twice postponed in the rainy spring of 1958, was contested on a dry, sun-scorched track. There were no heats, and starting positions were determined by time trials. The homestretch at Langhorne was downhill and fast. The great challenge at the time was to take the first corner (nicknamed "Puke Hollow") flat out, and the midgets were putting on a tremendous show as they entered the long bend at more than 100 mph, sliding through, wheel to wheel, at unreduced power. On his qualifying lap, twenty-two-year-old Nick Duino of New Brunswick, New Jersey, hit the inside dirt between the first and second corners. The soft surface threw the car into a series of rolls. Duino was declared dead on arrival at the hospital.

When the June 29 race was run, Bobby made the field as the eighth-fastest driver. However, he did not finish in the top ten. Bill Homeier captured first place in the race.

Chapter 17
Record Man (1958)

A Sam Nunis–promoted race at Trenton, New Jersey, on Sunday, August 3, proved a banner day for Bobby Marshman, the ARDC, and the prestige of midget racing. On the fast, one-mile track, Nunis featured a 100-mile NASCAR Sportsman race, along with 25-milers for the ARDC and the URC. Time trials had been completed the previous week, before the feature was postponed by a rainstorm. Trenton in 1958 was a typical paved oval. (The track's well-known "kidney bean" shape came ten years later.)

In front of his friends from the URC, Bobby was the man of the moment at Trenton, capturing his first ARDC feature win at the fastest speed yet recorded for a midget race in America. Bobby averaged 104.706 mph, just beating Tony Romit and Len Duncan to the line. Bert Brooks won the URC race, averaging 82.13 mph, and NASCAR winner Bob Malzahn of Keansburg, New Jersey, averaged 78.89 mph.

The crowd of nine thousand was said to be in a near frenzy, and the ARDC event was pronounced the race of the day, with the battle for the lead contested hard from start to finish. No more than a car length separated Bobby and Tony Romit for the entire fifty-lap race. Out of the last corner on the last lap, Bob exited on the inside and ran side by side with Romit to the finish, where Bob claimed victory. The excitement moved race enthusiast Raymond Sabourin of Flushing, New York, to step out of the crowd and present Bob with a twenty-dollar bill. Sabourin dipped in his pocket again for another twenty for car owner Harry Hespell. Dr. Sabourin was known as a great supporter of racing, as both an entrant and a sponsor.

Carl R. Green, lead editorial and technical writer for *NSSN*, was still acclaiming the achievement two weeks later. Green, seldom drawn to superlatives, made this enthusiastic comment: "The diminutive midget race cars with motors of 107 cubic inches, or less, ran faster than the 300 cubic inch stocks or sprint cars, and established a new track record for all types of race cars, a contest between refined design and Swiss watch workmanship against main strength and awkwardness." His conclusion was interesting: "The story of Trenton, New Jersey, August 3, 1958, is worth giving deep thought, which would greatly benefit both racing engines and regular passenger cars, and mostly their engines."

Green was making the larger point that Europeans were building cars with efficient, small-displacement, lightweight engines, and making inroads in the American market. He also harkened back to the earliest days of American car production, when each builder strove to build an engine five inches larger, or more, than their competitors before Henry Ford came along with his small Model T and "took most of the business, and money too."

A week later the hero of Trenton was in the stands at Williams Grove to pay tribute to his deceased friend at the URC's Lucky Lux Memorial Sweepstakes. The Sunday, August 10, event was won by Lou Johnson. The night before, at the Orange County Sweepstakes in Middletown, New York, Bobby had come home in fifth place, with the win going to Chuck Arnold.

At Seekonk, Massachusetts, on Saturday, August 16, the Hespell team was waiting for Wayne Doerstler to arrive to complete the four-car team when news arrived that he had suffered serious injuries in a road accident. Doerstler had actually crashed his Lincoln sedan into the rear of a truck on Route 422 near Allentown, Pennsylvania, late Thursday night but the news had not been relayed to the team. His injuries included a fractured skull, two broken arms, and five broken ribs. On very short notice, the seat in the Hespell midget went to Bert Brooks, who drove the car to victory.

On Labor Day weekend, the ARDC had a race on Friday night at Freeport, New York, and a Fair date on Saturday, August 30 at Flemington, New Jersey. A fourth in his heat was all Bob managed on the fifth-of-a-mile Freeport track. His best result for the weekend was a fourth in the Flemington feature in a race won by teammate Len Duncan in what was described as a "fierce battle."

When the ARDC returned to Hatfield on September 6, George Marshman was promoting the return of son Bobby "who had helped build the track." Bobby lived up to the hype, earning a *NSSN* headline that said it all: BOB MARSHMAN SETS NEW RECORD—FIRST WIN ON TRACK HE HELPED BUILD. The story lead wasn't bad either: "Bob Marshman, handsome 23-year-old [*sic*] son of race director and former competitor George Marshman, sped to a new track record at the Hatfield-Hi Speedway Saturday night to capture his first feature event checkered flag on the half-mile oval he helped to build."

Bob had chased Chuck Arnold of Stanfield, Connecticut, for the first nine laps before taking

the lead to win the twenty-lap feature in a time of 7:57.27, breaking Wild Bill Randall's record of 8:01.14. It was becoming clear to many observers that the still-only-twenty-one-year-old had a special affinity for the fastest tracks.

For the proud George Marshman, a poignant moment came the following week when he closed Sanatoga Speedway. George had run the track since 1951, and the venue held many family memories. Bobby had virtually grown up at the track.

Back on the Long Island venue at Freeport for a Friday night show on September 19, Bob managed fifth in his heat and a second in the consi. The next day the teams returned to Hatfield, where Wild Bill Randall won and, with a time of 7:26.08, reclaimed his record that had been broken by Bobby Marshman just two weeks previously.

On Sunday, October 5, the ARDC was again at the fast Trenton Fairgrounds Speedway, this time for a 100-mile contest. Bobby was one of six drivers who shared the lead throughout the race. In time trials Bob had been eighth-fastest, but the trials were rendered meaningless when the twenty-nine-car field was inverted for the start. Len Duncan, running without a pit stop, won the race, with Chuck Arnold, second; Bill Randall of Stoneham, Massachusetts, third; Dick Linder of Pittsburgh, fourth; and Bobby Marshman, fifth.

At Pennsylvania's Bloomsburg Fair the following Friday, October 11, Bobby won his heat and was third in the feature behind winner Jiggs Peters and Tony Romit. The day was marred by the death of Bobby Boone of Springfield, Massachusetts, driving for Ken Brenn. When Boone ran wide out of turn four on the fourth lap of the first heat, his right rear wheel touched the barrier, causing the tire to explode and pitching the car into a flip, followed by a series of vicious end-over-ends. Boone, still strapped in the car, was dead by the time help reached him. Despite the close battle in the feature race, news reports described fans as stunned and unresponsive because of the terrible accident that had befallen Boone.

Len Duncan had clinched the 1958 ARDC championship by virtue of victory the previous week at Trenton. The veteran driver, known as "the old smoothie," had driven the Hespell No. 9 car to eight wins during the season, and totaled 3,085 points, well clear of Ed "Dutch" Schaefer of Floral Park, New York, with 2,385. Bobby Marshman, who turned twenty-two in September, had distinguished himself with a third-place finish in the championship, with 2,125 points. He was also named winner of the ARDC's "Most Improved Driver" award for 1958.

Doug Stearly again entered Nassau for the Bahamas Speed Weeks in December, but this time he changed his Mercedes-Benz 300SL Gullwing for a new 300SL roadster. Bob was unable to accompany Bill Reiff on the drive to Miami. Instead, Bobby arrived by air in time for the races. He accompanied Bill in the truck on the long haul home.

"You had to hang around there a week or more because they couldn't take all the cars at the same time," recalled Bill. "You had to wait for your place on the boat to get the cars to Miami. I had left home the day before Thanksgiving, and we got back the day before Christmas."

Chapter 18
Winning Wedding Week (1959)

For 1959, the USAC and the ARDC announced continuation of their cooperative sanctioning of midget events in the Northeast. The mutually beneficial arrangement provided the USAC a strong presence in the East while protecting the ARDC from having choice dates "cherry-picked" by the larger sanctioning body. Essentially the USAC could be granted no sanctions in ARDC territory—newly described for 1959 as east of a line on the map extended south of western Pennsylvania—but USAC-licensed drivers were free to enter such races.

Fred "Jiggs" Peters in the Smiley's "Golden Arrow" won the season opener on Hatfield's high-banked asphalt half-mile track on Friday, May 1, by coasting home with a broken motor on the twentieth and final lap of the feature, just edging out Bert Brooks for the win. Gig Stephens was third, and Bobby Marshman, fourth. Bob had finished third in his heat. On Sunday afternoon the same weekend, Bob managed a win in the semi at the banked, paved, quarter-mile Empire Raceway at Menands, New York, near Albany. He did not place in the feature won by the popular "Flying Dutchman," Ed Schaefer.

The ARDC drivers were busy every day of the May 8–10 weekend, and the Friday night show at Hatfield may have been the biggest disappointment of Bobby Marshman's season. Leading the race by more than a straightaway on the twelfth lap of the twenty-lap feature, Bob exited turn four to see a red flag displayed at the start/finish. His teammate Wayne Doerstler had gone through the turn-one fence, attempting to avoid the spinning car of Tony Bonadies. Doerstler required stitches and the Hespell car was badly damaged. On the restart, Bob had lost his hard-earned lead, and Bert Brooks, Jiggs Peters, and Len Duncan all managed to get by him before the finish. It was a race he would recall as "one that got away."

Bob was not prominently placed in the race the next day at Old Dominion Speedway in Manassas, Virginia. The twenty-five-lap feature was won by his teammate Len Duncan on the three-eighths-of-a-mile asphalt, high-banked oval. Duncan won again on Sunday, May 10, on the state fairground half-mile dirt track at Richmond, Virginia, with Bobby placing fifth.

Bobby's Hespell teammate, Wayne Doerstler, in a great comeback from his major automobile accident the previous year—as well as his recent stitches from the Hatfield crash—won the Memorial Day race at the fifth-of-a-mile paved track at Roanoke, Virginia. Bobby made it a 1-2 finish for the Hespell outfit. The two men had finished in the same positions in their heat.

NSSN's Jim Lunt announced in his "Benzine Banter" column that "world record holder for midgets, Bobby Marshman" would marry Miss Janet Fairlie on Saturday, June 6. Lunt concluded with "Happy honeymoon, folks!" The wedding took precedence over the ARDC race at Danbury, Connecticut, the same day, but Bob's luck held when the race was washed out and the rain date was set for the following day.

• • •

It was two weeks after Janet Fairlie's graduation from East Stroudsburg State Teachers College that the young couple met in front of friends and family in historic Augustus Lutheran Church—established in 1743—in Trappe to profess their vows of marriage. Jay C. Miller was best man, and maid of honor was Janet's sister, Ann Louise Fairlie. Bridesmaids were Janet's college friends Linda Kalbhenn and Sally Rizek. Janet's sister Fredericka and Bob's sister LaRone (both fifteen) were junior bridesmaids. Reverend John A. McConomy officiated, and the vocalist was Bob's cousin, William H. LaRone. The bride's father, Mr. Frederick W. Fairlie Jr., gave her away in marriage. Bill Reiff, George Horrocks, and Laverne "Jake" Miller were ushers. Bob's sister Elaine's husband Dick Heist would have been an usher but he had injured his foot and G. William Yeagle pinch-hit for him.

Nancy Norris, social editor for the *Norristown Times Herald*, commented, "Although they didn't attend the same high school, the romance of Janet and her more-than-six-foot sandy-haired bridegroom began in high school days." (Bob's actual height was just a half-inch under six feet.) Ms. Norris also reported that "A summery color scheme of frosted green and white accented by pastel hues in bouquets was an effective one at the nuptials."

Two hundred and fifty people attended the wedding, and the reception afterward was in the church's social rooms. The evening before the wedding, the rehearsal dinner for thirty guests had been held at the Marshman home.

"We didn't have any money, so we went racing on our honeymoon," said Janet. They drove to a hotel in King of Prussia, Pennsylvania, Saturday night. "The next day," Janet recounted, "we drove up to Danbury for a race on Sunday."

On the first full day of their marriage, Bob and Janet were in Danbury for the postponed ARDC race and, in a fairy-tale outcome, Bob swept the day, winning not only the feature, but his heat and a semi as well. The team immediately loaded up and headed to New Jersey for a race that same night at Old Bridge. Bob's winning ways continued with victory in his heat. He was then third in a match race between the three heat winners, Bert Brooks winning, with Red Marlowe, second. A seventh-place finish in the feature was a disappointment, although his teammate Al Herman won.

After the race, the newlyweds headed to Bob's aunt Cora's house on Cape May at the Jersey shore.

Chapter 19
Moving Steadily Ahead (1959)

The young, newly married couple—Bob was twenty-two and Janet was twenty-one—initially moved in with the Marshman household in Yerkes. They were away at the races a great deal of the time, and Janet recalled the multigenerational families getting along well. In August they found a small house to rent in Sanatoga owned by Janet's brother-in-law's father. "It was remote," said Janet, "on a gravel road. We were happy there, although the early years were lean in terms of income."

The weekend of June 26–28 was busy, with three races. On Friday night at his Hatfield home track, Bob won his ten-lap heat and was second to Red Riegel of Reading in the match race of heat winners. Riegel also won the feature, with Bob unplaced. At Wall Stadium in Belmar, New Jersey, the next evening, Bob's best finish was a fourth in his heat. It all came right for Bobby Marshman on Sunday afternoon at Heidelberg Raceway, southwest of Pittsburgh. *NSSN* called Bobby the "big gun" as he won his heat, and in the fifty-lap feature on the half-mile dirt oval, he won by a half-lap margin over teammate Len Duncan. It was an impressive win as he moved steadily from his seventh starting position to pass race leader Dutch Schaefer on the fifteenth lap, going by "like a mail train," according to an *NSSN* reporter. (Some reporters were now calling Bob the "Collegeville Comet," which was somewhat closer to home than the "Pottstown Flyer" or "Pottstown Flash," as he was frequently referred to by the press.) A serious injury during the race was suffered by Bob Dittrich of Pittsburgh, Pennsylvania, who rode over the wheel of another car and flipped the White Brothers' Offy nine times.

The July 5 ARDC midget race at Williams Grove Speedway was a crowd-pleaser. The lead changed seven times before Jiggs Peters claimed first, just 35 yards ahead of Len Duncan. Pushing hard only 100 yards behind was third-place finisher Bill Homeier. Jimmy Davis was fourth, and Bobby, fifth.

On Saturday, July 18, and Friday, July 24, Bob had races at Hatfield, where he was third in the feature both times. Jim Packard won the Friday race, with Al Herman second. Finishing fifth, in a rare midget appearance, was Eddie Sachs. Sachs, who had married Nancy Ann McGarrity just a week before Bob and Janet's wedding, was a longtime friend of George Marshman's. Sachs, who already enjoyed a national reputation and was an Indianapolis veteran, had taken an interest in Bobby, and would continue to be a mentor to the younger man.

In a twenty-five-mile feature on the fast Trenton track on July 26, Bobby finished a close second to Gig Stephens. In winning, Stephens broke the record set by Bobby the previous year, pushing the new record to 104.9. In a race where the leaders were described as being "under a blanket" the entire way, it was Bobby on the last lap who made a final bid for the lead, only to slide wide and settle for second.

•   •   •

Sam Nunis made every midget race on the fast one-mile Trenton circuit an exercise in how to promote a race. Coming up at Trenton on August 23 was a 250-mile USAC/ARDC-sanctioned race with a purse in excess of $17,500. In his pre-race announcements, Nunis was featuring as favorites the "handsome" Gig Stephens of Reading, Massachusetts, and "the kid," Bobby Marshman. "Two top-notch auto racing jockeys whose talents are channeled against the greatest collection of motor maniacs ever gathered," Nunis said. In the event, it was Jiggs Peters in a Ken Brenn car who won the race, while Bobby was classified a DNF in eighteenth place of the thirty-nine starters. Not long after, on September 5, Bobby won his heat in a Sam Nunis promotion at Flemington; he was fourth in the feature.

It was a whirlwind schedule, and Bob was fortunate to be employed by his father, who understood, more than anyone, that racing took precedence over time on the job. Almost all of the races were within a day's drive of home, and Janet attended most of them with Bob.

Back at Hatfield on Friday night, September 11, Bob was leading the first heat when he felt the steering snap. Braking hard, he was hit in the tail by the car behind him. Bob's car flipped over, landing with the cowl on top of the guardrail before rolling down the embankment. Fortunately, Bobby was uninjured. The next day George Marshman had Bobby hard at work fixing the damage to the fence and guardrail.

At Reading on Saturday night, September 19, Bobby came away with a third in his heat, and was third in the feature behind winner Bert Brooks and Dutch Schaefer. The next day the teams were at Trenton for a 100-mile midget contest. The race was stopped after 99 miles when leader Bert Brooks was badly burned. Bobby had retired with mechanical trouble after seventy laps while running third. Jim Shaffer of New Castle, Pennsylvania, was declared the winner.

For his twenty-third birthday on Thursday, September 24, Bobby was at Springfield, Massachusetts, where he finished second to Bill Randall. Two days later Bobby switched things up, stepping back into the Ellis Brothers URC sprint car to contest the Atlantic Rural Exposition Sweepstakes on the third-of-a-mile Richmond, Virginia, track. Bobby was impressive, winning his heat and the feature in dominant fashion. As *NSSN* told it, "Midget star Bobby Marshman turned to his first love last Saturday afternoon, strapped his long lean frame into the bucket of the Ellis Bros. Red Ram sprinter, and blazed through a stellar field." The result demonstrated how his time in the fiercely contested midget battles had sharpened his skills and added to his confidence. When he left the URC, barely two years before, he had become a competitive driver with the chance for an occasional win. On this day, he demonstrated that he had taken a major step forward as a driver.

On October 11, Bobby held his own in the USAC Sprint Car (Eastern) race at Williams Grove Speedway. Driving the Caruso Offy, Bobby finished eighth in the fifty-lap feature from a thirteenth starting position after winning the consi. Race winner Tommy Hinnershitz led all the way home in his Pfrommer Offy, nailing his seventh USAC Eastern Championship. Contender Eddie Sachs, who was the fast qualifier, spun out on lap 36, damaging his car but escaping injury. Gene Hartley claimed second and Jiggs Peters, third.

Bob was in Raleigh, North Carolina, on October 17, to again drive the Ellis Brothers No. 8 car in the URC season final, but torrential rains forced cancellation of the event.

Bobby and Janet were among the 534 people attending the November 21 ARDC banquet at Somerville, New Jersey's, Fair Hills Inn, where he was awarded a trophy as fifth-place finisher in season points. He was also named the ARDC's most improved driver of the year. With 2,610 points, he trailed his teammate and champion Len Duncan's 3,120 points. Bob had been third in points going into September, but his end-of-season results dropped him two positions. It was disappointing only in that he had been third the previous year. The reality was that he had enjoyed another great season in a fiercely competitive series. The thirty-eight races in the series averaged thirty-one starters per race.

Racing wasn't over for the winter. The American Three Quarter Midget Racing Association (ATQMRA) sanctioned indoor racing for three-quarter (TQ) midgets at two prominent East Coast venues. The winter season opened in December on Sunday afternoons at the Island Garden Arena in West Hempstead, New York, and was scheduled to run every week into March. A parallel series was set to debut at the Armory in Teaneck, New Jersey, the first Saturday of the coming new year, and was also scheduled to run into March.

Bobby had arranged a drive in the TQ car of prominent entrant Jack Dowie. Although purses were small in the TQ races, the combined series attracted top drivers. Many maintained that they ran the small cars primarily to stay sharp and in shape over the winter months. This was likely the truth, as the race purse was usually $750. The Hempstead track was one-tenth of a mile around, the tight circuit requiring precision driving and a willingness to push and shove to get to the front. These circumstances often resulted in feuds that erupted in fisticuffs after, or even during, the race card.

Despite a second-place finish in the semi at the Hempstead opener on December 13, Bobby only managed an eleventh-place finish in the feature, won by defending indoor TQ champion Jim Lacy. Bobby had better luck on December 27, with a second-place finish in the consi and a third-place finish in the feature, won by Len Duncan.

Janet's first year of teaching had begun in September at West Pottsgrove Township Elementary School, where she taught second grade. They were a two-car family, with Bob driving their new Volkswagen Beetle and Janet driving a 1937 Plymouth to school. "To start it you had to put up the hood, open the air filter, put a screwdriver in the carburetor, shoot a spray of ether, close it up, and get back in to start it," said Janet. "When I would be at school I would park it at the top of a hill and pop the clutch when it got rolling." While racing income was minimal in the winter months, Janet's stable job made the difference, and she remembered it as a happy time. Best of all, they were expecting a child in 1960.

Chapter 20
More Three-Quarter Midget Adventures (1960)

The January 6, 1960, issue of *National Speed Sport News* splashed a welcome new year headline: BOBBY MARSHMAN TOPS HEMPSTEAD TQ FIELD. After finishing second in the heat and again second in the semi, on January 3 Bobby drove Jack Dowies's car to victory in the first race of the season. From a seventh-place starting position, Bobby was second by the seventh lap to race leader Bob Albert of White Plains, New York. The two men swapped the lead in the following laps until lap 29, when Albert was caught up in a spin with backmarkers. Bobby drove on for the win. He was said to be, at twenty-three, the youngest driver in the race.

The following weekend, Bobby was fourth in the Saturday night feature at Teaneck in a race won by Russ Klar. It was the evening of the URC banquet in Trenton, where a telegram from Bobby

and Janet was read expressing their regret that the race conflict had caused them to miss the event. The next day at Hempstead, Bobby led the first ten laps of the twenty-lap feature, only to spin. He charged back to finish second to race winner Jim Lacy.

"At Teaneck you didn't want to sit too high in the bleachers because the ventilation wasn't too good, so they would open the doors and you would sit in there, freezing," explained Bill Reiff. "If you were up too high, you could hardly see the race cars because of all the fumes and the fog."

"I didn't often go to Teaneck for the TQ races because I couldn't stand the fumes," said Janet. "They would open the Armory doors about five or six inches to try to get the exhaust out but it didn't help much, and just made the place cold. It was an ordeal, particularly with me being pregnant."

On a memorable drive home after one of the Teaneck races that Janet did attend, the little VW showed its mettle with Bob at the wheel. "Bobby Hillis was with us, and so was Laverne Miller. Laverne was big, and so was Bobby Hillis, and Bob was pretty big, and I was in the back seat, pregnant," recalled Janet. "It was snowy and icy, and we're going around a traffic circle when the Beetle just toppled over and rolled again onto its tires—no seat belts then, remember. It was a slow roll through the snow, and everybody was okay. Bob explained that the circle was banked the wrong way, and, of course, we all bought his story."

At Teaneck on January 16, Bobby won his heat and overcame a lap 7 tangle of cars in the feature to take a fourth-place finish. Indianapolis drivers Johnny Parsons and Jack Turner attended the race

as spectators, and, as reported by Chris Economaki in his *NSSN* column, they declared that Bobby Marshman was "the smoothest driver on the floor."

At Hempstead on Sunday, Bobby won his heat and was awarded second place in the feature four hours after it was over. He finished fifth on the track, but ATQMRA officials decided that apparent winner Jim Lacy had passed on a yellow flag and disqualified him, along with his brother Joe Lacy and Tony Romit for the same infraction. The ruling gave the win to Fred Clifton of Paterson, New Jersey, and awarded Bobby second.

In January, Bob Marshman and Bill Reiff received their military draft notices from the Selective Service Commission. The boyhood friends were now both married with pregnant wives. They traveled together to Norristown to report as ordered, each carrying a small satchel to be ready, should they be taken immediately. They explained that their wives were pregnant and came home with paperwork to be filled out by the physicians. The procedure included providing a birth certificate when the child was born. Sadly, Bill's wife Charlotte miscarried. While Bob was deferred from military service, Bill was soon called into the Army for a two-year stint. The draft was taking married men, but not those with children.

LARRY MENDELSOHN · presents
THE 2nd RACE OF CHAMPIONS

MIDGET AUTO RACES

indoors
with Indianapolis Drivers

BOBBY MARSHMAN, KUTZTOWN, PA.

7 RACES - 50 LAP FEATURE

DON'T MISS THE TOP AUTO RACING DRIVERS IN THE WORLD.
OVER 40 CARS AND DRIVERS INCLUDING

LEN DUNCAN	JOHNNY COY	CHARLIE BETTMAN	BOBBY ALBERTS
TONY BONADIES	TONY ROMIT	JIM LACY	SONNY SANDERS
DUTCH SCHAEFER	BOBBY MARSHMAN	FRED CLIFTON	SY KABACK
RUSS KLAR	GORDEN EISENHOWER	KING CARPENTER	AL KEMP

and many others

Starter: JOHNNY ZEKE   Announcer: NAT KLEINFIELD

1 NITE ONLY - FRI., JAN. 20th 8:30 P.M.

indoors
in the multimillion dollar

LONG ISLAND ARENA

Admission: $2.00, $2.50, $3.00
Children ½ price

At Teaneck on January 23, the feature was described as "a particularly rough race." Bobby was caught up in a lap 1 tangle, but struggled back to finish tenth in a race won by Len Duncan. He had finished second in his heat and won the semi. The next day at Hempstead, he was fifth in the feature, with the win going to Jim Lacy.

After dropping out of his heat at Teaneck on January 30, Bobby finished third in the semi to qualify for the feature, finishing second behind Len Duncan. On Sunday, Bobby won his heat and then finished third in the Hempstead feature behind Jim Lacy, who won, and Duncan, who took second. At the halfway point in the Teaneck indoor series, Bobby was in a tie with Fred Clifton for third place, with 336 points. Len Duncan was leading with 392, and defending champion Jim Lacy was in second, with 344.

On February 20 at Teaneck, Bobby was eliminated in a multicar pileup. At Hempstead the next day he was second to Len Duncan in the feature.

The March 2 cover of *NSSN* declared in bold: MARSHMAN MASTER AT TEANECK, to describe the outcome of the February 27 Teaneck TQ race. It was a satisfying comeback for Bobby after the trouble the previous week. Inside the weekly newspaper, the race story was topped with the headline: IT'S MARSHMAN IN WILD ONE AT TEANECK. The opening sentence of the story described the melee: "The wildest TQ midget auto racing program ever seen at the Teaneck Armory saw cars overturned, another vault the guardrail, one driver carted off to the hospital, multicar crashes, and a brilliant victory carved out by Bobby Marshman." Bobby had kept his cool and driven through all obstacles while battling Len Duncan throughout. Duncan had won both the heat and semi just ahead of Bobby, but Bobby Marshman had it when it counted most, in the feature.

After a two-week break to host a boat show, Hempstead was expected to run the last four races in its series. The ATQMRA was not satisfied with the preparation of the facility; certain safety features that had existed before the break were now not in place. Promoters Lou Figari and Larry Mendelsohn were unable to persuade management of the arena to work out their differences with the ATQMRA, and the balance of the series was canceled with little notice.

On March 5, Teaneck ran the final race in its series as scheduled. The 100-lap feature awarded double points, and the purse was boosted from the usual $750 to $1,000. Bobby ended his TQ season with a sixth-place finish. He had been forced to pit to change his left rear tire, and the stop dropped him from contention for the lead. Tony Bonadies won the race, with Len Duncan second.

In April the ATQMRA announced the final point standings, recognizing Len Duncan as the indoor TQ champion, with 1,712 points, which combined points earned at Teaneck and Hempstead. Jim Lacy was second, with 1,528, and Bobby Marshman, third, with 1,514.

Chapter 21
Welcome, Robbie (1960)

Getting a ride and making the next step up the ladder is the near-constant preoccupation of most serious race car drivers. One frustration for Bob was close at hand. Doug Stearly, a good friend who lived right next door in Collegeville, was an active entrant of championship and sprint cars.

"Bobby couldn't understand why his friend Doug didn't give him a shot in one of his cars," recalled Bill Reiff. "I was working for Stearly Motor Freight and I knew Doug's feelings on the subject. He wouldn't let Bobby run his race car because he knew what the outcome of things in racing could be, and Bobby and George and Doug were friends. Doug told me, 'If something happens, I [couldn't] live with it.' And I'm glad, because he had some bad luck with drivers. He was simply too close to the Marshman family."

ABOVE: Bobby drove Frank Calandrillo's famous Frankie Cal Offy in the USAC sprint car races at Reading in August. He did not finish the feature. (IMRRC / KEVIN HUGHEY COLLECTION)

Janet recalled the pressure that came from many people outside the racing fraternity.

"Those were hard years of getting started, 1955 until 1961. Those tough years were hard for Bob—people were always questioning him, when he was going to do this or that. They didn't know how difficult it was to get a ride. They had no idea what that even was."

The ATQMRA held its awards dinner at the Friar Tuck Inn in Cedar Grove, New Jersey, on April 16. Bobby and Janet wanted very much to attend, but could only make a brief appearance because the next day Bobby had a drive in the Cal-Offy for the USAC sprint car race at Reading. The Cal-Offy, owned and entered by Frankie Calandrillo, was an older car that had started life as a Kurtis-Kraft midget and was stretched in the mid-1950s to sprint car specifications. Bobby qualified the car sixteenth out of twenty-six entrants at Reading. His time was 26.87 seconds compared to the fastest qualifiers—Don Branson at 24.91, and A. J. Foyt, at 24.93. Bobby's third-place finish in the consi earned him a thirteenth-position starting place of sixteen cars qualified for the feature. The Cal-Offy was unready to make the start, and Bud Tingelstad, the first alternate, moved into the starting field while Bobby watched the feature from the sidelines. The Easter Sunday race was won by A. J. Foyt, with Jim Hurtubise second. Len Duncan, Bobby Marshman's friend and teammate on the Hespell midget team, was driving the Stearly Motor Freight Special, and also failed to make the start of the feature.

Bobby was back in the No. 4 Hespell midget for the ARDC season opener at Hatfield on May 6. He was third in his heat, and in the feature was eighth behind winner Ernie McCoy and second-place Len Duncan.

At Williams Grove on May 15, after winning his heat, Bobby was third behind winning driver Gig Stephens and Len Duncan. On this day Bob's friend Eddie Sachs put the Dean Van Lines Special on the pole for the Indianapolis 500.

Williams Grove was on a Sunday, and Janet did not attend, as she was close to her due date. Bob's friend Bobby Hillis accompanied him, and because it was a daytime race, they returned early.

"Bob hadn't been home ten minutes when I said to him, 'I've got to go to the hospital,'" recalled Janet. "So we drove to the Norristown Hospital. We had no plans for the possibility that Bob may not have been there when the baby came. Thank God he wasn't a drinker, or he may have stopped somewhere on the way back. But he didn't drink at all, and Hillis didn't either."

George Robert Marshman Jr. was born the same day. Rob—or Robbie, as he was always known—was a healthy and happy baby. In his earliest weeks, the infant didn't attend his father's races, but stayed home with Janet.

· · ·

After a weekend of rainouts at Reading and Old Bridge, Bob spent Memorial Day weekend as a spectator at Indianapolis for the forty-fourth running of the Indianapolis 500. While at the Speedway, Bob visited friends who were in the thirty-three-car field, including Johnny Thomson and Al Keller. Eddie Sachs, despite being in demand as pole sitter, and one of the race favorites, made certain that Bob met some of the influential figures who owned or crewed cars in the field. Sachs also pulled off an arrangement that was the highlight of Bob's weekend. Bobby Marshman got to sit in the back seat of the official Oldsmobile 98 pace car driven by Sam Hanks on the pace lap, with the thirty-three starters following.

"Eddie Sachs, who has done much for me in racing, knew a guy who knew a guy, and I was invited to make the spin in the pace car. Sachsie, of course, was right behind us, driving from pole position," Bob told Red McCarthy of the *Norristown Times Herald*.

Bobby witnessed one of the greatest races in Speedway history. After Eddie Sachs dropped out of the race with magneto problems, Rodger Ward and Jim Rathmann battled for the lead in a suspenseful finish, with Rathmann the eventual winner. Bobby's friend Johnny Thomson had a great race, too, as he pressured Ward and Rathmann from third place before falling back with engine troubles, settling for a fifth-place finish.

Bobby came home from Indianapolis with the firm resolve that next year he would move from a ride in the pace car to a drive in the show.

Chapter 22
Moving On (1960)

On the weekend of June 3–5, Bobby Marshman was back in the seat of the Hespell No. 4 midget. At New York's Freeport Speedway on Friday night, he was second in the Class B contest behind Russ Klar and ahead of Andy Furci; Bob's friend and teammate Al Herman won the ARDC feature. Saturday the ARDC teams were at Danbury, Connecticut, and Bobby had the misfortune in the semi to be one of four cars to come upon water spilled from Len Wrobel's Ford-powered car when it blew its engine on the entry to turn one. Jiggs Peters and Bobby both hit the fence, ending their day; Bob Courtwright and Red Marlowe hit each other, and although both cars flipped and put the drivers out of the race, neither Courtwright nor Marlowe was badly injured. Tony Romit won the feature. The third ARDC race of the weekend was at Hatfield on Sunday. Ernie McCoy won the feature, and Bobby took third in his heat and was eighth in the feature.

ABOVE: The program for the opening sprint car race of the season at Reading in March of 1960. (RMA)

Bobby got the best of a spirited duel with Al Herman for third place in the feature on June 11 at Old Dominion Speedway in Manassas, Virginia. Ernie McCoy won the race, with Dutch Schaefer second.

Just a week later, darkness fell upon the Hespell team and the entire ARDC family when Al Herman died in a ten-car crash on the first lap at West Haven, Connecticut. Herman vaulted a slowing car and flipped into the infield. He suffered a broken neck and skull fracture and died in Saint Raphael Hospital in New Haven. Allentown, Pennsylvania's, Homer Gerald "Al" Herman was thirty-three years old and left behind his wife, June, and nine-year-old son Jimmy. He had raced in the Indianapolis 500 every year since 1955, when he was named Rookie of the Year. The racing world was further shattered when legendary driver Jimmy Bryan died the next day in a first-lap crash at Langhorne Speedway. Thirty-four-year-old James Ernest Bryan of Phoenix, Arizona, was a three-time National Champion and winner of the 1958 Indianapolis 500.

The Hespell team paid tribute to Al Herman by not running their No. 3 car in the two races the following weekend. The first, at Danbury on Saturday, June 25, was won by Tony Romit, with Bobby Marshman managing only a third in his heat. The following day at Reading, the twice-rained-out race promoted by Bobby's brother-in-law Dick Heist was finally run. Bobby managed only a second in his heat. The feature was won by Chuck Arnold. Bobby expressed to intimates his disappointment in the car's engine.

Bill Holland, winner of the 1949 Indianapolis 500, joined the Hespell team for the 100-lap race at Williams Grove on July 3, in the No. 3 car previously driven by Al Herman. Bobby did not qualify for the feature, and the reason was apparent to most observers: Nick Nicolosi in *NSSN* stated that

Bobby's car seemed to be running on three cylinders. Tony Bonadies captured the 100-lap feature. The next day on the half-mile dirt fairground track at York, Pennsylvania, things were not much better, although Bobby managed to make the feature with a third-place finish in the consi. He did not place, after being caught up in a multicar crash.

In what turned out to be Bobby Marshman's last race in the Hespell No. 4 car, he won his heat at Danbury, Connecticut. Despite that good effort, the car was not right for the feature. Bob enjoyed close ties with Harry Hespell and the entire Hespell operation, but, having suffered numerous disappointments all season with his car, now felt the need to move on.

Bobby accepted an offer to drive the Konstant Hot midget from the racing stable of Bruce Homeyer of Caldwell, New Jersey. Homeyer was also an entrant of sprint cars and championship cars, all carrying the Konstant Hot moniker, the brand name for Homeyer's electric water-heating and -dispensing products. The No. 19 midget was bright yellow with black trim.

Bobby was moving on. There are times when a driver has to make a change, however difficult it may be on a personal level.

Chapter 23
Konstant Hot on a Hot July Day (1960)

The debut race for Bobby Marshman in the Konstant Hot car was the July 24 Trenton 300, in the longest and richest midget race of the year. On a hot summer day, Bobby won in spectacular fashion, and was the only driver in the race not to require relief. At the finish he was twenty-six seconds ahead of Chuck Arnold and Jiggs Peters, who had shared the driving in Ken Brenn's car. The 300-mile distance—Red McCarthy in the *Norristown Times Herald* called it the "longest small auto event ever held, and a feat of driving and physical endurance"—took its toll on everyone, including Bobby. He collapsed in the winner's circle shortly after accepting the trophy and accolades, and was taken to Helene Fuld Hospital in Trenton where he was released after receiving fluids.

"Everything was fine through the race. I was real steady through the late laps, didn't feel woozy or anything. But after it was over and the relaxation set in, I just caved in," Bobby told the press. "The doc said I was dehydrated, and I remembered that I didn't take the time to get a real drink the two times I pulled into the pits. Under those same conditions, I'll make sure I get a good drink next time."

The race lead changed eight times, and Bobby first took the front spot on lap 84. He led until lap 133, when he stopped for thirty-four seconds for fuel and tires. Jiggs Peters took the lead and held it until he stopped on lap 190 for fuel and to turn the car over to Chuck Arnold. Bobby resumed the lead and held it to the finish. He completed the 300 laps of the one-mile paved Trenton track in 3 hours, 8 minutes, and 27.14 seconds, an average speed of 95.514 mph.

Twenty percent of the $15,160 purse ($3,032) went to the race winner. Based on the standard owner–driver agreement of a 40 percent split of winnings to the driver, Bobby would have taken home $1,212.80. Considering that this was by far the richest purse of the ARDC season, the figure brings home the need for drivers to maintain a steady job outside of racing. Bobby used most of his share of the purse to pay off the loan on the family VW.

" 'It couldn't have been won by a nicer guy,' was the word of almost every car owner and mechanic Sunday, after Bobby Marshman, the mild-mannered easygoing midget chauffeur copped the longest midget race ever run at a speedway," wrote Nick Nicolosi in his *NSSN* column.

"Bobby, who had experienced poor luck all season, couldn't be denied Sunday, as he outdrove and outlasted a field of many midget greats," Nicolosi continued. "All year long the youthful Bobby had many a misfortune in his No. 4 Hespell mount. The change, although we know he hated to do it, was perhaps the best move for him and those concerned with the best interests of the sport."

In a race won by Dutch Schaefer at Danbury, Connecticut, on August 6, Bobby was second in his heat and fourth in the semi, but did not make the feature. At Freeport Municipal Stadium on

Long Island in a Thursday night, August 11, show, he was third in his semi but again did not make the feature. Tony Romit flipped his car in the race and was taken to Freeport Doctors Hospital to recover from his injuries.

On Saturday afternoon of the same weekend, at the Erie County Fair in Hamburg, New York, Bobby was third in the first heat and ninth in the feature, won by Ernie McCoy. Back "home" at Hatfield on Sunday, he enjoyed the best result of the long weekend, finishing third in the feature behind McCoy and Len Duncan. Bobby and Duncan waged a terrific battle for the second spot, and earlier in the day Bobby had the satisfaction of winning a three-man match race over McCoy and Dutch Schaefer.

Bobby and car owner Bruce Homeyer ventured west to contest the Milwaukee Midget Century, a USAC 100-mile race on the famed Milwaukee Mile in West Allis, Wisconsin, on August 27. Tony Bettenhausen of Tinley Park, Illinois, won the race, and Bobby's fellow ARDC driver Jiggs Peters brought Ken Brenn's midget home second. Don Branson was third in the star-studded field, and Bobby finished eighth of the thirty starters, just ahead of Parnelli Jones in ninth. Bobby afterward compared Milwaukee to the similar one-mile track at Trenton, saying the Eastern track was faster on the straightaways, but that Milwaukee was more uniform and easier to drive. Al Krause for *NSSN* singled Bobby out for praise, saying, "Another talented young Easterner who looked real good was Bobby Marshman driving the Konstant Hot Offy. Marshman started well back in the field but forged through steadily and wound up in eighth place."

In September, the ARDC ran two back-to-back midweek events in different states. Tuesday, September 13, found Bobby at Reading, Pennsylvania, where he had a second-place heat finish on the half-mile dirt track and a ninth in the feature. The next day, Bobby competed at the Upper Marlboro, Maryland, track, which ran double features of twenty-five laps each. For the first Maryland event, Bobby won his heat and finished seventh in the feature. In the second feature, he was involved in a three-car crash on the second turn of the first lap with Ernie McCoy and Tony Bonadies that put him out of the race. Earlier Bobby had prevailed with a win in a three-car match race over Bill Randall and Bert Brooks.

Chapter 24
Venison on the Table (1960)

The weekend of September 24–25, Bobby Marshman was entered in a sprint car race at the Allentown Fair in Lehigh County, Pennsylvania, and in a championship race at Trenton; in both events he drove cars owned by Ray Brady. Brady, a Studebaker dealer in Norristown, Pennsylvania, was a frequent entrant in the Indianapolis 500. In the Allentown sprint car event on Saturday, Bobby was in Brady's Kurtis-Offy and drove to a sixth-place finish in the semi. It was not good enough to earn him a start

in the feature. The race was won by Jimmy Packard, a friend of Bob's. Packard had enjoyed great success since they first met in the URC and appeared to be on the cusp of stardom. A week later, Packard died in a crash in a midget race at Fairfield, Illinois.

The historical importance of the Allentown race is the death of the enormously popular Johnny Thomson. Thomson was the driver that Bob Marshman most looked up to and admired. The "Flying Scot," as he was popularly known, was one of the leading drivers of the time, a pole position at the 1959 Indianapolis 500 among his achievements. He lived in nearby Boyerstown, Pennsylvania, and had befriended Bob. At Allentown he was in a car owned by Doug Stearly. Stearly had recently purchased the sprint car from Sam Traylor, who had previously run a pair of cars for Mike Nazaruk and Charlie Musselman.

Although Bill Reiff was in the Army, he had worked for Stearly Motor Freight, and had come home on leave the day of the race. He was too late to attend the Allentown race, but recalled the circumstances of the crash as told to him by Doug Stearly.

"Johnny Thomson was without a drive, and Stearly took the car he had just purchased from Sam Traylor to Allentown. Doug told me that he didn't like the look of the track conditions and was in favor of not running the race. He told Johnny, 'Let's park this; it's too dirty out here.' Thomson said, 'No, the car will win this show.' He went into the boards and it cut his legs and he died."

Doctors worked on Thomson for five hours in an attempt to save his life. The impact of his death was felt throughout the American racing world. The Flying Scot had made friends everywhere he went and impressed all with his personality and remarkable talent. He was survived by his wife Evelyn and four children: Dale, ten; Dana, six; David, four; and Daryl, three.

"Johnny Thomson was a great guy, and it was devastating to Bob when he died," said Janet. "Johnny and Bob mirrored one another for temperament."

• • •

The mood at Trenton the next day was one of sadness as news of the outcome of Johnny Thomson's crash spread through the pits. Bobby Marshman was in Brady's champ car for the Trenton 100-mile USAC championship race. Brady had both an older Kurtis-Kraft 4000 dirt car and a roadster, and the team was one of many that chose their dirt car for the paved one-mile Trenton track.

Bobby was one of twelve drivers, including Parnelli Jones and Lloyd Ruby, required to run familiarization laps and take the Trenton driving test the morning of the race. His qualifying time of 37.26 seconds was only the thirtieth-fastest of the thirty-four cars entered; Don Branson's pole time was 34.90. Only twenty-two cars qualified, leaving Bobby on the sidelines. This was nevertheless an important event for Bobby—his first shot at the Big Time. The race was won by Eddie Sachs in the Kuzma-built Dean Van Lines dirt car, followed by Rodger Ward in the Watson-built Leader Card roadster, and, in third place, A. J. Foyt in the Kurtis-built Bowes Seal Fast roadster.

OPPOSITE: Bob's Konstant Hot midget on display today at the Eastern Auto Racing Museum. (EASTERN AUTO RACING MUSEUM)

Back in the yellow-and-black Konstant Hot midget at the Bloomsburg Fair in Pennsylvania's Columbia County on Saturday, October 1, Bobby won his heat and then finished fourth in the feature behind race winner Al Keller of Green Acres City, Florida. Bobby and Keller and their families were becoming close friends. The next day Bobby finished fourth behind race winner Ray Brown in the 100-lap feature at Old Bridge, New Jersey. Chuck Arnold and Red Marlowe were second and third.

In a promotional blurb for the upcoming TQ race at Commack, New York, Bobby was identified as from Reading, Pennsylvania, and touted as "one of the greats of Indianapolis in the years ahead." While the unidentified writer missed on Reading, he or she proved prescient regarding Bob's future as a star at the Brickyard. At the Commack race on November 5, Bob was fourth in his heat in a Triumph-powered TQ and second in the semifinal. He finished eleventh in the fifty-lap feature. Fred Clifton of Paterson, New Jersey, was the race winner.

Bob and Janet were among the 710 people attending the ARDC annual dinner dance at the Far Hills Inn in Somerville, New Jersey, on November 19. ARDC president Dutch Schaefer was also the series champion for 1960; Bob was ninth in points. On the front of the November 23 issue of *NSSN* covering the event, a Chris Economaki photo pictured Bobby arm in arm with Red Marlowe. They were featured as the oldest and youngest winners of features during the season: Marlowe was fifty-nine, and Bob, twenty-four.

That winter Bobby took up a new interest. Growing up he had never been a hunter, but the practical issues of a tight family budget inspired him to get involved.

"Next to auto racing, he would rather stalk deer than anything else," said Janet. "Bobby had his first kill in December 1960. We lived on venison that whole winter. My sister Kay and her husband Don had a vegetable garden—they had the vegetables, and we had the venison. Every once in a while we would get a pound of ground meat and add it to our ground venison, and that was living high on the hog. It was communal living at its finest. I was teaching, but still, you had to watch everything."

Chapter 25
Portent of Change (1961)

Just as the new year of 1961 would bring recognition and new opportunities for Bobby Marshman, so too was it a pivotal year for American racing, with a portent of change in the air. Bobby's transition was perhaps more obvious: He started the year in an armory racing three-quarter midgets, but by May was in the field for the Indianapolis 500. On the larger scene, when Jack Brabham and the rear-engine Cooper made a more than credible showing in the 500, many in the racing industry shrugged it off as an anomaly. More-thoughtful observers saw it as the first step into a new era.

Rear-engine cars had appeared at the Speedway in the late 1930s, and as recently as 1951, but none of those efforts were as successful as Jack Brabham's turn in the Cooper. When the Australian

Brabham, who had won the Formula One World Championship in 1959 and 1960, appeared at Indianapolis in October of 1960, he was received with respect even among those unimpressed with the funny-looking rear-engine Formula One car. Team owner John Cooper and Brabham—taking advantage of being in America for an international Formula Libre race at Watkins Glen, New York, on October 9—took the opportunity to fit in two test days at Indianapolis. The speeds they achieved with the 2.5-liter (155-cubic-inch) Formula One Coventry Climax engine, although not record-breaking, were competitive, and the source of great interest and conjecture. Throughout the winter, speculation abounded on how such a car might perform with more horsepower, and whether the Cooper team would return in May for the 500.

Bobby Marshman's focus at the start of the year was the opening round of the 1961 ATQMRA series at the Teaneck Armory on Saturday night, January 7. The eight-race series would run into late March. According to Nate Kleinfield in *Illustrated Speedway News*, "the show was big in every respect with as wild a program as has ever been since the sport made its local debut in 1951." Some among the overflow crowd couldn't find a place to park and chose to leave their vehicles outside the main entrance. Police and firemen, as well as state troopers, were summoned. Fourteen cars were towed, and the organizers were threatened with suspension of their license to operate events at the Armory. Bobby was third in his heat and third again in the eighteen-lap semi, where Kleinfield credited him with "some nifty drifting." But Bobby did not finish the feature.

The following Saturday, January 14, thirty-five cars appeared for the Armory race. Bob's car was looked after by Norm Smizer, who owned the cars driven by Len Duncan and Dutch Schaefer. The race was reported as the closest finish in the ten years the TQ cars had been running at Teaneck. The first half of the race featured a fierce battle between Bobby and Duncan for second place. Duncan got away from Bobby and caught race leader Ernie Borelli, providing the action over the last half of the race. Borelli prevailed by an incredibly close margin, and Bobby Marshman was third.

•　　•　　•

Area temperatures below zero degrees accompanied by three- to five-foot snowdrifts presented a challenge, but the January 21 races went on as scheduled. Bobby was third in his heat and second in the semi. Starting eighth in the feature, Bob was soon up to third place. Late in the race he was held up by cars he was lapping and fell to fifth. On the last corner of the last lap, he whipped out of the corner on the low side to pass two cars and finish in third place.

On an eventful evening, Len Duncan won the January 28 Teaneck feature, with Bobby second. He had run sixth in his heat in a Noll Crosley owned by Norm Smizer. (Between the heat and semi, Smizer sold the car to Mel Carnival and Pete Reimuller, for $2,000.) Needing a strong result in the semi, Bobby fought hard to move up from seventh to second by the start of the last lap, and, as told by Nat Kleinfield in *NSSN*, "roared off the fourth turn at the finish flag to win, perhaps by inches, over Sy Kaback." Bob had brought victory to the new owners in their first race with the car, and was leading the series in points.

The Teaneck race on February 18, the Oilzum Trophy Sweepstakes, carried double prize money and drew forty-seven cars, the largest entry up to that time for an East Coast TQ race. The race had been scheduled for February 4, but blizzard conditions caused the event to be moved to February 18. (February 11 was a scheduled break for the TQ cars, as the Armory had a conflicting event.) Bobby, now in the Dowie Triumph, missed making the final by one position in the semi. In order to protect his point lead, an arrangement was made with Don Morris, who, having qualified for the feature by winning his heat and the semi, sportingly allowed Bob to take over his seat. All the effort was for naught, as Bobby dropped out of the 100-lap race on lap 37.

The very nature of racing on a tenth-of-a-mile track almost guaranteed fierce and rough driving. The February 25 show at Teaneck featured hard-nosed racing, including some fistfights. Bobby stayed clear of the fights, but after qualifying for the feature, again did not finish. Chris Economaki commented in his *NSSN* column that "Teaneck shows are getting wilder and wilder on and off the track."

As the Teaneck TQ series began to wind down, Bob was still hopeful of winning the series championship. On March 4, he took the feature lead on lap 2 from Jerry Wall, but a six-car pileup behind them forced a restart. Bob was second, but re-passed Wall for the lead and held it until lap 19, when Len Duncan passed him. Bobby immediately took back the lead and held it until lap 23, when Duncan took the top position for good. By race end, Bobby had dropped to third behind Jim Lacy, who took second. The point standings now showed Lacy with 676, Duncan with 620, and Marshman third, with 616.

Bobby's final hope for the championship was doused in the March 11 show when he was black-flagged in the semi because his car was smoking and dropping water. This left him out of the feature, which denied him the chance to stay in the points chase. In the final Armory TQ show on March 18, Bobby won the consi to make it into the 100-lap final. He was running second early in the race but did not finish. Philadelphian Len Duncan won the race, but Lacy of North Belmore, New York, clinched the championship.

Chapter 26
Upside Down at Trenton (1961)

Bobby now found another opportunity to drive a sprint car in races at Reading and at Trenton just two weeks apart, in late March and in early April. The car was the Iddings Meyer–Offy, owned and built by Henry Meyer and sponsored by the Iddings Auto Parts and Glass Company of Greenville, Ohio. The car, powered by a 220-cubic-inch Offenhauser, could be converted from an 85-inch (sprint car) wheelbase to a 93-inch wheelbase in order to be eligible to run as a championship car. Meyer, from Dayton, Ohio—who was to play a crucial role in Bobby Marshman's career—was a highly regarded car builder.

On the historic Reading Fairgrounds track on March 26, Bobby made a big impression in the USAC sprint car race by setting the fastest qualifying time of the day. He was said to have "electrified the crowd" on his qualifying run when he was the only man in the 25-second range, with a time of 25.76. *NSSN*'s Jim Lunt wrote in his column, "Guess the happiest man at Reading was Jay Miller, who saw his pal Bobby Marshman out-qualify the nation's best drivers. Bob handled the long-wheelbase Iddings just as easily as he does those record-breaking midgets at Trenton and elsewhere. If ever a man was ready for Indianapolis, here's one."

At the Reading feature, Bobby was alongside A. J. Foyt on the second row of the starting field. Don Branson and Jim Hurtubise were on the front row. Engine trouble quickly dropped Bob down the field in the race, and he finished twelfth. Foyt won the race, with Hurtubise second and Alvin "Cotton" Farmer, third.

On April 9, Bob was back in the Iddings car for the Trenton 100, the opening championship race

of the season. The event was significant for Bobby, representing the first time he qualified for USAC's championship series—he was twentieth-fastest of twenty-two starters from a field of thirty entrants.

In the 100-lap race on the one-mile track, all was going well for Bob until the thirty-seventh lap, when a brake broke on the back straight, throwing the Iddings car into the wall. *Illustrated Speedway News* reported that "the car went into a long sideways slide, struck the outer retaining wall first—bounced—struck the wall with the front end—flew into the air and flipped over—came down upside down on the rollbar—rolled over several times, and came to rest against the wall on all four wheels." The day after the race, the *Indianapolis Star* spotlighted the crash with two photos on the front page.

Bobby described the experience inside the car to Red McCarthy of the *Norristown Times Herald*: "The spot brakes exploded going into the third turn. With no brakes, I lost it, the car spun, climbed the fence, and flipped three times." Bobby was knocked out and had to be lifted from the car. He had suffered a concussion and was confined to Trenton's Helene Fuld Hospital for a week.

Later Bobby told Ed Broomhead of Philadelphia's *Evening Bulletin* that he didn't remember much of the accident. "I remember having brakes on the backstretch, but when I went to apply them in the third turn, they just weren't there. I also remember ducking down into the cockpit, and the next thing I can recall was waking up in the hospital."

The Trenton season opener for the championship series was won by Eddie Sachs in the Dean Van Lines Special, with Jim Hurtubise second in the Sterling Plumbing Special, and Troy Ruttman third, in the John Zink Trackburner.

111

Once out of the hospital, Bobby test-drove a midget at Hatfield to get back in shape for racing. While recuperating at home he received a phone call from Andy Granatelli inquiring how he was doing. They discussed Bob's upcoming trip to the Speedway to seek a ride in the 500. Granatelli had recently completed the purchase of the famed Novi enterprise, and in the *Indianapolis Star*, Bill Eggert wrote that the beloved Novis "have a new owner, new interest and new ideas."

Just two weeks after being upside down at Trenton and a week after being released from the hospital, Bob was racing at Langhorne in the 100-mile ARDC/USAC National Midget race. Bob told Red McCarthy, "At Langhorne it's just horsepower and nerve. It's what we call a 'flatten-out' track. You flatten-out the throttle, sit, and steer." Bob was driving Bruce Homeyer's Konstant Hot Special, and said to McCarthy, "It's number nine this year; last year we were number nineteen. And we have a good chance because that car just flies."

At Langhorne on April 30, Bobby qualified on the front row: He and Ernie McCoy were equal in time at 35.84 seconds, and they also shared the distinction of being the only qualifiers to exceed a 100-mph average. The track conditions were described as fast despite high winds and cloudy skies. In the race, Bobby led the first thirty laps, setting a record average pace at 100 mph for ten laps,

twenty laps at 99.861 mph, and thirty laps at 99.241. He pitted on lap 31 for a right rear tire, and Jiggs Peters went into a lead that he never gave up. Peters's tires had lasted the distance while most other top contenders stopped for a right rear tire. Bobby finished second, but a lap down to Peters, with Bill Randall third. The last twenty laps of the race featured a huge battle between Bobby and Randall for second place, Bobby taking the spot on the last lap when Randall ran low on fuel. Peters's Ken Brenn car was running on different Firestone tires with harder rubber than the other cars. Peters was said to have driven a shrewd race; however, his right rear was in shreds at the finish. He won the race at an average speed of 98.041 mph.

Bobby Marshman was gaining national notoriety. The week before Langhorne he had visited the offices of *National Speed Sport News* in Ridgewood, New Jersey, where he was photographed with staff pointing to an earlier front-page photo of his flip at Trenton. The resulting photo appeared on the front page of the May 3 issue. The caption credited him with being the Langhorne pacesetter before tire wear forced him into the pits.

PART 3 / LURE OF THE BRICKYARD

Chapter 27
The Phone Call (1961)

The garages at the Indianapolis Motor Speedway were the center of the racing world during the month of May. While many teams were housed there year-round, the remaining spaces were filled by late April, or the first few days of May, by as many as sixty or seventy teams from around the country. All were hopeful that their combination of car and driver would be the ticket to make the show as one of the thirty-three qualifiers for the 500.

Most teams were set with an established driver, but many entrants were open to trying a driver in their car who they believed, or hoped, could show the car's full potential. It was not uncommon for a team to try several different drivers over the month. As a result, the garages were populated with drivers hoping to break in to the big show. Some were rookies and others veterans. What they had in common was their lack of a seat for the biggest show in racing. There were never enough cars—particularly competitive cars—for all, and most went home disappointed.

Bobby Marshman numbered himself among those seeking a ride in 1961, and he and Janet had an agreement.

"We had a pact," said Janet. "He could go for one week. We couldn't afford any longer."

The first of two weekends of qualifying was May 13 and 14, the time when pole position is decided and when most of the major teams and drivers make it into the field. The following weekend was to fill the remaining spots in the thirty-three-car field.

Bobby Marshman drove the family Volkswagen from his home in Sanatoga, Pennsylvania, to the Speedway in early May. In the *Indianapolis Star* on May 3, Bill Eggert wrote that "Bobby Marshman, Pottstown, Pa., driver, has been added to the car-hunting list."

Bobby made the rounds of the garages where he was well received because of the many people he had come to know. Bill Marvel was one such contact who took a special interest in Bob. "We had met at a midget race a couple of years before he came to the Speedway," Marvel said. "We seemed to have a lot in common and became fast friends." During the month of May, Marvel worked for the Speedway as a volunteer press attaché in the media office headed by Bob Laycock. Marvel, also a motorsports journalist, had a wide range of contacts throughout the racing industry, and helped Bobby in every way possible. Marvel later became general manager of Pocono International Raceway in Pennsylvania and Texas World Speedway.

Bobby spent time with Eddie Sachs, who had arranged his ride in the pace car the year before. The well-connected Sachs likely passed along ideas and made introductions on behalf of his younger friend.

Another important stop was the garage of the Hoover Motor Express team. Eph Hoover of Nashville, Tennessee, was the team owner and Joe Langley, who resided in Southport, Indiana, a suburb of Indianapolis, was the crew chief. The crew chief was the most powerful person on a race team during this period, and was often the face of the team to the media and public. He made the decisions on cars and mechanical setups—the crew chief often had built the cars—and in most instances could hire and fire drivers. Bobby's contact in the Hoover garage was Henry Meyer, who had given him the big chance in his car at Reading and Trenton. Meyer thought highly of Bobby and likely had encouraged him to come and meet the team when he was at the Speedway.

On Friday, May 12, Bobby headed home. He had spent an exhausting week at the Speedway and nothing had come of it. He told his friend Bill Marvel, "Well, I might as well go back home and come back here and try it next year." With qualifying beginning the next day, it was apparent to him that all the seats were full and there was no place for him that year.

His early departure from Indianapolis had deprived Bob of seeing his friend Eddie Sachs capture pole position. Bob's soon-to-be teammate Don Branson was second, and Jim Hurtubise completed the front row. Parnelli Jones was the highest-placed rookie, in the fifth spot on the starting grid.

"When Bob came back from Indy that weekend he was really depressed," said Janet. "He came home on Friday, because if you don't have a ride by Friday, forget it. We took the car over to Euwe Buehl, the local Beetle specialist. Bob could tell on the drive home that the car needed a valve job, so we went there right after Bob got home."

Longtime pal Laverne Miller came by on Saturday to cheer Bob up. To take Bob's mind off his disappointment, they all, including one-year-old Rob, went to the enormous outdoor market known as the Gilbertsville Sale. "We went home after and were sitting around in the living room when the phone rang," recalled Janet. "It was Henry [Meyer] calling to urge Bob to return to the Speedway, as an opportunity had presented itself."

Inexplicably, Bob told Henry he had to think about it and hung up. "He asked them if he could call them back. I had a fit! He hung up the phone; he said, 'Well, I thought I'd think about it.' I said, 'We just spent all that money so you could be out there for a week and now you're going to think about it? You want to be one of those guys that gives up?' Laverne was sitting there watching this.

ABOVE: A handful of cars at Indy's Gasoline Alley, ready for practice in May of 1961. (MARSHMAN FAMILY COLLECTION)

PREVIOUS PAGES: Bobby drove a great race in the Hoover Motor Express car, moving steadily through the field from the back row to finish seventh. (PHIL REILLY COLLECTION)

117

He gave me a look and said to Bob, 'You've got to call them back.' Bob said, 'Now?' and I said 'Now! It doesn't sound like you're serious—*Can I call you back?*—there's guys standing in line, waiting.'"

At the Speedway Don Branson had qualified the Hoover Motor Express primary car—No. 3—in the middle of the front row. The team had a spare car—No. 31—which had been kept in reserve in case Branson might need it. Both Hoover cars were built by Quin Epperly, who had embraced and perfected the laydown Offy roadster. The design was radical for the time, but effective. The No. 3 car that Branson drove was brand new, having been built in Epperly's California race shop in time for the 500. The backup car was built in 1959 and had been driven to fourth place at the Speedway by Tony Bettenhausen.

With Branson safely in the field, the spare was available, and drivers were lining up for the seat. Henry Meyer urged Joe Langley to give the chance to Bobby. What may have clinched the seat for Bobby was the word of friend and fellow driver Bob Wente. Wente was being considered for the drive when his wife had a medical emergency back home in St. Louis. As he was departing, he was asked by Joe Langley for a recommendation from among those drivers interested and Wente recommended Bobby.

Plans were made in Yerkes for an immediate return to Indianapolis. The Beetle was not an option as the engine was apart in the VW shop. Bob's mother Evelyn saved the day by offering the use of her new Nash Rambler—just purchased from her brother Floyd, who owned the local Nash dealership.

"We left that same day and drove all night to get there," said Janet. "We met Bill Marvel at the track and he had us fixed up with credentials. It was something else, it really was. Laverne and I were there until three or four p.m. Sunday and we had to turn around and head home. I was home again Monday morning for school."

Chapter 28
Smooth like Wilbur Shaw (1961)

When Bobby Marshman climbed into the No. 31 Hoover Motor Express Epperly roadster on Monday morning, he had never previously been in an Indy roadster, nor had he driven a single lap around the Speedway. If these things bothered him, he didn't show it.

To race at the Speedway, drivers must first pass the driver or rookie test, where judges look for consistency and control. Beginning Monday, May 15, for two consecutive days, Bob was put through the traditional forty-lap test, in four ten-lap increments, beginning at 120 mph and increasing by 5 mph each stage, to the final ten-lap run, at 135. Bob was remarkably steady, and fast, and one veteran official stated that he had not seen anyone as smooth and consistent since Wilbur Shaw. (A three-time Indy victor, in 1937, '39, and '40, Shaw had always made it look easy.)

"When Bobby was taking his driver's test he was cool and relaxed about the whole thing," said

Bill Reiff. "He still was wearing his Konstant Hot coveralls—what he wore when he drove the midget. They were yellow with a black stripe."

Until a driver is given the seal of approval, his car must wear stripes—called rookie stripes—on the back of his car to warn other drivers that they are approaching an inexperienced driver. Bobby was proud to go through the ritual of peeling off his stripes, and the May 17 *Indianapolis Star* featured a Frank H. Fisse photo of Bobby performing this significant ceremony with the caption: "Now He's Ready." Dick Wallen, in his classic book *Roar from the Sixties*, said that Bobby "showed from the start that he belonged at the Speedway."

On Tuesday, the track was shut down for half an hour in silent tribute to Tony Bettenhausen, a giant of the sport, who had died in a practice crash the previous Friday. It was a quiet day at the Speedway, as most drivers, mechanics, and car owners were at the funeral services in Chicago Heights, Illinois, and the burial at Tinley Park, Illinois, near his home. Jack Beckley and J. C. Agajanian were

ABOVE: Bobby got his big Indy 500 break in 1961 when Eph Hoover's crew chief Joe Langley hired Bobby to drive the team's backup Epperly Champ car at Indianapolis. (FIRST TURN PRODUCTIONS)

INDIANAPOLIS MOTOR SPEEDWAY CORP.

RECORD OF FAMILIARIZATION RUN

CAR NAME _Hoover Spe_ DATE _May 15 1961_

CAR NO. _31_ DRIVER _Bob Marshman_

120 MPH LAP TIME 1:15		NO. LAPS RUN
LAP 1	1:14:84	120.789
" 2	1:14:12	121.435
" 3	1:13:44	122.549
" 4	1:13:46	122.561
" 5	1:12:84	123.558
" 6	1:12:88	123.491
" 7	1:14:50	120.805
" 8	1:14:34	121.065
" 9	1:13:70	122.117
" 10	1:13.74	122.050

125 MPH LAP TIME 1:12		NO. LAPS RUN
LAP 1	1:11:70	125.523
" 2	1:10:62	127.443
" 3	1:10:46	127.732
" 4	1:10:78	127.155
" 5	1:10:80	127.119
" 6	1:10:76	127.191
" 7	1:10:12	128.351
" 8	1:10:66	127.371
" 9	1:10:90	126.939
" 10	1:10:72	127.262

130 MPH LAP TIME 1:09		NO. LAPS RUN
LAP 1	1:08:24	131.887
" 2	1:08:04	132.275
" 3	1:08:10	132.159
" 4	1:08:66	131.081
" 5	1:08:16	132.042
" 6	1:08:06	132.236
" 7	1:08:40	131.579
" 8	1:07:70	132.999
" 9	1:08:04	132.275
" 10	1:08:12	132.120

130 MPH LAP TIME		NO. LAPS RUN
LAP 1	1:06:42	135.501
" 2	1:06:52	135.298
" 3	1:06:38	135.583
" 4	1:05:58	137.237
" 5	1:05:44	137.531
" 6	1:06:04	136.281
" 7	1:06:06	136.240
" 8	1:06:56	135.216
" 9	1:06:46	135.420
" 10	1:06:10	136.157

COMMENTS: _____

_____

pallbearers. Bettenhausen was survived by his wife Valerie and four children: Gary, nineteen; Merle, seventeen; Susan, fifteen; and Tony Lee, nine.

Bettenhausen was driving for car owner Lindsey Hopkins and crew chief Jack Beckley. The team had been favorites for pole position as well as for the race win. One of Bettenhausen's best friends was Paul Russo, who was driving Doug Stearly's latest acquisition, the Watson roadster, which had won the 1959 Indy 500 for Leader Card Racing in the hands of Rodger Ward. Russo was having trouble getting the car up to speed and asked his friend Tony to try the car to see what he thought.

"Doug [Stearly] was in a difficult position that day because his crew chief Ken Hickey wasn't there, and he was trying to handle things by himself with just one helper," said Bill Reiff. "I was on a two-week leave from the Army to help Doug and Ken, and was on my way to Indianapolis from my post in Virginia when the crash happened. Russo couldn't get the car going fast enough; he said, 'I never drove an A. J. Watson car before.' Russo went to Bettenhausen without asking Stearly. [When he found out] Stearly wasn't too happy about the whole idea, and Hopkins and Beckley weren't either, but Bettenhausen did what he wanted to.

"It was a bad situation," continued Reiff. "When I got there about an hour after the wreck, it took me a long time to find Stearly—he had my pit passes. After the USAC was done with their inspection of the car—it was in two pieces—I put the pieces on the trailer and I brought them home to Pennsylvania and took it down to Hickey's place. He took the motor out; it wasn't hurt. I went back to the Speedway and just hung out there, mostly with Bobby."

With a few words of advice from teammate Don Branson, Bob soon had the No. 31 Hoover car recording 140-plus-mph speeds. Observers were impressed at how quickly Bobby picked up the feel of both car and track. "Don helped me a lot," Bobby told the *Pottstown Mercury* reporter. "I wasn't quite getting it at first, but after he showed me how, it was easy."

Branson was generous in response to the same newsman: "I just gave him a couple of pointers and he took it from there. He ranks with the best young drivers I've seen."

Illinois native Don Branson was the perfect teammate for Bobby. He was one of the leading drivers of the time, and at age forty, was just coming into his prime. The World War II veteran had a calm and thoughtful demeanor and, confident in his own skills, was unruffled by setbacks. Branson had, like Bobby Marshman, come up through the ranks of midgets and sprint cars. He was a rookie at the Speedway in 1959, the same year he won the USAC sprint car championship, and was fourth in the 500 in 1960. He was considered tough and canny and brilliant on dirt. He clearly was an important factor in Bobby's success as a rookie at the Speedway. "Don Branson epitomized a father and a grandfather," said Janet. "He was a wonderful person."

"This is a chance of a lifetime for me," Bob told the *Nashville Banner*. "Folks tell me that no one has gotten a break like this around here since Bill Holland in 1947. I'm really indebted to the Hoover people and the way they've helped me and accepted me. Don, Eb, Joe, all of them. They've taken me right in and made me feel right at home."

The first weekend of qualifying had placed twenty-seven drivers in the field. On the following Saturday, May 20, six more drivers qualified to complete the thirty-three-car field. Now that thirty-three cars were in, additional qualifying attempts could be made to "bump" one's way into the field by exceeding the speed of the slowest qualifier. Doing so would bump that driver off the grid. (Pole-day qualifiers line up on the grid first. Second-day qualifiers go behind them, even if their speeds were faster. Third-day qualifiers follow second-day qualifiers. Once thirty-three drivers qualify for the race, the car with the slowest speed—regardless of current placement—is considered "on the bubble," and at risk of being bumped. If a driver is bumped, the bumper is merely added to the bottom of the grid. He doesn't get to take the bumpee's grid position, which is one reason why drivers try to qualify as early as possible.)

Parnelli Jones was the highest-profile rookie at the Speedway in 1961. He was one of the drivers to have qualified the first day and among the favorites to win the race. Jones, who was born in Arkansas and grew up in Torrance, California, came to the Speedway with a big reputation. He had been one of the top sprint car drivers in 1959 and in 1960, when he won USAC's Midwest sprint car championship, winning seven of the thirteen races. At Indianapolis he was driving J. C. Agajanian's No. 98 Watson-Offy.

Chapter 29
Qualifying for the Big Show (1961)

The most-talked-about car in the 1961 Indy field was the rear-engine Cooper driven by Jack Brabham. After encouraging results in the October Speedway test in their regular Formula One car, the Cooper T53, the team had returned to their Surbiton, Surrey, England headquarters. There, they developed a one-off version of the T53 Cooper, the T54, specifically designed for Indianapolis. Among many other detail changes, the new car featured an offset suspension, and the Coventry Climax engine was extended to 2.7 liters (or 166 cubic inches). An Offenhauser, by comparison, was 4.2 liters (or 255 cubic inches). The Cooper weighed only 1,050 pounds compared to 1,700 pounds for a typical roadster. The USAC permitted a special exemption, resented by many Speedway regulars, for the car to be under the mandated 96-inch minimum wheelbase, and the Cooper arrived at the Speedway at 92.5 inches. The Cooper was down significantly on top speed compared to the traditional roadsters, but because of its lightness could run very deep into the corners; its sophisticated suspension gave it superior handling through the corners as well.

Arguably, the most famous and successful race driver at that time was England's Stirling Moss. On March 8, longtime Indianapolis entrant Al Dean telegrammed Moss offering him a seat in the

500 in his choice of either one of the Dean Van Lines Specials—one, an A. J. Watson car, and the other, designed by Eddie Kuzma. Several weeks earlier, in a talk to the SCCA membership in New York, Moss had said he was open to the idea of running at the 500. As reported by Jep Cadou Jr. in his column in the *Indianapolis Star*, the offer included the services of crew chief Danny Oakes, who was the mechanic on Jim Hurtubise's record-setting car, and had won Mechanic of the Year at the Speedway in 1960. Dean concluded his telegram, sent to Moss at Twickenham, Middlesex, England, saying, "Please consider this offer in the interests of better Anglo-American relationships and in the hope that Jack Brabham will enjoy your company."

Within a week, Moss—whose father Alfred had raced in the 1924 Indy 500—replied that he would only be interested in competing at the 500 if he could do so in a British car. Al Dean replied in turn that he would consider sponsorship of a British car if Moss could line one up.

When Brabham claimed thirteenth on the first day of qualifying, he became only the third

foreign driver to make the field for the 500 since World War II. Luigi Villoresi had finished seventh in the 1946 race, and Alberto Ascari had qualified a Ferrari in 1952, but did not finish the race. After qualifying, Brabham immediately caught a plane for Europe so he could race in the Monaco Grand Prix the next day.

·　　·　　·

With their number-one driver already qualified in the middle of the front row, the focus in the Hoover Motor Express garage was to prepare Bobby Marshman for qualifying. Henry Meyer was in charge of the car, while crew chief Joe Langley concentrated on Branson's car, but now all of the team's resources were directed at helping Bob get up to what was believed to be the speed necessary to qualify.

During practice on Wednesday and Thursday, Bobby was able to turn laps at a consistent 142 mph, but the speed wasn't going to be fast enough to make the field. Don Branson tried the car and turned a lap at 144, which, it was clear, was what would be needed. At this point, Branson—some sources suggest it was Henry Meyer—had the idea to put a two-inch-thick block of wood under the driver seat to change Bob's perspective in the cockpit. They did so, and Bob went out and immediately was in the 144-mph range. The change had provided Bob a better view of his front wheels and simply made him more comfortable behind the wheel.

There were at least twenty drivers trying to get their cars up to speed to be one of the six to fill the field on Saturday or Sunday. There were several crashes and engine blowups during the week as cars were pushed to their edge and beyond.

Qualifying for the big show at Indianapolis requires more than the ability of car and driver to turn one fast lap. The qualifying speed is an average of four consecutive lap speeds. The driver has the track to himself, but he must put together four fast laps around Indy's oval—ten miles in all—before his task is complete.

Floyd Clymer, one of the great historians of the sport, expressed the "drama, comedy, heartbreaks, and tragedy" of attempting to qualify for the 500 in the month of May at the Speedway. "Friendships are made and friendships are broken; careers are made and careers are ruined; a very few fortunes are made and many are lost," he said.

Janet, back in Pennsylvania, described herself as being "on pins and needles" while Bob was out at the Speedway. "We had recess at ten in the morning," she recalled. "I would be thinking, Now it's nine out there—they're just starting."

Bob was staying with Bill Marvel and his family at their home on the northwest side of Indianapolis. Bill and Bernice Marvel put up many members of the Marshman family during the qualifying weekend and the race itself.

"John Pfrommer from Pottstown had a car at Indy, and his son Johnny, a senior in high school, planned to come down on that Friday after school in his dad's new Ford Thunderbird. Along with my sister Freddie, who was also in high school, the three of us drove out to Indy," recalled Janet, who was teaching first grade in the Pottstown School District at that time. "Evelyn kept Robbie. We left after school Friday and got there Saturday morning."

Janet liked to sit right behind the pits on the inside of the track. "You could go down to the pits and talk to your driver through the wire fence," she recalled. She was watching from behind the pits on Saturday when Bob drove the handsome orange Hoover Motor Express on to the track to make his attempt. Fog had delayed the track opening for half an hour. Bobby was first in line, but his initial lap was uncompetitive, at 142.135 mph, so he aborted the try. Penetrating wind and rain shortly after Bob's attempt caused the track to be closed for the next two hours and forty-two minutes.

When the rain stopped and the sun came out, the track reopened. There was a rush to practice and qualify, with seventeen cars on the track and thirteen qualifying attempts made. Lloyd Ruby, in the Lindsey Hopkins Epperly-Offenhauser that Tony Bettenhausen was to have driven, was fastest of the day, with an average speed of 146.909 mph. With the six remaining grid spots now filled, all other drivers, including Bobby, needed to bump their way onto the grid. As it turned out, Bobby had to wait a day for his second try: At 6:03 p.m., with Bobby the next in line to attempt to qualify, the track was closed. At 5:30 p.m., officials had announced a rule (rightfully dubbed "confusing" by the *Star*) stating that the normal closing time of 6:00 p.m. was to be extended another hour because of the bad weather earlier; however, the same rule stated that the session would end immediately when a car came up for its second try that day. Thus, because Bobby was on his second try, the extension automatically came to a close.

On Sunday, May 21, Bobby was first in line, and when trials began at the stroke of noon he was on his way. His first lap was somewhat disappointing at 143.665 mph, but he then found his pace and ran the last three laps at 144.300, 144.811, and 144.370 mph, respectively, for a qualifying average speed of 144.283 mph.

He was safely in the race.

Although he was the thirty-third and the last car on the grid, there was little chance of him being bumped. Bob was faster than four cars that had qualified in previous days, so they all would have to be bumped before he would be on the bubble.

On that final day of qualifying, Bobby and Norm Hall were the only drivers to make it into the field. Bobby had bumped Bob Cleberg from the race and Hall bumped Paul Russo. (Russo had found a spot driving for Bryant Heating and Cooling after his intended ride in Doug Stearly's Watson had been destroyed in the Bettenhausen crash.)

Jep Cadou wrote in the May 22 *Indianapolis Star*: "Marshman, a 24-year-old Pottstown, Pa., neophyte, made the grade on his second strike in the No. 31 Hoover Motor Express Special at 144.283.... This was a real achievement, because Marshman first took to the 2 1/2 oval just six days previously. Marshman . . . was the only rookie of 1961 who needed only 40 laps to complete the 40-lap test with a perfect record."

"It was not surprising that Bobby did so well on his driver test and in qualifying because he was so good on high-speed tracks," said Bill Marvel. "He had won his major midget races on fast tracks like Trenton. He was very good at that."

With the 500 on its traditional Memorial Day, May 30, date—falling on a Tuesday in 1961—they had a full nine days to wait for the race after qualifying ended. No activity was permitted on the track all week until Saturday morning, when the cars went out for what were officially called "fuel tests," also known as carburetion day.

Janet left the Speedway on Sunday afternoon, May 21, after Bob qualified, again riding in the Thunderbird with her sister and Johnny Pfrommer. They arrived home early Monday morning in time for classes, and at the end of the school week, Janet returned to Indianapolis. (Janet was completing her teaching obligations for the school year, but had resigned her position for the following year.) With the family VW now out of the shop, Janet drove it to Indiana with Robbie, who had celebrated his first birthday on May 15. They arrived for the final weekend before the race.

Chapter 30
Golden Anniversary (1961)

The Indianapolis 500, then and now, is second to none for pageantry and honoring tradition. In 1961 the Speedway was celebrating the golden anniversary of the first Indy 500. The race had been held every year since 1911 except during World War I and World War II. For the fiftieth anniversary, track owner Anton "Tony" Hulman Jr. pulled out all the stops. On May 10, the official opening day of the Speedway, thirty-three Ford Thunderbird convertibles, decked out in gleaming coats of gold, lined up in rows of three and followed the official Golden Thunderbird pace car on two laps of the track. Then, with help from 500 Festival Queen Diane Hunt and uniformed trumpeters, Tony Hulman inserted the golden key into the golden padlock to officially open the garages and signal the opening of race activities at the Speedway.

It is no exaggeration to say that Tony Hulman saved the Speedway from extinction after World War II. When Hulman purchased the facility from Eddie Rickenbacker in 1946, it was in poor condition, having suffered from neglect during the war years.

Rickenbacker himself had been an influence for good at the Speedway when he purchased it in 1928 and made important upgrades. Rickenbacker first came to national fame as a Medal of Honor recipient and was America's "ace of aces" as a pilot in World War I, having shot down twenty-six enemy aircraft. He had earned the nickname "Fast Eddie" as a driver in four Indianapolis 500s before the war. The colorful Rickenbacker achieved success in business after the war in the automobile and aeronautical industries, and his tenure as owner of the Speedway had ensured its continued success up to World War II. However, Rickenbacker's preoccupation with his role in the World War II effort, and the absence of races at the facility, left the Speedway in great need of infrastructure upgrades.

Although Tony Hulman was a sportsman as well as a successful businessman, his initial motive in purchasing the Speedway was more community-driven than any desire to operate a racetrack. Hulman understood the vast economic impact the Speedway had on the entire region of central Indiana and the prestige it brought to the city of Indianapolis. At the urging of his friend, Wilbur Shaw, a three-time winner of the 500, Hulman took on the sizable challenge of bringing the facility up-to-date and maintaining the 500's position as America's greatest race. By 1961 much of the work had been achieved, but Hulman never stopped upgrading facilities. For the golden anniversary, a new paddock grandstand was completed, plus a new grandstand on the main straight called Paddock C, replacing a wooden stand built before World War I.

Hulman, born in 1901 in Terre Haute, Indiana, and a graduate of Yale University, was head of Hulman & Co., perhaps best known for producing Clabber Girl baking powder. In 1961, Clabber Girl had 50 percent of the American market for baking powder, and was a product Tony Hulman personally had built into prominence when he came into the family-owned company as sales director in the 1930s. Hulman was also known for a high standard of ethics and was a great friend to race drivers. Examples abound of drivers and their families who were quietly, without publicity, helped by Tony Hulman. His personal philosophy, as told to Wayne Fuson for the *Indianapolis News*, was, "Whether in sports or business, play the game fair and you'll succeed."

Bobby Marshman was the youngest driver in the golden anniversary race, but he commanded respect, particularly on his team. Don Branson told the wire services that Bobby rated with the best of the young drivers he had seen. Joe Langley added, "Everybody says Bobby's been the smoothest driver out there this week; he has come along real well to have had only four days to get used to the car." In the same press story, Bob said, "I like the car fine. In fact, I like the whole setup fine. The car, the crew, the way I've been accepted and everything. Don Branson has helped me a lot, and so has Joe Langley and everybody. Everything has been to my favor."

No one who saw Bobby Marshman drive a race car ever doubted his talent and commitment. First impressions by others, though, did not always conform to their idea of a race driver. Red McCarthy of the *Norristown Times Herald* described Bob as "a gentlemanly, personable chap, whose appearance and conversation foster the Ivy League graduate impression." When Bobby made the rounds of sports desks, more than one writer initially assumed, from his athletic but slim stature, that he might be a baseball player or a track athlete. Frank Gianelli of the *Arizona Republic* had an even more extreme impression, writing, "Bob Marshman pops into the office and you peg him for an athlete—kind of small, maybe a jockey. Which is right thinking, wrong track . . . don't rate him

Another rookie wife at the luncheon was Mrs. Bobby Marshman, a fragile-looking young blond who teaches first grade in Pottstown, Pa.

"I have an understanding principal," she explained. She will not be back in the classroom until June 7 since she, her husband and their year-old son, Robby, will go to Milwaukee after the Speedway. While Mrs. Marshman was at the luncheon, Indianapolis friends, Mr. and Mrs. Paul Yerger, took care of Robin.

as puny [when] he gives you a knuckle-bending handshake." It is a curious description, considering that Bob was just under six feet tall.

When Janet and Robbie arrived over the weekend before the race, Janet was thrown into a round of parties and receptions.

"Jo Ward, Rodger's wife, was one of the first people to welcome me to the Speedway. She made a special effort to make me feel part of it," said Janet. At the wives' luncheon, Janet was seated at a flower-decked table with Mrs. Bob Wente, Mrs. Don Branson, and Mrs. Gene Hartley. Janet made friends easily and soon was an integral part of the close-knit group.

"I had teas and receptions to go to," said Janet. "There was always a microphone in your face. Eddie Sachs's wife Nancy and others, when the press would want to interview people at the functions, one of the women would say, 'Talk to her, she's a schoolteacher.'" In fact, Janet's outgoing personality and communication skills made her an ideal spokesperson.

In the May 30 *Indianapolis Star*, Janet's photo was among the twenty-four head shots of drivers' wives, alongside a feature by Mary Waldon headlined reactions are varied for wives of 500-mile race drivers. Mrs. Bob Marshman told the writer: "This is our first race, so I don't really know what to expect, but I am terribly keyed-up."

Janet and Bob had a cheering section of family and friends. Also attending the race from home were Janet's sisters Freddie and Kay and Kay's husband Don Scheffey. Bob's mother Evelyn was there, although George stayed home to look after his promotions. Evelyn told John Dell of the *Philadelphia Inquirer*, "It's much harder for me with Bob than it was with George. I guess I'm a little older now and a little more nervous. I'm really proud of Bob, but concerned, too. He's been around racing ever since he was a baby. We always took him to the races. I sort of used the wrong psychology, I guess."

Chapter 31
The 1961 Indianapolis 500

On Monday, the day before the race, Bobby was among the drivers assembled for the formal drivers' meeting conducted by chief steward Harlan Fengler. A number of veteran drivers were introduced and Eddie Rickenbacker was invited to say a few words. Captain Eddy shared memories of races at the Speedway before World War I, including a description of his driver's test. He related being instructed to go out on the track and keep driving until his right rear tire blew. This would demonstrate his ability to control the car in a slide.

The festival parade on Monday evening before the 500 was said to rival the Pasadena Rose Parade for size and quality. The track opened at 4:00 a.m. Tuesday and the crowd streamed in, providing their own color and excitement. The golden anniversary theme was picked up by the fans with golden hats, dresses, and shoes in abundance. Even a golden beer cooler was spotted.

Before the race Bobby maintained his cool despite an endless stream of well-wishers and the distractions of the festivities. He suited up in a uniform that had fifteen candy mints attached to the front. Janet had sewn them on the night before so he would have something to chew on during the race.

Race day at the Speedway was closely scheduled. At 8:00 a.m. the cars were expected to be out of the garages and parked in their respective pit boxes. At 9:30, a parade was led by the Purdue University Marching Band, featuring the Golden Girl and other baton twirlers. They were followed by high school bands and the American Legion band. By 10:00 a.m., the race cars were assembled on the track while the Purdue band played "On the Banks of the Wabash," followed immediately by the presentation of celebrities, including Jayne Mansfield, Connie Stevens, Mel Tormé, Gloria DeHaven, Dan Blocker, and Lorne Greene, who all were driven around the track in the golden Ford Thunderbirds.

Just after 10:00 a.m., three historic race cars and their original drivers, all veterans of the Speedway prior to World War I, were lined up inside the pit wall at the starting line. First in line was the No. 10 Duesenberg, sporting a red tail, white body, and blue hood as driven in the 1914 race by Eddie Rickenbacker—who was also driving it on this day. Next was Earl Cooper in the white Stutz, with a red No. 8, that he had driven to fourth place in the 1915 race. Bringing up the rear was Ray Harroun in his famous yellow No. 32 Marmon Wasp, in which he had won the first Memorial Day 500-Miler ever held, exactly fifty years before. The three veteran drivers wore golden race suits for the occasion and thrilled the crowd as they circled the 2.5-mile circuit.

The National Anthem was played by the Purdue band. To honor Memorial Day, the anthem was followed by a moment of silence, and then, "Taps," in tribute to the men and women of the armed services who died for their country.

Ten minutes before the start of the race, Mel Tormé sang "Back Home Again in Indiana" as the air filled with masses of multicolored balloons. When Tony Hulman said, loud enough for everyone in the 225,000-strong crowd to hear, "Gentlemen, start your engines," the teams went into action, firing up the cars. With not a cloud to be seen in the clear blue Indiana sky, the cars rolled off on the pace lap at 10:54, forming eleven rows of three cars each behind the Thunderbird pace car.

Bobby Marshman—at twenty-four, the youngest of the thirty-three drivers to take the green flag from starter Bill Vandewater—was starting on the last row. By plan Bobby drove steadily but not aggressively at the back of the field for the first thirty of the two hundred race laps.

At the front, all was not well for Bobby's teammate, Don Branson, who dropped back almost immediately after the start from his front-row position and was in the pits and out of the race after the second lap. *NSSN* reported that "Branson was a cool customer. When he pulled in with a blown engine he took off his helmet, put on a baseball cap, lit up a cigarette, and said, 'What happened, chief?'"

In the stands behind the pits, Janet had a good idea of what had happened to Branson.

"There was little screening between the grandstands and the racetrack at that time," said Janet. "Most of the trash, papers, programs, go up in the air, and one of those papers landed in his radiator, and that was why Don was out of the race so quickly."

Janet also caught an earful of speculation.

"Most of the people around me in the stands didn't know me, and they were saying, 'Oh, I wonder if they're going to bring Marshman in and let Branson take over.' Henry Meyer had explained it to me: 'It's a team; they are in that side of the garage, Joe Langley is the crew chief, and I am on Bob's car.' Later Don said to me, 'Janet, I wasn't going in that car. That's Bobby's car.'"

Jim Hurtubise in the Demler Special led the first thirty-five laps before stopping for a scheduled pit stop. Bobby pitted for the first of his three stops on lap 47. He took on fuel and the crew changed both rear tires and the right front. He was back on his way in twenty-seven seconds—a decent time

for a pit stop in 1961. With A. J. Foyt in the Bignotti-Bowes Seal Fast Special, Eddie Sachs in the Dean Van Lines Special, Troy Ruttman in the John Zink Trackburner Special, and Parnelli Jones in the Agajanian-Willard Battery Special all battling for the top position, Bobby was gradually improving his race position.

On lap 52 Bobby did an excellent job avoiding a chain-reaction crash that involved five cars. No one was injured, but Jack Turner in the Bardahl Special flipped end over end. At the 200-mile mark, Bobby was up to seventeenth place. He continued to drive well within his capabilities, and later expressed regret for not having pushed harder.

Bob's sister LaRone remembered his disappointment. "He felt his lack of experience kept him from pushing harder, and that he could have finished anywhere from third to fifth without stressing the car."

Bill Marvel also recalled Bob's feeling on his race pace. "It was easy for him because he felt comfortable on those long racetracks—he wasn't bragging; he wasn't that kind of guy. He just wasn't pushing as hard as he realized, after the race was over, he could have gone."

Parnelli Jones had charged to the front of the race on lap 45, and for a time was the fastest man on the track. Shortly after the restart following the yellow flag for the five-car crash, he was struck just above the eye by a piece of metal thrown up from the track.

"Right away my goggles filled up with blood," Jones told Bill Libby for his book, *Parnelli*. "I yanked my goggles away, emptying the blood out, driving one-handed, but every time I put my goggles back on, the one began to fill up with blood again, just like someone pouring wine into a glass, and half blinding me." Parnelli persisted, but eventually the Offenhauser engine in the Agajanian Watson went on three cylinders and he dropped from contention, finishing twelfth.

Bobby made his second pit stop at lap 117, stopping for thirty-one seconds to take on all four tires and fuel. On lap 127, tragedy struck. Eddie Johnson, running in the top ten in the Jim Robbins Kuzma, spun after contact with another car in the northwest turn. Johnson was uninjured, but the car was stalled in the middle of the track. Caution lights came on and the emergency crew was quickly on the scene. During the cleanup, track worker John Masariu was killed when he fell out of an emergency vehicle and a fire truck backed over him. Masariu was the principal of Ben Davis Junior High School in Indianapolis.

By lap 140 Bobby was up to ninth place with fellow rookie Jack Brabham in the Kimberly Cooper-Climax just behind him in tenth. Bobby made his third and final pit stop on schedule, on lap 167. This time he was stationary for only twenty-four seconds. In addition to fueling the Hoover car the crew changed the two rear tires and the front right. Sachs was leading the race, hotly pursued by A. J. Foyt.

The race finish was dramatic. Eddie Sachs appeared a certain winner when, with just three laps to go, he was forced to pit to replace his right rear tire. A. J. Foyt—who had seemed a likely winner earlier, until he fell back when he had to make an extra, unscheduled stop for fuel—now came through to win the 500, with Sachs second, just 8.28 seconds behind. It was the second-closest finish to date in the history of the 500. The closest finish had happened in 1937 when Wilbur Shaw finished 2.16 seconds ahead of second-place Ralph Hepburn.

When Bobby came past the pits for the next-to-final time before completing the 500 miles, his pit crew held up a blackboard that read well done. The track originally announced Bobby as finishing sixth, but the Hoover team thought he was fifth, and lodged a protest. The official scorers reviewed the tapes carefully and Bobby was neither fifth nor sixth—he was officially seventh.

Chapter 32
Sharing Rookie Honors with Parnelli (1961)

"There was no driver at the Indianapolis 500 any happier than Bobby Marshman," wrote LeRoy Fitz for the *Pottstown Mercury*. "He was the youngest driver in the field and one of only three rookies to finish." Bob, whose face was smudged with black from the oil and rubber, told Fitz that only his hands were a little tired after the 500-mile grind.

"Marshman said he was there to learn," wrote Fitz. " 'I didn't try to move up until after the first 75 miles,' he said. 'I would have liked to do better but I learned a lot of things out there today. I got a lot of help from my teammate, Don Branson.'" Branson had offered advice during the pit stops and was also on hand in case Bob needed a relief driver. "I had no trouble with the car," he told Fitz. "I was a little excited at first, but I felt better as the race went on."

The press wanted to know what Bobby was thinking during the race. "I thought about the fellows in the accident; I wondered if any of them were hurt," Bob replied. "Then later on I was thinking of buying Robbie, my little boy, a wading pool. I knew he would get a kick out of it."

The Hoover team was among the first to experiment with two-way radio communication between the driver and the crew. Bobby responded to LeRoy Fitz's inquiry on how it worked out. "It was working in this sense—they, the crew, could hear me, but the earphones weren't working and I couldn't hear them."

History was made when twin Rookies of the Year were named. Bobby and Parnelli Jones were the first drivers to share the honor, because the committee charged with naming the winner of the award was deadlocked. They went to the award sponsor Stark & Wetzel to ask them to break the tie. The company generously made the decision to award both men the honor. It was no small gesture: Stark & Wetzel, a meat company in Indianapolis, provided the winner a year's supply of meat and a check for $500.

The honor often, but not always, has gone to the highest-finishing rookie. Bobby had finished seventh and impressed all observers with his smoothness and talent from the day he had arrived at

the Speedway. Parnelli had arrived with a much bigger reputation and had impressed throughout the month. He had qualified fifth and had been a major factor in the race itself, leading many laps. His ultimate finish in twelfth position was all that kept him from claiming the award solely for himself.

The outcome was applauded in the motoring press and considered a fair and generous decision. Nick Nicolosi in *NSSN* said, "They made one of the fairest gestures remembered in the history of the great classic. Hats off to the voters." At the presentation ceremony the day after the race, the attractive Stark daughters did the honors: Marcia Stark presenting to Parnelli, and sister Diane to Bobby. The two drivers also received duplicate Rookie of the Year rings, a special award of which Bob was very proud.

·   ·   ·

The Victory Dinner on Thursday, June 1, was a large part of the Indianapolis tradition. Tony Hulman presided in distributing the record purse of $397,910.00. Each of the thirty-three drivers was introduced and presented his check by Sam Hanks, 1957 winner and director of racing at the Speedway during the month of May. The seventh-place share was $9,550.00, and Bobby received the standard 40 percent, or $3,820.00. The amount the Marshmans took home from this race was on par with the annual salary of a first-year teacher.

At the dinner, Jack Brabham, who had finished ninth in the Cooper, said, "There have been three great things happen to me in racing—the first two were winning my two world championships, and the third has been participating at Indianapolis. I never drove against more wonderful chaps. I'm very, very pleased."

While the peculiar undersized Cooper had not been welcomed with open arms in every corner of the Speedway fraternity, the team itself, and Jack Brabham and John Cooper in particular, were admired and well-liked. Many individuals stepped forward to welcome this team from another world of racing. Rodger Ward, who had helped Brabham at the test back in October, was especially notable in offering all possible support. A. J. Foyt called Brabham "a real pro."

"Jack Brabham was a gentleman on and off the track," said Janet. "He was the only one who ever obeyed the move-over flag. Bob liked him very much."

Days later, Bobby Marshman's smooth driving technique was still the talk of the Speedway. The consensus was that he had appeared to have the race gauged and he stuck to his plan. Russ Moyer, the Reading race organizer, was moved to say, "Mark my words—this boy Marshman is going to be a great one." Legendary driver Tommy Hinnershitz said of Bobby, "A nice smooth chauffeur who knows what he can do and then does it. He never sticks his neck out, and I have to rate him as one of the smoothest drivers to come along in a few years." Hinnershitz added that Bob was "likable and quiet; he doesn't go around all the time telling everyone how good he is." Hinnershitz also rated Parnelli highly.

Jim Lunt in his *NSSN* column said, "All of their friends in the East are mighty proud of Eddie Sachs and Al Keller [Keller finished fifth in the Konstant Hot Offy] for their terrific showings in the big set to. The honor of sharing the Rookie of the Year with Parnelli Jones is indeed a most illustrious one for Bobby Marshman. With all that meat pouring into the Marshman refrigerator, Bobby will have to watch his weight."

"Stark and Wetzel got us this great big chest freezer," Janet recalled. "I would just go to a local store and pick out what meat I wanted. It included poultry, Long Island ducklings—they were great." She continued, "It was so fun to watch this refrigerated semi come up that steep little gravel road to our house bringing our meat. It wasn't just for one year. When we moved into our new home on Foust Road in 1963, the freezer went with us and the meat still came."

One of the most enduring thrills for Bobby was being presented by the Champion Spark Plug company with the much-sought-after 100-Mile-an-Hour Club jacket. The rules were rigid and specific: To be part of the Club, a driver had to have completed all five hundred miles at an average speed in excess of 100 mph. Bobby wore the jacket with pride.

Chapter 33
Rocks Fly at Langhorne (1961)

With the third round of the USAC championship coming up in just five days at Milwaukee, there was little time to savor the accolades from Indianapolis. The happy news was that Bobby's performance at the Speedway had earned him a seat in the Hoover Motor Express Epperly roadster for the balance of the championship season on the faster paved tracks. At least half of the twelve races for the USAC national championship were on dirt tracks where roadsters were not usable. Most teams had both an upright dirt car and a roadster. While this was true for Hoover, who ran a Kuzma-Offy on dirt for Don Branson, the team did not field a second car in those races. Bobby secured a seat with Wally Meskowski of Competition Engineering in his dirt car. It was, in fact, a plum drive, as Meskowski was seen as a premier builder of championship dirt cars and sprint cars.

Bobby, Janet, and Robbie drove directly from Indianapolis to Milwaukee in the faithful Volkswagen Beetle. The Milwaukee 100, on the historic Milwaukee Mile in West Allis, Wisconsin, was a fixture on the USAC championship calendar. Coming just a week after the intensity of the 500, the race benefited greatly from the national attention and spotlight on the cars and their drivers. If the drivers weren't famous before the Memorial Day classic, thanks to the Speedway's media "machine," they were now. The race, on Sunday, June 4, drew a crowd of more than 30,000, exceeding the attendance of 18,000 for a Major League baseball doubleheader the same day between the home team Milwaukee Braves and the St. Louis Cardinals.

There were forty-one entrants vying for the twenty-two spots on the Milwaukee starting grid.

Bobby qualified twelfth in the Hoover Epperly roadster and finished thirty-four laps before his Offenhauser blew. His teammate Don Branson finished sixth, while Rodger Ward won for the Leader Card team. Al Keller was second in Bruce Homeyer's Konstant Hot roadster.

It was Bobby in a Konstant Hot race car the following Saturday night, June 10, in the ARDC midget race at Hatfield. The fifty-lap feature was promoted by George Marshman as the George Fonder Memorial, honoring the veteran Lansdale, Pennsylvania, driver who had been fatally injured at Hatfield on June 14, 1958. George also promoted Bob's return to his home track, emphasizing his Rookie of the Year status in the 500. Bob finished third in his heat, and led the early laps of the feature, only to drop out on the sixteenth lap with mechanical trouble. Len Duncan won the race.

With Bob's race calendar all in the Northeast until August, the family enjoyed a two-month respite from traveling race to race. It helped, too, to be close to home after the outcome of the 100-mile championship round at Langhorne on June 18. In this race Bobby made his first drive for Wally Meskowski of Competition Engineering.

Meskowski was a veteran champ-car mechanic and car builder who operated his Competition Engineering business out of a shop behind his Indianapolis home, just a couple of blocks from the Speedway. His most famous creation was the dirt car he built for A. J. Foyt that dominated for years. Meskowski was said to be hard to drive for, as he expected immediate success, and had a reputation for firing drivers if their speeds fell off on a given lap.

The one-mile Langhorne dirt track—a perfect circle—was feared by many as a driver killer. Some prominent drivers simply chose to scratch it from their calendars, championship points or not. Bob respected the famous track but did not fear it, having been consistently fast and successful there. In the brand-new No. 44 Meskowski, he was immediately up to a competitive speed and started the race in fifth position. Running in fourth position on lap 33, just ahead of Parnelli Jones, he was struck over the eye by a rock, thrown up from the track. In great pain, blood streaming down one side of his face, he brought the car to the pits and was quickly transferred to an ambulance. Meskowski put Californian Chuck Hulse, whose car had been forced out earlier, in the seat, but the team had trouble restarting the race car and it was in the pit for four laps. Hulse took over, but the car developed a rear suspension problem and was forced out of the race. Hulse and Bobby were classified with an eleventh-place finish. The race winner was A. J. Foyt, with Parnelli Jones number two.

Blood had entered the anterior chamber of Bob's eye, causing severe irritation. He was taken to a hospital in Bristol, Pennsylvania, where he remained for a week. He told a reporter from the Reading *Eagle* that he would rather be recuperating at home, and added, "Whatever it was, it hit me just above the eye. The terrific impact jarred the optic nerve and I got cut in the eyebrow above the eye—they sewed it up but they were a little worried about the blood in there. I don't know what hit me, but there is no danger to my eye or anything else. I expect to be ready to race at Trenton."

"I had words with that ophthalmologist," said Janet. "He was absolutely ignorant toward Bob, condescending and rude and talking down to him. 'Well, what are you doing this for anyway?'—that kind of stuff. I told the doctor, 'Just a minute; if you don't want to deal with this, tell me now.' My uncle—an ophthalmologist—was only an hour and a half away in Allentown, and he was president of the AMA. The doctor said 'Oh sure, you know a doctor.' I told him, 'If you want to call Robert Shoemaker, you can, but I will call him, and he will come right down.' He changed his tune. Bob got some respect."

Chapter 34
"One of the Superstars of the Speedways" (1961)

The Trenton race Bob had been anxious not to miss was a USAC/ARDC 250-mile midget race on July 2. Bob was again in Bruce Homeyer's Konstant Hot midget, the same car in which he had won the Trenton 300 the previous year. Nick Nicolosi in his *NSSN* column reported that the Marshman family washing machine had broken down the night before the race. He quoted Janet as saying she had told Bob not to show up at home after the race without the money for a new machine.

Bobby won at Trenton, demonstrating once again his command of fast ovals, but this time he needed the help of Jimmy Davies of Gardena, California, who relieved him late in the race. Bobby was one of nine drivers requiring relief in the blistering 110-degree heat. Davies, who had been the 1960 USAC midget National Champion, had captured pole position and led the first 9 laps of 250 before his Howard Linne Offy blew a piston. Jiggs Peters of Neshanic Station, New Jersey, driving the Ken Brenn car, took over the lead and held it until lap 127, when he stopped to replace the fuel pump. Bobby, who had been running at a steady tempo and staying in the top five, pacing his race well, now took the top position and immediately increased his speed until he had a lead of three laps. Well past the halfway mark, Bobby pulled in for fuel and tires, and also for relief, turning the car over to Davies. The change went like clockwork. Led by Bruce Homeyer, the crew had the tires on and fuel in the car in thirty seconds, and the driver change took an additional twenty seconds.

When Davies rejoined the track he had a one-lap lead, which he maintained to the finish. It was a busy day for Davies. After his early retirement he had relieved Bob Wente in the Leader Card Offy on lap 64, and was then relieved in turn by Gig Stephens on lap 73. When he relieved Bobby he finally found himself in the winning car. Bill Randall of North Reading, Massachusetts, finished second, and Tony Bonadies of Bronx, New York, was third. Despite the relief turn by Davies, Bobby was the picture of exhaustion at the finish, receiving oxygen while he lay on the ground with his driver suit open to his waist. "He was attended to quickly and was able to participate in the post-race ceremonies," AP reported.

On the familiar grounds of Old Bridge Speedway, New Jersey, on Friday night, July 14, Bob took the Konstant Hot midget to victory in an ARDC event, also winning his heat. Bob took the lead on the third lap and was never headed to the finish of the twenty-five-lap feature, despite being hard pressed throughout by Len Duncan and Al Keller. The *NSSN* reporter said Bobby was "rapidly becoming one of the superstars of the speedways."

In August, Bob was back in the Midwest for four races over nine days. On Saturday, August 12, he was in the Konstant Hot midget for a 100-mile USAC race at the Milwaukee Mile. Parnelli Jones (who celebrated his twenty-eighth birthday that day) won the race with a new track record of

99.99 mph. Bobby had qualified eighth and was fourth of the twenty-seven finishers, behind Jones, Len Sutton, and Jim Hurtubise.

The next day Bobby was in Wally Meskowski's sprint car on the half-mile, semi-banked dirt track in Terre Haute, Indiana. He was only fifth in his heat, so a strong finish in the consi was essential to make it into the feature. Bobby came through with a second-place finish to Don Branson, placing him in the feature, where he finished eighth of fourteen starters.

The following weekend featured back-to-back championship races at Springfield, Illinois, on Saturday and Milwaukee, Wisconsin, on Sunday. With twenty-eight cars attempting to qualify for only eighteen spots in the Springfield race, Bobby placed the Meskowski dirt car eighth, with a time of 34.62 seconds to pole sitter Parnelli Jones's 34.21.

During qualifying at Springfield, veteran driver Rex Easton, driving the Stearly Motor Freight Special, suffered severe injuries when he crashed heavily into the guardrail and flipped over. He was thrown from the car and taken to St. John's Hospital, where he was in serious condition with a basal skull fracture. The popular Springfield driver had been seriously hurt at Berlin Raceway in Marne, Michigan, in 1959, and had only recently returned to racing. Easton recovered, but the Springfield accident effectively ended his racing career.

The 280-mile trip after the Saturday race in Illinois, to make the race in Wisconsin the following day, was a thrash for the teams. Weather added a new twist to the challenge. At Springfield, with qualifying complete and the cars on their pace lap, the rain came. The race was rescheduled for Monday, August 21, which meant turning around after Milwaukee and retracing steps to Springfield.

For the Milwaukee 200 on Sunday, August 20, Bobby was back in the Hoover Motor Express roadster. With thirty-nine drivers vying for the twenty-six available starting positions, he did well to place the Epperly-Offy twentieth in the starting field. His teammate Don Branson captured pole

position but spun out of the race on lap 36, when he lost his brakes. Bobby managed 184 laps before retiring with mechanical issues. He was classified fifteenth. The race was won by Lloyd Ruby, his first-ever championship victory, in the John Zink Special.

The teams returned to Springfield on Monday to pick up where they had left off on Saturday before the rain began. Bob made a big impression in the race from his eighth-place starting position. *NSSN* reported, "Bobby Marshman moved the Meskowski Special high on the rim and started his countdown." Jep Cadou commented in the *Indianapolis Star*: "Marshman, co–Rookie of the Year at the Speedway, did a fine driving job to move up to second but had to stop when his hood came loose." It was lap 33 when the problem forced Bobby and his No. 44 Meskowski car into the pits. But he was soon back. *NSSN* noted that "undaunted, the Dutchman picked up the pace and wormed his way back into ninth." Bob was one of many drivers with a German heritage to be given the "Dutchman" sobriquet. The win went to Jim Hurtubise, with A. J. Foyt second.

After the race, Don Branson announced that he was leaving his seat in the Hoover Motor Express lead car, saying he was "looking for another ride." Although Branson had consistently shown the car's speed with front-row and pole-position qualifying times, he was disenchanted with persistent mechanical problems on the No. 3 car. Branson soon landed a seat in the Lindsey Hopkins–owned Autolite Special, replacing Dick Rathmann. Within weeks, Roger McCluskey of Tucson, Arizona, was announced as the new driver of the No. 3 Hoover car.

Chapter 35
Success in Big Cars and Winning in Midgets (1961)

Despite being hospitalized after taking a rock to the face in his previous appearance at Langhorne, Bobby Marshman once again excelled at the tough one-mile dirt track. On August 27, Bobby was in the Meskowski sprint car for the Twin 50s—two fifty-lap races around the 'Horne. Jim Lunt in *NSSN* said, "Bobby Marshman, co–Rookie of the Year at Indy, turned in the most accomplished job of 'move-up driving.' He drove the Meskowski '14' in expert fashion but unfortunately spun out of the first feature. Starting the second 'featch' in fourteenth spot he had the crowd screaming as he passed car after car to wind up third behind Parnelli. He gained several seconds on the leader but was too far back to overcome the deficit in time and space. The spunky driver from Pottstown has emerged as one of racing's top performers."

Jim Hurtubise won both fifty-lap races and therefore was the champion of the combined Langhorne event; Parnelli Jones was second, and Roger McCluskey, third. A. J. Foyt did not start the second fifty-miler after being struck in the face by a rock in the first race.

The Du Quoin State Fairgrounds Racetrack in Du Quoin, Illinois—site of the Du Quoin "Magic

Mile" clay oval—had scheduled a big Labor Day weekend of USAC racing.

"Bob and I really liked it at Du Quoin," Janet said, "but we had a terrible experience there our first year: Somebody broke into our brand-new Mercury station wagon, parked outside the motel, and stole our clothes. They just scooped up everything hanging on a rack in the back seat. Robbie was home with a friend, so we figured we had extra space in the back for packing. Most of my clothes were stolen, and so was Bob's clean uniform—he had to wear his dirty one. I had borrowed my sister's favorite white eyelet dress and it was stolen, too. She and I still talk about how neither of us ever got to wear that dress again.

"After the break-in, we didn't want to stay at the motel, so somebody told us about a B and B," she continued. "The people there were so nice; they even went out and found clothing for me. We stayed with them every year after that."

The Du Quoin kickoff event on Saturday, September 2, was a twenty-five-lap sprint car race. Sunday featured a stock car race. The big event, a 100-mile race for the USAC championship, was on Monday the fourth.

On Saturday, in the Meskowski sprinter, Bobby finished second to Jim Hurtubise in his ten-lap heat and was sixth in the twenty-five-lap feature behind winner Elmer George, Parnelli Jones, Hurtubise, Al Keller, and A. J. Foyt. The feature race finish was chaotic and resulted in numerous protests. Starter Pat Vidan had failed to throw the checkered flag after the twenty-fifth lap and the drivers raced on. Elmer George had been in the lead at the end of the regulation twenty-five laps, with Don Branson close on his heels. On the twenty-sixth lap George's car brushed Branson's and spun, and Parnelli Jones came through to take the checker. Branson, in the Hyneman Offy, flipped numerous times and was taken to Marshall-Browning Hospital for treatment of facial lacerations and a split finger. When the dust settled and the protests had been heard, George was declared winner because he was leading after the officially specified distance. The finish order reverted to the end of lap 25.

On Sunday, Paul Goldsmith won the 100-mile USAC stock car race. Bobby did not compete in this event.

Monday's Du Quoin 100 for the big cars had only eighteen available starting spots, and Bobby neatly put the Competition Engineering Special, No. 44, into the race in tenth starting position. In so doing, he maintained his fine record of qualifying for every championship race of the season. The race itself was relatively uneventful, and Bobby brought the car home in eighth place; the race was won by A. J. Foyt.

Back east at the end of the week, Bobby joined the Competition Engineering team on Friday night, September 8, at Lancaster, New York, for a round in the New York State Sprint Car Championship. Although the team was not contesting that championship, it was an available date to run the sprint car on the same weekend the team's big car would be entered in the championship

144

round at Syracuse. It took winning the consi to place Bobby in the fifteen-mile feature. Foyt won the feature, with Hurtubise second, Hal Rettberg, third, Bobby, fourth, and Parnelli Jones, fifth.

The fairground track at Syracuse, New York, had a storied history of intense racing and huge crowds. The Saturday, September 9, race attendance was adversely affected by a polio epidemic in the Syracuse area. Lower attendance always had a direct bearing on the race purse. The standard USAC arrangement called for 40 percent of gate revenues going to prize money, with a minimum guarantee. It was a period when the Teamsters union was attempting to organize race drivers. They had little or no luck with the fiercely independent USAC drivers of the period. Another factor in their lack of interest in organizing was the USAC's excellent insurance plan that covered death and injuries.

The Teamsters did, in this same period, make some initial inroads with NASCAR, as star driver Curtis Turner joined with Teamsters head Jimmy Hoffa to form the Federation of Professional

Drivers, offering pensions and insurance. Bill France, founder and then head of NASCAR, took a successful stand against the movement, banning any union members from ever competing in a NASCAR event. At the same time, he gave lifetime suspensions to Turner and Tim Flock. Turner's suspension was lifted in later years, but Flock never raced in NASCAR again.

•　　•　　•

In the 100-mile national championship race at Syracuse on September 9, twenty-eight cars were attempting to break into the eighteen spots available. Eddie Sachs was among those failing to make the field. Bobby qualified tenth in the Meskowski Offy and finished seventh. Rodger Ward won the race in the Leader Card Watson-Offy. The next day, at New Bremen Speedway, Bobby time-trialed fifth out of a field of twenty-three, and finished second in the second heat, driving the Meskowski Offy. However, he finished fifteenth in the feature after starting sixth. Parnelli Jones in the Fike Chevy was the winner of the fifty-lap USAC sprint contest on the half-mile dirt oval.

The Hoosier 100 on September 16 at the Indiana State Fairgrounds, one of the most popular events in the USAC championship series, was a great race for Bobby Marshman. Bobby qualified on the front row as the only other driver beside pole sitter A. J. Foyt to beat thirty-five seconds in time trials. A major crash in qualifying by A. J. Shepherd made headlines and seriously injured the veteran driver from Mitchell, Indiana. Shepherd's car went through a chain-link fence and flipped four times, and Shepherd was thrown from the car. He had a long convalescence in Indianapolis Methodist Hospital, recovering from head, neck, and back injuries.

At the race start, Foyt got high on the track, moving Bobby up and to the outside against the fence. "I just got into that first corner too fast," A. J. told Jep Cadou Jr., sports editor for the *Indianapolis Star*. "I went into a wide slide and almost got into Marshman and the fence." Parnelli Jones from row two took the opportunity to pass them both and held the lead in the early laps.

With the outside drift on the start, Bobby had lost momentum and dropped to fourth. Foyt took the lead on lap 17 from Parnelli, who ran strong until a driveshaft broke on lap 78, moving Bobby into second place, where he finished, with Jim McElreath third and Len Sutton, fourth. McElreath and Bobby were praised by the media for making "remarkable showings" as rookies in the race.

Bobby was named Hoosier 100 Rookie of the Year, and team owner Wally Meskowski told Cadou for the *Star*, "The kid did a good job, and the car appeared to run perfectly." The Hoosier 100 boasted the second-biggest purse (after the 500) in the National Championship, and brought Meskowski and Marshman $6,802. Foyt's winning portion of the total $41,425 purse was $12,615.

Chapter 36
More Midget Heroics and Change in the Air (1961)

It became a memorable weekend for Bobby when he won the Trenton 100 for ARDC midgets the day after his outstanding performance in the Hoosier 100. It took a heroic drive through the night to do it, as told by Nick Nicolosi in *NSSN*: "Despite an all-night drive from Indianapolis, blistered hands, and tough competition, Bobby Marshman and the Konstant Hot Racing Team remain the team to beat on the paved one-mile fairground track here." Nicolosi also called Bobby a "personable driver" and Janet "pert and pretty."

In winning at Trenton, Bob set a new national record for a 100-mile midget race at 98.633 mph, breaking the year-old record of 98.100 set by Tony Bettenhausen at Milwaukee. The first forty laps had been a back-and-forth battle between Bobby and Bill Homeier, and on lap 40, Bobby took the lead to stay, although Tony Romit and Tony Bonadies kept the pressure on. Romit, who drove an outstanding race from the back of the grid, had a smaller fuel tank and was forced to pit on lap 69, taking some of the pressure off Bobby. Homeier finished second, the only car on the lead lap with Bob. Romit of Cliffside Park, New York, was third. This marked the third-consecutive long-distance midget race won by Bobby in Bruce Homeyer's Konstant Hot car, and it was his fourth Trenton midget win.

The following weekend, on September 24, was the autumn Trenton 100 for USAC championship cars. Now back on the East Coast, Bob, Janet, and sixteen-month-old Rob were able to spend time in their own house. Bob qualified the Competition Engineering car fifth of twenty-two spots, with thirty-nine cars and drivers attempting to qualify. Engine problems put him out of the race on lap 29, and he was classified nineteenth. Bobby was not long out of the Meskowski car before being asked to relieve Johnny Boyd in the Leader Card Special. Bob spun out of the race on lap 57, becoming a spectator for the second time that day. Eddie Sachs won the race, with Jim Hurtubise second.

After receiving the winner's laurels, Eddie announced to the media and all present that it was his last race for the team. He said, "I've been fired by Dean Van Lines." Apparently the previous Tuesday, while running Firestone tire tests, Eddie was told by crew chief Cliff Brawner that he was being released for the last two races of the year because he wasn't fast enough on dirt tracks and needed to stick to pavement. The upcoming Sacramento and Phoenix races were on dirt. Sachs said that Brawner told him he drove dirt like he drove asphalt, gliding into turns instead of "dumping" it in. It developed that he had been removed from the Dean Van Lines car only for dirt races. He continued to be their driver on paved tracks and, in fact, despite all the publicity, Sachs did drive the dirt car for Dean Van Lines in the races at Sacramento and Phoenix.

•   •   •

Bobby Marshman was deeply involved in his sport, not just as a personal passion, but as a profession made up of other committed individuals. He had a strong sense of his place in the racing world, and made it a point to help others. Long sensitive to the needs of injured race drivers and their families, Bob would often be the first to organize benefits, even going into the stands at a race to collect donations from race fans.

In the early autumn of 1961, after visiting injured drivers in the hospital, he brought back to the race pits encouraging comments about the progress of both Wayne Weiler, who had crashed with severe injuries at Terre Haute in June, and A. J. Shepherd, who was injured in the recent Hoosier 100. The two men recovered, although their racing careers, at least at the top level, were over. Both men died in 2005.

Bobby personally considered himself one of the luckiest drivers in the race world, telling *NSSN*'s Bob Maginley, "I have always been lucky in getting machines that fit me. The Konstant Hot midget has felt like an old glove to me, and I get all out of it that's possible. You can only do this when your machine feels comfortable and properly set up." Bob continued in response to questions about Indy cars: "The only type I have driven, the only one, as a matter of fact, was the Hoover Motor Express car. I liked its feel, and although I would have liked to have gone faster, I was really pleased with its handling qualities. The other guys have talked about the stand-up type engine machines, and next season I would like an opportunity to try one for a few laps at the Speedway."

The news from Indiana was that the Indianapolis Motor Speedway was having the last strip of bricks paved over. When the Speedway opened in 1909, it was surfaced with crushed stone and tar. By the time of the first 500 in 1911, it was paved entirely with oversize bricks; hence, the popular term "The Brickyard." In 1937 the turns were resurfaced with asphalt and the back straight was paved in 1939. Bobby, in 1961, had experienced the last year that a substantial part of the Speedway was brick. In October, the last of the original 3,200,000 bricks—a 2,142-foot strip on the main straightaway—were paved, leaving only a symbolic yard of bricks at the start/finish. Tony Hulman told the *Indianapolis Star* that the change was recommended by drivers and race officials in the interest of safety. "Greater speed is definitely not our objective," Hulman said, "but new records will be a distinct possibility."

Henry Banks, USAC competition director and a former championship-winning driver, told Jep Cadou Jr. of the *Star*, "The drivers will have much better control of their cars on the main straightaway and going into the first turn than they did on the bricks. Those bricks were quite treacherous when they got oil or moisture on them, and the brick surface had been getting rougher and rougher in recent years."

There was more change in the air as the USAC struggled with myriad important decisions that had to be made for the future. The board had voted at their September 15 meeting to reduce engine sizes for sprint cars for the 1962 season, with Offys reduced from 237 to 222 cubic inches, and stock

blocks, from 366 to 305. More controversially, the board also announced that they would recommend reduction of championship engines from 256 cubic inches to 183 (3.0 liters), and possibly limit wheelbase from 96 to 90 inches. There was sentiment within the USAC to align their engines with FIA rules, and the 3.0-liter limit would have accomplished that by 1966.

At the same time, there was an even larger group who detested the idea, the main opposition coming from the Championship Car Owners Association, a group that had recently voted 40 to 3 against any reduction. Bob Bowes, owner of the Bowes Seal Fast Special, was one of the most vociferous opponents of the engine size change. Bowes told George Moore for *NSSN*, "What do we have to do to make these people understand what we want," he said. "We don't want to change."

Chapter 37
Rugged Western Tracks (1961)

On Saturday, September 30, at the Bloomsburg Fair ARDC midget race, Bobby was in the Berks Offy. Al Keller, the driver for Bruce Homeyer's Konstant Hot sprint and championship cars, was now also driving the Konstant Hot midget that Bobby had enjoyed so much success with over the past two years. In qualifying Bobby broke the midget record for the half-mile dirt track, at 24.55 seconds. The fine effort came to naught when the organizers, overwhelmed with an entry of forty-four cars, halted qualifying runs and began running heats. It took winning the consi—which he did in style—to make the feature, where he started nineteenth. Bobby moved steadily through the field, *NSSN* describing his "rim-riding style as he passed one car after another." Late in the race, overheating slowed his progress, and he finished fourth behind winner Ernie McCoy, Bob Harkey in second, and King Carpenter, third.

The next day the ARDC midgets ran on the hard-packed, half-mile clay at Nazareth, Pennsylvania. Bobby in the Berks Offy was second to Len Duncan in his heat. In later warm-ups the motor in the Berks car developed trouble. The Bennett Brothers, who ran the pink No. 3 Fluid Chemicals Offy for championship contender, Johnny Coy, asked their driver to step aside so Bobby—now a very popular and well-known name—could please the crowd by racing in the feature. Coy himself was a top-ranked driver.

Bobby brought the car home third in the thirty-lap feature behind winner Len Duncan in the Ken Hickey Offy and Ray Brown driving the Darrell Villa Offy. Behind Bob in fourth was Red Marlowe in a Hespell car and Al Keller fifth in the Konstant Hot Offy. Gig Stephens lost the opportunity for a successful day when, while leading his heat, he mistook the white flag—signaling there was one lap to go—for the checker. He lifted off the throttle and was passed by every car in the heat before he realized his mistake.

On Saturday, October 7, Bobby competed in a night show at Hatfield, a fifty-lap midget race. He won his heat in the Berks Offy, but in the feature, Bob was running in third place on the nineteenth lap when mechanical trouble put him out of the race. The winner was Red Riegel, with Jim Hurtubise second, Len Duncan, third, and Parnelli Jones, fourth. Duncan's third place clinched for him the 1961 ARDC championship.

The next day Bobby was at Williams Grove, Pennsylvania, for the Ted Horne–Bill Schindler Memorial Race, a round in the USAC Sprint Car Championship. The October 8 race was a disappointment for Bobby: The clutch went out on the Meskowski Offy, and he was unable to make even a time-trial lap. The race was won by Parnelli Jones, who was enjoying another dominating year in sprint cars.

At Indianapolis Raceway Park on October 14 for a USAC sprint car race, Parnelli Jones saw the engine in his Fike Chevy blow during warm-up laps. Parnelli, who needed to protect his points lead in the USAC championship, went looking for a ride. Jep Cadou Jr. in the *Indianapolis Star* said, "Because Parnelli needed to clinch the sprint championship, his buddy, Bobby Marshman of Pottstown, Pennsylvania, agreed to let Jones take over the Offenhauser-powered No. 44 Competition Engineering Special which Marshman was scheduled to drive."

Parnelli qualified the unfamiliar Meskowski Offy tenth and then charged through the field to win. "I sure was lucky to get a chance to clinch the championship today, thanks to Bobby," he told Cadou. "I thought I'd probably just be a spectator today."

Next up for Bobby was Gardena, California, for an October 21 Ascot Park USAC midget race. Driving the Algon Fuel Injection Special, Bob won the first heat over standout Billy Cantrell. In the fourth and fastest heat, Cantrell beat Bobby and the rest of the field as he sped to a new eight-lap heat record. Bobby faded in the feature, finishing eighteenth and last. A. J. Foyt was the winner of the forty-lap contest on the half-mile dirt oval.

Bobby's chief purpose in traveling to the West was to compete in the final two races of the USAC championship series. The penultimate round was on October 29 at the California State Fairgrounds in Sacramento. High winds the night before the race had damaged the track surface, leaving it rutted and dusty. Although the track was freshly watered on race morning, the ruts began to reappear during qualification. There were thirty-two cars competing for eighteen starting positions, and Bobby placed the Meskowski Offy thirteenth. The ruts became even more extreme in the race, with great clouds of dust in the turns and down the backstretch. Bobby seemed less troubled than most, moving steadily through the field. A large hole developed on the track just past the start/finish, and cars were airborne after going through it. Bobby was mentioned by the *NSSN* reporter as one of the drivers "flying through the air more than on the ground." His perseverance paid off with a third-place finish behind winner Rodger Ward and Parnelli Jones, with Len Sutton behind him in fourth.

With the season finale at Phoenix coming up in just three weeks, Bobby stayed out West and looked to pick up rides while there. J. C. Agajanian was promoting a USAC midget race in San Bernardino at the Orange Show Speedway on November 4. Bobby drove a Ward Offy but did not feature in the race results. A week later, on November 11 at Ascot Park, a USAC sprint car race drew a crowd of over 7,500. Bobby had a drive in a Conze Offy but it developed injector trouble and he was unable to take it to the track for qualifying.

Bob, Janet, and Robbie also found time to take a family trip to Yosemite National Park. "On the way back, Robbie came down with bronchial pneumonia," Janet said. "We were sitting in a restaurant, not knowing what to do, because everyone we knew had already gone to Phoenix. The lady who was our server was so nice and told us of a doctor, who immediately put Robbie into a hospital in Fresno. Robbie's crib was right next to the nurses' station, and no one stopped at the desk without talking to him, so he got lots of attention. It was a beautiful hospital, but it was hard for Bob and me to see Robbie so sick—he was only a year and five months old at the time, and in the hospital for a week." When Robbie recovered, the young family moved on to Phoenix.

• • •

The Arizona State Fairgrounds in Phoenix was the site of the Bobby Ball Memorial, the final round in the USAC championship series, on November 19. The fairground track at McDowell Road and 19th Avenue in Phoenix had existed as a race car venue since 1908. Its one-mile dirt oval had been used since 1910 and had long been on the AAA, and later the USAC, Championship Trail. It was a rough dirt track that made recent conditions at Sacramento pale by comparison. During time trials, Ray Crawford (who didn't own a dirt car) tried to qualify his roadster, and crashed. His attempt was generally considered unwise.

Bobby Marshman's friend Al Keller, driving the Konstant Hot car, set pole position. On the forty-first lap of the scheduled 100-lap race in the heavily rutted fourth turn, Keller's car was thrown sideways and flipped six times, coming to rest on top of a six-foot chain-link fence in the infield near the pits. A yellow flag was displayed for just one lap, a decision that later elicited the wrath of many drivers and crews. With the cars racing, there was no way to bring an ambulance and other safety equipment to the place where Keller lay. The green flag flew until lap 49, when the race was red-flagged. Race officials justified their actions of not stopping the race sooner, or keeping the field under yellow, on the grounds that the racing surface was not blocked. Keller was said to have died instantly, but he was officially pronounced dead of head injuries at Saint Joseph Hospital.

The race action was suspended under the red flag for more than an hour, and during this time, grading equipment was used on the track to address the ruts. When the race resumed, Rodger Ward and Parnelli Jones dueled for the lead. The race was yellow-flagged again on lap 81 when Chuck Hulse of Los Angeles in the John Zink Trackburner flipped five times in the north turn. Hulse suffered a shoulder injury and head cuts. The accident contributed to the officials' decision to end the scheduled 100-lap race after lap 89. Jones was the winner, with Ward second. It was Parnelli's first championship win, and he did it in J. C. Agajanian's No. 98 Lesovsky-Offy.

Bobby Marshman had started twelfth and finished eleventh, with relief from Jim Hurtubise. Hurtubise took over the Meskowski Offy after the red-flag stop because Bobby had been struck in the face by debris.

Eddie Sachs told the reporter for the *Indianapolis Star*, "There are other tracks as bad or worse, but this one was throwing clods of dirt." Rodger Ward was more emphatic in his comment to the *Star*: "This is about as bad a track as I ever saw in my life."

Al Keller, a good friend of Bobby's from racing together in the ARDC, was very popular with fans and other drivers. His regular job was as manager of a marine supply company in Boynton Beach, Florida, and he was a special police deputy for Palm Beach County. He was survived by his wife Virginia and his eight-year-old daughter Beth Ann.

Janet Marshman accompanied Virginia Keller from Phoenix to the Keller family home in Green Acres, Florida. "Al Keller was one of Bob's best friends," said Janet. "I flew from Phoenix—Robbie stayed with Bob in Phoenix—to Miami with Al's wife, Virginia. I couldn't let her be alone. Once she was with her family I flew right back to Phoenix."

The year 1961 marked great achievement and recognition in the career of Bobby Marshman. He made the step into the "big leagues" of automobile racing when he qualified for the Indianapolis 500, and continued to distinguish himself all year. With his outstanding drive in the 500 he earned a position in the USAC's highest category, the National Championship series, where he consistently performed at a top level and secured his place with the best in his sport. His eighth-place finish in points for the championship was well earned, and he was one of only three drivers, along with A. J. Foyt and Don Branson, to have qualified for every one of the twelve races in the series. In addition, Bobby was second in number of laps completed in the series: Foyt was first, completing 1,108 of a possible 1,388 laps, and Bob was runner-up, with 1,093.

Chapter 38
Subpoena (1962)

Over the winter Bobby remained focused on his vocation, and keeping fit was a big part of it. He rode his bicycle when the Pennsylvania weather permitted, and he also worked with weights, practiced isometric techniques, and did floor exercises, including push-ups. Bob also had a special exercise device, inherited from his friend Johnny Thomson, which consisted of a chair and a steering wheel. The wheel was connected to a shock absorber that could be adjusted to various degrees of resistance. Thomson's widow Evelyn gave it to Bob shortly after Johnny's death. Bob would spend an hour or more every day in the chair developing strength in his forearms and wrists.

Janet recalled how active Bob was around the house. "He was always meticulous. His mother Evelyn, an excellent housekeeper herself, once shared with me that before Bob and I were married, she always knew when I was coming to visit because Bob would clean the house to his standard. He was like this about his cars and his clothes, too—he liked things to look right. Even after we were married, Bob was always making certain the house was neat and clean."

An indication of Bobby's growing celebrity was his inclusion at the sixteenth annual banquet of Lancaster sportswriters on January 22, 1962, at the Hotel Brunswick in Lancaster, Pennsylvania. Bobby was an honored guest along with Dallas Green, pitcher for the Philadelphia Phillies; hockey legend Gordie Howe; Baltimore Orioles baseball players Jim Gentile and future Hall of Fame member Brooks Robinson; and future Hall of Fame football player Art Donovan of the Baltimore Colts.

It was banquet season, and the Hub Fan Club held their ninth annual party on March 3 at Syracuse, New York. Bob was one of four honorees, including Gene Hartley, Hal Rettberg, and Ed Gallione.

Bobby finished fourth on March 25 in the USAC sprint car opener at Reading. Driving the Meskowsi car, Bobby was fourth in the first heat and, in a later heat, led from pole for three laps,

only to be passed by Parnelli Jones, who went on to win, with Bobby second. Starting fifth in the thirty-lap feature, Bob passed Elmer George for fourth and held the position to the end. The race was won by Jim Hurtubise in the Barnett Brothers Chevy-powered car, with Parnelli second and Don Davis, third.

On the following Saturday, March 31, Bobby was to be among the featured honorees of the Bloomsburg Midget Racing pre-season roast beef dinner banquet at the Methodist Church gymnasium. Bob and Janet were being put up in the Hotel Magee in Bloomsburg, the heart of square dancing in Pennsylvania. The opening round of the 1962 USAC championship season at Trenton was scheduled for the very next day, and practice was to be held on Saturday, the day of the banquet. A friend, Fred Heydenright, had volunteered to fly Bobby and Janet from Trenton to Bloomsburg in time for the dinner and back the next day for the race. The day at Trenton, with thirty-four cars out for practice, ran unexpectedly long, making it necessary for Bobby to phone with regrets for missing the Bloomsburg event that evening.

At Trenton, heavy Saturday night rains persisted into Sunday, causing the event to be put off until the following week. The Sam Nunis–promoted race was to be videotaped by ABC-TV for airing on April 15, a first for a USAC championship race.

For 1962 Bob had in place a lineup of drives similar to the previous year. He would continue to drive for Wally Meskowski's Competition Engineering team in sprint car and championship dirt races. The big change was in his car and team for the Indianapolis 500, although many of the faces remained the same. Bryant Heating and Cooling took over sponsorship of the Epperly-Offy that Don Branson had driven at Indianapolis the previous year as Bobby Marshman's teammate. For Bobby, it meant moving from the 1959-built Epperly to the car that Quincy "Quin" Epperly had built new for the 1961 season for the Hoover Motor Express team. Joe Langley remained as crew chief. "We just adored him," Janet said. "We called him 'Huggybear.'"

Bryant Heating and Cooling first entered a car at the 500 with Eddie Johnson, who finished ninth in 1958 and eighth in 1959. In 1960 their driver was Dempsey Wilson, who made it into the field in thirty-third position and finished in the same place. For 1961 they were with Len Sutton, who finished nineteenth. Bryant's 1962 car that Bobby would drive carried the number 54 to celebrate the fifty-fourth anniversary of the founding of the Bryant Heating and Cooling company.

The Bryant company hosted a press party on April 4 at the Embers on Meridian Street in Indianapolis. Phil Hedback was Bryant's Indiana distributor and was a gifted public relations and marketing man. Bobby and Janet received an invitation similar to those sent to the press and to industry figures.

The invitation was in the form of a subpoena—*served on*: Bobby Marshman, *dated* "Big Day of Bryant 1962." The invitation continued: "The Bryant Manufacturing Company orders you under the penalty of law to attend the 'Car 54' press party, April 4, 1962, at the Embers. Your wife or friend is hereby summoned as a supporting witness."

"What a sponsor these guys were," Janet recalled. "They couldn't do enough for their drivers and crew, and remained friends forever. When we were going to build our new house the next year, Bob took copies of all the plans [to Indianapolis] and Bryant's engineers set that house up with heating and cooling and filtering. And Phil said, 'Now Janet, if something's not right you've got to let me know.'"

The barely one-year-old Epperly-Offy, to be driven by Bobby, remained a competitive proposition. Although Don Branson had eventually left the team in 1961 out of frustration with mechanical failures, he had always qualified the car well, including in the middle of the front row for the 500. It was a "lay down" design, meaning its Offy engine was laid on its side. Doing so put the engine's mass as low as possible, reducing frontal area and lowering the car's center of gravity. The transmission had two forward gears. The body was all aluminum and the car carried a nine-gallon aluminum oil tank. It featured a Halibrand Engineering quick-change rear end, steering gear, and spindles. It was equipped with air jacks to allow a four-tire change and refuel in less than twenty seconds. The car weighed 1,650 pounds and was 168 inches in length, with a 96-inch wheelbase. The No. 54 Bryant Heating and Cooling car, with Bobby Marshman as driver, was the first entrant for the 1962 Indianapolis 500—another Phil Hedback PR coup.

Postponed by a week for rain, the Trenton 100, the opening round of the 1962 USAC championship series, was successfully run on April 8. Bobby Marshman qualified Wally Meskowski's No. 8 Competition Engineering car tenth from thirty-nine cars vying for twenty-two available starting positions. Trenton was a paved track, but most entrants chose to run their dirt cars. Although many teams preferred the gearing and general setup of the dirt cars at Trenton, others withheld their roadsters to preserve them for the upcoming month of May at Indianapolis. The race was won by the defending National Champion A. J. Foyt in the Bowes Seal Fast Special, with Parnelli Jones second. Rodger Ward, third in the Leader Card Watson-Offy, was the only contending roadster. Bobby ran a steady race, running no higher than ninth, and finished tenth.

Bob's final race before he headed to Indianapolis for all of May was on April 22 at Rossburg, Ohio, for a USAC sprint car race. Although he was second in the first heat, Bob in the Meskowski Offy did not place in the feature. The race was won by Stan Bowman of Covington, Kentucky, with Jim Hurtubise second and Parnelli Jones, third. The scheduled thirty-lap race was shortened to twenty-seven laps when rain interrupted the event.

Chapter 39
Qualifying on the Front Row (1962)

The day after Eldora, Bob helped to start the month-of-May excitement a week early. He met crew chief Joe Langley for a joint promotion with Bryant Heating and Cooling and the Ayr-Way East store at East 38th Street and Shadeland on April 23. Ayr-Way was a discount store affiliated with Indianapolis's L. S. Ayres department store. Ads in local periodicals promised the public an opportunity to see the race car and to meet and talk to its driver and crew chief. These promotions, arranged by Bryant's Phil Hedback, featured the lead advertising line: "Car 54, where are you?" This reference played on the popular American television show by the same name, and the connection would be promoted ever more strongly as the month went on.

Entries for the 500 had reached seventy-two, a number previously exceeded only in 1953, with eighty-four cars. In 1953 the entry fee had been $250, and when the fee was raised to $500 the next year, the entries had gone down. By 1962, the fee was apparently no longer a disincentive for entrants, and track officials were worried about having sufficient space to accommodate all the cars, even

though new garages had been built earlier in the year. In truth, there were often cars in the garages that had little expectation of doing much more than making a token run during the month. What $250, or $500, bought was access, passes, and the intangible feeling of being part of the insider scene.

The magic 150-mph lap—equal to exactly one minute on the stopwatch—was being predicted by the media as well as by teams and drivers, and with the front straight now paved in asphalt, the likely prospect of seeing it happen this year created tremendous fan excitement. The track opened officially on Saturday, April 28, and by May 3, Parnelli Jones in the No. 98 "Ol' Calhoun"—the J. C. Agajanian team's affectionate name for their Willard Battery–sponsored Watson-Offy—had turned a lap at 148.5 mph.

The days before the first weekend of qualifying, Bobby Marshman and Parnelli Jones were dominating the newsprint as the two fastest men at the Speedway. In fact, the previous year's co–Rookies of the Year were the only drivers to break the magic 150 through the entire month. Only Parnelli achieved it on the official time system, while Bob was caught at that speed in practice on numerous handheld watches. On May 4, Bobby appeared to have the fastest speed of the day when, half an hour before the track closed, he turned a 148.7-mph lap. With just two minutes to go, Jones ran a lap at 149.0. Bobby was the first man to reach Parnelli's garage to congratulate him.

Bobby gave credit to Freddie Agabashian, a longtime 500 driver from Walnut Creek, California, turned color commentator for the 500 radio network, as having provided him unique advice on going faster. Agabashian had been a front-row qualifier on three occasions in a 500 career that spanned from 1947 through 1957, and he had captured pole position in 1952. "I don't want to tell you exactly what he told me," Bobby told Jep Cadou Jr. of the *Indianapolis Star*, "but it involved my pattern of driving the track." After Bob's fast lap, he told Cadou, "It felt real good. I want to make a minor change, to slow down the steering a little."

When Cadou sought out Agabashian for his view on the exchange, he was told, "Well, I don't want to give away any trade secrets, but I'll put it this way: There are some fellows who have the gift of putting into practice knowledge gained from those who have gone before. Bobby is one of those. I just thought I may be able to help him just a little bit."

Bobby immediately went back on the track and ran faster than he had to date.

The lead headline in the *Star* on May 7 was MARSHMAN CLIPS WIND-BLOWN 149 LAP. "Man, I wanted to hit that 150 so bad I could taste it, but I just couldn't get it done," Bobby told the media. "It was too windy, and I didn't want to hang it on the wall. The wind sock on the north turn was standing straight out and there was too much sun in my eyes at the north end of the track. I was coming off the third and fourth turns like a snake."

"You're going to cause me to get fired," Troy Ruttman, who was driving the Jim Robbins Kuzma-Offy, joked with Bob. "I don't know what you are doing, but you are really flying through those corners." Ruttman was considered among the greatest "naturals" to ever drive in the 500. When he won in 1952 for J. C. Agajanian at age twenty-two, he was, and so remains to this date, the youngest-ever

Indianapolis 500 winner.

Bobby said he thought he could hit the magic 150 the next day if the weather cooperated. Clint Brawner, chief mechanic of the Dean-Autolite team, clocked Bobby at 141 through the southwest turn. Bob admitted to Cadou that he had a little difficulty trying to concentrate on his driving when he was coming down the main straightaway during his fast run, because his attention was diverted to the small army in the pits clocking him with stopwatches. "We'll try her again tomorrow, I guess," Bob told Cadou.

On May 11, the day before qualifying, Bobby did several laps over 149 mph and turned his second-fastest time to date. But Parnelli was the fast man of the day, with an average lap speed of 149 mph. Jim Hurtubise crashed hard in the No. 99 Demler Special, cutting his leg and severely damaging the car.

On the first day of qualifying, Saturday, May 12, practice opened at 8:00 a.m. and qualifying began at 11:00 a.m. It had been hot throughout May, but Pole Day was said to be the hottest of the month. People likened it to race day in 1953—the race that sixteen-year-olds Bobby Marshman and Bill Reiff had driven to from Pennsylvania to watch—when driver Carl Scarborough had died of heat exhaustion. The ambient temperature was in the high 90s, and on track it was measured by Firestone technicians at 139 degrees. During practice, before qualifying opened, Bobby was unofficially clocked over 150 and 151 mph on several laps.

The long-anticipated official sub-minute lap finally happened in the first hour of qualifying, and it was Parnelli Jones who did it, managing the historic breakthrough in spectacular fashion. Three drivers qualified before Parnelli had his turn, one being Len Sutton, who closed his four-lap run with a 149.900-mph flier, qualifying at 149.328, a speed that was ultimately good for fourth fastest. Parnelli rolled out onto the track at 11:39 a.m. and never ran under 150 mph, capturing pole position with an average speed of 150.370 in the Agajanian-Willard Battery Special. Fastest of his four laps was the first, at 150.729 mph.

Bobby's turn came at 12:03 p.m., and though second fastest at the time, he could not match Parnelli. Bob's official speed for the ten-mile run was 149.347 mph, with individual laps at 149.180, 149.576, 149.353, and 149.278. Later in the day, Rodger Ward put his Leader Card 500 roadster ahead of Bob with an average speed of 149.371 mph. But Bobby Marshman had claimed his place on the front row, and his third-place starting spot compared nicely with starting thirty-third the previous year.

Filling the second row with Sutton's Leader Card entry were A. J. Foyt in the Bowes Seal Fast Special and Shorty Templeman in the Bill Forbes Racing Team Special. Inside on the third row was Jim McElreath in the Schultz Fueling Equipment Special, fastest rookie and last man to qualify over 149 mph. Fellow rookie Dan Gurney was in the middle of the row in the Mickey Thompson–built Harvey Aluminum Special, and on the outside of the row was Roger McCluskey in the Bell Lines Trucking Special.

Master publicist Phil Hedback had promised 150 silver dollars to the first man to qualify at over 150 mph. In a much-publicized photo, he poured the silver dollars into Parnelli's helmet in the pit

lane. In addition to the marketing gain of having Bobby Marshman on the front row in a Bryant car, Hedback had, with his simple but effective stunt, neatly managed to share some of the pole sitter's "moment in the sun," shifting some of the publicity from master promoter J. C. Agajanian and his sponsors to the direction of the Bryant Company.

Eddie Sachs had been looking for his third consecutive 500 pole position but lost his left front wheel during morning practice. The car was made ready for his qualifying attempt, but his crew waved him off when his speed in the first two laps was only 146 mph. He ultimately made the field in the twenty-seventh starting position on the second weekend of qualifying.

The ferociousness of a high-speed wreck at the Speedway can be understood, in part, by the description of damage to the second Bill Forbes Special when Norm Hall, who survived, hit the wall. His crew chief Dave Laycock detailed for George Moore in the *Indianapolis Star* the extent of damage to the Forbes roadster, which was considered a complete write-off. The frame was horseshoed, the fuel tank ripped off the body, the left wheel broken and ground away, the rear torsion bars twisted and driven to the right, the rear end ripped apart with the bolt studs pulled away from the casing, the driveshaft twisted up into the universal joint collar, the front end pushed over with the steering linkage bent, and the body paneling bent and twisted over its entire length.

Hall was knocked unconscious, but his condition was pronounced fair at Methodist Hospital. His worst injury proved to be a broken left leg.

Chapter 40
Gurney Pushes Design Innovation (1962)

Despite international fascination the year before with the sport's technological change of direction (represented by the rear-engine Cooper driven by Jack Brabham), there had been no massive move by the Indy establishment to follow suit. In fact, again, only one rear-engine car was on the start line for the 1962 race. Though the engine did not attract quite the same publicity as the previous year, 1962 proved that it was here to stay.

It was rookie driver Dan Gurney who was most responsible for moving useful development forward in 1962 through his involvement with—it would turn out—three separate design engineers and their cars. It all happened in the month of May, even as Gurney was also focused on his racing program in Europe. He was leading the Porsche Grand Prix team—Dan's win that year at Rouen in the French Grand Prix remains the only Porsche victory in a world championship Formula One Grand Prix—and he was also a key driver on the Porsche sports prototype program contesting the World Championship for Manufacturers. With traveling to and racing at the Targa Florio in Sicily on May 6, and the Dutch Grand Prix at the Zandvoort circuit on the North Sea on May 20, Dan Gurney had a very full month indeed.

The spectacularly talented Gurney was already one of the stars of American and European road racing before he arrived at the Speedway at age thirty-one. Born in New York, he moved to Southern California in his teens and first came to notice in road racing in 1957. By 1958 he was in Formula One as a member of the Italian Ferrari factory team, moving on to the British BRM team and to German Porsche. His career as a driver eventually included success in every form of racing, both on ovals and road courses. As a driver, designer, and manufacturer, Gurney today stands in a pantheon among the most influential figures in the history of motorsports.

Gurney came to the Speedway in late April with entrant John Zink. The team goal was to make their innovative rear-engine turbine-powered Zink Trackburner a world beater. Because of Gurney's commitments in Europe, it was important to make it through his rookie test early in the week to maximize his time in the Trackburner. He utilized the team's well-used Zink Offy roadster for the test, which was completed on April 29, allowing Dan to spend his remaining available days at the Speedway bringing the rear-engine turbine Trackburner car up to speed. On May 9, the effort with the rear-engine racer reached its zenith with a lap at 143 mph—a good speed for a car with so many developmental issues, but not a speed that was going to put him in the starting field, an assessment proven correct when the slowest car on the 1962 grid qualified at 146.318 mph.

The second important innovator to become part of Gurney's 1962 adventure at the Speedway was Mickey Thompson. Thompson was a highly independent speed maven who had designed, built, and driven successful land-speed-record cars. In his first year at Indianapolis he brought three beautifully presented rear-engine cars powered by stock block Buick V8s and designed by Englishman John Crosthwaite. The highly modified small-block aluminum Buicks were putting out 330 horsepower, compared to 425hp in a typical Offy. At the same time, the light materials used in the chassis and engine meant the Thompson cars had a competitive power-to-weight ratio. George Moore in the *Indianapolis Star* estimated a ratio of 3.27 pounds per horsepower for the Thompson cars to 3.75 pounds per horsepower for a roadster. Jim Kimberly, who was sponsoring all three Thompson cars, told Moore, "The engine is back on the rear wheels for better traction. The fuel load weight is in the middle of the chassis where it belongs, and the independent suspension is easier to handle."

Gurney now switched to the Mickey Thompson No. 34 car and had it over 148 mph for three laps. On the first day of qualifying, he put the car in the middle of the third row at a speed of 147.886 mph. Neither of the other Thompson cars managed to reach qualifying speed.

All of this was impressive enough for a rookie driver, but Gurney made still another crucial connection that proved vital in the movement toward rear-engine race cars at the Speedway. Gurney returned to Europe for the Dutch Grand Prix at Zandvoort on May 20—the opening round in the 1962 Formula One World Championship series. (Formula One design had begun to move away from front-engine cars five years earlier, and the last Formula One victory for a traditional front-engine car was at the 1960 Italian Grand Prix, where American Phil Hill won for Ferrari in a 246.) At

Zandvoort in 1962, Lotus team owner and creative designer Colin Chapman introduced a new car that is ranked today as one of the most important design breakthroughs in racing history.

The Lotus 25 was the first successful application of a fully stressed monocoque chassis on a rear-engine single-seater. It consisted of two aluminum pontoons forming the sides of the car and also serving as fuel tanks. The resulting "tub" was held together on each end by a firewall, which, together with subframes for the front and rear suspension, formed the chassis. The V8 engine was installed as a stressed member to further increase torsional rigidity, which in turn increased tire efficiency. The rest of the car was made up of removable glass-fiber body panels, which provided easy access to all vital parts. The tub provided a low driving position.

Although the Climax-powered Lotus 25 in the hands of Jim Clark suffered clutch trouble and finished tenth at Zandvoort after leading the early laps, people with technical instinct recognized the car as representing a new era. Dan Gurney spent a great deal of time with Chapman over the race weekend, regaling him with his personal experience at the Speedway and persuading him that a state-of-the-art chassis with a decent motor could win the race. Gurney urged Chapman to come to see the race, but it wasn't until Gurney promised to underwrite the airfare that the famously penurious design genius agreed to attend.

Chapter 41
Toody and Muldoon (1962)

Back at the Speedway, the cars and drivers still remaining outside of the starting field spent a busy week leading up to May 19 and 20, the final days to qualify for the thirty-three-car field. There were only twelve spots still open on the grid, and twenty or more cars were considered capable of making the necessary speed. It was also a busy week for Bobby and others who had already qualified because after May 20, the track would be closed, with only May 28 available for final tuning before the May 30 race.

On Tuesday, May 15, Bob was out on the track, followed by Chuck Arnold, showing his friend and competitor from the ARDC his line around the track. On the same run, Bob was purposely wearing out tires at speeds between 144 and 148 mph to better familiarize himself with the discoloration of worn-out tires. Bobby ran a long practice session on Thursday and his friend Parnelli Jones took over the pit board to show him lap times. Bob noticed Parnelli and, according to Jep Cadou Jr. in the *Indianapolis Star*, on the next lap by, Bobby patted his helmet, signaling he wanted relief. On his long run he did forty-one laps, all at a speed of 147 mph or better, with a best of 147.5. This was a speed he hoped to maintain in the race, and in that forty-one-lap session, he showcased his steadiness.

Phil Hedback was not slowing down on his promotion efforts for the No. 54 Bryant Cooling and Heating car. In his well-received and highly effective promotion, Hedback played upon the enormous success of the comedy sitcom television series, *Car 54, Where Are You?* It ran on NBC from 1961 to 1963, and in May of 1962 was at the height of its popularity. Actors Fred Gwynne as Francis Muldoon and Joe E. Ross as Gunther Toody played New York City police patrolmen encountering hilarious daily incidents on their beat in their patrol squad car 54.

At the Speedway in May, Gwynne and Ross made numerous appearances in uniform as Toody and Muldoon, and their comedy was perfect for sight gags and photo opportunities such as arresting and ticketing Bobby in the race car. A local television channel set up an interview for Bobby and the actors in which Toody and Muldoon appeared to pull Bobby and the Bryant race car over for excess speed. When Toody said, "What's your name?" an unscripted Bobby replied "Parnelli Jones." It brought down the house with the live crowd.

On May 19, during the second weekend of qualification, Bob was walking through the garages when the public address system put out an announcement: "Bobby Marshman would like his bike back. Car 54 check for Marshman's missing bicycle." It was an inside joke, but one most of the drivers and crew at the Speedway that day would get: Bob came and went from the racetrack every day by bike from the house he and Janet rented for the season.

The house on Medford Avenue was close to the Speedway, and to friends. "Parnelli and all those guys were only a couple of blocks in different directions," Janet said. "Those were fun times." Janet added, "We weren't party people. We were probably a little bit boring for some people—Bobby didn't smoke or drink, and neither did I; plus, we didn't go anywhere without Robbie."

In fact, the Marshmans' toddler was a hit with the racing crowd. "Everyone was always arguing over who was going to spend time with him," Janet recalled. "Our dear friend Sid Collins always got such a kick out of Robbie," she continued. "Whenever he came over to the house for dinner, he would sit with Robbie afterwards and read with him. He was Uncle Sid to Robbie."

To listeners across the world, Robbie's Uncle Sid was the "Voice of the 500"—the chief announcer from 1952 to 1976. "The greatest spectacle in racing" was one of Collins's signature phrases, beloved by his fans. George Bignotti was also a frequent visitor at the Marshmans' Indianapolis house, often coming with Collins, Janet recalled.

In addition to commuting from the Medford Avenue house to the track, Bob used his bike to move around inside the enormous Speedway grounds, and it could typically be seen parked outside the Bryant garage. Bob's friend Parnelli Jones also used a bicycle for getting around during this period.

The bike was a great deal more to Bob than mere transportation. He had a strong work ethic, and long hard bike rides were an essential part of his near-daily workout regimen. He also continued to build arm and wrist strength using the special chair/steering wheel setup he had inherited from Johnny Thomson.

Bob never forgot his friends in Pennsylvania who had helped him on his way. A treasured signed photo of Bob in the Bryant No. 54 arrived at the home of Bill Blatt the week before the race, signed "To Shooey, Best Wishes, Bob."

When the field was complete on Sunday evening, May 20, it had a traditional look. Of the thirty-three cars, eleven were from the shop of A. J. Watson, and three more were built from an A. J. Watson design by other constructors. Five were from the Frank Kurtis shop, four from Floyd Trevis, three by Quin Epperly, and one each from Lujie Lesovsky, Judd Philips, Ed Kuzma, and Edgar Elder. Only one car had the engine in the rear, and that was built by Mickey Thompson. It was also the only car in the race not powered by an Offenhauser engine.

With ten days to go before the 500, the teams went over their cars carefully and practiced pit stops. George Moore in the *Indianapolis Star* reported that Joe Langley discovered a cracked transmission case on Bobby's car. Drivers signed seemingly endless numbers of autographs; Bobby Marshman always signed as "Bob Marshman." Friendly and well-spoken, Bob was kept increasingly busy with personal appearances, and on May 24 appeared at the Kroger store in the Meadows Shopping Center to draw the winning ticket for a lucky customer's new Ford Falcon. The same week he was pictured in a Kroger ad, captioned "Cooling off with a big pitcher of Kroger Frozen Lemonade." On May 30, Janet was featured in the women's section of the *Star* in a photo with Mrs. Dick Rathmann and Mrs. Len Sutton, all attending the annual Firestone luncheon honoring the wives of the drivers, an event held at the Holiday Inn.

Race drivers loved to kid one another, and Janet recalled how much the press made of the two young chargers on either side of the front row, sandwiching the older driver Rodger Ward. "Parnelli was on the pole and Bob was on the outside and Rodger was in the middle—these two young bucks and Rodger was forty-something—they called him Pop and Grandpop and all that." Parnelli was asked by the *Indianapolis Star* if he thought he or Bobby would lead the first lap, and Jones replied, "We've got to look out for Father there in the middle."

Bob's focus was on the big race. He was asked his chances of repeating at Trenton, four days after the 500, and *NSSN* reported his reply. "I'm gunning for the big one out here in Indianapolis. I'm feeling real chipper about starting third as compared to thirty-third last year, then I'm going all out to get my third win at Trenton. Can't see any reason why I can't do it again," he said.

"Last year after running second to Foyt in the Hoosier Hundred, you recall that I got little sleep, yet won a 100-mile midget go the next afternoon at Sam Nunis's plant," he continued. "This setup gives a couple of days to rest up after the 500, and that's plenty of easy time before taking on the guys in the 250-miler at Trenton."

Parties and banquets filled the time for the racing industry. On May 24, "the racing fraternity's most glittering social occasion," as the *Indianapolis Star* described it, took place. It was the Monroe Auto Equipment Company rookie recognition dinner at the Columbia Club. Co–Rookies of the Year, Bob and Parnelli, were honored along with fellow 1961 rookies Don Davis, Norm Hall, Roger McCluskey,

ABOVE: The front-row starters for the 1962 Indy 500, interviewed by June Ford for her show on WISH-TV, Indianapolis. (MARSHMAN FAMILY COLLECTION)

Ebb Rose, and A. J. Shepherd. (Jack Brabham was one of the eight rookies in the 1961 Indy 500, but he was not in Indianapolis for the 1962 gala.) The next day's *Star* featured a photo of Janet and Mrs. Allen Crowe talking with the host company's president and his wife, Mr. and Mrs. B. D. McIntyre.

The annual Champion Spark Plug Company's 100-Mile-an-Hour Club dinner was an event that Bob was especially proud to be part of. To earn entry in the exclusive club and receive the coveted jacket, a driver had to complete the entire five hundred miles of the race at an average speed in excess of 100 mph. At the 1962 dinner on May 25 at the Indianapolis Athletic Club, Bob was formally welcomed to the club along with Eddie Sachs and Chuck Stevenson. Also inducted but not present were Jack Brabham, Norm Hall, and Shorty Templeman. It was announced that Parnelli Jones—who was not yet a member of the club—would receive a diamond ring to honor his official 150-mph laps.

There had been no on-track activity for the cars since Sunday, May 20, the last day of qualifying. With the Indy 500 on Wednesday, May 30, the warm-up day was Monday, May 28. Parnelli Jones and Rodger Ward each did a lap at over 149 mph, while Bob again concentrated on maintaining a consistent race pace, running eleven laps in the 147-mph range.

Chapter 42
The 1962 Indianapolis 500: The Unplanned Pit Stop

The day before the race, chief steward Harlan Fengler conducted the traditional drivers' meeting, restating the rules of the road and other particulars of running the race. The meeting was always a time for informal, good-natured exchanges along with the serious briefings. The celebrities on hand added to the festivity, though when it rained in the middle of Fengler's briefing, many scattered. When it stopped, only legendary orchestra director Paul Whiteman remained. He told Jep Cadou Jr. of the *Indianapolis Star*, "I'm a little too old to run when it rains, so I stayed right here."

As the meeting came back to order, Sam Hanks, the director of racing for the Speedway who also served as master of ceremonies, began by saying, "It started to rain but Tony Hulman held up his hand and said, 'Halt!'" Bobby Marshman asked Fengler what the procedure would be in the case of rain. Fengler replied that if the minimum distance necessary to constitute a complete race (250 miles) had not been reached, he would have the option, depending on conditions, of running the cars under a yellow flag or stopping the race until the track was dry and restarting in the order they were in when the race was stopped.

On race day morning on the traditional May 30 Memorial Day holiday, the track opened to a light rain that had persisted all night. By 8:00 a.m. the skies had cleared, and it proved to be a warm day with no further hint of rain. The Studebaker-Packard Corporation brought out thirty-three current Studebaker convertibles to accompany their newest hope, the Avanti, which served as the honorary pace car—the actual pace car was a comparatively homely Studebaker Lark convertible. The proud name of Packard—a frequent 500 pace car in earlier years—had already disappeared as an individual marque and Studebaker would follow suit, with the company dissolving entirely within the next few years. The appealing and even groundbreaking Avanti continued in production until 2006, thanks to the efforts of private entrepreneurs.

The celebrities touring the track as part of the festivities included actress Connie Hines of the TV show *Mister Ed*; actor George Montgomery; Western TV star Dale Robertson; Jon Provost, star of the *Lassie* TV series; Marlene Schmidt, the 1961 Miss Universe; Jerilyn Jones, 1962 500 Festival Queen; Vince Edwards, TV's Dr. Ben Casey; actor/comic Morey Amsterdam; *Bonanza* star Dan Blocker; and TV duo Fred Gwynne and Joe E. Ross in costume as Toody and Muldoon of *Car 54, Where Are You?* fame.

When the cars were rolled out on the grid, chief mechanic Joe Langley had placed a message in the cockpit for Bobby, printed in bold red letters, that simply read, "Relax."

After the pageantry and pre-race excitement, Tony Hulman gave the traditional order, "Gentlemen, start your engines," and the thirty-three beautifully turned-out race cars made a breathtaking presence of color and sound as they circled the 2.5-mile track on their pace laps. Rookie starter Pat Vidan leaped high in the air as he threw the green flag to start the race and Parnelli Jones jumped forward into the lead, closely followed by A. J. Foyt from the second row and Rodger Ward. Bobby Marshman dropped to fifth on the first lap and appeared to be following a cautious strategy in the early laps as he slipped to sixth by lap ten. He was trailing Jones, Foyt, Ward, Len Sutton, and Jim McElreath, and was just ahead of Roger McCluskey, Dan Gurney, and Bud Tingelstad.

If this was a deliberate strategy, it did not serve him well. After the leaders lapped Jack Turner, Allen Crowe, Bob Christie, and Chuck Rodee, these four were caught up together in a major accident on lap 19 on the main straightaway. The first five cars had just gone by them, but Bobby was in the unfortunate position of seeing the wreck develop directly in front of him as he was preparing to lap them himself. Crowe and Christie bumped and spun, and then Turner went over one of the car's tires and flipped in the air. To avoid all this, Bobby had to slam on his brakes and take whatever measures he could to miss the melee. He made it through, but had damaged a tire, and headed straight to his pit. Turner suffered the worst injuries in the crash, with a broken pelvis and toe.

The incident effectively removed Bobby from any chance at winning the race, as reported in *NSSN* correspondent Gene Powlen's "Hoosier Hi-Lites" column. "While not involved in the early four-car tangle, it had its effect on Bobby Marshman, who finished fifth. Bobby had to lock his car up to avoid the accident and wore down one of his tires and had to make an unexpected pit stop. His crew wasn't ready for him, and in addition to necessitating four stops, he lost valuable time while they scurried around getting the air turned on for his jacks."

It was a long fifty-five seconds in the pits, changing both rear tires and the right front, along with taking fuel. His other pit stops were all in the low-thirty-second or twenty-second range. Even though the unplanned stop was under a yellow flag, Bobby lost his competitive track position. At that time, cars did not stack up behind a pace car during a full-course yellow. When the yellow was displayed, drivers all around the track were expected to reduce speed and maintain the same approximate distance from the cars ahead and behind them during the duration of the yellow. It was an imperfect system.

Once back on the track, Bob was well out of the top ten. However, he was back up to eighth on lap 80. Then, his next thirty-one-second pit stop for two rear tires, a right front tire, and fuel dropped him down the charts again. He next saw the top ten on lap 110, and moved up to ninth by lap 120. To his great credit, he never gave up the fight, and gradually regained much of the lost ground.

Through all of this, Parnelli Jones in the Agajanian No. 98 was completely dominating the race. On lap 75 he dove into the pits but did not stop as he had on lap 59, but only slowed to shout and gesticulate to his crew. Crew chief Johnny Pouelsen knew the problem. A section of the brake line had broken from vibration and Parnelli was running in the lead without brakes. When Parnelli came in again on lap 124, he could barely come to a stop, overshooting his pit box; the car finally halted after some manhandling by a crewman. (Rodger Ward then took the race lead and drove on to victory in Bob Wilke's Leader Card Watson roadster.) For his last pit stop, Jones bounced to a halt against a stack of tires piled up by his resourceful crew. Despite the challenge of racing without brakes—criticized by many rival teams—Parnelli Jones drove an extraordinarily well-judged race to finish seventh.

It was a great day for Rodger Ward and Bob Wilke, A. J. Watson the car builder, and Takeo "Chickie" Hirashima, the team's master Offenhauser expert. It was the second 500 victory for Ward, who had won in 1959. Len Sutton from Portland, Oregon—also of the Leader Card team—took second, making this the first 1-2 finish by a team at the 500 since 1947 and 1948 when Mauri Rose and Bill Holland had consecutive 1-2 finishes for Blue Crown. Ward took home $125,015.37 of the total prize money of $426,152.37. Sutton's second place earned him $44,566. When Studebaker presented the pace car to Rodger Ward, he became the first private owner of an Avanti, as it was the first one off the assembly line and the first delivered.

Bobby continued his strong effort throughout the race and finished fifth behind Ward, Sutton, Eddie Sachs in third—Sachs had driven a fine race coming from twenty-seventh on the grid—and Don Davis, fourth. Rookie of the Year Jim McElreath was just behind Bobby in sixth, and Jones, seventh. Bobby achieved his position despite making two more pit stops on laps 134 and 172. His four

stops were one more than any of the other front-runners, and the time lost was just too much to make up. The Bryant Heating and Cooling car with Bob at the wheel received prize money of $14,316.

Chapter 43
"You Don't Get One Second to Relax" (1962)

After the long month at Indianapolis and the 500, Bob, Janet, and Robbie—who had turned two at the Speedway—were happy to drive east to enjoy some time in their home in Sanatoga. The Trenton 250 on Sunday, June 3, was coming up, and Bob was heavily favored in the Konstant Hot midget. He had been dominant in these long-distance midget races, and went into the race with confidence. Jack Kiser of the *Philadelphia Daily News* devoted his June 2 column to speculating who would win.

"The crystal ball shows nothing more than a fuzzy picture of fish-tailing, pint-sized Offys scooting around the mile oval. Over half of them will limp into the pits with mechanical failures before the checkered flag falls on the winner, at least a lap ahead of the field. Who's the winner? The picture is hazy, but it looks like Bobby Marshman, the pride of Pottstown, Pa. The 25-year-old charger is the solid man in the 45-car field, and he has the physical and mechanical equipment to spread-eagle the field."

Kiser said that Bruce Homeyer's Konstant Hot Offy had been completely rebuilt over the winter. Bobby told Kiser that 250 miles in a midget at Trenton is more tiring than the 500 miles at Indy. "You don't get one second to relax," he said. "You've got to drive those little babies every foot of the way or you'll suddenly have the back end leading the way down the track."

Time trials were Saturday, June 2, with the race starting at 2:30 p.m. on Sunday. Prize money was guaranteed at $12,500. After taking the lead in the thirty-four-car field on lap 2 from Bill Randall in Ken Brenn's pusher midget, Bobby, again displaying his mastery of midgets on the high-speed tracks, led the next 120 laps when he pitted for fuel and tires. In a heartbreaking turn of events, the Konstant Hot car would not restart; the crankshaft had locked up. The race was won by Jiggs Peters in Ken Brenn's conventional midget.

The next round of the USAC championship division was the following weekend, June 10, at Milwaukee, for the Rex Mays Memorial 100-mile race. The field was dominated by roadsters, and Bob, in Wally Meskowski's upright Competition Engineering car, was one of only three dirt cars to make the race. The Indianapolis 500 was the only race of the season entered by the Bryant Heating and Cooling roadster.

Qualifying at Milwaukee was a near thing for Bobby. Thirty-five cars ran the time trials in an attempt to secure twenty of the twenty-two spots in the field; the final two spots were designated for the first two finishers in the twenty-lap consi. When qualifying ended, Bob's disappointing time put him on the outside looking in, along with Rodger Ward, Dick Rathmann, and others. But in the consi, Bob and Rodger both made a comeback. In what Al Krause in *NSSN* called "a thrilling duel," Ward won and Bobby finished second, qualifying both drivers for the start of the Milwaukee 100. The feature was won by A. J. Foyt, and Bobby brought the Meskowski Offy home twelfth to capture the last position granting championship points. Len Sutton had moved up to second by lap 80, only to be forced into the wall on lap 84 due to a broken left rear wheel cylinder. The Oregon racer was hospitalized for over a week recovering from vertebrae and lung injuries, and it was nearly two months before he was able to return to competition.

The June 10 Milwaukee race brought some attention to the issue of yellow-flag violations, particularly the tendency of drivers to "sneak up" on the car ahead during full-course yellows. Fines for this offense, ranging from $35 to $100, were levied by the USAC on eleven drivers. However, the biggest headline grabber after Milwaukee was USAC's $1,000 fine to race winner A. J. Foyt, for verbal abuse directed to race promoter Tom Marchese over the payout. A. J. accepted the reprimand graciously, acknowledging he was out of line, and promptly wrote a personal check to pay the fine, the largest fine ever levied by the sanctioning body up to that time.

On June 25, the scheduled Langhorne Century championship race was rained out after qualification. Before the rain came, Jim Hurtubise had captured pole position, with Bob fifth fastest in the Meskowski car, once again showing his talent on this toughest and most unforgiving of one-mile dirt tracks. His time of 34.163 placed him right in the hunt with Hurtubise at 33.540; second-fastest Don Branson, 33.605; A. J. Foyt, 33.644; and Parnelli Jones, at 34.095. Minutes after all entrants had posted a time and the eighteen-car field was complete, a heavy thunderstorm came into the area, forcing postponement of the race for a week.

On Saturday, June 30, the evening before the new date for the Langhorne championship race, Williams Grove hosted a USAC sprint car race. Bobby Marshman was in the Fike Plumbing Special normally raced by Parnelli Jones. Bob was involved in a four-car tangle on the north turn in the first lap of the consi, along with Jim Hemmings, Hal Rettberg, and Don Brown. All four drivers escaped injury. However, the incident ended Bob's race and kept him from showing his prowess in the car. Jiggs Peters won the race, with A. J. Foyt second.

The Langhorne championship race the following day, Sunday, July 1, was won by A. J. Foyt, followed by Parnelli Jones, Jim Hurtubise, Don Branson, and Bobby Marshman. Bobby held his fifth position until lap 59 of the 100-lap race, when he pitted for a relief driver. Elmer George finished the race in the Meskowski car, and the two men shared the championship points that went with the fifth-place finish.

For George, it was an eventful day: Just before relieving Bobby, he had already done a relief drive in the Jake Vargo Special, which had been started by Bob Mathouser of Omaha, Nebraska. When George took over the Vargo Special, he complained of bad handling, and was in turn relieved by Hugh Randall of Louisville, Kentucky. Randall, the car's third driver of the day, completed only two

laps before flipping violently in the section of the Langhorne track known as Puke Hollow. The car turned end over end several times. Randall was declared dead of numerous injuries at Lower Bucks County Hospital in Bristol, Pennsylvania.

Chapter 44
Good Friends, New Wheels (1962)

Hosting three races, the one-mile oval at Trenton, New Jersey, was the most active track on the 1962 Championship Trail. Promoter Sam Nunis, in a successful effort to attract more roadsters (many entrants thought their dirt cars had an advantage at Trenton), insisted on a 150-mile race for his July 22 event. Mother Nature intervened: Rain shortened the race to a yellow-flag parade from lap 132 until the race was called at 142 miles. Rodger Ward was the winner in the Leader Card Watson roadster, followed by Don Branson in a Leader Card, making it another 1-2 finish for Bob Wilke's team. Don Davis was third in the Rose Truck Lines Turner-Chevy. Their usual fellow contender Len Sutton was still recovering from his accident in the June 10 Milwaukee Mile. (Sutton was back at the Milwaukee track in August, and finished out the season.)

Bobby Marshman qualified sixteenth at the July 22 Trenton race, and had Competition Engineering's Meskowski dirt car up to eighth position on the sixty-third lap when the engine blew in dramatic fashion. Bobby impressed many with his cool in handling the high-speed moment. Nick Nicolosi in *NSSN* reported, "The entire car was enveloped in smoke at 110 mph and Marshman did a beautiful job in maintaining control going into a turn. The youngster from Pottstown, Pennsylvania, drove calmly into the infield despite blinding smoke pouring through the cockpit." Bobby placed twenty-first.

"When we went to Trenton, we'd stay at our Sanatoga home, and so would everybody else," Janet said, "plus as many as we could put up at my sister's house and my parents' house. Some of the drivers, like Cotton Farmer, became close friends of my parents, though they hadn't met before that. Parnelli would be down with my sister and her husband and Bill Marvel, and we'd have a big cookout. It wouldn't cost the guys anything except their travel."

Bob's years in the URC and the ARDC fostered this kind of camaraderie, Janet explained. "We had a closeness [with the other drivers] when we came East and stayed in Sanatoga," she said. But for most of the race season, Bob and Janet were home-based in Indianapolis. "It was the hub," Janet added. The Indianapolis house they rented, from April to October, was a practical choice for the young couple, giving them a more central base for race commutes.

After the July Trenton race, a split between chief mechanic George Bignotti and A. J. Foyt now played a profound role in Bobby Marshman's career. Bignotti and Foyt, despite their tremendous success together, were famously at odds on car preparation and long had carried on a love-hate relationship in running the race cars. Foyt was a self-taught engineer whose own instincts often clashed with Bignotti's method of preparing a race car. Foyt left the Bowes Seal Fast team in August to join the Lindsey Hopkins team. (When Foyt joined Hopkins's team, he took the coveted No. 1 for the reigning champion along with him, and bumped out Don Branson. Branson soon moved to the Leader Card team, where he scored championship wins at Langhorne and Trenton later in the year.) Around the same time Foyt left, Bignotti and his partner Bob Bowes Jr. sold the entire Bowes Seal Fast operation to William Ansted and Shirley Murphy. Although Bignotti was no longer a co-owner, he chose to remain as chief mechanic for the new Ansted-Murphy operation.

The newly formed Ansted-Murphy team quickly snapped up Bobby as their driver for the cars called Thompson-Rotary Specials. The dirt cars were Meskowski creations, and the team's roadster was a Trevis. As chief mechanic, Bignotti remained central to the operation.

Chapter 45
"Famous Indianapolis Driver" (1962)

Bobby's first race for Ansted-Murphy was set for August 18 at the Springfield 100. But between Trenton and Springfield, he was scheduled to run two back-to-back East Coast races: first, the August 11 George Fonder Memorial race at Pennsylvania's Hatfield Speedway track; and second, the August 12 midget auto race at Owego, New York's, Shangri-La Speedway.

Twice postponed, the George Fonder Memorial ARDC-USAC midget race finally ran on August 11. At his hometown Hatfield track, Bob claimed second place in dramatic fashion, overtaking third-place finisher Red Riegel on the forty-eighth lap of the fifty-lap race. Riegel was a tough man to beat, with an impressive ten victories to his credit on the Hatfield oval in the past two and a half years. Tony Bonadies finished first in the twenty-car field. Warren Howard wrote in the *Pottstown Mercury*, "Marshman—who drove a superb race—was the fastest thing on the track much of the time, and obviously displaying the prowess that won plaudits in both his Indianapolis appearances."

Bob's celebrity status was considered a major draw for the August 12 Shangri-La Speedway event. Promoters featured him in newspaper ads for the ARDC race: "Starring Bobby Marshman, famous Indianapolis driver and 1961 Co–Rookie of the Year."

At the newly refinished track in Owego, New York, Bobby was fifth in heat one but in the feature he dropped out on the eighteenth lap because of fuel injection troubles. On the twenty-third lap, ten cars experienced tire trouble at the same time, including one driven by Bob Harkey, who nevertheless took over the lead in that lap and went on to win the twenty-car, twenty-five-lap race.

Less than a week after Owego, Bob was in the Midwest for the Springfield 100 on August 18, competitively piloting his first drive for Ansted-Murphy in the No. 14 Thompson-Rotary Meskowski-Offy. He qualified tenth and finished fourth in the one-mile dirt circuit event. As reported by Jep Cadou Jr. in the *Indianapolis Star*: "Despite a dusty track with numerous holes, the race was accident-free and run entirely under the green flag before an Illinois State Fair crowd of more than 20,000."

The Springfield championship race featured a great battle between Jim Hurtubise and A. J. Foyt from the sixty-mile point until Foyt was forced to stop for fuel on the ninety-sixth lap, ultimately taking seventh in his first ride in the Hopkins Special. Hurtubise, driving the Barnett Brothers Kuzma-Offy, claimed first place twenty-three seconds ahead of Parnelli Jones in the Agajanian-Willard Battery Special. Don Branson took third in the Wilke Leader Card racer, with Bobby next in fourth.

Janet recalled the excitement of race weekends. "I had my own stopwatches, but that was for my own benefit," she said. "The men did the official timing. But since I didn't usually see Bob from morning to night, when he was finished I liked to be able to talk to him about his day. I always knew what his times were.

"We [the wives] had to sit in one area at the tracks—we couldn't be in the pits or anything," Janet continued. "Each track had slightly different rules. For example, at Trenton we weren't allowed in the infield—no one was, except the pit crew. Sometimes, if he wasn't having car problems, Bob would come over between heats to wherever I was sitting."

The drivers' wives were "a very diversified group," according to Janet.

"We all got along, and some of us were closer at times," Janet said. "Jane Hurtubise I just loved, more than anyone, because she was such a free person—it was a way that I could never be. And Jo Ward was really nice and welcoming. Two of the families I became fondest of were Len and Anita Sutton and Jack and Joyce Turner. But everyone was cordial."

Chapter 46
"Let's Go to the Fair, Bob" (1962)

August 18 was Springfield and August 19 was Milwaukee—approximately twenty-four hours and three hundred miles apart.

The August schedule was tight because it was fair season, and the races were popular events at the fairgrounds. "Our good friend Jay Miller usually helped with the driving between races," Janet said. "The three of us would take turns. If Jay or I were driving, Bob would be in the back with Robbie and they'd both sleep.

"I especially enjoyed the Springfield and Milwaukee fairs," Janet recalled. "I loved the movie *State Fair*, and these two fairs were the closest thing to it. They had cheese contests, and prizes for the food the women had put up, like mincemeat. It was so unique. I'd be in the infield watching the test drives and Bob's car would break—it broke regularly—and he'd pull in. I'd know he'd be in a bad mood, so I'd say, 'Let's go to the Fair, Bob.' If he didn't want to, I'd go with my sister. As long as I knew he was out of the car and okay, off I went."

Despite the often grueling travel schedule, Janet remembered these trips as "a wonderful time. That's because I was young. It just occupied all of our time. We loved it."

The Milwaukee 200-mile championship race on August 19 played out in front of a crowd of nearly thirty thousand at the Wisconsin State Fairgrounds on an exceptionally hot day. Competing in the Thompson-Rotary No. 14 Trevis roadster for the first time, Bobby captured pole position, clocking 34.606 seconds. He led the first two laps of the race until Parnelli Jones passed him on the backstretch on lap 3 and Rodger Ward got around him on the fifty-fourth mile. In what the *Indianapolis Star*'s Jep Cadou Jr. described as a "race as torrid as the 90-degree weather," Ward ultimately won in the Leader Card Special, nipping Foyt—who was driving the Hopkins Special roadster for the first time—by less than a car length. Bobby took third.

Thirty-two miles of the sweltering 200-miler were run under the yellow caution flag. Early in the August 19 competition, five cars were put out of the running by a tangle on the fifteenth lap, but there were no serious injuries. After the race, Eddie Sachs and Bob were both treated for heat exhaustion.

After Springfield and Milwaukee, Bobby moved up to fourth place in the point standings for the USAC National Championship, with 1,000 points, behind A. J. Foyt in third, with 1,070; Parnelli

Jones in second, with 1,209; and Rodger Ward in first, with 1,960.

On August 26, Bob made his next appearance with the Ansted-Murphy team in the 100-mile USAC championship race at Pennsylvania's Langhorne Speedway. His car was the former Bowes Seal Fast Special, now wearing A-M colors. On the extremely hot and humid day, Bob charged hard in the fast-paced contest, but was done in at fifty-three laps when he pitted for a tire, and was relieved by Elmer George, whose own car had thrown a rod during qualifying. Bobby started seventh and George finished the car ninth. Don Branson claimed first at the 'Horne that day, leading from start to finish at record speed in the Leader Card dirt car.

Chapter 47
An Upside-Down Shoulder Harness (1962)

Racing was a tough, unforgiving business. Serious injury and career-ending crashes were always a possibility, and all too often, a driver suffered fatal consequences.

The summer of 1962 was a grim one in terms of driver deaths. Tragic losses included Stan Bowman, who died in a warm-up lap at Terre Haute on June 17; Hugh Randall, on the fifty-ninth lap of the July 1 Langhorne 100; Peter Ryan, in a July 2 Formula Junior race in Reims, France; Don Davis, at an August 5 New Bremen Speedway sprint race; and Jackson Hagemeyer, in an August 12 time trial at Terre Haute.

Regrettably, two more fine drivers were killed on August 23. Clark "Shorty" Templeman and Jim Hemmings both died from injuries in an eleven-car crash in a USAC midget race at the Marion County Fairgrounds track in Ohio. Templeman was in second place on the second lap when his car hit the fence and flipped down the backstretch. Nearly the entire field became involved in the multicar crash that followed, and one car landed on top of Hemmings. Both Hemmings and Templeman were declared dead at Marion General Hospital. Five other drivers were hospitalized from the accident, but survived.

Bob, like most drivers, dealt with the reality of unpredictable losses in his own way. When fellow racers died, he responded by organizing financial help for their families. And when it came to his own racing, he was fully cognizant of safety issues, and did his part to allay these concerns.

In his "Midwest Racing Notes" column in *NSSN*, Bill Marvel wrote that since joining his new team, Bobby Marshman had adopted an eight-point harness system cued to the needs of a dirt track driver: It was designed to prevent the most serious injuries by keeping the driver strapped into the car, unlike the system in use, which, Marvel wrote, "threw the driver about like a rag doll."

Bob called this installation an upside-down shoulder harness, explaining that the idea came from drag racing. Sportswriter Marvel, a close friend of the Marshmans, said, "I pray that he never tests it."

Rather than tests, Du Quoin offered frustration for drivers on the Championship Trail in 1962. The September 3 race at the Du Quoin, Illinois, fairgrounds was scheduled for Labor Day Monday, until rain forced a postponement for the next day. When the downpour continued on Tuesday, the championship event was canceled altogether, a rarity for the USAC, and a disappointment to the 4,000-plus crowd of would-be spectators.

The next championship race was in Syracuse on September 8. Bobby was piloting the Thompson-Rotary Special at the New York State Fairgrounds' "Moody Mile." He started seventh in the 100-mile race and moved up to second place by lap 72, only to be forced out of contention by a broken shift lever a few laps later. He ultimately was classified thirteenth. Parnelli Jones suffered similar angst: After qualifying fastest at 99.9 mph and taking an early lead in the race, Jones blew a piston and was classified fifteenth. Rodger Ward captured first in his Leader Card Duo racer, setting a new track record of 95.571 mph for 100 miles. He was followed by A. J. Foyt, Troy Ruttman, Jim Hurtubise, Allen Crowe, and Roger McCluskey.

Bobby then left the East Coast for the Indiana State Fairgrounds and the popular Hoosier Hundred in Indianapolis. The September 15 USAC championship race started twenty minutes late, first because of a pace-car problem, and then because of pit stops by Bobby and by Chuck Hulse during the parade laps. When the green flag finally came down, a race of many duels evolved in front of a record crowd of nearly 28,000.

Early in the 100-mile race, Jim Hurtubise in the Barnett Brothers Special and Parnelli Jones in the Willard Battery Special traded first place until Jones stretched his lead to fifteen lengths at the end of forty miles, right before Hurtubise spun out and lost five laps. Bobby and Don Branson kept the pressure on Jones in the second half of the race until engine troubles pushed Bob back from second to sixth, with Branson passing him on the seventy-eighth lap.

Jones eventually lapped even second- and third-place contenders Branson and Jim McElreath, who fought their own intense battle for a number-two finish, until Branson dramatically grabbed second place on the final corner of the race. Rodger Ward and Roger McCluskey thrilled the crowd with their duel for fourth place in the final twenty miles of the race, with McCluskey prevailing and Ward following in fifth, despite a dragging radiator shell. Bob finished sixth after starting eighth, again driving the Thompson-Rotary Special.

Chapter 48
The Marshman Mile (1962)

Immediately after the Hoosier Hundred, Bob drove through the night to be in Trenton for the USAC-ARDC 100-lap midget race on September 16. He piloted the No. 7 Konstant Hot car to first place, claiming his fifth midget win at Trenton. He also set a track record when he averaged 99.958 mph on the one-mile paved circuit.

The event was viewed by many as an East versus West encounter, and Jim Davies from California, the National Midget Champion, took the lead on lap 1. Missourian Bob Wente ran second until lap 23, when he took over the number-one position. Wente held on to first until Don Branson of Illinois took the lead in the third turn of the forty-fifth lap. Bobby stayed on Branson's tail through all this, and then on lap 59, Pennsylvania's pilot passed Branson for good, winning the race for the East Coast. Behind Marshman at the finish were Chuck Arnold of Connecticut in second and Branson in third.

Bobby's commanding midget wins at Trenton were becoming almost routine, causing Bill Marvel to ask in his *NSSN* column whether Sam Nunis was thinking of renaming Trenton the Marshman Mile, saying "Bobby Marshman sure has Trenton for midgets down pat." Bob's strong finish in his next Trenton race, the USAC championship contest one week later, gave further weight to Marvel's tongue-in-cheek question. Starting in fourteenth place and finishing third, Bobby proved his prowess and his staying power in championship competition.

In fact, Trenton's September 23 USAC race boasted a dramatic jump in distance over previous years. Originally scheduled for 100 miles, the race became the track's first 200-mile event. It was a crowd-pleasing, hard-fought competition at the New Jersey State Fairgrounds as the race unfolded in front of twenty thousand fans. Don Branson prevailed for first in Bob Wilke's Leader Card dirt car, with Len Sutton second in Wilke's Leader Card roadster, and Bobby third in the Thompson-Rotary Special. Defending champion A. J. Foyt qualified fastest at 105.7 mph in the Hopkins car, and finished fourth.

Rodger Ward's fifth-place finish in Wilke's Leader Card roadster gave him the 200 points he needed to clinch USAC's 1962 national driving championship. In the lead from lap 27, Ward spun on lap 132, landing in the infield, but he restarted from there to finish the race. Later, Foyt and Lloyd Ruby protested that Ward had not returned to the pits before restarting, but USAC officials ruled that the pit stop requirement did not apply unless two or more cars were involved in an accident, and Ward's finishing position held.

Bob's October calendar opened with a midget race in Indiana, followed by a sprint car race back East in his home state.

On October 7, Bobby was at the wheel of the Leader Card Special in the Terre Haute Hundred USAC midget race. He started in twentieth place, and by lap 38 had moved to second behind Jim

Hurtubise, who was looking for his sixth straight win at Terre Haute. At that point, Bob's right rear tire went flat and he pitted. Although he battled hard to regain his position, he was forced to retire late in the race with a broken shock absorber. Ronnie Duman of Dearborn, Michigan, was the race winner.

On October 14, Williams Grove, Pennsylvania, hosted the annual Ted Horn–Bill Schindler Memorial race where USAC sprint cars made their final 1962 appearance on the East Coast. Cotton Farmer took first place in the fifty-lap event, approximately six car lengths ahead of Jiggs Peters in second. With his third-place finish, Parnelli Jones clinched the national sprint car championship.

Bob was involved in one of two accidents that day. He and Ohioan Bobby Marvin had a minor collision, but both drivers and cars were able to continue the race, with Marvin claiming thirteenth, and Bobby, fifteenth. In a separate incident, Roger McCuskey was unharmed when he flipped his car on the thirty-fifth lap, but was not able to complete the race.

Chapter 49
Musical Cars (1962)

The Foyt and Marshman late-summer car switches did a turnaround in the fall. For the October 28 Sacramento USAC championship race, A. J. Foyt returned to his old car, now known as the Thompson-Rotary Special, and Bobby took over the Hopkins Special.

It was the same car–new name for A. J., but there were in fact other significant changes. Although he was reuniting with crew chief George Bignotti, Foyt was returning to what was otherwise a very different team, with new owners Bill Ansted and Shirley Murphy.

Not long after Foyt's move to Ansted-Murphy, Bobby was brought on board by Lindsey Hopkins to finish the 1962 season, starting with the Sacramento race. The highly regarded Jack Beckley was chief mechanic / crew chief for the Hopkins team.

Beckley's ability to give his cars a fast edge was well proven. When Bobby joined the Hopkins team, Beckley had already prepared five front-row starters at Indy, including a winner in 1954, driven by Bill Vukovich. In 1955, Beckley joined forces with Lindsey Hopkins. Throughout his career in the 1950s, '60s, and '70s, Beckley was one of racing's most respected chief mechanics, and was later tapped to be the Indy 500 technical director.

George Bignotti was also a well-respected crew chief, with the 1961 Indy 500 victory already to his credit. By 1962, Bignotti had established himself as a formidable chief mechanic, and he and Foyt were viewed as the team to beat. As his career progressed throughout the 1960s, '70s, and '80s, Bignotti continued to earn laurels. He was credited with eighty-nine open-wheel victories, with his cars winning a total of seven Indy 500s as well as three USAC championships in a four-year period.

So when A. J. and Bobby changed teams in the fall of 1962, they also changed chief mechanics. For A. J., it was a reunion with Bignotti; despite their much-publicized differences, Foyt and

Bignotti were back together. And Bobby was now on board with Hopkins and Beckley. However the complicated relationship between Bignotti and Foyt played out, the Hopkins/Beckley opportunity was clearly a great career move for Bobby. Well-to-do businessman Lindsey Hopkins was a longtime Indy insider, and a much-respected car owner and sponsor. Known as the consummate Southern gentleman with "old money" credentials, Hopkins was considered a true sportsman by his peers.

Bob went out West for his first drive with his new team. On October 28, the twelfth annual Golden State 100-mile race in Sacramento was the next-to-last event on the 1962 Championship Trail. A crowd of over twelve thousand cheered the outstanding field of contenders, while the year's designated USAC champion, Rodger Ward, was watching from the press box. He was recovering from vertebrae injuries sustained during qualifying for the Los Angeles Times Grand Prix for sports cars in Riverside earlier in the month.

ABOVE: Posing for a photo at Ascot, California, with renowned promoter and car owner J. C. Agajanian. (MARSHMAN FAMILY COLLECTION)

Despite his new drive, Bobby encountered disappointment at the California State Fairgrounds. He spun and hit the rail in turn three of the forty-fifth lap of the race, eliciting a yellow flag for six laps. He escaped uninjured and was classified fifteenth in the Hopkins Special, after starting fifth. A. J. Foyt, in the Thompson-Rotary Special, won the race in track record time.

On November 3 and November 10, Bobby competed in USAC sprint car races at the Ascot Park Speedway in Gardena, California, driving the No. 5 Colvin Chevy in both events. Roger McClusky won the two races on the half-mile track driving the Konstant Hot sprint car. In the November 3 race, Bob started fifteenth and finished eighth. The November 10 event proved to be less successful for Bob, who started nineteenth: His car ran poorly in the feature, and on the thirteenth lap, throttle problems put him out of the running.

The Ascot Park races were not Bob's favorites, according to Janet, because that speedway was a sandy dirt track. "Bob was a rim rider," she explained, "and you can't do that on a sandy track because that stuff falls apart. There was nothing Bob liked better than a dirt track to pitch a car." He especially liked Terre Haute and Springfield, Janet recalled.

"You could always tell an Easterner from a Westerner," Janet continued. "The Westerners were going around the middle in a groove and the Easterners were up with the back tire high, just high up in the dirt and spitting it all over everybody. It looked neat—it really did."

Chapter 50
Victory Clouded by Injuries (1962)

In Phoenix on November 18, Bobby claimed his first national championship win in the final USAC race of the season. This victory was clouded by a serious accident on the track, the first in USAC's seven-year history to involve spectators, and the reason for ending the race just over halfway through the 100-mile challenge.

The Arizona State Fairgrounds event was named the Bobby Ball Memorial in 1954, after the death of the well-liked, up-and-coming young driver, a Phoenix native. Ball was considered one of the best midget drivers in the United States in the early 1950s, and was the fifth-place finisher in the Indy 500 in 1951. He died at age twenty-eight following an accident at Carrell Speedway in California. Well-mannered and bespectacled, Ball was sometimes described as looking like an "Ivy League type." He was viewed, as Bobby later was, as intelligent and clean-cut.

Since the Phoenix contest's inception, the coveted race win had been captured by an impressive list of racing greats, including Jimmy Bryan, Tony Bettenhausen, A. J. Foyt, and Johnny Parsons.

The start of the 1962 Bobby Ball Memorial was charged with positive energy as well as great expectations in the 12,000-plus crowd, thanks to a top-notch field lining up on the one-mile dirt track. In fact, over half the names on the roster were qualified Indianapolis drivers. "A fast race and a safe one is the hope of all here," wrote *Phoenix Gazette* sports editor Bob Allison in the event's race program.

Sadly for all involved, a mishap by Elmer George necessarily dominated the race and its after-

math. George was running his HOW Special mid-field when, in the forty-ninth lap, he bumped the back of Chuck Hulse's car and went into a spin. George's car flipped and smashed through a chain-link fence into an overflow crowd of spectators. The flagman waved the cars around for two more laps under the yellow flag, making it a complete race at fifty-one laps. The competition was stopped "in the interests of public safety," since the fence reportedly could not be properly repaired at that time.

Twenty-three people were injured in Sunday's accident, and on Monday, eight remained in the hospital, including two in critical condition, but there were ultimately no fatalities from the accident. George himself suffered deep shoulder lacerations and required stitches, but he vetoed any further work on himself until every injured spectator at the hospital had been treated.

The crash claimed headlines the next day, but Bob's skill in navigating his victory was also noted. *NSSN* described him as driving in "classy high-riding style."

Starting in fourth in the Hopkins Special, Bobby led the race from the thirtieth lap when he overtook the lead group of Parnelli Jones and A. J. Foyt. At the finish line, Foyt was second in the Thompson-Rotary Special, right after Bobby, with Texan Lloyd Ruby third, in the J. H. Rose Trucking Special, and Parnelli following in fourth in the Agajanian-Willard Battery Special.

Early press deadlines in the East led to inaccuracies in the initial published reports, showing Parnelli as third, with Ruby, fourth. The official results, released later, corrected the standings, placing Ruby in third and Parnelli in fourth. The confusion was most likely caused by the number of lapped cars between the two drivers.

Parnelli also spoke highly of Bobby's skill after the race, telling *NSSN* that "Bobby was sure haulin' her around there and I just couldn't hold him back." Jones added that Marshman and Foyt had put on a tremendous show for the fans. The previous year, 1961, Phoenix had marked Parnelli's first championship win, and in 1962, Phoenix marked the first for Bobby.

At season end, Bob was fifth in the USAC point standings, at 1,581. First-place National Champion Rodger Ward had 2,400 points; A. J. Foyt was second, with 1,950; Parnelli Jones earned third, with 1,760; and Don Branson was fourth, with 1,700.

Repercussions following the Phoenix accident included a proposal to place a ban on the track. Charles Garland, executive secretary of the Arizona State Fair Commission, said he would recommend auto racing be abandoned at the state fairground. As reported by United Press International (UPI), Garland stated that the track was in the best condition ever, but added that "it's still a dirt track, and dirt tracks are dangerous." Garland went on to say, "The fair commission makes very little money out of automobile racing, but we have kept providing one or two races a year strictly out of a sense of obligation to some 25,000 fans." Tom Binford, USAC president, said that the USAC would continue to sanction the race if a guardrail was placed in front of the grandstand.

Two years later, the Arizona State Fairgrounds traditional dirt track was replaced by a new paved venue: the Phoenix International Raceway, a one-mile oval.

For Bobby, 1962 was a year of accomplishment. From a strong fifth-place finish in his second Indy 500 in the spring to his first USAC win in the fall—plus his solid final championship placement—Bobby was coming into his own. The low-key Pennsylvania driver was earning high marks at many racing venues, and continuing to fulfill the promise racing enthusiasts had been seeing in him for many years.

ECONO - CAR
RENTAL SYSTEM, Indianapolis

PART 4 / A REVOLUTIONARY ERA

Chapter 51
Formative Years for a Revolution (1962–63)

Throughout 1962, rear-engine cars were much discussed, but generally dismissed, in America's open-wheel racing world. However, a handful of industry insiders found the new technology compelling enough to pursue, so that by the end of the following year, in 1963, the "funny cars" were emerging as serious agents of dramatic change in US racing.

Ford's role in rear-engine race car development became so central to the engine's success that it can be easy to forget that in the early 1960s, the car manufacturer was operating on a shoestring budget when it came to Indy 500 cars and rear-engine design.

Ford executive Donald Frey headed the company's efforts to reenter racing. It was Frey—working with a small team—who put the company in the 500 in 1963. But in May 1962, Frey and Ford engineer Dave Evans traveled together to the Speedway, along with Frey's brother, simply to spectate and speculate—and they were not disappointed. Frey and Evans returned to Dearborn with fresh ideas for Ford, and, it would turn out, for Indy racing.

Meanwhile, as noted earlier, Dan Gurney had prevailed upon Lotus founder and designer Colin Chapman to attend the same race. His visit, too, proved fruitful. After appraising the prize monies, and the competition, Chapman finally responded to Gurney's urging to design a Lotus entry for the Speedway.

Independently of one another, Frey was developing an engine and Chapman a chassis to place on the Brickyard's starting grid.

Returning from the 1962 Indy 500, Frey's central idea was to build a Ford engine to race at the Speedway. The notion was in line with Ford's new marketing focus on "total performance," which encompassed racing. Under the leadership of Lee Iacocca, general manager of Ford Division, the company announced in June that it was officially breaking with the Automobile Manufacturers Association ban on factory-supported racing, which had been in place since 1957. Ford then jump-started its stock car effort for the Daytona 500.

Frey continued to pursue his Brickyard goal that summer, enlisting the support of additional Ford engineers, including Bill Innes, before presenting the plan to Iacocca. In the company's search for the right chassis designer, Lindsey Hopkins and his chief mechanic Jack Beckley were among those brought in—not surprising choices, since Hopkins was already well-connected with Ford and was an early convert to rear-engine advantages. A. J. Watson, who was also a highly regarded Indy 500 car mastermind, was another expert who was invited to join the conversation.

In the midst of the Ford discussions, Gurney and Chapman showed up in Dearborn with a proposal from Lotus. The enterprising American racer and the renowned British designer sat at the table with earned authority: In May, Gurney had put a Thompson-Buick rear-engine racer in the middle of the third row in his first time at the 500, and that same month, Chapman had introduced the groundbreaking Formula One Lotus 25 at the Dutch Grand Prix. Meeting with Frey, Innes, and other Ford executives, Chapman presented a well-thought-out plan for what an Indy 500 rear-engine chassis should be, as well as an idea of what the engine needed in order to produce the power.

The July 23, 1962, meeting of Ford and Lotus was unplanned but fortuitous. This initial Lotus-Ford alliance moved ahead, albeit erratically, with the goal of creating a rear-engine racer to compete in the 1963 Indy 500.

Ford was not the only car maker taking on the rear-engine challenge with a vision of competing at the Brickyard. Grand Prix champion Jack Brabham had led the way in 1961, of course, when he drove Jim Kimberley's T54 rear-engine Cooper-Climax to an impressive ninth-place finish at the Speedway. Hopkins had unsuccessfully attempted to purchase a copy of the Cooper car for the 1962 Indy 500. Mickey Thompson created his own design: The champion of race-car innovation had his rear-engine racer, powered by an aluminum stock block Buick V8, in eighth place on the 1962

BELOW: Jim Clark and Dan Gurney in their 1963 Lotus 29-Fords. (RMA/CHERNOKAL)

PREVIOUS PAGES: Bobby sits proudly behind the wheel of the Econo-Car championship dirt car at Trenton in April. (RMA/IMLAY)

starting grid, with Gurney as pilot. And without a doubt, John Zink's 1962 near-miss rear-engine Trackburner was also significant in fueling the movement.

The Lotus-Ford collaboration initiated in the summer of 1962 progressed into the fall. In October, a Lotus 25 was shipped to the Speedway for a test drive by Formula One star Jim Clark, who had just driven to victory at Watkins Glen, New York, in the October 7 US Grand Prix, a Formula One World Championship race. The test car was the Lotus 25, which had been driven in the same Watkins Glen race by Clark's teammate, Trevor Taylor. Despite Clark's impressive display of speed and finesse in his first time at the Speedway, Ford ditched the project the very next month due to lack of funds, as well as internal feuding, only to revive it two months later.

All of this was a prelude to 1963. Jumping ahead, the Lotus-Ford team effort did prevail after many more bumps along the road, and met its goal for the 1963 Indy race. The team had second- and seventh-place finishers that year, both in Chapman-designed Lotus 29s fitted with Ford V8s. Thompson was not far behind them, with a ninth-place finish for his Chevy-powered rear-engine racer.

The rear-engine revolution, as it was dubbed, did not achieve its full potential until a few years after the Lotus-Ford debut, but 1962, 1963, and 1964 were undeniably the formative years in the new setup's evolution to power. From that time forward, rear-engine racers increasingly pressured the status quo. In much the same way that roadsters had gradually pushed out dirt cars in the 1950s, rear-engine racers were on their way to making roadsters virtually obsolete. No longer a distant rumble from European circuits, rear-engine cars were emerging as a transformational factor in US auto racing.

Bobby Marshman came to play a major role in the rear-engine takeover. Although he piloted front-engine racers in all of his 1962 and '63 competitions, Bob began his progress toward rear-engine driving when he became one of Ford's chief test drivers for the Lotus-Ford rear-engine prototypes starting in the latter part of 1963—and then piloted one in the 1964 Indy 500. A handful of individuals helped drive the rear-engine to dominance, and Bobby was one of them. Though the young driver had come up from the old dirt tracks and had never raced on a road course or in Europe, he became one of the key players in the vanguard of rear-engine success in the United States. He was the first homegrown American oval racer to make one of the funny cars go fast. Very fast—fast enough, in fact, to help power a revolution.

It is fair to say that Bobby Marshman was the first American dirt-car driver to make the rear-engine car a front-runner at Indy. With his steadiness as a test driver and his skill as a competitor, Bob was a central player in bringing about the changes that remade his sport in America. In turn, rear-engine cars and Ford would prove to be central to the last two years of his life.

Chapter 52
Ringing in a Happy New Year (1963)

1963 would prove to be a banner year for Bobby Marshman, with landmark achievements in both his personal and his professional life. For his young family: a new house complete with a checkered flag-patterned floor in the den. On the track: qualifier for the Speedway, and for every race on the Championship Trail. In other professional pursuits: steady test drives for the major tire manufacturers and, more importantly, for Ford, the newest Indy engine developer. And within the racing industry: a growing reputation as a young American driver on the ascent.

The new year even began on an auspicious note. On January 18, chief mechanic Jack Beckley signed Bobby Marshman to drive for the Lindsey Hopkins–owned race team, both for the 500 and on the mile tracks of the Championship Trail. The next day, the *Indianapolis Star*'s Jep Cadou Jr. quoted Hopkins, who was in town to attend USAC board meetings: "We think we have the best up-and-coming young driver in the business."

The full-scale contract with one of the industry's top teams was a well-earned coup for the highly focused twenty-six-year-old driver.

Bob continued the month in a spirit of camaraderie. On January 20, he braved winter winds with approximately three hundred other racing enthusiasts to take part in the Hoosier Auto Racing Fans (HARF) club's eleventh annual Hall of Fame dinner in Indianapolis. Rodger Ward and race promoter Joe Quinn were honored that night as inductees to HARF's Hall of Fame.

Bobby had a busy evening. On behalf of the Checkered Flag Fan Club, he took the podium to present Cotton Farmer with the club's award for sportsmanship. Later in the presentations, Bob came forward twice to accept accolades on behalf of Parnelli Jones, who was unable to attend. Jones was the winner of the 1962 National Sprint Car Championship, and was also awarded HARF's 1962 Driver of the Year Award. For the latter, Jones was chosen for winning his third-straight sprint car title, and for being the first driver to break 150 mph in qualifying for the 500.

Bob himself was the recipient of a new prize announced at the HARF gathering. The Lafayette, Indiana, *Journal & Courier* presented their first award "for the most cooperative driver toward the working press," naming Bobby the 1962 winner. "Bob was always polite to everyone," Janet noted.

Back in Sanatoga, Bobby and Janet took advantage of winter's relative downtime in the racing world to make progress on their plans to build a house a few miles away, in Fagleysville, Pennsylvania. Their new home would be close to Janet's sister Kay and her husband Donald Scheffey, who was the housing developer and builder, and their son Donnie. With Robbie's third birthday coming up in May, Bobby and Janet were pleased that they would all be close by. Donnie was just five weeks older than Robbie, and the two boys were already great pals.

Chapter 53
"This Is Great" (1963)

February had its own lures for race drivers, and Bobby unsurprisingly took the bait, traveling to Florida that month in search of a drive in the Daytona 500. Sportswriters from the *Pottstown Mercury* to the *Indianapolis Star* spread the word that Bobby—along with other experienced drivers—was looking for a "ride" in the 500-mile stock car race at Daytona Beach. In the Pottstown paper, Warren Howard reported, "Bobby Marshman notes that the late-model stock car 'rides' are much harder to get than USAC championship trail mounts, but he has a couple of prospects for the race."

When he arrived at Daytona International Speedway, Bobby landed a trial run in a Holman-Moody car. On Feburary 13, *NSSN* reported, "Youthful Bobby Marshman of Pottstown, Pa., a popular young USAC racing car charger . . . was given a trial run in a 1963 Ford factory car. . . . It was the first time Marshman had ever driven a racing stock car and after two laps around the Speedway, he grinned and said: 'This is great.'"

Bobby didn't confine himself to Daytona Beach during his stay in the Sunshine State. In mid-February, Bobby went to watch the races at the State Fairgrounds in Tampa, where his attendance alone earned him attention. In a full-length article in the *Tampa Tribune*, sports editor Tom McEwen reminded readers that this was "home" for the young driver, who attended Florida schools in the winters when his family lived there during his father George's racing season. In the *Tribune* photo, Bobby is wearing his brown leather 100-Mile-an-Hour Club jacket, now sporting two hash marks on the right arm, indicating that he had achieved the rare high-speed distinction twice. Also at the Tampa track, local artist Doris Briggs presented Bob with an oil painting showing him in action at Indy; she had used a postcard photo as the model.

Back at Daytona, Bobby got more wheel time on the two-and-a-half-mile paved tri-oval, but he wasn't in the lineup for the February 24 race, and did not attempt to qualify. Instead, Bobby practiced two cars on the track—the 1963 Ford, as well as a 1963 Plymouth for Norm Nelson. In mid-February, *NSSN* had reported that "USAC star Bobby Marshman" would be driving a 1963 Plymouth for Jack Smith, but the drive did not materialize.

NASCAR drivers were the top four finishers in the 1963 Daytona 500: Tiny Lund was the winner, with Fred Lorenzen taking second place, followed by Ned Jarrett in third, and Nelson Stacy in fourth.

Before the February 24 race, much was made of a feud between the USAC and NASCAR, but most of the fuss came from officials rather than drivers. USAC's Henry Banks made news early in the month by saying USAC drivers were superior to NASCAR drivers, and that he was confident of a "win-place-show" for his drivers in the race.

As it developed, the best results from the seven USAC drivers in contention at Daytona were fifth place from Dan Gurney and ninth place by Johnny Rutherford. Gurney was not even a USAC regular. In fact, Gurney could just as easily have entered the Daytona 500 with his FIA license—or his NASCAR license. Back in January, when he arrived for the Riverside 500 in California, Gurney discovered at check-in that he'd left his FIA and USAC licenses at home. He neatly solved the problem by joining NASCAR on the spot, and went on to win the California race under a NASCAR license.

After the Daytona 500, *NSSN*'s Tom Tiede addressed the USAC–NASCAR "rivalry" with driver interviews. When asked about the competition, USAC driver Paul Goldsmith said, "They [NASCAR] are fine drivers, and I don't know many drivers who'll tell you differently." NASCAR driver Ned Jarrett said, "There is no visible difference between the two racing groups," and fellow NASCAR pilot LeeRoy Yarbrough remarked, "Race drivers are all the same breed of people. How can you say one group of them is any better than another?"

Two weeks after the race, the *Pottstown Mercury* reported, "Bobby Marshman, who planned to drive in the recent Daytona, Fla., '500,' says of the high-speed track that it's the easiest he ever drove. 'All you do is stick your foot in it and go,' he says, 'and the guy with the best car wins.' Marshman was scheduled to drive with one of the factory teams, but the cars weren't 'prepared' in time."

Despite his disappointment in not hitching that sought-after ride, Bobby's time in Florida was not wasted. With his easygoing yet professional demeanor, Bobby made a positive impression on all those he met.

Chapter 54
"The Popular Pottstown Pilot" (1963)

Bobby took part in local events when his hectic travel schedule allowed. On March 2, he was the much-publicized guest speaker for the seventeenth annual Pottstown Father & Son Night held in the Pottstown Senior High School auditorium. Bobby talked about the Indy 500 to the 1,000-plus gathering and commented on films of his 1961 debut race at the Speedway.

"What Bob enjoyed the most when he was back in the area was when he was invited to go to things for the Boys Clubs and the Boy Scouts," recalled Janet. "He was a Scout himself. I still have a wood project that Bob worked on to earn a badge when he was a Boy Scout."

Bobby valued every racing award he received, Janet noted, but he had an innate concern for others. "Bob sometimes gave his trophies to a charity, so they could be auctioned to help those in need," she said.

On March 9, at the tenth annual awards dinner of the Hub Racing Club in Syracuse, New York, Bobby was made an honorary member. In mid-March, Bobby once again connected with racing friends, attending the second annual banquet of the Bloomsburg Midget Raceway, where he was the guest of honor. He told the gathering that sportsmanship is the key to success. Held in the social room of the Bloomsburg, Pennsylvania, Methodist Church, the event featured a showing of Indy 500 film footage.

Later in the month, "the popular Pottstown pilot," as sportswriters sometimes described Bob, was at another Pennsylvania event, and this time he was in his favorite seat, behind the wheel. He was competing in USAC's first sprint race of the season, held at Reading Fairgrounds. The 5,000-plus crowd enjoyed race day's pleasant weather after the region's rough winter, and the track was in good shape. The March 24 contest was won by A. J. Foyt, who had claimed pole position, driving the Competition Engineering Special Chevy. At the finish, Foyt suffered hand and leg burns when a hose blew loose from his car, pouring hot water all over him. He was treated at the scene and not hospitalized. Bobby started ninth and finished seventh in the KEY Chevy.

On March 28, Bobby was at the Brickyard, having fun tooling around the track, demonstrating the 1963 Indy pace car. Driving the turquoise-colored Chrysler 300 Sports Series Convertible, Bobby "turned in a lot of laps . . . for the benefit of the photographers in camera cars, a helicopter, and high in the stands," Jep Cadou Jr. reported in the *Indianapolis Star*. " 'I figure I'd better get used to the car,' said the confident Bobby. The pace car, of course, is part of the spoils awarded to the driver winning the race."

Three days later, Bobby was back in competition. But the March 31 USAC sprint race at Williams Grove was a disappointment. As AP reported, "[F]or one of the few times in his US Auto club career, Bobby Marshman, Pottstown, Pa., failed to make the feature race. He placed sixth in the 10-lap consolation race, too far back to qualify." Don Branson won the thirty-lap feature in the Beletsky Chevy.

Meanwhile, back at Ford headquarters, March had come in, not with a roar, but with some snags for the engineers assigned to develop an engine for the 1963 Indy 500. Colin Chapman and his team had the Lotus 29 chassis ready to mate with the car manufacturer's engine, but that engine ran poorly in Dan Gurney's test drive at the Ford Proving Ground in Kingman, Arizona. Disgruntled by the disappointing performance, Gurney and Chapman were prepared to move ahead elsewhere, until Ford engineers convinced them that they could resolve the difficulties. A new test phase was scheduled to start March 24, this time at the Speedway.

Jim Clark was at the wheel on the first day of the test week in Indianapolis and had the car up to over 146 mph before he had to return to Europe to race. When Gurney took over, some adjustments had been made, and he was soon up to 149 mph; then, he turned a dazzling 150.501, a Speedway lap speed second only to Parnelli Jones. The chassis/engine duo was clearly a go, and Ford and Chapman signed a contract for three cars. March ended on a more-congenial note than it had begun for this group, as they now moved ahead as a team.

Bobby Marshman was soon to become a key player in this inner circle of rear-engine innovators aiming for America's most famous speedway.

Chapter 55
Tragedy at Langhorne (1963)

On April 7, Langhorne Speedway's USAC sprint car competition featured a "twin 50" program, with two fifty-mile races on the one-mile dirt circle. The track was fast, smooth, and dust-free.

In the opener, Jim Hurtubise led the first forty-eight miles, only to run out of fuel with less than two laps to go. The victory went to A. J. Foyt, who had flown in from Texas for the race, with Roger McCluskey capturing second. For much of the race, crowd excitement was focused on a dramatic three-car battle among contenders Bobby Marshman, Bobby Marvin, and Allen Crowe, who finished third, fourth, and fifth respectively.

Tragedy struck in the second event of the day. On lap 41, Bobby Marvin's car clipped the outside guardrail, rupturing the fuel tank. The car burst into flames as it bounced across the track and on top of driver Bud Tingelstad's car. Tingelstad suffered minor burns from his efforts to pull Marvin from the crash, and Marvin died shortly after admittance to Lower Bucks County Hospital, with burns to 100 percent of his body. The twenty-four-year-old driver had been racing for four years, and had plans to make his first attempt at the 500 in a Novi the next month.

The Langhorne race was halted at forty-one miles because of Bobby Marvin's fatal accident, with Roger McCluskey in the lead. Foyt had led early in the race from pole position until mechanical problems forced him out on the eleventh lap, and McCluskey took over as front-runner, with Hurtubise right behind. Marvin had been running third on the same lap with McCluskey and Hurtubise when the accident happened. The final results put McCluskey in first, Hurtubise in second, Crowe in third, and Bobby Marshman in fourth.

Two weeks later, in response to the fatality, USAC's director of racing Henry Banks consulted with Langhorne promoters Irv Fried and Al Gerber to address safety concerns at the track. The chief issues of the meeting were inadequate guardrails, slow fire-protection response time, and poor telephone communications around the track.

Meanwhile, interest and speculation were surging for the 500. Though the race was a year-round presence in Bobby's life, Indy excitement typically took off in April—as Memorial Day suddenly seemed close enough to touch—and 1963 was no exception.

On April 16, Jim Rathmann, the 1960 Indy 500 winner, was announced as a driver for Lindsey Hopkins, alongside Bobby. Two days later, the Speedway's first social event of the year was held at Bryant Heating and Cooling's annual press party at the Speedway Motel. News also broke that the entry fee at the Brickyard had been doubled, from $500 to $1,000, to keep out non-competitive entries. As a result, a number of previous owners/entrants chose not to enter the 1963 competition.

On a related front, the *Indianapolis Star* reported on an April 18 talk by Lee Iacocca, general manager of Ford Division, who told the Inter-Industry Highway Safety Foundation of Michigan,

"A 500-mile race is far more than a test of speed. Much more importantly, it is a test of how a car handles and how it stands up to punishment." In contrast to General Motors and American Motors Corporation, Ford had become an outspoken proponent of automobile performance.

Indy buzz continued to build through April, including news about spectator-focused improvements at the Speedway. Over 14,000 new seats would enhance this year's race, thanks to a 10,000-seat extension to the paddock along the front straight, plus the erection of a new open stand in the northeast turn, bringing total grandstand seating close to 150,000. Another high-profile development debuting that spring was a $1.5 million motel / golf clubhouse behind the southeast turn. The Speedway Motel featured a commanding sign displaying the IMS winged wheel emblem on the outside, and on the inside, tables with chrome-plated crankshaft pedestals.

Bob and Janet and Robbie had their own lodgings well in hand for the 1963 race season. While work began on their house in Pennsylvania, they decided to be closer to Bob's spring and summer racing events, and signed on for a six-month rental in a new apartment building near the Speedway. In March, Janet and her sister Kay drove down to set up the apartment for the April-to-October stay.

"Moving to Indianapolis was easy," Janet said. "Indiana was the Midwest like everybody always told me it was, with the most receptive, the most nonjudgmental people. They treated us like neighbors."

Janet and Bob enjoyed the camaraderie among the apartment building residents. "So many of the drivers lived in the apartments, like the McCluskeys and Johnny Rutherford, and we were all friends. You're all thrown together and you have to stick together," Janet said, adding, "There were new horizons, too. Most of the people in the apartments were either with racing or attending Indiana University's medical school, right in Indianapolis. One of the med students, Julianna Simmons, remained a lifelong friend."

The apartment turned out to have other advantages. "The building was just outside of the fourth turn of the Speedway," recalled Janet. "We would sit up on the roof garden, and from there you had a view of the fourth turn and then down the straightaway and into the first turn. We could watch them warm up. It was really neat.

"The apartment owner liked being with the drivers and hearing all the racing stories," Janet added. "He was a nice guy."

And as Bobby told the *Pottstown Mercury*'s Warren Howard, "There's no place like home, but I like to live in the Midwest during the racing season, because you can accomplish so much more."

Chapter 56
New Jersey and Ohio . . . With Indiana on Their Minds (1963)

Indiana may have been on his mind, but New Jersey was next on Bobby's dance card. Not just another race, the ABC-TV 100-Mile National Championship Sweepstakes at Trenton Speedway marked the opening of USAC's 1963 championship racing season. The April 21 event was the first race on the Championship Trail, and the only championship race prior to the Indy 500.

A record 18,000 fans were on hand at the New Jersey State Fairgrounds' one-mile paved track. The race featured a spectator-pleasing contest between A. J. Foyt, Lloyd Ruby, and Eddie Sachs for first, with passes and re-passes throughout the first part of the race. Ruby was forced out on the forty-first lap by a broken gearbox on his rear-engine 2.7-liter Lotus-Climax. Then, on lap 75, Sachs—who was running second at the time—was forced out due to a broken piston on his City of Vancouver Special.

Foyt not only held the lead to capture first place in his Sheraton-Thompson Special, but also shattered his own previous track record with a new 100-mile record of 102.491 mph. And rear-engine pilot Ruby—despite being bested by the Offys in the race—set a new track record of 106.414 mph for one lap in qualifying. Ruby's rear-engine Lotus, owned by J. Frank Harrison of Tennessee, attracted great interest, weighing in five hundred pounds lighter than the roadsters, with an aluminum Climax FPF four-cylinder engine. The chassis was a modified Lotus 18, with an extended wheelbase to meet USAC requirements.

After Foyt in victory position at Trenton came Parnelli Jones in second, Jim Hurtubise in third, Jim McElreath in fourth, Troy Ruttman in fifth, and Bobby in sixth in the Econo-Car Rental Special.

A week later, Bobby was in Ohio for the New Bremen Speedway's sprint car program. On the same day, April 28, an *Indianapolis Star* photo showcased chief mechanic Jack Beckley working on "the Econo-Car Rental Special for driver Bobby Marshman" in the Brickyard garages. The caption also noted that Beckley "always has had top-flight drivers in his auto racing equipment." The Lindsey Hopkins team was one of the first to arrive at the Speedway.

Two accidents slowed the New Bremen fifteen-mile race, but there were no serious repercussions. Bobby Unser was uninjured when he hit the wall on the first lap, but was forced out of the race. He was driving the Fike Plumbing Special, which usually had Parnelli Jones at the helm. On the twentieth lap of the thirty-lap race, Zeke England hit the wall and collided with Bob Tattersall, whose car flipped several times. Both drivers were treated at the track. Jim Hurtubise took first place at New Bremen, with Don Branson second, and Bobby third.

As April drew to a close, Indy expectations and debates went into high gear, with rear-engine contenders generating much of the heat. Many in the racing establishment remained skeptical of the new European technology, expressing the belief that the speed Gurney showed in Speedway trials and the speed Ruby demonstrated at Trenton could be ascribed to soft tires. A. J. Foyt was firmly in this camp, saying, "If they'd let us use those soft tires to qualify on the Offys, we'd really show 'em some new track records." USAC rules for 1963 prescribed that teams must use the same type of tire to qualify that they would use in the race, including tread design, size, and hardness of compound.

Rodger Ward was one of the few who welcomed the so-called invasion, and his comments proved prophetic: "I feel there is great potential in the rear-engine cars. The Lotus-Fords already have proved they could be competitive. On the other hand, some of the drivers of these cars are relatively inexperienced at the Speedway. So are the crews—and the pit stops will be a deciding factor."

Foyt and other drivers expressed concern about the safety of the rear-engine cars, saying they were little more than a frame with an engine and fuel tank attached. Foyt said, "If one of them ever hits the wall here, man, I'd sure hate to be in that one. The driver would be cooked right now."

Len Sutton, on the other hand, was another driver who foresaw a future for the new technology, predicting that in three years half the 500 field would be made up of rear-engine cars. As we now know, he was more than right.

Adding to the conversation was Indy's leading car builder A. J. Watson, who said he'd had it in mind for several years to build a rear-engine car, but had been too busy supplying the demand for his conventional roadsters and hadn't gotten around to it.

On another design front, innovative changes were in the works for one of J. C. Agajanian's Indy-designated roadsters, engineered by chief mechanic Johnny Pouelsen, a pilot who owned a flying school in Compton, California. Drawing on his work with aircraft, Pouelsen was experimenting with a variety of aerodynamic features as well as modifications to deflect the air stream and create less drag.

In addition to the drama of the new, there was excitement over the return of the crowd-pleasing

Novis of Speedway lore. Under the auspices of owner Andy Granatelli, the famous Indy cars were coming back after a five-year absence, along with their singular engine roar—or scream, as many described the cars' shrill running sound. The legendary Novis raced only at Indy and were much revered among fans.

Innovation and anticipation were in the air. April was ending. The Speedway proving ground awaited.

Chapter 57
Size Matters (1963)

In 1963, May 1 was opening day at the Speedway.

The Lotus-Ford team was there in full force, including mechanics Jim Endruweit, David Lazenby, Colin Riley, and Bill Fowler. The Lotus-Ford race cars had been prepared in England and flown to Indiana for drivers Jim Clark and Dan Gurney. Unlike any other cars in Gasoline Alley, the Lotus 29 was of monocoque construction with a stressed skin body. It sported a sleek, low-slung chassis, and its rear engine was a Ford V8, a Fairlane-based stock block with a smaller (3.76-inch) bore to reduce the displacement to 255.6 cubic inches. Weighing in at 1,130 pounds, the Ford-powered Lotus was one of the lightest cars on the track.

But it wasn't the elegant Lotus chassis or the new Ford engine that were currently attracting attention at the Speedway—it was the car's tires.

To be more precise, tire size was the center of major controversy in the earliest days of the month.

The "Tire Wars" commenced when Chapman and Gurney announced on opening day that the Lotus 29-Fords would be running on Firestone rather than Dunlop tires. In fact, Firestone had produced special 15-inch tires for Lotus (as well as 12-inch tires for Thompson, which were the center of their own controversy later in the year). Outrage erupted over the Lotus 15-inch tires, which were slightly wider and lighter than the 18-inch tires then used on the rear of the roadsters (which traditionally used 16-inch tires on the front). The chief complaint of the roadster contingent was the ability of the wider 15-inch tires to run much longer without changing, potentially allowing Lotus to run the race with only one stop. In 1962, Ward had stopped three times during his winning drive, and Foyt, four times, on the way to his 1961 victory, making a possible one-stop run for Lotus a tremendous worry for the contenders on traditional tires.

On May 7, USAC president Tom Binford informed a meeting of owners, drivers, and mechanics that he did not believe it was up to the USAC to outlaw a tire which Lotus and other teams had previously been told they could run. In response, some owners considered petitioning the USAC board to hold a special meeting on the subject.

The next day in the *Indianapolis Star*, Jep Cadou Jr. chided the roadster group for trying to beat

Europeans at the conference table instead of on the track. "It seems that foreign participation is always welcome at the Speedway—until it becomes an actual threat to win the race," he wrote. "Then, it is bucked with vehemence at every turn."

J. C. Agajanian and Bob Wilke reportedly pulled out all the stops to have the 15-inch tires banned, contending that they and other teams had gotten a raw deal by not being told 15-inch tires would be available. Firestone's position was that they built the 15-inch tires specifically for the lighter-weight Lotus and could not recommend their use on the much heavier roadsters.

Goodyear soon entered the fray, teaming up with A. J. Foyt to test wider 15-inch stock car tires at the track. Although it had been over forty years since the tire company had been a competitive presence at the Speedway, a full crew arrived, headed by Goodyear racing division chief Ted Lobinger and designer Ed Long. Foyt's 15-inch Goodyears had a tire width of 7.51 inches, more than an inch wider than the 18-inch Firestones most cars were using. Foyt showed what they could do, running a 146-mph lap on an extremely windy day that was estimated to hold speeds down by up to 3 mph a lap. Goodyear soon scratched the effort for the 1963 race, but the racing bug had bit, and they were back at the Speedway in July for tire tests aimed at May of 1964.

There were repercussions in other quarters. California supplier Halibrand Engineering, with no

reason to anticipate a sudden clamoring for 15-inch rims, was suddenly expected to cast, machine, zyglow-test, and deliver enough wheels to meet the unexpected demand surge in a matter of weeks. In addition, the company was dealing with cancellations for the 18-inch rims they had already built.

Halibrand met the challenge, focusing its entire operation on supplying three hundred wheels before the May 18 qualifying deadline. Firestone, in turn, agreed to supply the roadsters with 15-inch tires. The scarcity crisis eased just after mid-May, and the supply of the sought-after wheels and tires began to catch up with demand.

Parnelli Jones was soon on board, saying that he had made up his mind to use the Firestone 15-inch tires in qualifying and in the race because he expected them to give much better wear due to their extra tread width. Eddie Sachs, known as "the clown prince of racing," brought some humor to the situation when he marched through the Speedway garage carrying an extra-wide dragster wheel with an inside rim measurement of 11 inches across, announcing that his chief mechanic Wally Meskowski was going to mount it on his Bryant Heating and Cooling Special.

Outside the tire-skirmish rink, fans and participants alike enjoyed the pre-race game of guess-the-winner. Jones was the pick of many sportswriters. And among the pros themselves, a poll of the 100-Mile-an-Hour Club showed Bobby as one of nine drivers touted to win on May 30, although Parnelli and A. J. were the two top favorites in the poll. In 1963, there were only seventy-one living members of the 100-Mile-an-Hour Club, and Bob was one of them. Indeed, he had proven himself twice.

Chapter 58
Early Days of May (1963)

Disputes and predictions aside, the real action was on the track.

On May 1, Eddie Sachs was the first man pushed through the paper start banner in the bright yellow-and-red Bryant Heating and Cooling Special, an A. J. Watson–built car owned by D. V. S. (George Deeb, Bob Voight, and Dick Sommers). Sachs was soon joined on the track by Bobby, Jack Turner, A. J. Foyt, Parnelli Jones, and Jim McElreath, all ready for an early shakedown. Although chief steward Harlan Fengler had imposed a speed limit of 140 mph, Jones clocked a 143.5-mph lap, while Foyt and McElreath both got over 140. The next day, Bobby was up to 144 mph, as was McElreath.

Along with his speed on the track, Bobby's weight was duly noted by the press. From an *Indianapolis Star* article: "At 167 pounds, Bobby Marshman is 15 pounds heavier than he was last year—looks tough enough to lift the Offenhauser up and qualify on his own horsepower." Bobby responded, "I've always wanted to gain weight, and the extra pounds make me feel better." When asked how he did it, Bobby credited Stark & Wetzel's Rookie of the Year prize, an ongoing supply of meat, saying, "I haven't eaten all of it, but I'm working on it." The *Star* added Bobby's regimen:

"He doesn't smoke or drink, he takes one vitamin every day, and squeezes a rubber ball when he isn't driving to strengthen his wrists."

In his "One Man's Opinion" column in *The Tennessean*, Raymond Johnson also commented on Bobby's fifteen-pound weight gain, starting with the headline MARSHMAN ANYTHING BUT HUNGRY. Johnson reported: " 'They always told me to get a hungry driver,' car owner Lindsey Hopkins remarked to a trio of scribes who were needling Marshman. 'When I signed Bobby last winter, he was skinny. Now look.' "

Not all the press attention was on Bobby's weight. The 1962 Formula One World Champion Graham Hill was on the track in the earliest days of May, taking his driving test in Mickey Thompson's Harvey Aluminum Special. Hill was the first rookie to pass, despite a slide in water overflow from his own car. However, he later bowed out of further contention for that year's race after determining that the car wasn't up to the task.

On May 3, Sachs was the top performer, turning a lap at just over 147 mph, with Bobby close behind as second-fastest, with a lap just under 146 mph. In another forty-eight hours, both Jimmy Clark and Bobby were running faster than 148 mph for several laps in an informal race of their own on the windy track.

Then on May 11, Jones clocked a lap at 152.027 mph, a new record for running on Firestone 15-inch tires mounted on an 8.5-inch-wide rim. The next day, in windy conditions, McElreath, who had been fast all month, did a 150.326-mph lap, and Bobby Marshman, a 149.8-mph lap, both on 18-inch tires. The two drivers had plans to try the 15-inch tires later in the week.

On May 15, the last of the sixty-six entries checked into the Speedway garages.

Bobby's May 15 schedule featured an important engagement that he wouldn't dream of missing: Robbie was turning three.

"Bob was a real family man," said Janet. "We weren't party people, but we had fun times." Bob and Janet celebrated Robbie's birthday in their Indianapolis apartment with friends from home and from the Speedway. "Jay Miller was there—he was best man in our wedding, and was always with us, all through Bob's racing," said Janet. "Doug and Laura Stearly from Collegeville were there with their son, and Johnny Rutherford and other drivers. The friends at Robbie's birthday were as close as family to us.

"The drivers all made a fuss over Robbie," Janet continued. "I think they missed their own kids, because many of the wives and families weren't able to be at the Speedway for the entire month. Parnelli especially would grab Robbie and be off having fun with him."

Back at the track the next day, Parnelli was more serious than playful, pulling off a 153.557-mph lap. The day was also marked by numerous mishaps, perhaps the most serious being when Curtis Turner spun and crashed his Fiberglass Special after sliding in oil and water dropped on the track by Art Malone's Novi. Turner gashed his leg and suffered other cuts and bruises, but the car fared far worse and was essentially totaled.

Chapter 59

"A Cooling Sip of Kroger Milk after a Hot Lap at the Track" (1963)

Suddenly it was Saturday, May 18, and the schedule was set for qualification, with Bobby third in line behind Jim McElreath and Ebb Rose. Over 200,000 fans showed up to watch. The day presented extremely gusty winds and a slick track, which left everyone complaining about their times.

Before qualifying began on Saturday, Dan Gurney had a spectacular crash on a practice run when he hit the wall going into the southwest turn and continued to slide for nearly eighty feet. His Lotus 29/2 was severely damaged and out of the running for the May race. Gurney was fine, and definitely in the running. He stepped into the Lotus 29/1—the Lotus-Ford team's backup car, or test mule—and qualified the next day, in the fourth row, behind his teammate Jim Clark in row two in the Lotus 29/3.

On the darker side of the sport, Jack Turner crashed dramatically on Sunday, rolling end over end five times and completely demolishing the Precision Piston Ring Special. Turner announced the end of his racing career from his bed at Methodist Hospital, where he spent nearly two months recovering from serious injuries, including severe back burns that required skin grafts. The Seattle native's accident made a deep impression on his friend Len Sutton, who rigged up a fire extinguisher in his own car, perhaps the first driver to do so.

Fortunately, Sutton did not have to test his precautionary cargo when he hit a wall himself on May 21. He was out of the car quickly and no fire ensued from the crash, but damage to his Leader Card Autolite Special demanded extensive mechanical first aid. Later, Sutton did qualify, only to be bumped twice, and in the end, the second-place finisher in the 1962 Indy 500 did not make the 1963 starting grid.

Bobby had better luck. On the first qualifying weekend, he claimed the seventh spot, third row, on the grid. Along with every driver there, he had given much thought to the ongoing controversy over whether to switch to the wider 15-inch tires. In the end, Bobby chose to qualify and race on the traditional 16-inch front, 18-inch rear setup.

Despite the intensity of qualifying, Bob made time for a few lighthearted sideline gigs. A newspaper fashion story showed Bobby and his car posed on the Speedway with several prominent local women modeling the latest dress styles, with Bob looking stylish in his racing uniform. Bobby also found time to take visiting land-speed record holder Craig Breedlove on a tour of the IMS Museum. In a different milieu, a full-page Kroger grocery ad on May 23 featured Bobby and Parnelli, with a picture of Bobby in his car, "refreshing himself with a cooling sip of Kroger milk after a hot lap at the track."

The next day, Bobby was indeed turning some hot laps, practicing in the 149- to 150-mph range. He also test-hopped the No. 31 American Rubber and Plastics Special vacated by Bobby Unser and got the racer up to 147.7 mph.

In another on-track adventure, Bobby learned that his pal Parnelli did not like the idea of another driver following his line. Bobby was doing just that on a fast lap when Jones took note of it and lifted suddenly, forcing Bobby to brake hard.

The competitive pace was more relaxed a few days later at the driver golf tournament where Bobby was teamed with Parnelli, as well as *Los Angeles Times* sportswriter Jim Murray and Speedway Christian Church minister Dr. Ray Montgomery, who frequently gave the invocation before the start of the Indy 500.

Parnelli Jones spoke of Bobby in a 2015 interview with J. C. Argetsinger, president of the International Motor Racing Research Center at Watkins Glen. Jones said, "Although we fought hard on the track, we were good friends." Parnelli remembered Bob as "an extremely talented and very likable young driver on his way up."

Chapter 60
A Fast Crowd (1963)

When the watches stopped on Pole Day (May 18), Parnelli Jones was on the pole at 151.153 mph, Jim Hurtubise second in the Novi, with 150.357 mph, and Don Branson third, at 150.188 mph. In the second row, Rodger Ward was in fourth position, with 149.800 mph, Jim Clark fifth, at 149.750 mph, and Jim McElreath sixth, with 149.744 mph. Bob was the last and slowest first-day qualifier. He qualified seventh, inside of the third row, at 149.458 mph, with laps of 149.800 mph, 150.000 mph, 149.007 mph, and 149.031 mph.

The rest of Bobby's row filled out on May 19, with A. J. Foyt in eighth, with 150.615 mph, and in ninth, Paul Goldsmith, with 150.163 mph. Fighting a slick and windy track, most of the drivers on the first qualifying weekend were disappointed with their speed. Bobby's speed would end up being the eleventh-fastest in the starting field.

On May 26, the last day of qualifying, the starting list appeared to be complete—but there were upsets to come. Len Sutton and Ralph Liguori were bumped in the final minutes: The two had tied at 147.620 mph, and only one could make the grid. As officials were extending the decimal figures to settle the tiebreaker, Ebb Rose spared them the decision. Rose outpaced not only Sutton and Liguori, but Troy Ruttman, too. Ruttman, who had bumped his way onto the grid earlier in the day, was pushed to the thirty-third spot, as Rose claimed thirty-second with a stunning last-minute 148.545-mph qualifying speed in the Sheraton-Thompson Special. The qualifying game for 1963 was over.

With positions now designated for the entire field, all spots on the eleven rows of three were named and claimed. After spirited weeks of practice and two adrenaline-driven weekends of qualifying, the final round of pre-race tension could commence.

The day before the race, the *Raleigh Register* reported that "Bobby Marshman said he had run more than twenty laps, after he qualified, at speeds between 149 and 150, indicating he expected to hit that pace and perhaps faster if necessary to stay in contention. Such speeds, Marshman admitted, would put a terrific strain on the motors and chassis of the race cars and could turn the race into an endurance run to prove the ability of pit crews and mechanics in preparing and keeping a car running."

At the annual drivers' meeting on May 29, chief steward Harlan Fengler emphasized that no car would be allowed to continue in the race without brakes, a transparent reference to Parnelli Jones's laps-long brake lapse the year before.

Eddie Sachs, as spokesperson for the drivers, singled out Andy Granatelli and Colin Chapman for special distinction. Speaking of Granatelli, Sachs said, "We are proud you brought the three Novis back and made them the great race cars they were in the past." To Chapman, he said, "We can't begin to tell you how glad we are you are a part of the race. We really want you here."

Chapman, for his part, was reportedly impressed by the standard of workmanship and

presentation of the roadsters. When asked about the long tradition of roadsters at the 500 versus the rear-engine racers of Europe, he replied, "Here the cars are designed and built by mechanics and there they are designed and built by engineers." His meaning is open to interpretation.

Celebrity well-wishers played their part at the meeting. Comedian Bill Dana entertained the gathering, and actress Connie Stevens told the drivers, "I'd like to wish you all Godspeed. I'm awfully glad to be here." Dan Blocker, who was at the height of his fame as Hoss Cartwright in TV's *Bonanza*, also wished the drivers well, as did the 500 Festival Queen, Linda Lou Mugg. Raymond Firestone offered his wishes for a safe race, as well he might, with every car on the starting grid riding on his company's tires.

Back to the business at hand, Fritz Duesenberg, chairman of the USAC technical committee, warned the gathering that "any car that liberates excessive fuel or oil will be black-flagged." His warning was repeated by Fengler.

The next day was May 30. And a memorable day it promised to be, with speeds for the record books already in place. The 1963 qualifying lineup was the fastest in Speedway history, averaging

149.033 mph, crushing the previous record of 147.339 mph from the year before. Even the slowest qualifying speed was higher, at 147.832 mph. It was indeed a fast crowd.

These thirty-three gentlemen were not only ready to start their engines, but primed to push them to a new level of speed, guaranteed to dazzle the eager fans.

Chapter 61
The 1963 Indianapolis 500—Abundant Spectacle, Amazing Speed

Exuberant pre-race hoopla was a hallmark of the Speedway, and the forty-seventh Indy 500 lived up to tradition. An impressive array of marching bands, drill teams, majorettes, color guards, and more came together to help create the vibrant, charged atmosphere so integral to the race spectacle.

At 10:15 a.m. on Thursday, May 30, the opening parade began, with Chrysler convertibles chauffeuring celebrities around the track, including renowned driver Stirling Moss, along with movie and television stars. And at the same moment that the convertibles began their circle, the thirty-three cutting-edge racing machines were pushed into starting formation, cheered on by a record crowd of more than 250,000.

Indianapolis was clearly the place to be on this cloudless, 65-degree Memorial Day.

At 10:50 a.m., the traditional release of a multitude of balloons filled the air with color, and three minutes later, Tony Hulman gave the signature command. The gentlemen started their engines—except for Ebb Rose, whose Sheraton-Thompson Special was slow to start, though he did catch up before the green flag. The other thirty-two cars followed the turquoise-colored Chrysler 300 Sports Series Convertible pace car as it orbited the track for the parade lap, with Project Mercury astronaut and air force colonel Leroy Gordon Cooper Jr. on board with Tony Hulman and Sam Hanks. Space pioneer Cooper, who had circled the Earth only weeks before, was not at the Speedway on behalf of the National Aeronautics and Space Administration (NASA), but had arrived without fanfare, to cheer on his friend, driver Jim Rathmann. After its lap, the honorary car pulled aside so the official pace lap could commence. The goggled gladiators headed for a flying 90-mph start.

At 11:00 a.m., starter Pat Vidan gave the green flag, and all thirty-three cars roared past, aiming for the first turn. The 1963 Indy 500 was off and running. It proved to be a riveting race—and also an injury-free one, despite accidents and spins that brought out yellow flags for almost an hour in total. Periodic slowdowns aside, the theatrics on the track never flagged.

Parnelli Jones thrilled onlookers with sizzling displays of speed in his Agajanian-Willard Battery Special, besting all records to date, and leading for 167 laps. Clark, in the invading Lotus-Ford, kept Jones on his game throughout the challenge, proving the old-timers right in fretting over the potential dominance of the upstart rear-engines. But not this day. The California Offy driver defeated the Scotsman and his new-breed entry, even though Jones made three pit stops to Clark's anticipated single stop.

Nevertheless, the Lotus-Fords did prove their prowess in their first assault on the Speedway. When Jones made his first pit appearance on lap 64, Clark and teammate Dan Gurney ran 1-2 for about a dozen laps. Gurney fell back, but Clark remained a threat to Jones for his entire drive for the checkered flag, even taking the lead for twenty-eight laps and closing the gap between them to under five seconds in the closing miles. At the finish, Clark was 33.84 seconds behind Jones for second, and teammate Gurney claimed seventh.

Other contenders pumped drama into the contest on every mile.

Roger McCluskey, in his Watson-built Konstant Hot racer, not only led for four laps of the race, but was also one of Jones's early challengers. He was virtually assured of third place until he suddenly found himself in a so-near-and-yet-so-far nightmare: On his lap 199 (and the leader's last lap), McCluskey skidded in oil and spun into the infield in the northeast turn, ending his hard-fought run.

Eddie Sachs, too, had to call it quits late in a day of competitive piloting. He had recovered from a spin on lap 179, but on lap 182, he lost a wheel on his Bryant Heating and Cooling Special and hit the wall. His duel with McCluskey for third had been one of the race's highlights.

Disappointment touched other challengers, including the three Novi drivers, Jim Hurtubise,

Bobby Unser, and Art Malone. Not one of the revered Novis made it to the finish line, with Unser and Malone exiting on the third and nineteenth laps, respectively. Hurtubise, however, grabbed the lead on the first lap, and even after losing the number-one spot, continued in the front pack, dueling with Foyt for third and fourth for many miles, and running consistently at 149 mph. Then, just over halfway through the race, on lap 103, Hurtubise was black-flagged because of an oil leak and taken out of the competition, shutting down the "wicked roar" of the Novis for the day.

Bobby had his own heartbreaks, despite an enduring contest with the top contenders, including Jones in the early laps. Bob was besting McCluskey in a duel for second when he made his first pit stop—and just barely missed colliding with Jim McElreath on the pit apron. Coming in just ahead of him, McElreath locked a brake, forcing Bobby to deliberately spin to avoid him. Floyd Clymer wrote in the *1963 Indianapolis 500 Mile Race Yearbook*, "The two cars gyrated around like a pair of dancers and never touched each other and then pulled up in front of their respective pits as crews scattered like pigeons." Next day's newspaper pictures of the pit-spin duet captured some of the breathtaking unpredictability of the high-speed race. Despite the dramatic photos, both cars made it back into the race, though Bobby lost a lap in his stop.

By lap 130, Bob was once again running with the top ten, in eighth position, until he pitted on lap 148. Back on the track, he was tenth and nursing a sick car after 160 laps, and yet moved into seventh by lap 175. Shortly after McCluskey's spinout, Bobby was running sixth on his lap 197 (and the leader's last lap) when his clutch gave up, forcing him out for good after completing 196 laps. "Early reports had said that his dropout with four laps to go . . . had been due to rear end trouble, but when tearing the car down, it was discovered that the six bolts in the clutch had sheared off," reported the *Pottstown Mercury*. Bobby was officially awarded sixteenth position, although early unofficial rankings placed him fifteenth.

After running with the lead pack through much of his third Indy race, Bobby missed completing the full 500-mile run by less than 10 miles.

The checkered flag came down to anoint Parnelli Jones the winner, in a record-blasting 143.137-mph average speed. Jimmy Clark claimed second, averaging 142.752. A. J. Foyt was third and Rodger Ward fourth, followed by Don Branson in fifth and Jim McElreath in sixth. All six of the top finishers beat Ward's existing record of 140.293 mph.

Dan Gurney finished seventh, completing the impressive debut of the two Lotus-Ford entries, arguably the most controversial and closely watched cars on the track. Another rear-engine racer was not far behind: Al Miller placed ninth in the Chevy-powered Thompson-Harvey Aluminum Special. Between Gurney and Miller was Chuck Hulse, in eighth.

Fourteen of the original thirty-three drivers were still running when Jones claimed first place. The final five were: Dick Rathmann, tenth; Dempsey Wilson, eleventh; Troy Ruttman, twelfth; Bob Christie, thirteenth; and Ebb Rose, fourteenth.

Chapter 62
Black Flags and Fisticuffs (1963)

Despite his hard-charging race, Parnelli Jones's Indy 500 victory elicited a checkered reaction.

Jones was barely out of Victory Lane before controversy erupted over his car's oil leak in the final laps—or, more pointedly, over the black flag that never waved him in.

There were no official protests during the race, although several crews, including Lotus-Ford's, reportedly contended to chief steward Harlan Fengler that Jones should have been stopped because he was leaking too much oil. Spray from a cracked oil tank hit Parnelli's exhaust pipe and smoke first appeared at 1:53 p.m., according to the minute-by-minute report in Floyd Clymer's *1963 Indianapolis 500 Mile Race Yearbook*. The black flag was taken out and was at the ready. J. C. Agajanian, the owner of Parnelli's car, and his crew chief, Johnny Pouelsen, were seen in what appeared to be heated conversation with Fengler during the final laps, when the black flag was still unfurled. Agajanian convinced Fengler that the car was smoking less and less because the oil leak was subsiding.

Officials decided not to wave the black flag at Jones as he powered home to victory at 2:29 p.m. By race end, the car had quit smoking. But the controversy did not subside. Immediately after the race, USAC officials checked the quantity of oil left in Jones's tank. Their conclusion, as noted in Clymer's *Yearbook*, was: "not enough oil used or lost to be a hazard." And Fengler told the *Indianapolis Star*, "You can't take this race away from a man on snap judgment," adding that other cars were also throwing oil. However, Eddie Sachs and Roger McCluskey both complained vigorously to the press, stating that Jones's oil leak was responsible for the accidents that put them out of the race so late in the game. Others took up the dispute with great verbal heat, and Jones and Sachs came to physical blows over their differences the next day before the Victory Banquet.

Fisticuffs aside, most of the anger was directed at the USAC for what many considered a flagrant display of partiality, with the Offy establishment getting special treatment at the expense of the rear-engine newcomers. Many reiterated the stern warning at the drivers' meeting that "any car that liberates excessive fuel or oil will be black-flagged."

Jim Clark said that during the race, he thought Jones would be black-flagged because of what Fengler had said at the pre-race meeting, and that he backed off so as not to be so close to the oil coming from Jones's car. However, Clark went directly to Jones's garage after the race to shake his hand, and later told Bob Renner of the *Indianapolis News* "that Parnelli is to be congratulated—he's quite a race driver."

Bobby had a comment on the matter for Sandy Grady of Philadelphia's *Evening Bulletin*: "I'd hate to take the race away from Parnelli after the hard work and great race he drove. But it's unfair to stop one driver [Hurtubise] for leaking oil and let Parnelli go ahead."

Flagman Pat Vidan told Grady, "I had the black flag in my hand, ready to wave Parnelli off the track; gee, I didn't want to. I was really happy when the stewards changed their minds."

When Grady asked Fengler what had transpired, Fengler answered, "I changed my mind on the black flag because Parnelli's car stopped spewing oil. The track was so slick by that time, I'd hate to take the victory away from Parnelli on a technicality. Oh, you'll always hear some sour grapes."

Andrew Ferguson, Team Lotus competition manager, later commented on the controversy in his book *Team Lotus: The Indianapolis Years*: "The man more experienced at the Brickyard had won. And Jones had not been short on skill. For others to blame him for their accidents on oil missed the point that he had driven over it safely . . ."

Chapter 63
June: Multiple Tracks and One Rest Stop (1963)

Bobby and his fellow drivers seemed undaunted by their hectic race schedules. Three days after the grueling Indy 500, many of the same competitors were in the starting field for the New Bremen, Ohio, sprint car race. Roger McCluskey at least left frustration behind at the Brickyard, winning the half-mile dirt track race on June 2.

Bobby's Ohio race was a disappointing one. He was in a two-car incident with Chuck Hulse on the sixteenth lap which put Bobby out of the race. Hulse continued and finished second, but he was fined $100 for unsportsmanlike behavior regarding the accident.

Early in the New Bremen race, a fatal accident brought great sadness to participants and spectators alike. Indy driver Allen Crowe crashed into a concrete wall on lap 11 and flipped. His car burst into flames after landing in the middle of the track, and was hit by several of the oncoming racers. Crowe died that evening in Dayton's Good Samaritan Hospital of chest and head injuries. The Springfield, Illinois, native had been a USAC competitor for five years, and made the starting grid for the 500 in 1962 and 1963.

Bobby's next race was a week away, and the respite was a welcome one. "After Indy and before

Milwaukee, we liked to stop for a few days to spend time with friends from home who had moved to Elgin, Illinois, outside of Chicago," Janet said. "The Glenns were the parents of my best friend from high school, and they raised Morgan horses, so I'd go riding with their kids. Bob liked horses but didn't care about riding them, so he'd stay at the Glenns' house and relax, and spend time with Robbie. It was a restful, calming-down period for Bob."

On June 9, Bobby was back on track, competing in Milwaukee's Rex Mays Classic on the Wisconsin State Fair Park's one-mile paved oval.

Played out before a record crowd of nearly 34,000, the Milwaukee 100-mile event was marred by numerous incidents, notably when Masten Gregory hit the wall in the qualifying race, tearing off the right front suspension of his Mickey Thompson Chevy-powered racer and breaking the rear wheel, knocking him out of a spot in the starting field. In the 100-lap main event, several drivers had accidents on separate laps that ended their races, including Johnny Rutherford, Jim Hurtubise, Roger McCluskey, and Al Miller. Parnelli Jones sat out the event because both sets of brakes went out on his Agajanian Willard Special before he could qualify.

During qualifying, Bobby spun on the north turn and started ninth in the 100-mile race, placing seventh in the Econo-Car Rental Special. Rodger Ward claimed first place in the Offy-powered Kaiser Aluminum Special, after taking the lead on the sixty-eighth lap and keeping it despite pressure from second-place finisher Eddie Sachs in the Competition Engineering Special.

The next day, Sachs was in a different hot seat, in a closed meeting with the USAC executive committee. He apologized for his criticism of the recent Indy 500 officiating, and was given one year's probation. Considered as merely a slap on the wrist, the probation meant Sachs could still race, but could make no unsupported comments that might reflect on the integrity of USAC officials.

Next up after Milwaukee was the Terre Haute "Action Track," with a thirty-lap sprint car feature on June 16 at the Vigo County Fairgrounds. It boasted the richest small-track race purse to date, but the day's prizes eluded Bobby when a broken piston dropped him to sixth in the first heat and kept him from the feature. It was a more rewarding day for Roger McCluskey, who not only did make the feature, but set a new record of 12:14.25 on the half-mile dirt oval, in front of 11,000 spectators. Second place was claimed by Chuck Hulse, third by A. J. Foyt, and fourth by Steve Stapp, the son of Indy driver Babe Stapp.

The 100-mile national championship ride at Langhorne Speedway was now on the horizon. Bobby described the challenging track to Warren Howard of the *Pottstown Mercury*: "It's a continuous left turn. A perfect circle. You're 'on it' all the time, continuously fighting the wheel in what they call a power slide."

Before the demands of the championship event, Bobby paused to put his driving skills toward a good cause on June 19. As he told Howard, "Parnelli Jones, Rodger Ward, Jim McElreath, and myself ran a special race at Indianapolis for the benefit of the Shriners' hospital." Bobby added that his chances in the upcoming Langhorne race were "excellent."

On June 23, a hot day at the 'Horne, Bob had a bittersweet run. He charged out of his sixth-place start and ran well in a relentless display of speed. Bobby caught early leader Jim Hurtubise on lap 28 and they began a fierce side-by-side battle until Bobby took charge on the thirtieth lap. He extended his lead to 9.5 seconds over A. J. Foyt, who had worked his way into second place. Then on lap 63, Bobby pulled into the pits with severe fatigue and neck cramping. In the Pottstown paper, Howard colorfully described Bobby's condition when he exited the car: "Marshman staggered about the pits like a drunken sailor, his stamina completely gone. His head lolled like a knockout victim after a ring brawl as he splashed his face with orange juice."

After a right rear tire change on the car, Don Branson took over for Bobby and finished the race. Branson's own Leader Card Special had delayed the race start for over half an hour while mechanics worked unsuccessfully to repair a fuel pump. Marshman and Branson finished fifth behind winner Foyt, with McElreath second, Hurtubise, third, and Jones, fourth.

Jack Kiser of the *Philadelphia Daily News* asked Bobby why he didn't slow down to finish the race at Langhorne and settle for second or third place. Bobby's answer: "Well, some people had said I was falling into a pattern of conservativism. That I'd set up a plan before the race and stick to it, even if the other guys were winging out front. So before the race I decided to do nothing but charge. Sure, I still had a pattern to follow, but that pattern consisted of trying to pass everyone in front of me when I saw daylight. . . . You've got to charge hard if you hope to have a chance against the likes of Foyt, Herky, Ward, Sachs, Jones, McCluskey, Hulse, Branson, and the others."

Back in the Midwest on June 28, Bobby competed in the first USAC midget race ever staged at the old County Fairgrounds in Columbus, Indiana, a half-mile dirt track event. Bobby was the second-fastest qualifier, at 28.24 seconds, behind Ronnie Duman, at 28.14 seconds. Four thousand fans crowded the stands to watch Bob Tattersall of Illinois take first and Tommy Copp of California, second. Bobby was sixth behind Mel Kenyon of Iowa, in fifth, Duman of Michigan, in fourth, and Bobby Grim of Indiana, in third.

Before the June 30 Raceway Century event at Indianapolis Raceway Park, the sports press touted Bobby as a top challenger to Roger McCluskey. However, thanks to a broken crankshaft, Bobby did not qualify for Raceway's first 100-lap sprint car race, despite putting in practice laps with other competitors the day before. Another non-qualifier of interest was Rodger Ward, who missed the starting grid because of a blown engine on a new car entered by General Motors engineer Mike Burnett. Powered by a Chevy engine mounted behind the cockpit, the machine was presented as the first rear-engine sprint car ever built.

On the track in the IRP contest, McCluskey and A. J. Foyt both ran nonstop races for the 62.5-mile distance on the 0.625-mile paved oval, with McCluskey claiming victory three seconds ahead of Foyt. Bud Tingelstad, the fastest qualifier, placed third.

Chapter 64
"Running the Track He Helped to Build" (1963)

Bobby spent much of July piloting on Eastern tracks—at least when the rain clouds parted long enough to run a race.

At the Williams Grove Speedway on July 7, Bobby had the eventual winner Roger McCluskey in his sights as he moved steadily up through the field in the USAC sprint feature, and at the finish, he claimed third behind Chuck Hulse. Later, Tommy Nicholson, Eastern supervisor for the USAC, told the *Pottstown Mercury*, "He [Bobby] was the only guy who could do a thing at Williams Grove. He started ninth, finished third, and would've won it in a couple more laps." But the race was thirty laps on the half-mile track, and McCluskey held first position from the second lap to the checkered flag, bolstering his lead in USAC sprint car standings.

Mother Nature dampened two racing events in one weekend: On July 20, a downpour at Hatfield Speedway forced a reschedule for the next Friday; and on July 21, torrential rains interrupted qualifying at Trenton International Speedway. The *Terre Haute Tribune* listed Bobby as one of "the dozen nationally famous performers who completed their time trials" before rain intervened. The race was rescheduled for the following Sunday.

For the Hatfield Speedway race, the *Pottstown Mercury* reminded its readers that Bobby would be "running the track he helped to build five years ago." The half-mile, high-banked oval boasted improvements for the July 26 USAC sprint car program, including additional lighting on the backstretch.

Bobby did not disappoint the home team in his first run at Hatfield in a sprint car. He won his heat, and in the thirty-lap feature, he poured the pressure on leader Parnelli Jones in the final five laps, ultimately finishing second behind Jones. Roger McCluskey was a distant third, with A. J. Foyt fourth, and pole winner Don Branson in fifth.

It was a rough go for many drivers that evening. A multicar accident on the ninth lap began when Cotton Farmer's car hit the fence, somersaulted, and landed on its tires, but not before involving Ron Lux, Chuck Hulse, Bob Courtright, and A. J. Foyt in the incident. Earlier, Jim McElreath, Ralph Liguori, and Steve Stapp experienced individual spins and flips. Despite all the drama, there were no injuries.

Engine troubles plagued Bobby two days later at the Trenton Speedway 150-mile championship race. He started in sixteenth position and finished nineteenth, with a broken piston putting him out of the action. A. J. Foyt had a far happier day, leading all the way to win the July 28 race, and thus claiming the lead in USAC point standings. Cheered on by over 18,000 spectators, Bobby Grim took second and Rodger Ward, third. In a pre-race mishap, Eddie Sachs was hit in a warm-up lap by Bob Wente's spinning car, sending Sachs to Helene Fuld Hospital where he was treated for internal injuries as well as jaw and shoulder fractures.

For the Daviess County Fair in Elnora, Indiana, Bobby was a drawing card for the July 29 midget auto races, but not as a competitor. Rather, he was highlighted at the top of the Fair program as the pace-car driver for the race.

Even with so much summer action on the racetracks, rear engines continued to be the hottest topic in the racing world. Less than a month after the 500, Ford Motor Company announced its commitment to return to the Brickyard in 1964 with new, more-powerful engines. Ford engineers were still developing their newest engine, and it was reported to feature a double-overhead camshaft design resembling the Meyer-Drake Offy four-cylinder, "much like a V8 Offy, if such an engine existed," according to press descriptions.

Janet's thoughts on the subject mirrored those of many fans. "I loved the noise of Offys," Janet said. "You knew with every driver when they lifted for a corner. And the Novis—there was a roar all

the time. But the rear-engine cars sounded like firing up an Impala—they were not sweet. The noise, the sound, is part of a race car."

Bobby was increasingly drawn to the rear-engine racers. According to Phil Sarno, sports editor of the *Hazleton Standard-Speaker*, Bobby predicted that rear engines would dominate the 1964 Indy 500 field. "They're the definite answer," Bobby said. "Those machines can run fast and it takes less effort to drive. And they are terrific on tire wear."

In fact, Bobby made up his mind early on that he wanted a Lotus. In July, he told Hugh Brown of the *Philadelphia Bulletin:* "I hope to drive one. They run so fast and effortlessly, they look like they're doing no work at all. What tremendous tire distance! That's because of their light weight, the engine in the rear, and the independent suspension that permits them to get wonderful traction." Bobby, a bona fide "old school" dirt driver despite his young age, was ready to embrace the new cars.

Not so for his racing colleague Parnelli Jones. "It irks me, all this talk about a new era," Jones told UPI, adding that the Lotus-Fords in the Memorial Day race weren't up to Indy standards. When asked if he'd like to try one out, Jones said, "No. I don't want to drive them because I feel they're unsafe."

Other drivers aired their opinions that summer. Rodger Ward told the *Indianapolis Star*: "I think that this [the rear-engine machine] is the kind of car it will take to win. I want to be in that car." But not a Lotus. Ward went on to tell the *Star* that he'd had overtures from Ford to drive in next year's 500, but said he'd rather drive a rear-engine Offenhauser.

And Al Dean, a man with four Offenhauser-powered racing cars in his Dean Van Lines stable, told *Sports Illustrated*: "I'm going to dump my junk. The Lotus-Fords have made my cars obsolete."

Chapter 65
"Wheeled through the Field of Top Drivers like a Comet" (1963)

Bobby's August race calendar was robust, with at least one race a week, and covered a generous swath of the Midwest, including Indiana, Illinois, Wisconsin, and Ohio.

On August 2, Bobby led all the way to victory in what *NSSN* called "a star-studded field" in the Columbus, Indiana, forty-lap USAC midget race. He was piloting the Harry Turner Special on the Bartholomew County Fairgrounds' half-mile dirt oval. Starting from the outside of the front row, Bobby took the lead in the first turn, and never let it go. Second in the "110-Offy" feature was three-time national midget champ Jimmy Davies, who had set a one-lap track record in qualifying. Roger McCluskey was third, followed by Bob Wente, the USAC midget point leader to date.

The entry list for the August 4 Salem Speedway sprint car program was called "a Who's Who of automobile racing" by the *Indianapolis Star*, with seven Indy 500 drivers, plus a full cast of top USAC sprint car drivers scheduled to compete in the thirty-lap race. It was Bobby's first start on the high-banked Indiana track, and he arrived early to familiarize himself with the setup. A quick study, Bobby finished third driving the Chevy-powered Econo-Car Rental Special. Don Branson was the race winner, three seconds ahead of number-two finisher Parnelli Jones.

Janet was a loyal fan and regular spectator. She sometimes attended Bobby's races with Robbie, sometimes with her sister Kay, and sometimes on her own. "When we were staying in Indianapolis during race season, I didn't always take Robbie to the races," Janet explained. "At some tracks, we couldn't go into the infield, and I didn't want him to be confined. Many people would say, 'Keep us in mind if you need someone for Robbie.' But usually, Robbie would stay with a good friend in Indianapolis who had young children. Robbie loved being with them.

"The racing was a good time. Bob made it a good time for me," Janet added. "My opinion of the tracks was colored by the way Bob felt about them. For instance, Bob loved to race at Terre Haute."

Apparently, the attraction was mutual. The *Terre Haute Tribune* praised Bobby and Chuck Hulse in a pre-race August 9 feature. "They look more like junior executives than they do race drivers," wrote the unnamed reporter. "Both are well-educated and can use the King's English without taking a meat cleaver to it. The obvious question is, 'Do these guys represent race drivers in general, or are they welcome exceptions?' Bobby's reply: 'We're like 99.44 percent of the drivers. We don't beat our wives or anything; we're quite a bit like you. It's just that other small percentage of drivers who give us a bad name.'" The *Tribune* writer continued: "Why do they continue in their admittedly hazardous profession? 'I love it,' says Hulse. . . . Marshman added, 'If they told me before the race that the promoter had absconded to Mexico with the gate receipts, I might cry a little, but I'd still go out there and race.'"

On race day, August 11, Bobby captivated the seven thousand fans at the Terre Haute USAC sprint race when he handily maneuvered through the pack from seventh place to arrive in the winner's circle of the thirty-lap battle. Roger McCluskey was leading the charge through much of the race and seemed poised to confirm his pre-race favorite status. But the spectators at the Vigo County Fairgrounds had their eyes on Bobby, who was forging ahead so fiercely that the *Terre Haute Tribune* dubbed him the "the Pottstown terror" the next day in admiration of how he "wheeled through the field of top drivers like a comet."

Bobby had first thrilled the crowd earlier in the day when he won the third heat after starting next to last. In the feature, he once again demonstrated his skill in the chase, moving from a seventh start spot to fourth position by lap 8, and to third place by lap 11. On lap 15, Bobby had fought his way to second place, and the crowd was with him. Steve Stapp's spin on lap 22 elicited a yellow flag, and when it was lifted on lap 25, Bobby and McCluskey fought neck and neck for the lead. Bobby grabbed the top spot on lap 26 and kept it, capturing first place on the half-mile dirt track—his first USAC sprint car feature win of the season. Second place went to McCluskey, third to Don Branson, and fourth to Bobby Grim, who had earlier set a track qualifying record.

Bobby's victory glow was overshadowed several hours later when he was told that his mother had been hospitalized after a heart attack. Fortunately, Evelyn Marshman was fine by the next day, though still confined to the hospital for observation. Bob and Janet immediately headed east to spend time with her.

Bobby and his mother had a warm and close relationship, Janet recalled. "Bob always looked after his mother. Evelyn was a self-sufficient person, but Bob always made sure she had good tires on her car, that sort of thing," Janet said. "If I had to pick a mother without my own wonderful mother in the pool, I would pick Evelyn, because she was a perfect mother to me. She was just the loveliest of people, and Bob took after her."

Bob and Janet were back in Illinois for the Springfield 100-mile national championship race on August 17. Bobby again charged hard and competitively. Starting from third, he was number one for over half of the 100-lap contest on the one-mile dirt oval. After holding the top spot from lap 6 to lap 58, the "pride of Pottstown" was pushed out of competition by magneto failure, and was fifteenth in the final standings. Over twenty thousand fans cheered Rodger Ward to first place after an intense duel with second-place finisher A. J. Foyt. Bobby was not alone in dealing with engine woes at the Illinois State Fairgrounds: Ralph Liguori, Bobby Unser, and Ronnie Duman were among other drivers sidelined by mechanical failure. A wreck put Jim Hurtubise out of the day's action.

Race officials had their own problems. When the Illinois State Fair Board's insurance policy was found to be well below USAC's minimums, the start of qualifying was held up. After a delay of nearly an hour, an acceptable policy was confirmed and the competition commenced.

A few days later, the USAC made a public statement addressing a more widespread and contentious dispute. The sanctioning body had been under pressure by a strong contingent of roadster loyalists to adopt a weight minimum rule, ever since the powerful displays of speed by the relatively lightweight rear-engine cars in May.

On August 21, USAC president Thomas Binford stated that the board of directors would not pass "any resolution or rule that might stand in the way of progress in the sport of automobile racing." He went on to say, "It is the official policy of USAC to encourage innovations from wherever they may come, providing only that they meet the safety requirements, wheelbase, tread, and engine-size limitations."

Binford also said that the final ruling on a minimum weight restriction would be decided by the board of directors in September.

Andy Granatelli—the force behind the return of the Novis in May—was a leader in the demand for a minimum weight rule, with the goal of banning the Lotus-Fords. At the same time that he was fighting to maintain the status quo, Granatelli was looking to the future with his own Indy car research. He arranged an August test day at the Speedway with the front-engine Harry Ferguson–designed P99 four-wheel-drive (4WD) racer. (Harry Ferguson was an engineer and inventor renowned for his innovations in agriculture, aviation, and motor racing.) Brit driver Jack Fairman was Granatelli's test driver for the Formula One car, which was powered by what *Motoring News* later described as a "very tired" 2.5 liter Coventry Climax engine. After Fairman turned laps at over 140 mph, Granatelli decided to try the car with a veteran Indy 500 pilot. Bobby did the job, and reportedly was quickly lapping over 141 mph, even though the car's handling characteristics were new to him.

"Although the car was running out of steam on the straights," wrote Ian Wagstaff in his book, *The British at Indianapolis*, "Marshman reckoned he could go through the turns flat out. Granatelli was convinced and declared he would be entering a 4WD Novi for the 1964 race." Granatelli hired Harry Ferguson Research Ltd. in Coventry, England, to build the 4WD chassis, and planned to power it with one of his supercharged Novi V8 engines.

Chapter 66
Lotus: Plague and Progress (1963)

No matter who might wish it so, the Lotus-Fords were not going away. The August 18 Milwaukee Mile championship race said as much, and more, as if in skywriting.

Still considered intruders by Offy defenders, the rear-engine racers had many fans applauding. According to the *Indianapolis Star*, pro-Lotus-Ford mail was arriving in USAC offices through the summer. The fans weren't all talk: A record crowd of over thirty-five thousand bought tickets to attend the 200-mile showdown at the Milwaukee Mile's one-mile paved oval.

The speed capability of the outsiders was undeniable even before the race. Word was out that Jimmy Clark and Dan Gurney had unofficially broken Don Branson's record on the Wisconsin State Fairgrounds track during practice the month before—by almost five miles per hour—driving the same Lotus-Fords they had powered to second and seventh places at the Brickyard in May.

And now they had official permission to compete in the Tony Bettenhausen 200 in Milwaukee. The FIA granted full international sanction to the event less than a week before the start. Gurney, equipped with both USAC and FIA licenses, could have run without the last-minute sanction, but now teammate Clark could accompany him in the 200-lap race.

If anything, the Lotus-Fords exceeded the pre-race buzz, moving solidly beyond threat to a stinging domination at the Wisconsin USAC championship race. As Bob Greenberg wrote of the race in the November 1963 issue of *Car and Driver*: "In a nutshell, it was all Clark."

Indeed, Jimmy Clark won impressively, leading from start to finish, with a record-breaking average speed of 104.452 mph. A. J. Foyt, the only driver not lapped by Clark, fought hard and brilliantly for second in his Sheraton-Thompson roadster. Gurney and Rodger Ward had their own fight for third, with Gurney ultimately taking it, and Ward following in fourth. The next day in the *Indianapolis Star*, Bill Eggert colorfully described Clark's performance: "His cigar-shaped green racer resembled a tabletop toy car as it scooted outside and inside traffic and threaded through holes that other cars could not enter."

Bobby was part of the Milwaukee action, qualifying twelfth, but he experienced frustration in the race. He ran fifty-six laps until a broken differential placed him with the spectators. He was twenty-second.

After their success, the Lotus-Ford drivers received their laurels, along with a warning from race officials. The team was told to raise their cars' exhaust pipes for safety reasons, or they wouldn't be able

to compete in the September 200-mile race in Trenton. The cars' protruding sharp-edged exhausts were at tire-top level, and considered a potential danger to a driver following closely behind.

But the real warning at the August 18 race was unofficial, aimed at the current American racing machines. Powerful and beloved as they were, the Indy roadsters could not match the agility and speed of the new, lighter-weight competition that so captivated the fans. *Car and Driver*'s Greenberg pronounced the verdict: "Yes, the magic, Offy-powered dragons have been slain."

Midweek after the drama in Wisconsin, Bobby was back in Illinois, competing in a USAC midget race at the eighty-eighth annual Fairbury Fair. The August 21 fifty-lap feature was the kickoff event at the Fair Speedway. Among other Indy drivers competing on the quarter-mile dirt track were Parnelli Jones and Bob Wente, who placed first and second. Bobby was eleventh in the feature, after winning a semi.

Bobby had a solid result in his last race of the summer, capturing second in the New Bremen thirty-lap feature. The New Bremen Speedway was newly

MIDWEST RACING NEWS

VOLUME 5, NUMBER 15   28   MILWAUKEE, WISCONSIN, WEDNESDAY, AUGUST 21, 1963   25 CENTS PER COPY

Record 35,096 Crowd Sees Clark, Lotus-Ford Win Fair Park "200"

(Stories on Page 3)

Ward Wins Springfield 100 Mile Big Car Race

(Story on Page 3)

Jimmy Clark, Duns, Scotland and his Lotus Ford (above) were the class of the field in Sundays 200 mile national championship speedway big car race at state fair park. Clark won the race at a record 104.48 miles per hour.

This was the closest the field came to Jimmy Clark and his No. 92 Lotus Ford (inside position, first row) as the 26 starters eased through the north turn on the pace lap of Sundays 200 mile big car race at state fair park. Once the green flag fell, Clark was off like a shot and won the race by nearly one full lap.

plowed and disced in preparation for the August 25 USAC sprint car program, promising a greatly improved surface on the half-mile track. Despite the repairs, the race feature was delayed for more than an hour and a half because of unsatisfactory track conditions.

On the second lap, Bobby and pre-race favorite Roger McCluskey tangled, and McCluskey exited the race with a damaged tire. Chuck Hulse took his first USAC sprint win for the season, with Bobby right behind to claim the number two spot. Arnie Knepper was third. Bob's race result put him in second place in the season point standings, overtaking A. J. Foyt, who did not compete in the Ohio race.

Chapter 67
"He Never Faltered" (1963)

Race fans were also following a different but related summer competition, between Firestone and Goodyear. In the latest iteration of the so-called Tire Wars, both companies were intent on developing the dominant racing tire for the future. Bobby spent much of his summer in the trenches for Firestone, and also tested for the competition.

In July, Bobby, along with Jim McElreath, tested nearly one hundred tires for Firestone at the Speedway. Both drivers recorded laps of 152.8 mph, Bobby in the Econo-Car Rental Special, and McElreath, in the Hotel Tropicana Special. Bobby averaged 151.8 mph for eight consecutive laps, more than 0.5 mph faster than the Speedway's four-lap qualification record posted by Parnelli Jones in May. A month later, while testing for Firestone at the Fort Stockton, Texas, track, Jim McElreath broke the world's closed-course record, running at 186.392 mph on a hot August day. He was driving the Bill Forbes Special on the 7.712-mile banked track.

Meanwhile, Goodyear was hard at work developing a new tire material with exceptional wear capabilities, conducting its own Speedway test series in July. A. J. Foyt, who was considered to be the driving force behind Goodyear's renewed racing interest, was the tire company's major test pilot. He turned a 149.6-mph lap at Indy on behalf of Goodyear's research.

Bobby also tested for Goodyear. In a Speedway test for the company at the end of July, Bobby Marshman had a near mishap driving the Novi racer piloted by Bobby Unser in the Indy 500. Marshman was averaging 148 mph in the test when the car threw a connecting rod and began to wobble, but he calmly drove the shaky chariot into the pits. In August Speedway tests for Goodyear, Bobby Marshman, A. J. Foyt, and Roger McCluskey all "experienced superior forward traction and side bite in the turns when they drove during the tire tests," George Moore reported in the *Indianapolis Star*.

Bobby was considered an ideal test driver because of his smooth driving style.

"The officials at the track explained to me why they wanted Bob to test," said Janet. "They told me they never saw anybody who was as consistent as he was. If he was to run 120, he ran 120. On the straightaways, on the turns, he never faltered. He wasn't on it and off it and on it and off it. That's why they wanted him."

Bob was testing pretty much year-round in 1962, '63, and '64, Janet recalled, first for the tire companies, and then, starting in 1963, for Ford.

"Bob tested all over—Texas, Arizona, the Speedway—wherever they wanted him to go," Janet said. "I went to almost all of Bob's races, but not to his test drives. You don't go to work with your husband."

Chapter 68
Fast and Furious (1963)

Labor Day weekend had come to mean the Du Quoin State Fair in downstate Illinois for Bob and Janet, and 1963 continued their tradition. That year the fair had a record number of 42,000 visitors, and in addition to a weekend-long race program, the entertainment roster featured Andy Williams and the Osmond Brothers. Bobby was there to run two races on the Du Quoin State Fairgrounds track, one on Saturday, August 31, and the other on Monday, September 2, and he also had one race scheduled in between, in Kansas City.

Bobby captured second place in his first challenge on Du Quoin's one-mile dirt oval, in the August 31 USAC sprint race. Bobby repeatedly challenged A. J. Foyt through the twenty-five-mile action, but Foyt held him off to lead all the way to first place. Chuck Hulse came in third. No times were kept for the race, according to officials, because of an accident on lap 7 when Johnny Rutherford spun three times, hit the protective bales lining the track, and spread hay all over the straightaway,

BELOW: Bobby dueled with Chuck Hulse and Don Branson at DuQuoin in September. He finished fourth ahead of Branson. (RMA/SCOTT)

forcing the race to a temporary halt. Rutherford was not injured.

On Sunday, Bobby traveled to Kansas City for a September 1 USAC sprint car race at Lakeside Speedway, where he suffered a mishap. In heat two, Bobby was hit in the right arm by a rock, and *NSSN* reported that "his arm swelled to twice its size and he was taken to a hospital for treatment." Don Branson placed first in the thirty-lap event on Lakeside's half-mile dirt oval, and A. J. Foyt was second. Although his injury put him out of the Kansas City feature, Bob was back behind the wheel in Du Quoin the very next day.

On Labor Day, the Du Quoin track hosted the 100-mile USAC championship race. "A highlight of the race was the three-car battle among Hulse, Marshman, and Branson, which lasted most of the race," according to Jep Cadou Jr. in the *Indianapolis Star*. At the end of the contest, Bobby was fourth, between Hulse in third and Branson in fifth. The 100-lap race was claimed by A. J. Foyt, with Rodger Ward second after leading for the first 42 laps. During qualifying, Cotton Farmer spun and flipped on the backstretch and was hospitalized for a neck injury.

A fellow Pennsylvania pilot posted stellar results over the same weekend. On August 31, relative newcomer Mario Andretti won three midget races in one day: an ARDC race in Flemington, New Jersey, in the afternoon, and two races in a Hatfield doubleheader that night. Both Mario and Bobby had their beginnings on the same Pennsylvania tracks some years apart.

In 2015, Mario Andretti spoke about Bobby Marshman in an interview with J. C. Argetsinger. "I was a rookie when Bobby was already an established driver," Andretti recalled. He went on to tell how it was Bobby's earlier success in three-quarter midget racing that persuaded his father-in-law to purchase the car in which Mario then drove to his own victories. Although running in the same races as Bobby by 1963 and 1964, Andretti said, "I was never competitive with Bobby." But from his experiences in those races, Andretti said he concluded at the time that "Bobby was destined to be a multi Indy car champion."

Chapter 69
Offy Time (1963)

As mid-September neared, the buildup began for the eleventh annual Hoosier Hundred, the USAC championship race at the Indiana State Fairgrounds. The September 14 contest on the one-mile dirt oval was dubbed a "rich race," thanks to its impressive $50,000 purse. Rodger Ward was the day's hero, leading from start to finish in the 100-mile race, and along the way, breaking the one-lap and 100-mile track records. Don Branson was second, and A. J. Foyt, third.

Bobby was a different kind of hero that day, and was presented a sportsmanship award at race end by Mechanics Laundry. Bobby had burned a piston in practice, and although he was qualified to run some slow laps at the start of the race, and thus collect eighteenth-place money, he made a different choice. He yielded his starting position to Ralph Liguori, who had been the nineteenth-fastest qualifier. Liguori's finishing position was sixteenth.

The next day Bobby was at Reading Fairgrounds for a USAC sprint car race. Driving the Meskowski Chevy, Bobby time-trialed ninth and was third in the first heat after a rough battle with Jimmy Maguire, whose car blew on the last lap. Although he qualified third, Bob did not line up for the feature. Roger McCluskey won the thirty-lap feature in the Bruce Homeyer Chevy.

The September 14 Hoosier Hundred continued to radiate a warm glow for Offy fans. After all, the roadsters had powered through the Indiana State Fairgrounds course at thrilling speeds. Yet the day before the race, in another part of the state, a USAC board meeting had cast a shadow over the future of the great American cars.

On the board's agenda was the much-debated proposal for a minimum weight restriction. Divided on what limit to propose, the committee studying the issue presented the board with a choice of either a 1,200-pound or a 1,250-pound weight restriction. In fact, both proposed minimums were above the weight of the Lotus-Fords, and would effectively ban them from competing. The Lotus-Ford was not the only car at risk; Mickey Thompson's rear-engine creations would also weigh in under the recommended minimum. Thompson had been vociferous in his protest against the weight requirement, asserting that the proposed ban would put him out of business.

On Friday, September 13, the USAC board rejected the weight-limit proposal, ten to three, with three directors abstaining. The rear-engine cars could not be pushed off the USAC championship circuit because of their ultra-light weight. In the same meeting, two other controversial proposals—regarding wheel size and protruding fuel tanks—were sent back to the rules committee for further study.

The roadster/rear-engine feud was about to face a major showdown at the September 22 Trenton championship race. Just a month before, on August 20, Jimmy Clark in his Lotus-Ford had set an unofficial one-mile track record of 109.1 mph on the asphalt Trenton Speedway. In a later practice session on the track, Clark crashed when he experienced mechanical failure in the steering mechanism of his Lotus-Ford and slammed into a guardrail. He was uninjured, and was still aiming for the September 22 battle in New Jersey.

The day before the Trenton face-off, many of the championship competitors were racing in a USAC sprint race at Pennsylvania's Allentown Fair. With a crowd of seven thousand watching the September 21 event on the half-mile flat dirt track, Johnny White commanded the lead all the way to claim first, with A. J. Foyt five seconds behind him. The race was scheduled as a thirty-lap event, but a track official accidentally waved a white flag instead of a yellow flag when Steve Stapp spun on the twenty-seventh lap, and the race was stopped after twenty-nine laps. Bobby placed eleventh in the fourteen-car field.

The next day, September 22, the Trenton Speedway hosted the second annual 200-mile USAC championship race. Over 32,600 fans were in attendance to witness the confrontation between the

Offy roadsters and the Lotus-Fords. And in a related competiton at the event, close observers noted that more cars on the Trenton track were competing with Goodyear tires than with Firestones, marking the first time in recent racing history that Firestone did not hold sway at a championship event.

Jimmy Clark set a new mark of 109.356 mph in qualifying. On race day, he and Dan Gurney in the Lotus-Fords appeared to be in place to win the battle, dominating early on, with Roger McCluskey running behind them in third. Bobby, A. J. Foyt, and Parnelli Jones were the crowd-pleasers as they maneuvered for fourth position in the first portion of the race. Then on lap 49, Clark was out of the race with a broken oil line. Bobby had made his move to fourth when a broken throttle put him out of the race at lap 63. Gurney led through lap 146, and then two laps later, he was forced to drive his smoking car into the pits, ending his run courtesy of an oil leak. Foyt grabbed the lead from Gurney on lap 147 and kept it. With his win, A. J. clinched the USAC National Championship for the third time. Bud Tingelstad was second in the race, and Troy Ruttman, third. Bobby started ninth and finished twentieth.

At the end of the day, the Lotus-Fords had once again dazzled onlookers with their speed before they retreated to the pits, and the Offys had once again claimed victory. But they had not reclaimed the status quo.

Reporting on the Trenton race in the December 1963 issue of *Road & Track*, Brock Yates included Bobby's opinion of the Lotus-Fords: " 'They are faster everywhere on the track,' said Bobby Marshman, the precise, intelligent young driver of Florida millionaire Lindsey Hopkins's roadster after the race. 'The slight speed advantage our cars had on the chutes at Indianapolis is gone. Their independent suspension gives them tremendous bite on the tighter, more cramped corners of a mile track, and they exit onto the straightaways at tremendous speeds.' "

Near the end of his Trenton postmortem, Yates added, "It has been a long time in coming, but there is a new wave enveloping American championship racing."

Change was pressing in, and Bobby was in place to help lead the charge forward.

Chapter 70
A Colorful Month (1963)

The Ted Horn–Bill Schindler Memorial on October 5 could be described as more contentious off the track than on. Bobby was not involved in any of the disputes at Pennsylvania's Williams Grove Speedway. For him, it was a disappointing day: He was twentieth of twenty-eight cars in time trials, missing out on the starting field for the thirty-mile USAC sprint race. However, Bob was there to observe the dramas that marked the event.

The first conflict erupted early in the day's schedule, after a heat run, when A. J. Foyt approached Johnny White, who subsequently accused Foyt of hitting him while he was still in his car and then clamping him in a headlock. Foyt denied the charges, saying he simply grabbed White when he got out of the car, so he could complain to White about "chopping me off" in the corners, which Foyt alleged White had been making a habit of doing, not only that day but in other recent races. Foyt was also accused of making a rude gesture to the booing crowd, which he explained was nothing more than a bow he made to the assemblage with his fingers outstretched. The USAC soon took up the misconduct charges against Foyt.

At race end, another conflict unfolded after New Jersey driver Jim Maguire crossed the finish line first, followed by A. J. Foyt. Maguire's win was immediately protested because his car was oversized in engine displacement and therefore illegal. Officials upheld the protest, though Maguire's Chevy-powered car was only six cubic inches over the USAC limit. Thus URC regular Maguire, who had led the entire race, was disqualified from first place and Foyt was declared the winner. Not only stripped of his win, Maguire "had to borrow $15 from Sam Veezia to get to Thompson, Connecticut, for a midget race the following day," according to Tom McGeehan in *NSSN*.

In fact, most of the drivers were focused on getting to their next race after the feisty events at Williams Grove. For Bobby, the following day's race was in Terre Haute—over six hundred miles away.

Bobby arrived for the October 6 Terre Haute midget race with a reputation for dramatic driving, earned in his August 11 sprint car win on the same track. The *Terre Haute Tribune*'s October pre-race story reminded fans that less than two months before, Bobby had "put on a show the likes of which hasn't been seen on the Action Track since the great Tommy Hinnershitz retired." An immensely popular sprint car driver from the 1930s, '40s, and '50s, Hinnershitz was dubbed the Flying Farmer, and wore his famous overalls to win 7 Eastern sprint car championships and claim 103 feature victories.

The Terre Haute midget race played out on a slick track at the Vigo County Fairgrounds' half-mile dirt circuit, with a crowd of 4,500 in attendance and twenty-four cars in the starting field. Bob Wente, the USAC midget champion, won the 100-lap contest, though Don Branson had looked like the sure winner. After leading for 77 laps, Branson ran out of fuel on lap 99, and subsequently dropped dramatically to a seventh-place finish. Jim Hurtubise was second and Billy Woods, third.

Bobby was involved in a first-lap accident in the Terre Haute race that had repercussions in the final results. When Bobby slid out on the first turn and Chuck Wyant flipped over his spinning car, the accident forced a restart. Bobby and Wyant escaped injury, but their cars didn't. "Marshman got back into action in another car," AP reported. The race was restarted, with several slow laps while debris was cleared from the track. After the race, Branson filed a protest contending that his fuel was depleted in the slow laps of the restart. The USAC denied his protest a few days later, and the standings held. According to UPI, "supervisor Bob Stoud said the delay was necessary to remove the wrecked cars and allow Marshman to catch up with the field." Bobby finished ninth in a Kenyon racer after qualifying twenty-fourth in a Nowicki car.

The Foyt–White altercation at Williams Grove came to the forefront again when the USAC suspended Foyt on October 7. Two days later, Foyt sped to a new unofficial world's closed-circuit course record of 200.457 mph on Goodyear's San Angelo, Texas, test venue, a five-mile-long track with 18-degree banking. The same day, the USAC temporarily lifted Foyt's suspension "until more facts can be gathered," releasing the three-time national driving champion and speed wizard to compete in California's Riverside Grand Prix. Foyt persistently and vehemently denied that he had slugged White, even urging a lie detector test to prove his innocence. Finally, at a USAC hearing on October 31, Foyt was officially absolved of misconduct allegations because "there was not sufficient evidence to substantiate the charges," according to USAC president Thomas Binford.

In another arena of the sport, it looked like the USAC had resolved the wheel

Page 2   NATIONAL SPEED SPORT NEWS

Maguire Beats USAC's Best At Grove, But Foyt Gets Cash

Maguire's Steak Turned To Beans After W-G Win

By TOM McGEEHAN

MECHANICSBURG, Pa. — When Jimmy Maguire pulled into victory lane after winning the USAC Horn-Schindler sprint car feature Saturday night, he had visions of celebrating the victory with a big steak dinner.

GETS BAD NEWS

But the steak turned to beans when Maguire later learned that his Chevy-powered mount had a 314 cubic inch engine, which is six inches over the USAC limit. The United Racing Club sprint car circuit, in which Maguire regularly competes, has no limit on cubic inch displacement.

So the disappointed Maguire and Venezia crew had to forfeit the $1200 first place money and their hard-earned victory. The young crew cut chauffeur had to borrow $15 from Sam Venezia to get to Thompson, Conn. for a midget race the following day.

In discussing the disastrous turn of events, Maguire talked about his thoughts during the course of the race, when A. J. Foyt, the USAC champion, was breathing down his neck for the entire 30 laps. He told Sam Venezia, "You guys think you had it bad . . . some guys were waving me outside and some mentioned me to the inside. I finally took Joe's (Venezia) advice and ran the inside groove. I figured he (Sam)

guire outran the best USAC had to offer.

Other Grove sidelights included a scrap between husky A. J. Foyt and Johnny White. Foyt claimed that White was using him as a "hang-board" in the second heat race, by drifting to the outside and carrying Foyt with him.

FEARLESS FOYT

After the heat was over, Foyt came blasting into the pits. He jumped out of his car and ran over to White, who was unfastening his safety belts. Fearless Foyt then grabbed White in a headlock, and pulled him out of the car. Bystanders quickly pulled the pair apart.

Later they shook hands. When asked about the scrap, Foyt said that White had done this on several occasions. "It's better to settle something like this off the track rather than on it," Foyt concluded.

When the announcer gave Foyt's name in the feature line-up, he received many boos from the crowd, while White's name was cheered. Foyt then walked alone to the center of the track, amidst the boos of the crowd, and did a few bows, which was met with louder boos and a few Bronx cheers.

When questioned about the incident, White didn't seem to know what the argument was all about.

USAC DRIVERS PROTEST

The complaint was presented by a member of the pit crew of the Hoffman Hot Special, owned by Bruce Homeyer, out of Cedar Grove, N. J. It charged that Maguire's car, the Venezia Brothers Special, was oversize in engine displacement and therefore illegal. Several drivers, including Foyt, put up the protest money.

Members of the technical committee had removed the tear-down a garage for teardown when car owner, Sam Venezia, Fanwood, N. J., admitted that the car was oversize. The officials, under the supervision of Tom Nicholson, USAC Eastern Zone Supervision, had no alternative but to disqualify Maguire and his car and award the victory to Foyt. Maguire and Venezia also had to forfeit their night's earnings.

In the feature action, Maguire had starting position and romped into the lead following a real traffic jam on the first lap. He moved in front going up the backstretch and was never behind again.

Repeated attempts by Foyt to overtake the young lad were stopped as

(Please Turn to Page Fourteen)

Hometown Bo[y] In N.C. Grand

RANDLEMAN, N. C. — It was a sweet homecoming for Richard Petty here Saturday as the local driver scored an impressive victory in the 200-lap NASCAR grand National race.

Petty maneuvered his 1963 Plymouth into the lead at 186 laps on the quarter-mile paved oval after a neat but rough duel with Freddy Lorenzen's Ford.

Lorenzen's car later had to withdraw when a driveshaft gave way but returned to take fifth spot.

size issue, only to stir up further dissent. On October 2, the board of directors voted to restrict the wheel size on all championship and sprint cars to a minimum of 15 inches, stating that 12-inch wheels constituted a safety hazard. Mickey Thompson, whose innovative cars famously sported 12-inch wheels, immediately disputed the decision. The car maker's outrage over the ban was backed by his sponsor Harvey Aluminum Company, a major metals producer and substantial investor in Thompson's radical designs, as well as by Sears, Roebuck and Company, a newcomer to racing, and the company supplying the tires for the controversial 12-inch wheels.

Nevertheless, USAC officials said the board action was final, effective January 1964. However, Thompson was told he could request that the issue be further considered at the May 1964 rules committee meeting, a concession that didn't exactly support the complex preparation of a car for the Indy 500.

But Memorial Day was months away, and there were still races to run in 1963.

At the California State Fairgrounds on October 27, over fifteen thousand fans were on hand for the thirteenth annual USAC championship 100-miler in Sacramento. Winner Rodger Ward took the lead from Johnny Rutherford when Rutherford's front axle failed on the thirteenth lap. Ward led to the finish, claiming his third "Golden State 100" win, following his 1957 and 1961 victories. Foyt claimed second in the Sacramento competition, Jim McElreath, third, and Lloyd Ruby, fourth. Although the race was slowed by four yellow flags lasting a total of twenty-two laps, there were no injuries. Bobby started third but was out after five laps, plagued by a broken piston, for an eighteenth and last-place finish.

Chapter 71
Green Means Go (1963)

Test drives pushed on as October moved into November. Firestone and Goodyear continued the fall leg of their research with a number of Indy drivers, including Bobby, putting the tire companies' products through their paces.

With paving of the Speedway's new tunnel still under construction, Goodyear began its tests in mid-October at nearby Indianapolis Raceway Park. After talking to Goodyear's racing division project manager Chuck Blanchard, the *Indianapolis Star*'s George Moore reported that "testing was not just to try and see if they could keep going faster all the time, but to determine just where they were standing in respect to tire compounds, tread contour, and body construction."

Firestone had first dibs on the Speedway when paving was completed ahead of schedule. Bobby was part of the four-day test action, along with Rodger Ward, Jim McElreath, and Chuck Hulse. The October 16–19 session included some disquieting moments. At one point, just as Bobby was starting to push his speed over 146 mph in his Econo-Car Rental Special, a crack developed in the engine block. He switched to Don Branson's Wilke-owned Leader Card Special, but on turn two, he put the car into the concrete, tail first, setting the roadster on fire when the fuel tank burst. Fortunately,

Bobby's injuries were minor. As for the car, the frame was not bent, and a new fuel tank installation put everything right for the next day's testing. Bobby made no excuses, but told the *Indianapolis Star*'s George Moore, "I just lost it. And I was more mad than scared." Fellow testers also experienced minor mechanical troubles in the Firestone tests, and they agreed that the track was "greasy" and slippery, keeping their speeds down.

In his October 30 *NSSN* "Midwest Racing Notes" column, Bill Marvel wrote, "Bobby Marshman, after his wreck in the recent tire test at Indianapolis, stated, 'One of those spins every 2,000 miles around here is plenty.' It was the Pottstown, Pa., veteran chauffeur's first such experience, and you can bet he is hoping it will be his last."

In other fall testing news, Ford and Lotus had three days at the Speedway in late October, with Jimmy Clark and Dan Gurney trying out the team's latest rear-engine developments aimed for the Indy 500. A few weeks later, Ford announced it would be running its new quad-cam engine at the Brickyard in May.

Ford was eager to increase its test miles before May, but both Clark and Gurney had full race calendars through the end of the year. Ford again turned to Indy expert and rear-engine enthusiast Lindsey Hopkins, his skillful chief mechanic Jack Beckley, and the team's undeniably quick young driver Bobby Marshman to work with Lotus and Ford as they prepared for an extensive winter test program.

Hopkins "had one of the bright young stars of American racing in Marshman," Leo Levine wrote in *Ford: The Dust and the Glory*.

In addition to his driving acumen, Bobby's personality was also a good fit for the team effort. As Andrew Ferguson wrote in *Team Lotus*, Bobby was given the highest of compliments when described as being "in the Jimmy Clark mould" by David Lazenby, a key figure in the new car's development. The exceptional Lazenby had joined Lotus in 1961 and was assigned to be Clark's senior mechanic for the 1963 Indy 500.

In his book, Ferguson recounted Lazenby's description of Bobby's first encounter with the car at the test track. "He mumbled under his breath when, on arrival to test for us, he discovered the car he was to drive was Jimmy's, resplendent in its British Racing Green." The Indy community, including Bobby, had long considered the color green unlucky.

Ferguson added, "Colour preferences aside, Bobby was not slow to recognise the Lotus as the car with which to succeed."

Levine concurred: "By the late summer of 1963 he [Bobby] was ready to make his bid for bigger things. The Lotus was the car that could do it for him, Bobby felt."

Chapter 72
A Checkered Flag Floor and an Icemaker (1963)

The fall of 1963 was also a pivotal time in Bobby and Janet's private life. Their house in Fagleysville was completed at the end of the summer.

In his October 2 "Speed Talk" column in *NSSN*, Bob Maginley wrote, "Bob and Janet are moving back east this week and will occupy their new home," adding, "Bobby seems to obtain more polish as a driver each time we see him run."

In fact, Bobby had test drive commitments, and it was Janet who drove back to Pennsylvania with Robbie to get the family settled into the new house.

"Since Bob was working, testing at the Speedway, I took care of moving us in," Janet said, "My brother-in-law had built the house, and Bob and I had gone over the plans with him over the past months. Bob had a cousin who did woodworking, and he did our entire kitchen."

The young couple had help from other quarters as well. "The building on the house had started in the spring when we left for Indianapolis," Janet recalled. "When we got to Indiana, Phil Hedback of Bryant Heating and Cooling Company took over the plans, and his engineers then did all the mechanical work—the heating, the air-conditioning, that sort of thing. They contacted their Bryant distributor near our home and went over it with him, and they just took care of the whole thing. It was really great. Mr. Hedback and his wife were pretty top-rate. We used to go up to Lake Wawasee with them, way up in northern Indiana. They were old enough to be our parents, and that's how they treated us. I was only twenty-five at the time, and Bob was twenty-six. We really liked both of them."

The new house was special to Bob and Janet. "The back of it was right up against a mountain, with fields all around," said Janet. And the distance to her sister Kay's home was "just about the length of two fields." That meant Robbie and his cousin Donnie could play together daily.

Bobby's father made a surprise installation for the three-year-old boys.

"George Marshman had two old-fashioned telephones that cranked," Janet recalled, "and he put one in Robbie's bedroom and then went down the road and put one in Donnie's bedroom. George installed all the wiring and the two boys could call each other. It was just the neatest thing."

The following spring, a news item in the May 24 *Philadelphia Inquirer* described the Marshmans' "new stone-front colonial home . . . in a rural section of Montgomery County." The unnamed reporter observed that Bobby's "mailbox is topped by a chrome silhouette of a racing car and below his name are the words 'USAC driver.'" The writer added that the young driver had already "accumulated enough trophies to fill the den of his new home," and the article made special note of the floor in the paneled room: "Inlaid in the floor tiles is a checkered flag, such as the one that signals victory on the track."

This striking interior feature—a checkered flag floor—was suggested by some of the workmen, said Janet. "The men who were installing a tile floor for us in the den asked if they could create a big waving checkered flag on the floor," Janet explained. "I didn't know how they were going to do it, but they wanted to, and Bob said yes. It was really nice of them to do. I picked out cork tile because I liked the texture, and then they laid the floor in the den and on into the utility room. Their checkered flag design was right in front of the fireplace. I think the people who bought the house later took out the floor, but it didn't have the significance to them that it did to us."

Bob insisted on only one detail. "When it came to picking things out for the house, Bob would stand back and let me decide," Janet recalled over fifty years later. "But he told me, 'The only thing I want to pick out, and not anything else, is the refrigerator.' He wanted an icemaker. GE [General Electric] had just come out with their first automatic icemaker, and so we got the top-of-the-line model, only because it came with that icemaker. Whenever Bob called, he would always ask me first thing, 'Did the refrigerator come?' I still have it, the same refrigerator, and I'm still using it."

Chapter 73
Tire Testing and Championship Racing (1963)

Bobby's November schedule held a wide variety of events.

Bobby was a guest at a gala in Indianapolis on November 11. The Speedway's annual press, radio, and television party was held at the new Speedway Golf Course Clubhouse, with 350 people attending. In a key announcement at the press party, Phil Hedback disclosed that Bryant Heating and Cooling Company would be sponsoring a rear-engine Offenhauser built by Rolla Vollstedt of Oregon, with Len Sutton as the driver. Their bid for the 1964 Indy 500 grid looked promising: In Speedway tire tests the week before, Sutton had the car up to 152.2 mph.

In fact, test drives dominated the month for many of the top Indy drivers, including Bobby.

Braving the uncertain weather conditions of November at the Speedway, Firestone and Goodyear could be called tireless in their 1963 testing regimens—except, of course, they brought an overwhelming supply of tire options to put through the rigors of a racetrack test.

Goodyear's engineers wrapped up their fall Speedway sessions on November 9, reportedly pleased with the results. The company's number-one test driver, A. J. Foyt, had grabbed headlines during the program when he hit a 153.1-mph lap, a breath under the unofficial record of 153.5 mph set by Parnelli Jones in the spring. Len Sutton, Eddie Sachs, and Don Branson also tested for Goodyear.

Firestone's Speedway test session started later in the month, with Rodger Ward, Jim McElreath, Chuck Hulse, and Bobby again trying on a multitude of experimental tires for wear, tread design, contour, compounding, and construction. In one test drive, despite adverse weather, Ward upped his speed from the 145 mph he ran on the 1963 tires to 149–150 mph on the experimental version. On November 20, the *Indianapolis Star* reported: "Bobby Marshman turned in one of the hottest laps of

the current Firestone tests, hitting 152.2 unofficially yesterday at the Speedway. According to Chuck Barnes of the Firestone test group, Marshman wound up with a five-lap average of 151.7." Bobby tested in the Econo-Car Rental Special.

Engineers from both companies went home to apply their research to the big decision: What tire should they build for the Brickyard in 1964?

On November 26, a newcomer entered the rubber mix, when Mickey Thompson arrived at the Speedway to test tires created for him by Sears, Roebuck and Company. After the USAC banned the 12-inch wheels Thompson had previously used on his cars in the 1963 500, he converted two of his Speedway racers to conform to the new 15-inch wheel ruling. This required changing the suspension units and the hubs on the cars to accommodate the larger wheels and tires, and Thompson wanted to determine whether these modifications affected the handling of his rear-engine cars. Thompson's new, custom Sears tire conformed to the USAC's mandatory 15-inch wheel size, but it was nonetheless unusual, smaller in overall height than the standard 15-inch racing tire. The height reduction was achieved by making the sidewalls narrower.

Still steaming from his October run-in with the USAC over their 15-inch wheel requirement, Thompson said he was also running the new tires at the Speedway so the USAC could not ban them for lack of a test program. Indy veteran Duane Carter was his test driver.

Even though so many drivers were heavily booked up with tire testing, their main focus was still racing. The Bobby Ball Memorial race in Phoenix on November 17 was a key event: The 100-mile contest on the Arizona State Fairgrounds track was the final race of the year for the USAC National Championship. In recent years, the track had been in notoriously poor condition, with serious accidents marring the 1961 and 1962 championship races, but for 1963, welcome improvements were in place.

Bobby was the Bobby Ball Memorial race winner in 1962, but this year his efforts were blunted by mechanical trouble, and he finished last after qualifying third. Rodger Ward claimed first after taking the lead on lap 31 and holding it. There were no serious injuries, despite two caution flags—first, when Jerry Weld spun on lap 2, and then when Lloyd Ruby flipped and was forced out of the race on lap 42. Chuck Hulse placed second, and Jim McElreath, third.

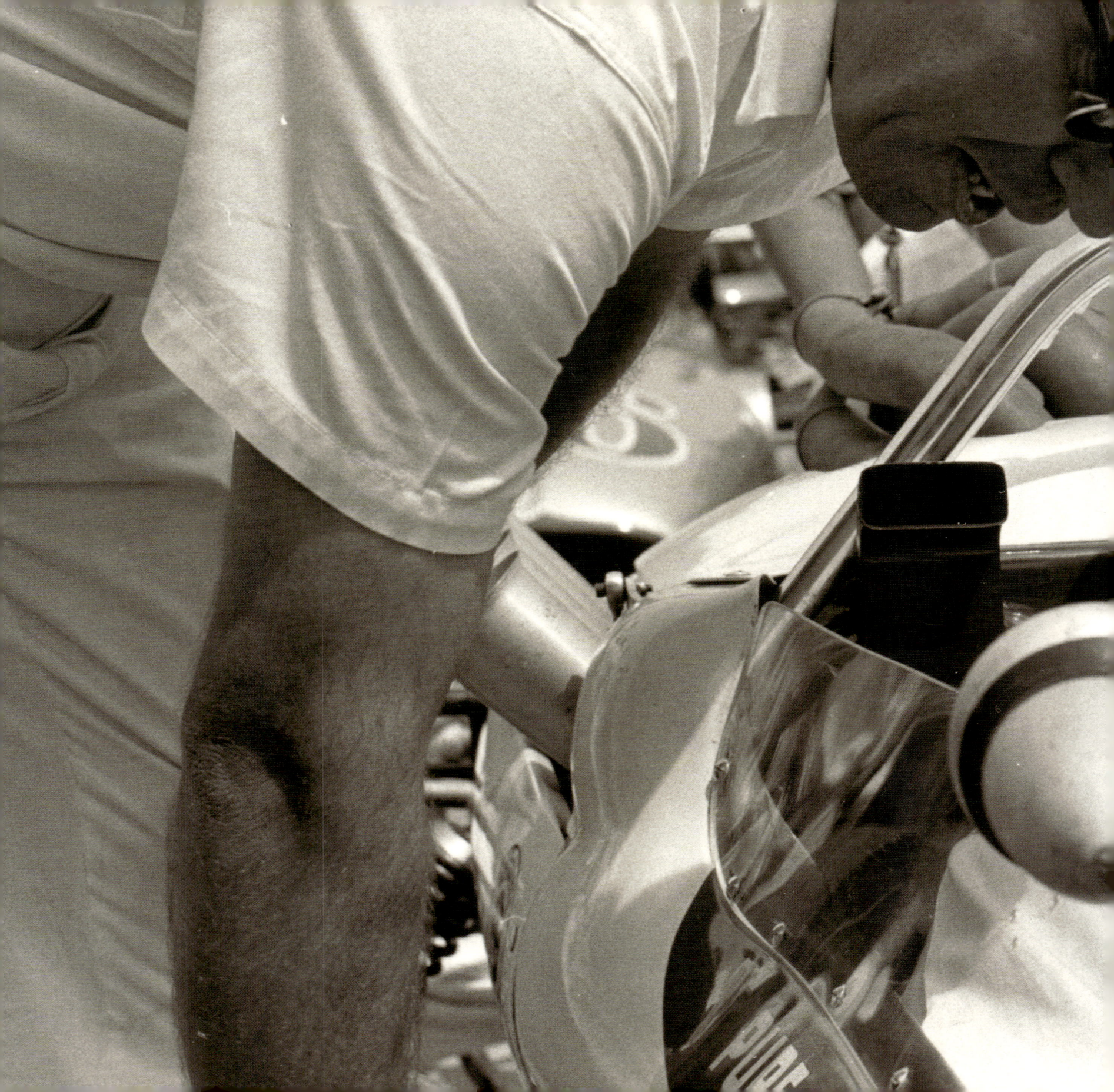

PART 5 / THE MAN TO BEAT

Chapter 74
Testing, Testing . . . (1963)

n 1963, the Lotus 29 encompassed the groundbreaking features that had the racing fraternity spinning. With the 500 so nearly won, Ford and Lotus continued to forge ahead with new developments, all aimed at conquering the Brickyard in 1964.

Bobby racked up enormous mileage totals, testing experimental engines for Ford through November and December of 1963, and into the following year. With continual refinements, the Lotus 29–derived test mule evolved into the Lotus 34. Although it was team drivers Jim Clark and Dan Gurney who would eventually race the Lotus 34s in the Speedway showdown, it was Bobby's driving acumen and intuitive knowledge of racing cars that were crucial in the 34's development process.

Ford was pleased, as reported in February by *Los Angeles Times* auto editor Bob Thomas. One official in Dearborn told Thomas that the company was very satisfied with the engine test results from Bobby's runs at Kingman, Arizona. The *Indianapolis Star*'s Jep Cadou Jr. had already reported that Bob tested the Lotus-Ford "in December at the Kingman [Arizona] Proving Grounds at more than 190 miles an hour."

In the test program, Hopkins's crew chief Jack Beckley also displayed his mechanical skills alongside Bobby in developing the new-to-them machine. At the start, according to Leo Levine in *Ford: The Dust and the Glory*, Bobby knew little about driving a rear-engine car, and Beckley had little idea how to set one up. As testing progressed, Levine wrote, "Everyone got the hang of it. Marshman learned how to make the car go quickly, Beckley found out what to do with the camber, the castor, and complicated plumbing, and the engineers kept producing more power."

Bobby's intensive test sessions with Lotus and Ford were a compliment to his skill and to his status as a top-notch American driver, but they were also a welcome opportunity on behalf of his own racing future. For the entire 1963 season, Bobby had campaigned for Lindsey Hopkins in a front-engine roadster. However, by the time Memorial Day 1964 came into focus, he would have thousands of miles of seat time in the rear-engine Lotus-Ford, the very car that was leading the future.

Bobby also tested for Firestone in front-engine roadsters in the closing months of 1963. As late as December, the stalwart team of Bobby, Rodger Ward, and Chuck Hulse braved chilling Speedway conditions to demonstrate surpassing speeds for the company. On December 19, a Franklin, Indiana, *Daily Journal* photo showed the three gutsy veterans wearing fearsome mask-like gear for protection

PREVIOUS PAGES: Bobby in the pits at Indianapolis with Jack Beckley. (MARSHMAN FAMILY COLLECTION)

from the unforgiving winds that chased them as they whipped around the Speedway.

ABOVE: In 1963 and '64, Bobby did plenty of tire and engine testing for Lotus and Ford. (RMA)

With testing demands, frequent travel was a fact of life at Bobby's professional level, even when race season ended. He also enjoyed time at home with Janet and their precocious three-year-old son, settling into their new Fagleysville house.

"When Bob would call us from a test track, he'd say, 'Tell Robbie we're going to clean the garage when I get home,'" recalled Janet. "Bob was meticulous, and the garage was brand-new, so there wasn't really anything to clean. That was just something he enjoyed, and he wanted to share it with Robbie."

The move to the new house was a pleasant adjustment all around for the young family. In fact, movement and adjustment seemed to be everywhere in Bobby's world. The world of speed had witnessed a year of undeniable change in 1963, and the speed of change would only increase in the coming year, with Bobby helping to set the pace as a key player in the evolution of rear-engine racers.

Chapter 75
"A Truly Illustrious URC Graduate" (1964)

As 1964 began, Bobby Marshman was already a key figure in his sport. And as the year progressed, Bobby stood out even more, becoming the first driver to claim rear-engine technology for America's dirt-trained oval race drivers.

Bobby's 1964 calendar reflected the life of a successful professional driver, with over three dozen races planned for all four seasons—including Memorial Day at the Speedway. He was also committed to miles of test drives for the racing industry's leading innovators.

Bob was also a popular presence at race-related events throughout the year. On January 11, he took part in the sixteenth annual URC banquet as one of the presenters of the 1963 season awards, along with his father George and other prominent racing personalities. A record crowd attended the Saturday night affair at the Stacy-Trent Hotel in Trenton, New Jersey.

Reporting on the event for *Illustrated Speedway News*, Nat Kleinfield noted that Jim Maguire was handed his 1963 URC Championship Trophy "by a truly illustrious URC graduate, Bobby Marshman, now an Indianapolis great as everyone knows." Kleinfield added that "Marshman's little talk in presenting Jim with the URC trophy was excellent in crediting the Club with his [Bobby's] development in the earlier years."

Four days later, Bobby was a featured guest—along with Rodger Ward, Jim McElreath, and Chuck Hulse—at a Firestone presentation in the Los Angeles Statler-Hilton, where president

Leonard Firestone unveiled the company's new, wider tire designed for the demands of the Indy 500. Firestone claimed the new product would make the distance on only one pit stop and pump up speeds by five miles an hour. The new tire was approximately 1.5 inches wider, with a softer compound and lighter body construction, than the tire used by Parnelli Jones in his 1963 Speedway victory. Reporting on the LA fete in the *Indianapolis Star*, Jep Cadou Jr. wrote, "Firestone hopes with its well-publicized unveiling of its new tire to avoid any repetition of the misunderstanding and controversy over the 15-inch tires that occurred last May. The tires were designed for the lightweight, rear-engine cars, but operators of the conventional roadsters protested they hadn't been informed of the new tire."

There was no shortage of public information this time. At Firestone's buffet dinner, the four Indy veterans shared their experiences with the new product with 200-plus members of the racing community and press. The drivers had collectively put in more than seven thousand test miles developing the tire, at IMS as well as at the Trenton State Fairgrounds Speedway and Firestone's Fort Stockton, Texas, test track. During the IMS tests, Bobby had delivered the fastest turn speeds, charging through the corners of the Speedway at more than 150 mph. "Marshman described the new tires simply as 'fantastic,'" added the *Star*'s Cadou.

January was much more than banquets and dinners for Bobby. He was also continuing test programs at Ford's Arizona Proving Ground in Kingman, working closely with Lotus lead mechanics David Lazenby and Colin Riley. Andrew Ferguson recalled in *Team Lotus* that "Lazenby found Bobby a quiet and reserved character . . . and very likeable."

Chapter 76
Winter Travails Under Sunny Skies (1964)

Test drives were a welcome sideline for professional drivers, augmenting incomes and track time. "Bob kept a record of his hours and other expenses, and I'd end up doing the billing," Janet said. "He tested pretty much year-round."

Janet recollected one test gig in early 1964 that proved to be an exercise in frustration. "In January, Ford sent Bob and three or four other drivers to Mexico City, with Speedway cars," related Janet. "The plan was to shake 'em down on a track there. But they never got the cars in because the Mexican government would not guarantee Ford that the cars would get out. Bob was staying in a room with a bare lightbulb on a long cord hanging down from the ceiling, not exactly first-class accommodations." She recalled that Bob and the other drivers were stuck in Mexico City for weeks while Ford and the Mexican government negotiated.

Adding to the frustration, Bobby's first drive in the Daytona 500 was on the horizon, with the opening phase of competition scheduled for February 8. Bobby waited unhappily in Mexico City for the resolution of a situation outside of his control, and was eager to get to Florida.

"Bob didn't know when he'd get back from Mexico, so I drove his mother, Evelyn, and Robbie to Florida to meet him there," Janet said. (The timing was close, Janet recalled, but Bob made it to the February 8 race.) "After the race, Bob drove home with us.

"We all stayed in a motel in Ormond Beach," Janet continued. "This was Bob's idea and it was fine with us. All the other drivers were in Daytona, but Bob didn't want to stay with everybody else. He liked all the guys, but not so much collectively, because he often found that someone would get hurt when things got a bit carried away. Bob figured it would be too wild in Daytona."

For the Daytona International Speedway races, Bob had been lined up since early January to drive a Ford Galaxie for Holman-Moody. Bobby's car sported the HM logo, as did the cars of Fireball Roberts, Freddy Lorenzen, and Larry Frank.

Despite the predominance of Fords in the starting field, Plymouths and Dodges were the sensation of Speedweeks at Daytona Beach in February 1964. Roughly six months after Chrysler had publically disavowed its Automobile Manufacturers Association pledge to stay out of racing, the company's cars were not only on the track, but were leading the pack at record-breaking speeds, topping 171 mph. Directing the impressive Chrysler offensive was Ron Householder, a former Indy driver, who now headed the factory team of Plymouths and Dodges.

The February 8 NASCAR Grand National race was a fifty-mile non-championship event that determined the pole position for the second 100-mile qualifying race on February 21. Bobby finished sixth, with Richard Petty claiming first in a 1964 Plymouth, a prelude of things to come.

On February 21, two 100-mile qualifying races on the Speedway's 2.5-mile paved tri-oval set the stage for the Daytona 500, with Plymouths and Dodges sweeping the first three finishing slots in both races. In the first race, Junior Johnson was number one in a 1964 Dodge; in the second race, fellow Dodge pilot Bobby Isaac was the victor in a three-car photo finish of Chrysler products. Bobby Marshman started seventh in race two, and finished eighth.

The February 23 Daytona 500 marked the sixth annual 200-lap NASCAR Grand National race. Fans cheered Richard Petty, son of the first Daytona 500 winner, Lee Petty, to victory at a record-breaking average speed of 154.334 mph. Twenty-six-year-old Richard Petty led a Plymouth

sweep of the top three places, with Jimmy Pardue second and Paul Goldsmith, third. Petty the younger went on to claim seven Daytona 500 wins along with seven NASCAR championships.

It was a disappointing day for Bobby, who suffered a mishap when a newspaper flew out of the stands and blocked his radiator, causing the engine to overheat and putting him out of the race after completing seventeen laps. He placed thirty-fifth after a sixteenth-place start. Hard luck also plagued fellow Indy drivers A. J. Foyt, Parnelli Jones, Jim McElreath, and Johnny Rutherford, who all suffered mechanical woes or crashes, including a spectacular—and injury-free—flip on the backstretch by Rutherford when he collided with Ned Jarrett. Out of seven Indy competitors, only Goldsmith (third) and Dan Gurney (fourteenth) finished the race. Bobby's fellow Holman-Moody pilots had mixed results: Frank did well, starting fourteenth and finishing eighth; Lorenzen was out on lap 50 with engine troubles; and Roberts was out on lap 14 with transmission problems.

Chapter 77
Successes and Mishaps (1964)

On March 3, the *Pottstown Mercury* alerted its local readers to Bobby's front-cover status on *Cars: The Automotive Magazine*. The photo showed a smiling Bobby in the cockpit of the Lotus-Ford test car with the new double overhead cam (DOHC) engine fitted behind him. Also strapped to the car was a plain gray metal toolbox containing the data acquisition equipment. Inside *Cars*, a feature article by Roger Huntington gave a detailed breakdown of Ford's new powerplant.

March 22 marked an early opener for the 1964 USAC championship season, and also marked the first professional race on the newly built Phoenix International Raceway with its beautiful mountain and desert vistas. The one-mile paved oval replaced the old dirt fairground track, where conditions had been protested and criticized in the past.

Track officials reported attendance at 12,450 for the debut event. The spectators braved blustery weather, with 35-mph winds blowing desert sand across the track and tumbleweeds over the grounds. Bobby, piloting the Epperly roadster for Hopkins, started thirteenth and by lap 57, was up to sixth position. Later, when his rear tire was bumped by Bobby Unser, it was Unser who was out of the game after completing seventy-two laps. Marshman held on to finish seventh. Driving the Sheraton-Thompson Special, A. J. Foyt was the victor, giving Goodyear its first win in USAC championship racing.

The first USAC sprint car race of the season was held one week later at Pennsylvania's Reading Fairgrounds, with A. J. Foyt once again the victor, winning the thirty-lap feature with half a lap over Jim Maguire in second. The March 29 event was marked by multiple accidents. Defending national sprint car champ Roger McCluskey ran into trouble on his second qualifying lap, when his car spun and flipped end over end, sending him to Reading Community Hospital with a concussion and compound fractures. In the feature, Don Branson, Jim Hurtubise, and Bob Harkey were injured in separate incidents by flying dirt and rocks, but only Branson was hospitalized, causing speculation over whether he and McCluskey would recover for Indy competition in May. On the fourteenth lap of the Reading feature, Bobby attempted to come in low to pass on the third turn, and crashed through the wooden retaining fence. He escaped with bruises, and the accident put him out of the race. He had started tenth after winning one of the heat races earlier in the day.

Throughout March, the racing world's tire competition revved up in anticipation of Memorial Day. Goodyear and Firestone were the chief powerhouses, and though Bobby was primarily a Firestone man, he test-drove for both companies at the Speedway and other testing grounds. Dunlop, looking to Indiana from across the Pond, was also a competitor for race performance notice, as was Sears, supplying Sears Allstate tires exclusively to Mickey Thompson.

At the Speedway, March snowstorms and extreme winds were a challenge to car owners, mechanics, and drivers taking part in a wide range of test programs, as well as to the track's snowplow crew. Powerful wind gusts caused the first accident mid-month, when Don Branson slid into the infield on the southwest turn and struck a steel post, severely damaging his new rear-engine racer, built by A. J. Watson. Fortunately, Branson was not injured. There was heartbreak for the popular Novis when a March 31 fire in Gasoline Alley caused extensive damage to the two cars, one of which had arrived from England only days before. Undaunted, owner Andy Granatelli kept his focus on May 30, and had the cars flown to Santa Monica, California, for repairs.

Bad luck and fickle weather did not overshadow accomplishments at the Brickyard, and track speeds were noteworthy. Bobby made headlines when he pushed the Lotus-Ford past the 153-mph mark on March 23, the day after the Phoenix race. Len Sutton held the record for the month, at 154.9 mph in the Bryant Heating and Cooling Special.

During this period, engine debates were as heated as the tire wars. The rear-engine versus front-engine argument was still the hot topic wherever speed sport enthusiasts gathered. Recently dismissed and even denigrated, rear-engine machines now not only dominated conversations but, increasingly, influenced car preparation. A wide range of new rear-engine designs were emerging for the 1964 Brickyard showdown, and would eventually account for twenty-four of the sixty-one entries. In addition, many Offy-powered front-engine racers were shedding weight: Their builders sought ways to change from steel to aluminum and other relatively light metals, looking at brake rotors, crankshafts, and various components. The indisputable advantages of the lighter "funny cars" had not gone unnoticed.

Ford continued to hold sway as the rear-engine leader, and exercised tight control in distributing its new DOHC V8 engine to Indy 500 competitors. Only Team Lotus, with drivers Jim Clark and Dan Gurney, would have Ford support. But Ford selected a few teams to receive the new engine on loan. In addition to Clark and Gurney, the drivers who ultimately lined up on the

'64 Brickyard starting grid with the new DOHC V8 engine were: Bobby for Lindsey Hopkins; Rodger Ward for Wilke-Watson; Eddie Sachs for DVS; and Eddie Johnson and Dave MacDonald for Mickey Thompson. The groundbreaking Ford engine came with strict terms from Dearborn. One directive stated that all mechanical work on the DOHC V8 engine must be done exclusively by Ford's Engine and Foundry division, and by no one else. (This particular demand proved to be a hot button come May.)

In the fall of 1963, Hopkins had purchased a Lotus 29 for Bobby to drive, by most accounts the Lotus 29/2, the same car Dan Gurney put out of action in his practice run crash at the Speedway on Pole Day morning, May 1963. The majority of commentators have agreed with Leo Levine, who wrote in *Ford: The Dust and the Glory*, that Ford sold Hopkins "one of the 1963 cars (actually the one Gurney crashed just before qualifying, now rebuilt). This was not only to be used for racing in 1964, but was also to serve as a mobile test bed for engine development through the fall and winter months."

In *Team Lotus*, Andrew Ferguson questioned the consensus that Bobby's car was the 29/2, and at the same time, acknowledged Lotus's—and the era's—lack of detailed records. Ultimately, Ferguson noted that the number designation for Bobby's Lotus "remains uncertain," adding that "the Ford test vehicle, whether run by Ford or by Hopkins, could have been any one of the three existing Type 29 chassis." What is clearly on record is that the three Team Lotus chassis for the 1963 Indy 500 were the Lotus 29/1, the Lotus 29/2, and the Lotus 29/3. For the 1963 race, Jim Clark drove the Lotus 29/3, and Dan Gurney raced the Lotus 29/1 after crashing the Lotus 29/2 during practice and relegating the damaged car to the sidelines for that year's race.

Whichever Lotus 29 became Bobby's car, he was undisputedly the driver who worked with Ford and Lotus to develop the new engine that was currently so in demand. And now his car would have its own Ford V8. Jack Beckley was in charge of modifying the Lotus 29 chassis in the Hopkins

stable to accommodate the hot new powerplant. Ford shipped the engine to Hopkins on February 20. Hopkins signed with Pure Oil to run its petroleum products, and Bobby's red-on-white Pure Firebird Special was on its way to becoming a reality. It was a beautiful car, but one that proved to be unreliable—consistent only in presenting Bob with problems throughout the 1964 season.

Despite the allure of rear-engine technology, the front-loaded Offy was still a formidable contender, revered not just out of sentiment, but for its power and reliability. With this in mind, as May 30 drew closer, the top teams hedged their bets by providing both a rear-engine racer and a conventional roadster for their drivers, allowing them to make the final choice for the 500. In the Hopkins stable, Bobby would be able to select from either the rear-engine Lotus 29 or the Hopkins roadster he drove in 1963.

When Memorial Day came, twelve rear-engine racers and twenty-one front-engine cars lined up on the 1964 Indy starting grid.

Chapter 78
Pre-Indy Spring Fever (1964)

As was customary, the Speedway closed for the month of April for repairs. However, Indy speculation remained wide open. Nearly every race and test result in April was viewed through the lens of the big race to come.

At this point, the Firestone–Goodyear rivalry only intensified, and the companies' aggressive test programs were setting new records. On April 4, while testing for Firestone at Trenton International Speedway, Bobby was unofficially timed at 31.94 seconds (112.711 mph). This was a significant—and much noted—chip off the official track record of 32.92 seconds (109.356 mph) set by Jimmy Clark the previous fall. Bobby was driving the rear-engine Watson-Offy, subbing for the injured Don Branson.

The next day, April 5, the first USAC Midwestern sprint car race of the season kicked off at Eldora Speedway in Rossburg, Ohio. Bobby made an exceptional showing on the half-mile dirt track, finishing second in the McDermott Special. Johnny Rutherfold took first in the thirty-lap event, driving the Key Enterprise Chevy, and Chuck Hulse was third in the Fike Plumbing Special. The drama of the afternoon's action included four accidents, but fortunately, the drivers suffered only cuts and bruises.

For the April 12 Williams Grove USAC sprint car race, the *Lebanon Daily News* named A. J. Foyt as the man to beat, but noted that "the opposition will come from such fine Eastern stars as Jim Hurtubise, Bobby Marshman, Jimmy Maguire, and Mario Andretti." In qualifying, however, Bobby timed twentieth in his Woodies Chevy, missing the fourteen-car field. Foyt in his Chevy won the thirty-lap feature over Johnny White, Jimmy Maguire, and Jud Larson.

BELOW: The start at Trenton in April, with Foyt and Hurtubise on the front row and Bobby on the inside of the second row, aboard Hopkins's Epperly roadster. (RMA/CHERNOKAL)

With Indy already in mind, sportswriter Joe Hendrickson asked 1957 winner Sam Hanks for his prediction, and reported in the April 17 *Pasadena Independent*: "Hanks believes the champion will come from six big names—Jones, Clark, A. J. Foyt, Rodger Ward, Sachs, and Bobby Marshman. While Clark will go with the new Ford creation, Marshman will stick with the machine that Clark pioneered last year in the tight duel with Jones."

On April 19, Bobby piloted the Hopkins Special to an excellent third place in the 100-mile USAC championship event at Trenton International Speedway, the second race of the season on the Championship Trail. A. J. Foyt claimed victory, and the only drivers finishing on the lead lap with him were Jim Hurtubise in second and Bobby right behind him. Bobby had his choice between the Epperly-Offy and the Lotus, and in the end drove the roadster.

The Trenton race was thwarted by a downpour on the thirty-ninth mile, forcing a two-hour halt. After the restart amid showers, Bobby thrilled the crowd as he chased Lloyd Ruby, and once past him,

went after Chuck Hulse. In *Roar from the Sixties*, Dick Wallen described Bobby's race as "spectacular." Wallen wrote: "[Bobby] couldn't get a good shot at the Dean Van Lines chauffeur [Hulse], however, until they came up to Bob Harkey and Norm Hall on the fifty-ninth lap. Without blinking, the Pride of Pottstown took all three and put the two lapped cars between him and Hulse. It wasn't the last time he would make such a move."

Also of note at Trenton that weekend, Mario Andretti made his championship debut in Doug Stearly's Elder roadster. It was rumored that if Bobby chose to race the Lotus, Mario might drive the Hopkins roadster, but this did not come to be.

Meanwhile, back at the Speedway, April track improvements to the tune of approximately $600,000 were on schedule for May activities. Changes included eighteen thousand new grandstand seats, a thirty-four-by-sixty-seven-foot scoreboard, a three-lane vehicle tunnel for easing traffic flow in and out of the infield, and extensive new fencing geared toward spectator safety. New buildings were also under construction in Gasoline Alley.

In addition, elaborate preparations were underway to enable the advent of live, closed-circuit TV viewing for the 1964 race, via pay television in 160 theaters nationwide. Jay Michaels of MCA-TV directed the necessary track installations, including eighty-seven miles of cable and twelve camera

257

stations. Michaels told the *Indianapolis Star*'s Jep Cadou Jr. that he expected to have a 100-plus telecast crew on hand, featuring TV sportscasters Charlie Brockman and Bernie Herman, as well as Indy insider (and 1957 winner) Sam Hanks. The venues for the telecast would range from the 16,000-seat Los Angeles Sports Arena to smaller theaters across the country. Many racing personalities were involved in the closed-circuit viewing enterprise, with J. C. Agajanian holding the most franchises, in major cities throughout California. Bobby Unser and Len Sutton were on board with franchises in the Southwest and the Pacific Northwest, respectively. Bobby Marshman and his father George shared four franchises in Pennsylvania and New York State.

Bobby did his part to get the word out for the telecast. In the May 21 *Democrat and Chronicle*, George Beahon wrote: "The note at the desk said Bobby Marshman would be in Rochester later this week to meet the press. Obviously, the reason would be to help promote the first closed-circuit (MCA) telecast of the Indianapolis '500' at the War Memorial on Memorial Day. I'm out in front on this one, because it was my distinct pleasure to meet Marshman at what used to be the old 'brickyard' about a year ago. . . . Marshman, a friendly, then 24-year-old crewcut, had just finished a test spin around the track. . . . He stopped to talk at length and seriously with another driver, then went to the other's car for an extended conference about something inside the other's machine. When he finished I asked whether he had been helping the other? Answer affirmative. Then I wondered out loud why he or any other driver would go to such [an] extent to assist the opposition. He had a pretty decent answer: 'When someone gets in trouble out there, it could involve anyone and everyone. The less trouble, to anyone, the less risk to yourself. Furthermore, a relaxed driver is a safe driver. If a guy is happy and friendly out on the track, he isn't likely to look for any trouble. I want every man and car out there to be trouble-free.'"

Chapter 79
Wrangling a Rattler (1964)

On April 16, three days before the Trenton championship race, Bob set another unofficial track record, this time clocking 30.355 seconds at the Phoenix International Raceway in a Lotus-Ford test car. (His own Lotus-Ford was being readied for Speedway practice in May.) There was added excitement during the testing, as reported by Jep Cadou Jr. in the *Indianapolis Star*: "On his last lap there, Marshman ran over a four-foot-long diamondback rattlesnake with eleven rattles which was lying coiled up in the 'groove' of the track."

Rattlesnakes were an ongoing challenge at the Arizona test site, Janet recalled. "Bob wasn't worried about snakes, but the drivers did have to be careful," she explained. "If you have front wheels without fenders like the race cars were built, and if you hit one of those snakes with a front wheel, you'll throw it into the cockpit."

Bob had his own method for dealing with the problem, Janet added.

"One time, Bob saw a six- or eight-footer," she recalled. "He went down the track and had to skid, almost, in order to miss the snake with the front, and then he had to bring the back around again to run over it. That was his whole idea: He didn't want to hit the snake with the front; he wanted to hit it with the back, and he did it. He cut the rattles off—there were ten—and brought them home for Robbie. I still have them in a jar."

Not every drive that spring hit the mark for Bob. In the 150-mile USAC stock car race at Langhorne Speedway on April 26, he qualified eighth and finished eighteenth, driving a 1963 Ford. Recent heavy rains had left the track in poor condition, with excessive dust and poor visibility, and only nine cars from the nineteen-car field finished. Jim Hurtubise was the winner, ahead of Norm Nelson in second, and Herb Shannon in third, with all three driving 1964 Plymouths.

The April 26 contest was Bobby's first USAC stock car race. The week before, the *Pottstown Mercury* reported: "Bobby Marshman, Pottstown's contribution to the popular auto racing sport, tries on a 'new shirt' next Sunday at the Langhorne speedway. Marshman, who at 27 is already established in Indianapolis, sprint, and midget mounts, will try his hand at late-model stocks."

In the Yankee "300" at Indianapolis Raceway Park, his last race before the Indy 500, Bobby finished eleventh, driving a 1963 Ford owned by Rudy Hoerr of Illinois. The May 3 USAC stock car race was won by Fred Lorenzen, with Parnelli Jones in second after leading for 97 of the race's 120 laps. In a pre-race promotion, Bobby, Gary Bettenhausen, Troy Ruttman, and Curtis Turner spent two evenings making personal appearances at separate auto dealerships, where they handed out free autographed photos. Bobby did his stint at the Bob Phillips West Side Ford dealership.

At this point, Bobby, Janet, and Robbie had moved into their Indianapolis apartment for the season, May through October. "We were in the same apartment as the year before," Janet said. "The owner kept it open for us, and we were surrounded by friends, people we knew."

Before they left Pennsylvania for Indiana, the wholesome young family was photographed on the porch of their new Fagleysville home for an article that ran in the Sunday, May 10, *Philadelphia Inquirer Magazine*. The picture of Bobby, Janet, and Robbie—as well as a photo of Bobby in his Lotus 29—illustrated a full-page feature by Robert Salgado, an *Inquirer* staff writer and photographer. Salgado covered Bobby's racing heritage, his fast-paced racing career, and his upcoming drive in the 1964 Indy 500.

At the end of the article, Salgado wrote: "Bobby's petite blonde wife, Janet, is not as calm about her husband's profession, but she has accepted it as something he wants to do. . . . Whenever she can, she watches him race. . . . 'I don't like not to go to the track,' said Mrs. Marshman, a former schoolteacher. 'You worry more if you don't watch.'"

Chapter 80
"Lead-Foot Bobby Marshman" (1964)

On a sunny May 1, 1964, the Speedway opened for official practice. For the first two days, Henry Banks, USAC director of competition, imposed a 145-mph speed limit, but the pace to come would soon best all previous trials.

Ever-increasing speeds marked the entire month. New tire compounds and engine technologies honed over the past months contributed to the miles-per-hour leaps from the year before, but tires were probably the biggest factor behind the enhanced speeds. The size change was visible, progressing from tall tires in 1962, to the wider tires that had been a bone of contention in 1963, to Firestone's still-wider tire iteration of 1964. The new tire was broader and stockier in profile, a full inch and a half wider than in previous years.

All of these changes added up to a measurable difference in speed: The final starting field on the 1964 Indy grid boasted an average speed of 152.571 mph, compared to 1963's qualifying average of 149.033. Nearly all were on the new Firestones.

But in early May, the fierce competition was just beginning to take shape, with sixty-one entrants signed on to make their bid for a grid spot.

The first day of practice, Len Sutton beat out Eddie Sachs as the number one driver to roar down the track. Jim McElreath was fastest, at 145.2 mph in the Novi-Ferguson, one of the cars damaged in the March garage fire. On May 6, A. J. Foyt pulled off the fastest unofficial lap ever, at 154.189 mph, in his Sheraton-Thompson Special, but he was still undecided about whether to choose the front-engine Offy over his rear-engine option. The same day saw the month's first accident when Jim Hurtubise crashed and hit the wall, skidding over 1,500 feet. He escaped serious injury, but faced extensive damage to his car, the DVS Tombstone Life Special, which he and his brother Pete had built over the winter.

On May 7, tire company rivalry played out between A. J. Foyt on Goodyears and Parnelli Jones on Firestones, with Jones setting a new unofficial Speedway record of 156.233 mph in his roadster, called "Ol' Calhoun." The next day, Goodyear's main man was wooed away by the faster speeds of the competition's tires: On May 8, A. J. officially switched to Firestones on his front-engine racer, probably the most publicized tire change in history. The remaining entrants on Goodyear tires followed Foyt's example, pushing Firestone into dominance on the track. Goodyear returned to Akron, and A. J., who had almost single-handedly brought the tire company back into Indy racing, expressed his long-term association by continuing to wear his Goodyear driving suit.

Jep Cadou Jr. of the *Indianapolis Star* devoted his entire May 8 column to "blond haired, blue eyed Bobby," as he described him. Bobby told Cadou it was ten to one that he would choose the Lotus 29 over the lay-down roadster in the Hopkins garage. "I was pretty well sold on the Lotus-Ford before

Hot-Line Hot-Dog

Bullet-Bobby Marshman

coming to the track," Bobby said. "That Ford engine is going to do a fantastic job in both performance and durability. I tested on one Ford engine for almost 3,000 miles."

While fans were reading the story, Bobby was busy making headlines for the next day's *Star*, which shouted across the top of the page: MARSHMAN CLOCKS 153.5 IN FORD. Indeed, Bobby's May 8 run was the fastest lap ever by a Lotus-Ford on the Speedway, despite wind gusts up to 28 mph. With this speed, Bobby not only outpaced Jim Clark's 149.750-mph record lap in a Lotus from the year before, but also topped Parnelli Jones's 1963 race lap record of 151.541 mph. The head of Ford's racing effort, Dave Evans, came to the garage immediately after the speed display to congratulate him. Bobby told the *Star*'s Cadou: "We're very happy the way things are going. When qualifying starts, we'll be there."

"Lead-foot Bobby Marshman" again scored a banner headline in the *Star*, this time for gunning the fastest speed for Saturday, May 9, when he hit 152.5 mph. Conditions were reportedly too windy

for true top speeds. Pedro Rodríguez struck bad luck the same day in a flaming crash, hitting the wall in his rear-engine MG-Liquid Suspension Special at 145 mph. He was hospitalized, and although not seriously injured, was sidelined from the race. The same weekend, Parnelli declared his choice: "Ol' Calhoun" would be his mount on race day. A big score for the front-engine contingent.

When Cadou canvassed drivers for a pole-speed prediction, Bobby forecast 155.2 mph, and A. J. said 156.5 mph. Len Sutton said 157.7 mph, and Jim Hurtubise predicted 158 mph, adding, "and it's going to be me." Then on May 12, two days after the story ran, Bobby broke Parnelli's unofficial fastest lap with three laps in a row over 157 mph, with the fastest at 157.178 mph. After that, Bobby upped his prediction, telling the Associated Press, "I feel 158 is possible under ideal conditions." Cadou in the *Star* attributed Bob's new record to a switch from gasoline to alcohol fuel by Beckley.

On the track May 13, Bobby ran the fastest lap, 156.794 mph, once again winning what Cadou called the "steaks race," the daily competition for free dinners. Parnelli ran 154.879 mph before his engine blew. Rodger Ward, who had been over 155 mph earlier in the week, followed suit and blew his Ford. Jim Hurtubise, on the track for the first time since his crash, was soon up to 151.5 mph. Dan Gurney and Jim Clark were back from Europe. Gurney was dealing with injuries he had suffered at Monaco, and despite limping on a badly burned left leg, still turned laps at over 153 mph. Clark, on the other hand, had a gearbox blow up when he headed out for practice. Both drivers were piloting the new Lotus 34s.

May 14 was a newsworthy day in many ways. Bob once again fired up the crowd as the day's fastest man at 156.822 mph, and A. J. was close behind Bobby, at 156.2 mph. The same day, A. J. chose his roadster, which he affectionately called "Old Betsy," for his May 30 drive—more cause for celebration among Offy devotees. In addition, there was "jubilation in the Lotus-Ford factory garages," according to the *Star*, when Clark and Gurney both got up to qualifying speeds. Jim did a lap at 155.4 mph, and Dan, at 154.75.

The next day, the track sizzled with speed. On May 15, Bobby set an all-time practice record of 158.758 mph in No. 51, and Parnelli hit 158.298 mph in No. 98.

Saturday, May 16, was the first day of qualifying. It was a first-in-line, first-to-go system. Chief steward Harlan Fengler reminded teams that crews could start lining up at the entrance on Friday evening, half an hour after the close of the track, to claim a spot in the qualifying order. Colin Chapman was shouted down when he suggested that cars with the fastest practice times get prime qualifying spots. Some drivers urged a drawing to determine placement, but despite these feisty suggestions, the traditional system stood. At least for 1964. A bit of rowdiness among the crews at the entrance gate convinced Fengler that it was time to consider a more-dignified system for the future.

Chapter 81
160.085 on the Electric Eye (1964)

Fan interest was unprecedented. On May 16, Pole Day, over 250,000 people filled the stands—not only the largest crowd ever for qualifications, but a larger crowd than any race day. Safety director Joseph Quinn was prepared, with 1,100 safety patrolmen on hand in addition to over 400 state, county, and city police to help direct traffic.

Twenty-seven-year-old Bobby Marshman was a star player during the intense, speed-obsessed weeks of May, captivating onlookers and the press alike. Indeed, there were other stars and a colorful supporting cast as drama unfolded on the track in anticipation of Memorial Day. But Bobby was increasingly the crowd favorite. It wasn't hype that captured their imaginations. It was action—namely, his consistent high-speed runs throughout practice.

A May 16 *Indianapolis Star* headline shouted 3 FAVORED IN POLE BATTLE, with Bobby's photo topping the page under the banner "The Challenger" and a photo of "The Champion" Parnelli Jones directly underneath. A. J. Foyt rounded out the trio named by Jep Cadou Jr. and Rick Johnson.

In Cadou's own annual "pole poll," he asked twelve key Indy personalities to name their picks for pole position. Bobby was the favorite, eight to two, since Speedway president Tony Hulman and director of racing Sam Hanks diplomatically declined to vote. Bobby's supporters for pole position represented the inner circle of the 500. From the Speedway: chief steward Harlan Fengler, referee Don Cummins, safety director Joseph Quinn, steward Paul Johnson, and press liaison Bob Laycock. And from the USAC: technical committee chairman Fritz Duesenberg, director of competition Henry Banks, and chief observer Walter Myers. Parnelli scored two ballots, from Speedway publicity director Al Bloemker and from Larry Bisceglia, traditional first fan in line for the race.

During morning practice on the first day of qualifying, Bobby proved what he could do: He set an unofficial lap record of 160.085 mph, caught on the track's electric eye. It was the first lap over 160 mph in Speedway history, and was eagerly trumpeted by the press. The feat had "considerable shock effect," according to Bob Ottum in *Sports Illustrated*. Ottum reported: " 'He did it in . . . *what*?' choked one driver over his coffee and doughnuts in the cafeteria under the grandstands. 'Isn't that just great! This is liable to turn into one hell of a day.' "

Despite so much promise and so much delivery, there was heartache for the popular Pottstown driver and his fans. Winds thwarted Bobby's times later in the day when the official qualifying watches were ticking, and he failed to match his morning speed, the unofficial record. That said, Bob's performance remained outstanding, as he finished with a record-breaking 157.867-mph average. However, later the same day, Jim Clark topped him at 158.828 mph, claiming the pole. Bobby was second on the starting grid, the middle man in the front row.

Bobby's four lap segments were 157.370, 158.117, 157.425, and 158.562, averaging 157.867

mph. Clark's were 158.339, 159.337, 159.179, and 158.423, averaging 158.828 mph. Jim Clark was the first foreign driver to win the pole since René Thomas in 1919.

After qualifying, AP quoted Bobby: "I had quite a bit of trouble with the wind and the front end. I tried a little too hard. But the wind did come up."

UPI reported: "Marshman, a slender 150-pounder from Pottstown, Pa., who at 27 looks more like a college sophomore than a professional, year-round race driver, was the top favorite for the pole position. . . . He was bitterly disappointed when he had to settle for runner-up honors." The report added that Bobby's "disappointing" speed was more than six miles per hour faster than last year's best by Parnelli Jones.

Bobby told UPI: "I feel like I missed the show, even though second spot is a good one. I wanted to win the pole especially for Jack Beckley, my chief mechanic, for whom it also would have meant a lot. Now I'm more determined than ever to win this race, and I think we have a real good chance."

Bobby consistently maintained a positive attitude. During non-driving hours, he sported a red baseball hat with "158" stitched to the front with white embroidery. He told *Sports Illustrated*'s Ottum, "I've already got one made up with 160 mph on it for when I make it official."

There were twenty-one qualifiers after the first weekend of trials, sixteen on the first day and five on the second. Ford V8-powered cars commanded the first three spots with drivers Jim Clark (158.828 mph), Bobby (157.867 mph), and Rodger Ward (156.406 mph), marking the first time in forty years that an Offy did not make the front row of the Indy 500.

In the second row, two front-engine racers were breathing hard against the rear-engine leaders, with Parnelli Jones (155.099 mph) in fourth and A. J. Foyt (154.672 mph) in fifth. Filling out row two, in sixth, was Lotus-Ford pilot Dan Gurney (154.487 mph)—and in this election year of '64, his fans showed their support with DAN GURNEY FOR PRESIDENT lapel buttons and bumper stickers much in evidence.

In row three were Lloyd Ruby (153.932 mph), Len Sutton (153.813 mph), and Don Branson (152.672 mph). Walt Hansgen (152.581 mph) was tenth, in row four, the fastest rookie in the field, and also, at age forty-four, the oldest driver to date to qualify as a rookie. Alongside him on the fourth row were Jim Hurtubise (152.542 mph) and Dick Rathmann (151.860 mph).

Chapter 82
"We Forbid Them to Tear the Engines Down" (1964)

Off-track dramas heightened tensions for both qualifying weekends. For one, Ford's iron-fist control of its engines stirred up some ire on several fronts.

A. J. "Gus" Scussel, manager of Ford's special engine department, explained Ford's perspective to *Sports Illustrated*'s Bob Ottum: "We do not tell these people [the teams] how to run the race; that is their business. We have eight of our new engines down here. We loan them to these people and we take them back and study them when they are through. We forbid—understand that, now—we forbid them to tear the engines down. They are too intricate and there isn't enough time to train mechanics to do the job. If an engine blows up, or collapses, we simply pull it out of the car and install a new one. This program is still new."

Perhaps inevitably, there was some pushback to what some called a "Big Brother" approach.

The *Indianapolis Star* noted resistance in the Hopkins garage. Ford wanted to take Bobby's engine back to "freshen it up" right before the first qualifying day, but "the crew wouldn't give it to them," the *Star*'s George Moore reported. Lindsey Hopkins and his chief mechanic, Jack Beckley, told Ford they preferred to leave the engine alone until after qualifying because the engine was giving no indication of problems, despite having 2,500 miles on it. Beckley explained that the engine had gone 410 miles since it was last overhauled, and that the mileage in part explained why this particular engine was running free. "We don't have much frictional resistance," said Beckley. "With the miles we have on it, the engine is beginning to loosen up, and this is giving us more power."

Bobby's car had been purring along at record speeds in the hard-charging practice weeks, but other Ford engines had not been going as well. The Hopkins team's success rated Beckley and Marshman a front-page photo above the fold in the main edition of the May 16 *Star*.

A few days later, it was a group of Indy race mechanics who were grumbling about Ford. They complained of preferential treatment when the USAC allowed Ford to return several qualified engines to its factory for inspection there rather than subject the engines to the routine teardown and measurement at the track. The reason given was that IMS lacked the necessary equipment needed to inspect the new engines. Director Henry Banks assured competitors that there was no cause for alarm, since the Ford engines were sealed by USAC inspectors before and after measurements were taken at Dearborn, and were accompanied there by USAC technical committee members S. A. Silberman, Fritz Duesenberg, and Jack Brant.

On-track tire woes also caused consternation. Team Lotus had qualified on May 16 on the faster Dunlops, despite a bit of pressure from Ford to go with the greater endurance of the Firestones. Then on May 18, the Dunlops began to throw off rubber after twenty-two laps of testing by Dan Gurney at speeds in the 150-mph range. This mishap was duly noted by USAC officials and other observers, including the press.

The *Indianapolis Star*'s Rick Johnson reported: "Lotus car builder and crew chief Colin Chapman said he was not in the least bothered by the rubber chunking off. 'We have no tire problem,' he said. 'We plan to run the race on one set of tires.' Calmly, Chapman dismissed the incident, and with a wave of his hand, said 'It is normal. Now if you'll excuse me, I want to talk to this chap.'"

When asked if Lotus would be allowed to switch tires for safety reasons, USAC director of racing Henry Banks told the *Star*: "Only if the tires failed completely would we allow that . . . these tires just blistered. They won't be allowed to alter the types of tires or the compound of their tire now. This is set forth clearly in the entry blank." There were no Dunlop officials on hand for comment.

In contrast to the unflappable Chapman and the unwavering Banks, the *Star*'s headline screamed tire trouble may doom clark, gurney. The coming race would tell the tale.

George Moore pointed out in the *Star* that the entire Dunlop operation consisted of four guys working from the back of a rented truck parked at the north end of the garage area. Dunlop's US representative Peter Smith and tire engineer Vic Barlow obtained a wheel balancer, which they mounted in the back of the truck. Dunlop wasn't working with a host of competitors like the American tire companies, but rather, was at the Speedway primarily to support the 4WD Novi because of Dunlop's contracts with the car's builder, Harry Ferguson Research Ltd. (In the end, the entire Granatelli Novi team, including the team's 4WD Ferguson-built Novi, qualified and then raced on Firestones.)

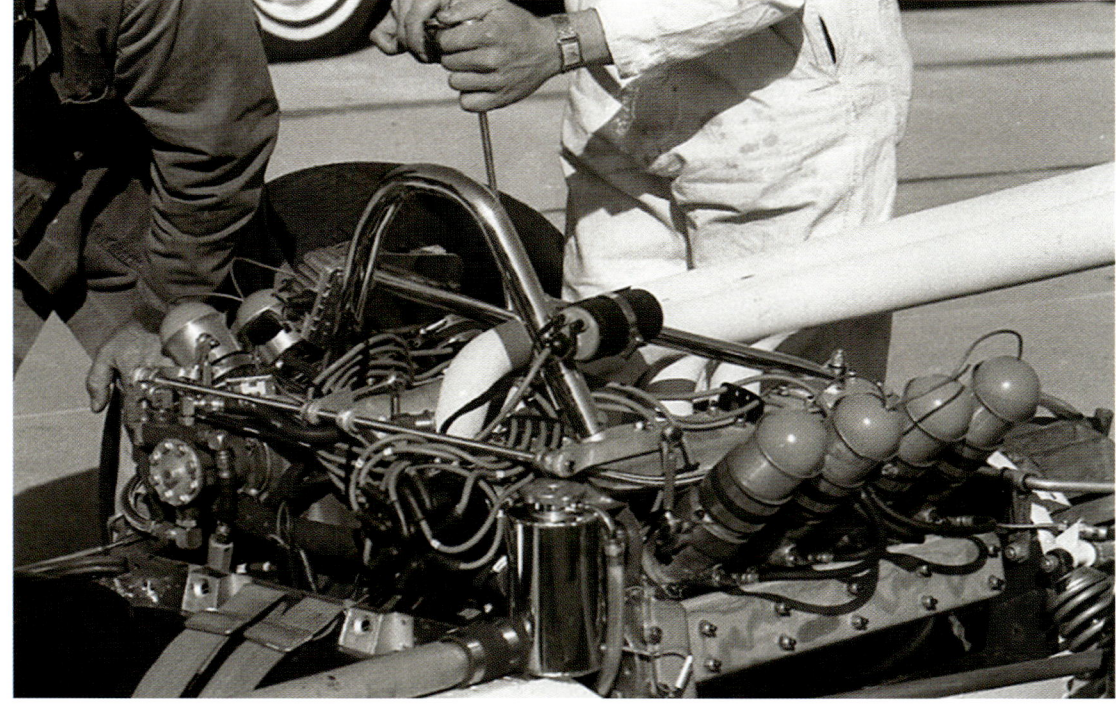

Dunlop did not even have a binding agreement with Lotus.

Indeed, Chapman had almost reversed his confidence in Dunlop only a few days earlier, making his final decision in his own inimitable manner. Close to the first day of qualifying, Chapman was torn between using Firestones or Dunlops, and he instructed Team Lotus competitions manager Andrew Ferguson (no relation to Harry Ferguson) to set up a private meeting with Firestone immediately. Andrew Ferguson went to great lengths to reach the two top racing directors at the tire company, who were in meetings in New York, and they extended themselves in turn, flying directly to Indianapolis in their corporate plane to meet with Chapman that evening.

Minutes before they were due, Ferguson recounted in *Team Lotus*, Chapman told him, "I've changed my mind. I won't need to talk with them now—you deal with it." All too soon, Ferguson said, the two Firestone executives arrived at his motel room door as promised, geared for a game-changing conversation with Chapman. Alone and left holding the proverbial bag, which was now empty, Ferguson wrote, "I fumbled my selected speech and went straight in. 'I'm very sorry, but I'm afraid the meeting is off.' Before I could get any further, both turned and walked away without a word. The sheer discomfort of that occasion has remained with me ever since."

Back on the track, practice continued during the week between qualifying dates. On May 21, Jim Hurtubise, Parnelli Jones, and Bobby ran full-fuel load tests in the 150-mph range, with Bob fastest, at 152.6 mph. He didn't slow down the next day, but again paced the fastest speed, at 155.4 mph.

Meanwhile, corporate sponsors were heralding success. In the May 18 *Indianapolis Star*, Pure Oil ran a one-third-page ad showing Bobby at speed under the headline MARSHMAN QUALIFIES PURE FIREBIRD SPECIAL 157.867 MPH! Later in the month, Marathon ran a dramatic half-page ad in three Indianapolis newspapers that proved to have a more-somber meaning. Over a photo of Eddie Sachs in his American Red Ball Special, the headline read KEEP YOUR EYE ON EDDIE SACHS. HE'S RIDING ON EIGHT GAS TANKS . . . AND THEY'RE *ALL* FILLED WITH MARATHON!

Chapter 83
33 (1964)

Always a high-pressure hustle, the final qualifying weekend of 1964—May 23 and 24—had the added stress of treacherous winds and threats of rain.

On Saturday, Jack Brabham claimed the inside of the ninth row with apparent ease, despite threatening skies, and a series of complications. His initial frustration came on the Speedway's first qualifying weekend: Brabahm had been next up on May 17 when the closing gun went off and officials waved him off the track. More than a slight inconvenience, this near-miss forced him to make additional cross-Atlantic commutes—first, his planned flight between Indiana and Holland in order to qualify for the Dutch Grand Prix, and then an unplanned return flight to Indianapolis from Holland for Indy's final qualifying weekend. On May 23, Brabham made the starting grid with finesse and still maintained his tight race schedule: He was first on the track on Saturday, ready to roar at 11:00 a.m.; by 11:10 a.m. he had qualified at 152.504 mph; in another twenty minutes Brabham was speeding to the airport, with a police escort, to catch his next transatlantic flight, at 12:06 p.m., to Zandvoort for the Dutch Grand Prix on May 24.

At the Speedway, May 24 was the final day of qualifying. On that Sunday, approximately fifty thousand fans cheered as the third Novi made the field when Art Malone qualified at 151.222 mph, despite gusty winds. Bobby Unser and Jim McElreath had already qualified the other two Novis the day before. There was only one bump on the final day, when rookie Bob Wente took out Paul Russo, veteran of fifteen Indy starts.

The lineup was complete. The drivers for the 1964 Indy 500 were proof that records are meant to be broken. Thirty contenders topped the 150-mph mark, and twenty-six qualified faster than the 1963 record set by Jones, at 151.153 mph. The group's average speed was 152.571 mph, making it the fastest field ever to compete in the 500.

There were five days between Sunday's final qualifying and race day on Saturday. At the end of the week, Bobby was picked as the favorite to win the Indy 500 by members of the American Auto Racing Writers and Broadcasters Association at their annual meeting. Bobby received fourteen votes, Jim Clark took ten, Rodger Ward, nine, and A. J. Foyt, seven.

Bobby and Rodger Ward made headlines for their prowess in the final practice session on

Thursday, May 28. In the next day's *Indianapolis Star*, George Moore noted, "The hopes of the Ford Motor Company to win its first 500-mile race are resting squarely on the shoulders of Bobby Marshman. And the Pottstown flyer is being backed up by another Ford product in the hands of Rodger Ward." Bobby had impressed with 157-mph speeds, and Ward had traveled at 155.2 mph the same morning.

Some of the other qualifiers were struggling with mechanical problems before the race, including A. J. Foyt, Jim Clark, and Dan Gurney, whose crews were busy with their cars on the final practice day. In a more-positive development, Norm Hall picked up a sponsor at the final session. His popular "Nothing Special," in which he had qualified thirty-first, would become the Hurst Special.

Troubles or no, race day was about to dawn for the entire field. Eleven rows, three abreast.

Thirty-three men had claimed what were arguably the most sought-after thirty-three positions in the nation that weekend, on that exceedingly selective grid, the Brickyard.

ABOVE: Bobby was selected by the experts as the favorite to win the 1964 500. (FIRST TURN PRODUCTIONS)

Chapter 84
"This Should Be My Year" (1964)

Throughout the spring, Bobby had approached the coming 500 with confidence. As early as mid-April, he told Ed Broomhead of Philadelphia's *Evening Bulletin*: "I have everything going for me. These Ford-Lotus cars are terrific. They have double overhead cams on each side and approximately 430 horsepower. We have had very little trouble with the car in its tests, and if I'm ever to win the Indianapolis race, this should be my year."

In mid-May, Bobby was further quoted about the coming race in Michigan's *Holland Evening Sentinel*. "For me it's flat out from the start all day long," he said. "We are sure we have the dependability and performance of a car that will go all the way at top speed."

Bobby added, "If I had to pick my top rival on race day, it would be [Jim] Clark, who has done a fantastic job and is a real credit to racing. But A. J. Foyt, Parnelli [Jones], and [Rodger] Ward will be right up there too." Bobby also revealed that the team plan was to make just one pit stop at mid-race, for fuel only, adding that they were prepared to change tires if needed.

In the May 25 issue of *Sports Illustrated*, Bob Ottum quoted Bobby: "This will be an all-out speed race. My only strategy is to get ahead and stay there."

In the same article, Ottum referred to Bobby as "Pennsylvania's frail leadfoot." It was an undeserved comment, given Bobby's athleticism and strict training regimen, and the unfairness bugged him. Mild-mannered Bobby dealt with the insult in his own way. Janet recalled that when they next encountered Ottum, at Milwaukee, "Bob shook his hand and gripped it so tight, the man had tears in his eyes. Bob never said a word, but he made his point. It was very subtle." And she added, "The Marshman family has never bought a copy of *Sports Illustrated* since."

Bobby was known for his modest, thoughtful personality.

"He had this quiet strength," Janet said, "but he was absolutely outgoing and welcoming to new people. He treated everyone the same." Friendly and unassuming, Bob was well-liked by his fellow drivers. And the feeling was mutual, according to his longtime friend Bill Reiff, who said, "Bobby liked everybody."

Bob enjoyed exchanging practical jokes with his close friends, Janet recalled. When Johnny Rutherford met a lovely nurse, Betty, who was a member of the Speedway's volunteer medical team, Bobby knew she was the love of his pal's life. At that time, drivers were often stereotyped as Lotharios, and Betty had made sure Rutherford was single before dating him; she had also assured her father of this, since he was quite strict, as Janet recollected. Bobby knew this background, so when Betty brought her parents to the track the first time, Bobby was ready for some good-natured teasing, along with pal Chuck Hulse.

"Bob waited until Johnny was with Betty and her parents," Janet recounted, "and then he got on the PA and tapped on it, and said, 'Johnny Rutherford, Johnny Rutherford, you're wanted at the entrance—your wife and children are here.' Not another word. Johnny wasn't married, of course, but his future in-laws were very staid. Still, they all took it in the spirit of fun. But that was the kind of kidding Bob was known for."

Bobby was also known in the racing community as a colleague who sought out support for drivers and their families when the need arose. In May, for example, Bob and Janet and their good friend, writer and filmmaker Dick Wallen, were working together to organize a movie benefit to help cover medical treatment for Jimmy Maguire. The young driver had lost his right arm when it was severed in an accident during the May 3 USAC sprint race at New Bremen Speedway. A few days before the 500, Bob called *Illustrated Speedway News* publisher Walter Bull to enlist the newspaper's help for the July fund-raising event. Bobby's efforts were later described by Red McCarthy in the *Norristown Times Herald*: "Bobby put in hours and miles traveling the circuit of smaller tracks, asking hat collections for funds that would provide Maguire with an artificial arm and provide his family with the wherewithal until Jim could get physically adjusted again."

Among his many qualities, Bobby was empathetic, he was fun, and he was fast. He was also articulate. Bill Reiff recalled that Bobby was frequently tapped for speaking engagements, sometimes at the last minute.

"There used to be a large Firestone plant on the edge of Pottstown, and when Bobby was in the area, someone would get ahold of him and say, 'You've got to come over to the plant today for lunch,' because some big wheel or another was coming in, so he'd go over and speak during their lunch. He was in demand."

Reiff's recollection is corroborated by Nat Kleinfield, who wrote in his column for *Illustrated Speedway News*, "The last conversation I had with Eddie Sachs, he told me how Bobby was progressing in the art of making luncheon speeches to various groups, how he was getting to be an excellent after-dinner speaker in demand because of his racing success."

Bobby was increasingly sought out by the press. He was often approached as a spokesman for high-speed driving, largely because of his sheer mastery of the sport. But also because he gave thoughtful answers. As Janet put it, "people were catching on that Bob was not just quiet, but also smart."

What's more, Bobby's personal story was the real deal, and people were eager to watch it unfold. Fans reveled in the way he turned possibility into reality: Before their eyes, the 1961 co–Rookie of the Year had moved from his last-row start in his first Indy race to his middle-of-the-front-row slot in 1964, with Indy races both years in between. This clean-cut, small-town boy gave life to the cherished American belief in meritocracy. With guts, grit, and talent, Bobby had become one of the sport's best competitors, a dirt track pilot equal to anyone, in any car, and on any track.

Along with his thirty-two brethren, he was primed and ready for Memorial Day, 1964.

Chapter 85
The 1964 Indianapolis 500

The forty-eighth running of the Indianapolis 500 turned from gaiety to gravity in what seemed like an instant. Those who were there have said they will never forget the long, unnatural silence that settled over the 300,000 fans—the haunting silence, and the horrific black clouds darkening the upper end of the main straightaway, where the worst had happened.

Earlier in the morning, the Speedway was still bright with sunshine and success, with a record crowd, a record purse, and record speeds throughout May. The exuberant annual festivities kicked off, and the spectators exploded with high spirits and great expectations. Taking part were a roster of celebrities, including French actor and singer Maurice Chevalier, television hosts Art Linkletter and Ed Sullivan, orchestra leader Skitch Henderson, actress Marilyn Maxwell, and singer Keely Smith. In the track's traditional pre-start spectacle, a bonanza of colorful balloons soared, along with the fans' eager anticipation of the race to come.

With Tony Hulman's traditional command of "Gentlemen, start your engines," the competition began. The dynamic Ford Mustang paced the pack of thirty-three, starter Pat Vidan waved the green flag, and the race was on. Pole sitter Jimmy Clark grabbed the lead on the first lap, setting a new first-lap record of 149.775 mph. Bobby was right behind him, pushing hard. As the field roared into the second lap, the race seemed to be in motion to fulfill all its promise.

Tragically, just minutes after the flying start, a fiery crash on the second lap proved fatal to two drivers and injured five others. When Dave MacDonald hit the inside wall coming out of the northwest turn, his car exploded and slid toward the center of the track in front of Eddie Sachs. With no time to maneuver, Sachs slammed MacDonald's car broadside in a flaming collision. Ronnie Duman, Johnny Rutherford, Bobby Unser, Chuck Stevenson, and Norm Hall were also entangled in the enveloping fire to different degrees. The race was immediately halted. Much-loved veteran Sachs and promising rookie MacDonald both died as a result of the blazing accident, and the other five drivers suffered injuries of varying severity. The Speedway had never witnessed a tragedy of such magnitude, nor had the 500 ever before been stopped, except for rain in 1926.

The shocked crowd waited uneasily for nearly two hours before the race was restarted. Eddie Sachs's death had been almost immediate, and was announced during the waiting period. Dave MacDonald's death at Methodist Hospital became known a few hours later.

The remaining twenty-six drivers waited in a limbo of personal sadness and professional demands to return to the oval arena.

Return they did, and the chase was on once again, the culmination of all their hard work in May and the preceding months.

At the restart, Jim Clark in the Lotus 34 again seized the lead position, but on lap 7, Bobby in

BELOW: Clark, Bobby, and
Rodger Ward lined up behind
the pace car, ready for the
start. (RMA/KNOX)

his red-on-white Lotus 29 took command over the yellow-on-green racer, shooting into first place. By the eighth lap Bobby had a three-second lead over Clark. Bobby had been preparing for this moment all year, and he was making it happen, steadily increasing his lead over second-place Clark, and lapping cars at will.

All spring, Bobby had been driving to the beat of the song "Hello, Dolly," recalled his friend Bill Marvel, sportswriter and Speedway publicist. "Bobby liked the tune and he'd put it into the rhythm of his driving."

No matter to what tune, Bobby and the No. 51 Pure Firebird Special were sizzling, undeterred by Jack Beckley's pleas on the pit board to cool it. The crowd was with him. Wallen described the enthusiasm of "the far-from-impartial crowd" in *Roar from the Sixties*: "The gloom of the disaster and the boredom of the long wait for the restart were forgotten as Marshman took every corner in a smooth, sweeping arc, lapping cars as if they weren't there. He might be in a 'furrin' car, but he was one of their own giving the driving lesson to the World Champ-een."

Bobby soared on. By the tenth lap, his average speed was 153 mph, and by lap 20 he had increased it to 154.601 mph. By lap 25 he had established a fourteen-second lead over Clark, and five laps later

had gained a twenty-three-second lead over the Scot. Bobby's thirty-lap average speed also rose to 154.888 mph, and he edged ever closer to a thirty-second lead over Clark.

On lap 39, Bobby was bearing down on fourth-place runner A. J. Foyt, with full intent to lap the year's winningest driver. "Bobby and A. J. were never enemies, you know," said Marvel, "but they were great rivals on the track." Bob was almost upon his powerful opponent and was poised to lap A. J. as soon as he lapped the slower car between them. Then bad luck struck.

As he prepared to lap thirteenth-place Johnny White for the second time, Bobby found only one option for a safe pass. He was forced to dip below the white line, a maneuver that ripped out the car's oil and water plugs. Bob's longtime friend Merit O'Neal commented on what he saw: "Johnny White was a rookie, and he pulled down in front of Bobby as [Bobby] moved left to pass him—what [White] should have done was move to the right. It left Bobby no place to go." Boyhood friend Bill Reiff added: "At that time the Speedway was paved very smooth all the way to the white line, but below the line the quality of asphalt was considerably worse." The maneuver "knocked everything off the bottom" of the car, Beckley said in the *Terre Haute Tribune*.

The *New York Herald Tribune* described Bobby's dilemma: "Bobby Marshman . . . was eliminated in the following manner: He was diving into a turn on the tail of a slower car driven by an inexperienced competitor. He had two choices—either force the slower car out of the groove and thereby perhaps endanger the driver, or go around onto the grass and pass him on the inside. Marshman chose the grass, and as a result ran his low-slung machine over an obstruction and an oil line [broke]. When the fluids ran out, Marshman was finished."

With the oil and water plugs torn out, Bobby had no choice but to pull off the track, coming to a stop on the infield grass inside the fourth turn. He was not black-flagged, but reportedly would have been if he had made it past the starting line. There Pat Vidan had the black flag in hand because Bob's car was leaking oil.

It was a drama with a disappointing ending. After leading in spectacular fashion from lap 7 to lap 39, Bobby was out of his dream race in his dream car.

With Bobby in the infield, Jim Clark took the lead until lap 47, when his left rear Dunlop tire shredded, setting up a vibration that broke the rear suspension. Parnelli Jones then led until lap 54, when A. J. Foyt began to duel with him for top position. Parnelli pitted on the fifty-fifth lap, and as he pulled back out, a fire erupted in his car. He leapt out of the cockpit and was taken to the hospital with first- and second-degree burns. Dan Gurney was called out of the race by Colin Chapman on lap 111 because of overheated rubber, with whole pieces of tread peeling off from the center of his Dunlops. Thus was the prediction from the *Star* fulfilled, that the Dunlops might doom the race for Clark and Gurney.

Twelve cars were still running at the end of the race. A. J. Foyt was the winner in his front-engine Watson-built Sheraton-Thompson roadster, reaffirming Offy dominance. Rodger Ward was second

in his rear-engine Watson-built Kaiser Aluminum Special, the only Ford-powered car to complete the race. Lloyd Ruby in his Forbes Watson-Offy was third. Fourth was Demler Watson-Offy pilot Johnny White, later named Rookie of the Year. In order of finish, the remaining drivers still running were Johnny Boyd, Bud Tingelstad, Dick Rathmann, Bob Harkey, Bob Wente, Bobby Grim, and, in eleventh place, Art Malone. Walt Hansgen was also running at the end of the race and completed 176 laps; however, Hansgen placed thirteenth, behind twelfth-place Don Branson, who completed 187 laps before his transmission failed.

Bobby placed twenty-fifth, but he set the fastest race lap ever run in the Indy 500, at 157.646 mph—57.09 seconds—on lap 15. He also established ten-, twenty-, and thirty-lap race records. In addition, his run placed him in the Autolite "500 Pacemaker Club" as an Indy 500 race leader. Accolades all, but perhaps small consolation.

The evening after the 500, Bobby spoke by phone to his father George, who was running the closed-circuit television screening of the race in Rochester. Bobby's sister LaRone Marshman Innes later recounted the conversation to racing historian Brian Brown. Bobby told his father: "My feet got ahead of my brains. I was within two seconds of lapping Foyt and could see him right in front of me and just got overanxious. I knew if I went by him he would jump right out of his seat, and I wanted that more than anything."

The *New York Herald Tribune* described Bobby after the race: "Marshman was examining one of the hose connections that had been picked off the track. He was thinking about the big payday this automotive horseshoe nail had cost him. 'If I had to do it over again, I still think I'd go underneath him,' he said."

Janet recalled why Bob likely felt that way: "You have to understand that the terrible accident had only just happened," she said. "It was horrible—all you could see were billows of smoke from the fourth turn. Bob knew [Johnny White] was a rookie—so Bob worried that he might be nervous, since the crashes had really just happened. Also, Bob knew Johnny White was in a front-engine car and that it was harder for a front-engine driver to hear a rear-engine car coming. Since he was

ABOVE LEFT: Bobby raced hard with Clark in the 500. (BRIAN BROWN COLLECTION)

ABOVE RIGHT: Until making his mistake by going too low, Bobby looked like a runaway winner. (RMA / WAYNE BRYANT)

OPPOSITE: Jim Clark takes the lead at the start of the 500, chased by Bobby, Parnelli Jones, Foyt, and Rodger Ward. (RMA/KNOX)

driving one of the few rear-engine cars, Bob was afraid he would startle Johnny White if he passed him on the right. It happened so fast.

"Bob never begrudged Johnny White," Janet continued. "He said, 'The guy is a rookie.' Bob didn't judge." In fact, two weeks later when White suffered life-changing injuries during qualifying at Terre Haute, Bobby was very sympathetic, and helped spearhead a fund drive for White and his family.

Later on race day, a spectator approached Bob and Janet. "He was holding the water flange that had flown off Bob's car when he went out," Janet recalled. "The guy told us, 'I was in the stands and this hit me on the head. I thought you might want to have it.' Bob caught on quickly that the guy wanted to keep it as a souvenir, and so Bob told him he could."

With the race's tragedy on everyone's minds, the post-race mood was reportedly subdued. In the June 2, Columbus, Indiana, *Republic*, Larry Lee wrote, "The speeches were short at Sunday's '500' Victory Dinner, and there were two reasons in one—Eddie Sachs wasn't there. . . . Jim Clark, Bobby Marshman, and Parnelli Jones, three pre-race favorites, were unusually quiet and short in their acceptance talks." But Lee went on to say that "Jones 'escaped' from the hospital to be at the dinner."

The shock of the inferno was immediate and its effect long-lived. Gasoline was quickly blamed for the severity of the second-lap crash, and a ban on the fuel was almost immediately proposed—and hotly contested. Sachs and MacDonald had both been driving gasoline-powered cars. In the separate pit-fire incident, Jones was using a mixture of alcohol with a small percentage of gasoline. All season, fuel mixtures had been the subject of debate and experiment, but the deaths of Sachs and MacDonald

confirmed drivers' worst nightmares of racing with gasoline. Compared to the methyl-alcohol fuel traditionally used for the Indy 500, the gasoline-based mix was known to be more combustible and unstable. Second-place finisher Ward was driving the only Ford engine running on methanol on race day.

By the end of the year, the USAC and the Indianapolis Speedway had put in place safety regulations aimed primarily at fire prevention, but a ban on gasoline was not adopted. The new rules included limits to the amount of fuel that could be carried, as well as a requirement for drivers to refuel at least twice during the 500. Among the other changes were new specifications for fuel tank construction and materials, as well as a ban on placing fuel tanks in front of the driver.

Before and after the 500, 1964 was a race year marred by tragic fire incidents on many tracks. The men who died were never statistics to their fellow drivers or their fans. Each loss was deeply felt. The two drivers who died in the 500 were mourned by all who knew them, and knew of them. Dave MacDonald, twenty-seven, was rushed to the infield hospital where a team of six doctors tried to save him, performing a tracheotomy before he was flown by helicopter to Methodist Hospital. He was pronounced dead an hour later. Eddie Sachs, thirty-seven, a great favorite of Speedway fans and fellow drivers, died in the cockpit of his flaming car. Medical examiners later determined that his death was caused by a fatal chest injury from the impact of the collision.

Later that day, the Gasoline Alley Highland Pipers paraded with their bagpipes before the Tower Terrace and played "The Rowan Tree," a mournful Scottish dirge reserved for those who are loved and will be greatly missed.

PART 6 / AT THE HEIGHT OF HIS CAREER

Chapter 86
June: Wisconsin, Indiana, Pennsylvania (1964)

The calendar page turned, bringing the Rex Mays Memorial 100, scheduled on June 7 at the Wisconsin State Fairgrounds.

Bobby was set to pilot the Pure Firebird Special in the Milwaukee Mile USAC championship event, but during a practice session, he crashed nose first into the concrete retaining wall. Bobby was not hurt but the car was severely damaged. The *Indianapolis Star*'s George Moore reported, "The crash bent the front suspension members and tore the upper A-arm on the left side from the wheel. The front part of the body, which constitutes the frame on this Lotus-Ford, was bent to the right. In addition, the radiator was smashed . . . An extremely dirty track was held to blame for the accident. The asphalt surface of the Milwaukee paved mile oval was covered with a fine layer of dirt which billowed into the air as the cars went past. Marshman said the car just got away from him on the slippery pavement. 'I just lost it,' he said, 'and there was nothing I could do about it.'"

Although the Lotus 29 was out of the running, Bobby was not. Teammate Bob Veith stepped aside so Bob could drive the Hopkins Epperly roadster, which Veith had qualified eighteenth.

However, engine troubles put Bobby out after completing twenty laps, giving him a twenty-first-place finish.

As the 100-mile race unfolded on the Milwaukee Mile, Rodger Ward, A. J. Foyt, and Jim Hurtubise fought a ferocious nose-to-tail battle until misfortune struck the threesome on lap 52 in dramatic fashion. Hurtubise later described the accident: "Rodger was leading when his clutch went out. His car just stopped. Then Foyt ran into him and was thrown my way and I ran up on top of his rear. Then I don't know what happened." What the 35,600 fans saw happen was Hurtubise's car launching from the right rear of Foyt's car into the wall, where Hurtubise's fuel tank split on impact, causing his roadster to burst into flames. The crash broke up the rear end of Ward's car, putting him out of the

race, but Foyt was unscathed and drove on, eventually winning.

In the accident, Hurtubise was hit in the chest by his front tire, breaking several ribs and puncturing his lung, and he suffered second- and third-degree burns over 40 percent of his body. Bobby, who was out of the race at that point, jumped into the ambulance to be with his friend and attempted to take Hurtubise's mind off the pain as they were taken to the West Allis hospital. Because of the severity of his injuries, Hurtubise was then flown to the Burn Center of the Brooke Army Medical Center in San Antonio. It was the second time in two weeks that the DVS team had been affected by the tragedy of fire—first by the loss of Eddie Sachs, and now, by the severity of Hurtubise's injuries.

After the June 7 race, Bobby's badly damaged Lotus 29 had to be shipped back to Cheshunt, England, for extensive repairs. Although sources conflict on this point, it appears that Lindsey Hopkins then purchased a replacement Lotus 29 for Bobby to drive for the rest of the season. Based on the limited documentation of the era, it seems likely that Hopkins acquired the Lotus 29/3 to replace Bobby's damaged car.

Whether it was the racer he crashed in Milwaukee that had been rebuilt or a different chassis number, it was a Lotus 29 that Bobby drove for the remainder of 1964, both for racing and for testing.

Next stop on Bobby's June schedule was the Terre Haute Action Track where he had claimed victory the previous August. Driving the Competition Engineering Special in the June 14 USAC sprint car race, Bobby earned a third-place finish after some skillful maneuvering around veteran Jud Larson and newcomer Mario Andretti. A. J. Foyt won the fifteen-mile race on the half-mile dirt oval, lapping the entire field except for Johnny Rutherford in second and Bobby in third. Tragically, this was the race where Speedway Rookie of the Year Johnny White suffered a debilitating accident during qualifying. He hit the fence on the second turn of his first lap and barrel-rolled along the rail, ending upside down outside the track. The thirty-two-year-old father of four sustained a major spinal injury and was paralyzed from the neck down. Bobby and other drivers helped raise funds for the driver and his family.

At a press conference at Langhorne Speedway on June 18, Lee Iacocca vowed that Ford was committed to staying in racing, "hitting back at General Motors Corp.'s anti-racing campaign," according to the Salisbury, Maryland, *Daily Times*. Ford vice president and general manager of Ford Division, Iacocca told the paper, "We have great tracks for developing automobiles. What's wrong with us adding a few more auto race tracks. Bobby Marshman does a better job of testing than a dynamometer."

On June 21, Langhorne Speedway hosted the first dirt track USAC championship race of the year. Some drivers—including Rodger Ward and Parnelli Jones—gave Langhorne a pass, but Bobby chose to test his mettle once again on the infamous one-mile dirt venue and was rewarded with a third-place finish.

A sweltering race day at Langhorne saw more than twenty-five thousand fans in attendance. Bobby qualified fifth in the Hopkins Special and finished number three on the lead lap behind winner A. J. Foyt and runner-up Don Branson. The event was the last championship race on the intimidating 'Horne, with its challenging circular dirt layout. By 1965, the Bucks County, Pennsylvania, track was paved and reconfigured.

A week later, Bobby was scheduled to drive the pace car for a benefit URC-ARDC midget race at Williams Grove. The June 28 event was organized on behalf of Jim Maguire, who had lost his right arm in a May 3 race accident at New Bremen Speedway. Thanks to the commitment of Bobby and many others, the proceeds from over five thousand ticket sales went to the Maguire rehabilitation fund.

Chapter 87
Midsummer On and Off the Circuit (1964)

At its midway point, 1964 was already regarded as a mean year for the racing community, marked by driver fatalities.

On July 2, Glenn "Fireball" Roberts died at Memorial Hospital in Charlotte, North Carolina, where he had been since May 24. He ultimately succumbed to complications from burns that covered over 70 percent of his body following a fiery crash in the World 600 NASCAR race. The three-car accident also involved Junior Johnson and Ned Jarrett, who pulled Roberts from his burning race car.

Roberts was one of racing's true superstars. "Fireball was the idol of all drivers," Jarrett told an AP writer, adding, "He was a gentleman and a sportsman, all that a man in our profession should be." Still mourning the death of two-time National Champion Joe Weatherly in January at Riverside, NASCAR had now lost two of its top drivers.

Also on July 2, Jim Hurtubise held a news conference at Brooke Army Medical Center where he remained in serious condition, still almost completely immobilized from the effects of burns suffered at the June 7 Milwaukee Mile.

"When I race again, you can bet I'll wear a lot more clothes," he told an AP reporter. "I might be a little warmer, but I'll be better protected. If I had been wearing gloves my hands wouldn't have gotten burned." He called for new safety measures, including mandating lower fuel loads. Hurtubise did return to racing the following year, and continued his driving career into 1980.

On July 5, 1964, Tony Bonadies was killed in an ARDC midget race at Williams Grove Speedway. The veteran Eastern driver and two-time runner-up for the ARDC championship died instantly after being thrown from his car when a rear axle snapped.

Competing in the July 12 Milwaukee Mile 200-miler, Bobby drove a '64 Ford owned by Vanda Hurst of Milwaukee, and was teamed with USAC stock car star Don White for the Wisconsin State Fairgrounds event. Bobby crashed when he and Lloyd Ruby collided on the thirty-eighth lap, setting off a five-car pileup. He and Ruby, along with Ralph Baker and Gordon Gorman, escaped serious injury, but the accident sent Johnny Rutherford to the hospital, where he was later released in satisfactory condition. The multi-racer tangle halted the USAC stock car event for twenty minutes. The race winner was '64 Mercury pilot Parnelli Jones, a single second ahead of teammate Rodger Ward. Bobby finished thirty-first in the field of thirty-eight.

Bobby faced additional disappointment that month when he failed to qualify in two USAC sprint car races, in Ohio and Pennsylvania. His car was a Clyde Gutzwiller Chevy for the July 5 Eldora Speedway race won by Jud Larson. For the July 18 Williams Grove Speedway race won by A. J. Foyt, Bobby's car was the Walter Beletsky Special.

However, July's highs were memorable.

Trenton was next on Bobby's competition schedule, and his presence at the July 19 race was eagerly anticipated. The *Asbury Park Press* in New Jersey wrote: "Bobby Marshman has been installed as favorite to win the third annual Trenton 150." The Hazelton, Pennsylvania, *Standard-Speaker* featured a photo of Bob in the Pure Firebird Special at Indy, with the caption: "Bobby Marshman, sensational driver from Pottstown, is shown in the world's fastest Lotus-Ford [160 mph]."

Trenton's July 19 USAC championship race was billed as another rear-engine racer vs. roadster showdown. In fact, the rear-engine cars seemed to be in command. First Bobby qualified in the Pure Firebird Special in 32.38 seconds, topping A. J. Foyt's record run of 32.44 seconds. But then Rodger Ward in the rear-engine Kaiser Aluminum Special set a new record, at 32.27 seconds. Next Jim McElreath in the Zink-Urschel rear-engine Offy clocked 32.12 seconds and took pole.

The early miles of the July 19 Trenton 150 were promising for Bob. After a third-place start, he passed McElreath on lap 12 to take over the lead. Then, after completing twenty-two laps, a torsion bar broke and Bobby was out of the race. But not for good. Ward was running at the head of the pack until lap 105 when he pulled in for relief from the relentless 100-degree heat and Bobby took over. Despite two pit stops for fuel, Bob brought the car home for a seventh-place finish for Ward and himself.

Front-engine pilot Foyt was the Trenton winner, setting a new track record of 105.590 mph in his Sheraton-Thompson Special. Afterwards he offered his insights on the roadster victory, telling Dave Overpeck for the *Indianapolis Star*, "The rear engines have been going faster than us, but we've been holding up and they haven't. That's why we've won."

Later in the month, this assessment of rear-engine speed was echoed in the *Fresno Bee*, where Omer Crane quoted USAC's Henry Banks in a conversation about the recent Indy 500: "I feel Bobby Marshman [driving a Lotus Ford] probably would have averaged well over 150, except for his one miscalculation."

Amid competitive grit, the sport's camaraderie was ever-present. This spirit came through in an open letter from Jim Maguire printed in the July 21 *Illustrated Speedway News*. Maguire wrote in part: "To say thank you to everyone who sent me letters, etc., would take the rest of the racing season. So, to all of the people who helped me through Norwood Arena, Williams Grove, the Bobby Marshman and Dick Wallen movie party . . . and gave me encouragement to get well as soon as possible, they will always be remembered . . . I wish the people of the outside world could know how warmhearted the real racing crowds are."

Chapter 88
Two Wheelers (1964)

Committed as they were to an intense and demanding profession, the drivers were young men, and they always found ways to have a good time. Janet remembered that in the summer of 1964, the drivers were into motorcycles.

"Bobby had a Honda; he did some public relations work for some people in Fort Wayne and they gave him the motorcycle," she said. "All the guys had one of a different make. For instance, Johnny Rutherford had a Kawasaki. A. J. had a different one. They were like little kids with them.

"I told Bobby I wanted to drive the bike," she continued, "and he said, 'No, no, not on the road—it's not safe.' Fortunately at the apartments where we lived out there, the parking lot was almost empty during the day because people were working or in school, and it gave me plenty of room to learn how to ride it. Bobby loved that motorcycle and he took it home with us when we moved back to our house in the fall."

Tire testing continued to keep the top drivers busy—and provided a relatively reliable source of income. Firestone had engaged a first-rate test crew, including Bobby, A. J. Foyt, Rodger Ward, Parnelli Jones, Jim McElreath, and Lloyd Ruby.

In one of the Firestone test runs at the Speedway, Bobby narrowly escaped injury. He was driving the Hopkins roadster at approximately 143 mph when a torsion bar came loose and punched a hole through his right rear tire on the southwest turn of the track. His car spun three times, brushed the wall, and finally stopped when it backed into the concrete. Bobby was unharmed and the car damage was minor.

The very next week, Firestone tests at Trenton Speedway resulted in separate crashes for Rodger Ward and Parnelli Jones, with both smashing into the same guardrail on the second turn, about an hour apart. Jones's collision was caused by a malfunction in his car's front suspension system. The rear-engine Offy caught fire and was badly damaged, and Jones himself was treated for burns to his right arm at Helene Fuld Hospital. Ward was not injured and told AP reporters afterwards that he couldn't account for the cause of his crash.

Throughout the summer, driver safety was the focus in many quarters. Spurred by the catastrophic Indy 500 fire in May, the USAC was working on new rules geared toward safety issues, such as limiting fuel capacities. During this same period, Goodyear was leading in the development of a fire-protective racing suit, with plans to test their design in the coming months. In the fall, a California company, Protection, Inc., demonstrated its prototype fireproof racing suit at the Central Indiana Firemen's Convention and expressed its intention to have an affordable retail model available for the 1965 Indy 500.

Chapter 89
"I Thought He Was Going to Pass Everybody in the Place" (1964)

August held a full lineup of races for the Pottstown pilot.

On August 15, Bobby competed in a USAC sprint car race on the Allentown Fairgrounds' half-mile dirt oval. He won his eight-lap qualifying heat and started seventh in the thirty-lap feature, finishing sixth in the fourteen-car field. Ahead of Bobby were winner Jud Larson, followed by Mickey Rupp, A. J. Foyt, Don Branson, and Bud Tingelstad.

The next day, Bob chauffeured Vanda Hurst's '64 Ford in the August 16 Milwaukee Mile USAC stock car race. He started ninth and finished twenty-seventh. Nearly two-thirds of the way into the 150-lap race, Bobby was caught up in a three-car accident. Defending champion Don White hit the wall, and as he came off the spin, was hit by Rich Kleich (who was driving a car he had just taken over for Sal Tovella), and then Bobby crashed into both cars. All three drivers were uninjured. Parnelli Jones was the race winner.

On August 20, the battle was again at the Milwaukee Mile, for a 200-mile USAC stock car race.

Bobby again drove the Hurst Ford. He started eighth but was plagued by engine problems, for a twenty-ninth-place finish. Parnelli Jones and Rodger Ward were declared co-winners of the contest: Jones had taken the helm of Ward's car on the ninety-fifth lap after his own Mercury blew its engine while he was leading on the eighty-eighth lap; in Ward's Mercury, Jones took the lead back from the field at lap 114 and kept it to the end.

The next challenge in the USAC championship lineup was the August 22 Tony Bettenhausen Memorial at the Illinois State Fairgrounds. In the 100-lap competition on the one-mile dirt oval, Bobby was piloting the Hopkins Offy. He captured second place in an intense wheel-to-wheel battle with first-place finisher A. J. Foyt in his Meskowski Offy.

As the green flag dropped on the Springfield race, Bobby charged to the lead, outpacing pole sitter Rodger Ward. On lap 25, Bill Horstmeyer, who was new to the USAC but a twelve-year racing veteran, clipped the outside rail as he exited turn four. His Kuzma-Offy flipped several times, landing upside down in the middle of the front stretch, and then burst into flames, with Horstmeyer trapped inside by the fence where the car had halted. He was rushed to St. John's Hospital where he died several hours later from burns and injuries.

ABOVE: Bobby poses prior to the 100-Miler at Du Quoin in September, where he finished second to A. J. Foyt. (RMA/SCOTT)

After Horstmeyer's crash, the cars continued under a full-course yellow flag before racing again on lap 42. A few laps later, Bobby pitted with a shredded right rear tire, after leading for forty-nine laps. Jud Larson then took the lead until lap 66, when Foyt passed him. At that point, Bob was back in, and threatening Foyt. On his charge back toward the front, Bobby impressed Foyt's crew chief George Bignotti, who said, "I thought for a while he was going to pass everybody in the place."

The Marshman–Foyt duel lasted to the finish, thrilling the crowd. Bob surged ahead in the corners only to have A. J. storm ahead again on the straightaways. On the last lap, the two drivers exited the final turn with Bobby in the lead by inches—but under the checkered flag, Foyt was ahead by a wheel to claim his seventh consecutive victory on the 1964 Championship Trail.

Chapter 90
August Angst and Action (1964)

Determination in competition wasn't confined to drivers. Goodyear reappeared at the Speedway in the early part of August for more testing, despite being jilted in May, when not a single car ran the Indy 500 on Goodyears. Looking ahead to 1965, engineers for the tire company told the *Indianapolis Star* they believed they could develop a racing tire as good as or better than the competition.

Elsewhere, trial runs netted some notable success. On a practice day at Trenton Speedway on August 17, Parnelli Jones set an unofficial record speed on the one-mile oval at slightly over 113 mph, driving the Lotus 34 that Jim Clark had put on the pole in May for the 500. Yes, Parnelli, the outspoken critic of the entire rear-engine revolution. Just days before, J. C. Agajanian had announced that he was entering Parnelli in a Lotus-Ford in the driver's next two races because the new rear-engine Offy built for Jones had been damaged beyond repair in recent Trenton tire tests.

Actually, Parnelli's conversion was born of a determined and lengthy effort by Team Lotus. As Andrew Ferguson explained in *Team Lotus*, "The deal to secure Parnelli . . . firstly meant dealing with his car owner, J. C. Agajanian, whose extrovert personality hid as bright a business mind as one could find anywhere." Next Lotus had to gain Ford's approval to the contract stipulations. Finally, Parnelli was on board.

Walt Hansgen had also been chosen by Team Lotus, even before Parnelli signed on. Hansgen and Jones were the Lotus team's carefully-thought-out stand-ins for Jim Clark and Dan Gurney, who were scheduled to race in the Formula One Austrian Grand Prix the same weekend as the Milwaukee USAC championship race. It was this highly visible August 23 American race that Lotus and Ford viewed as a crucial proving ground, to oust the memory of their May disappointments.

Unfortunately, Hansgen's practice drives for Team Lotus ended in accidents, with the second on August 20 putting him in the hospital with a concussion and burns on his right arm. With three days to go before the Wisconsin face-off, Team Lotus now had Parnelli in place—and one unmanned

reserve car. The overriding question was: Who would climb into the empty cockpit for the August 23 running? The chosen driver for the Ford-powered Lotus 34 turned out to be none other than the year's most famous front-engine racer, A. J. Foyt. As unexpected as the match appeared, the truth was that Ford had been wooing Foyt all year. Ferguson wrote: "With the Texan now present at Milwaukee the pressure was on to reach a suitable agreement without delay." Thus, with the race nearly upon them, the deal was finalized, and Foyt was the newest Lotus-Ford pilot in the pits.

Lots of action in the upper Midwest, and the drivers weren't even on the grid yet.

Chapter 91
Milwaukee and More (1964)

Traveling the Championship Trail in August demanded a quick, long-distance turnaround. The day after the Springfield, Illinois, championship race, Bobby and most of his competitors were again revving their engines at the August 23 Wisconsin championship contest in Milwaukee.

The Milwaukee 200 race drew a record crowd of over 38,450, despite rainy conditions that delayed the race start by over an hour, and brought out yellow flags during the running. Driving the Hopkins Lotus 29, Bobby qualified seventh. In the race, he led for five laps, but a blown engine forced him out on lap 38, relegating him to a twenty-fourth-place finish. A. J. also had a bad luck day: He ran only one lap in his debut Lotus-Ford drive before a jammed gearbox on lap 2 not only put him out of the race, but ended his spectacular run of consecutive victories on the championship circuit. He finished twenty-sixth.

The race winner was Lotus-Ford pilot Parnelli Jones, who led for 195 laps and flew under the checkered flag two laps ahead of runner-up Rodger Ward (driving another rear-engine machine, a Watson-Ford for the Bob Wilke team). In *Team Lotus*, Andrew Ferguson recounted, "Ford was delighted with this result, and congratulatory cables became the order of the day."

The glow dimmed a bit a few days later. On August 28, USAC director of competition Henry Banks reprimanded both Jones and Ward for running too fast under yellow flags in the Milwaukee 200, slapping Jones with the largest fine ever assessed by the USAC, set at $1,100, and fining Ward $600. Banks explained that Parnelli's fine was higher because as leader, he was responsible for setting the pace for the field. Banks also said that yellow-flag violations had been an increasing problem and needed to be stopped.

The same day, the USAC disqualified Parnelli from an August 26 midget race win at the Fairbury Fair. On lap 40 of the fifty-lap race, Jones lost a wheel due to a broken radius rod, but ignored the black flag waving him off the track; instead, he continued his race, crossing the finish line first, on three wheels. Now USAC was officially dismissing his gutsy victory. Bobby placed eighth in the Fairbury feature, after winning the ten-lap semifinal.

Bobby ended the month of August with two first-place finishes. At Eldora Speedway's August 29 USAC midget race, Bobby took the lead on the first lap and never looked back. Driving the Ralph Wilke No. 4 car, he captured first place in the forty-lap contest on the half-mile dirt oval ahead of runner-up Mel Kenyon, who had set a track record of 19.80 seconds in qualifying. Bobby claimed victory again the next day in the Allen Crowe Memorial 100 at the Illinois State Fairgrounds. In the August 30 USAC stock car race, he was powering a 1964 Ford owned by Vanda Hurst. After running third for most of the contest, he moved in and captured the lead with eight laps to go in the 100-lap battle. Thirty-one starters crowded the Springfield one-mile dirt oval, and Bobby was first of the nineteen finishers, at an average speed of 94.41 mph; teammate Don White was second, also piloting a 1964 Ford.

Chapter 92
September at Speed (1964)

For Bobby, September started at the Du Quoin State Fair, where he competed in the three Labor Day weekend races scheduled on the fairground's one-mile dirt track.

A USAC midget race on September 5 jump-started the Du Quoin competitions. Although he was running with the leaders in the early laps of the 100-mile race, Bobby finished tenth in the Mataka Offy. The winner, in the Tornado Automotive Special, was Don Branson, who had crashed heavily just two days before in Firestone tire tests at the Speedway.

Bobby finished in the top three in each of his next four races, including two at Du Quoin and one each at the Indiana State Fairgrounds and at Langhorne Speedway.

In the first of these Du Quoin races, Joe Leonard won the 100-mile USAC stock car contest on the dusty oval ahead of Dodge teammate Len Sutton. Bobby followed in third piloting a Ford, with Norm Nelson fourth in a Plymouth, and A. J. Foyt, fifth, in a Dodge. The top five all finished on

the same lap. The September 6 race marked the first USAC stock car win for Leonard, a three-time national motorcycle champion.

The finale of the Du Quoin Fair's hard-charging race weekend was the Ted Horn Memorial USAC championship race. Bobby finished second in the September 7 competition behind winner A. J. Foyt. Just before the green flag of the 100-miler, it was Don Branson on the pole in the Wynn Friction Proofing Special, with Foyt starting second in the Sheraton-Thompson Special, and Bobby starting fourth in the Hopkins Special. By the end of the second lap, Foyt and Bobby were one and two. After fifteen laps, Bobby lost his brakes but remained in the chase until two-thirds into the race, when he backed off in order to retain a secure number-two finish. Foyt led from start to finish, but Bobby had the satisfaction of being the only driver on the same lap with him at race end. Bobby and A. J. had both lapped Branson, who finished third. With his victory, Foyt clinched the National Championship for the fourth time. It was also A. J.'s twenty-fifth championship race victory, tying him with Rodger Ward for the distinction of all-time lead.

Two days later, in a USAC stock car race at the Indiana State Fairgrounds, Bobby was on the pole with a new track record time of 40.76 seconds (88.322 mph). In the September 9 race itself, Bobby roused the 13,500-plus crowd with a dynamic display of skill. Driving a 1964 Ford, Bobby led the first three laps of the 100-miler before dropping to second behind Parnelli in a Stroppe Mercury. On lap 17, Bobby lost ground when he was forced to pit after a cut to his left rear tire, but he then blazed his way through the pack to joust with the front-runners, ultimately claiming third place. Foyt was first in a Nichels Dodge, and Don White, second, in a late-model Ford. A crash put Parnelli out of contention on lap 60.

• • • •

It was still 1964, and the old 'Horne was as yet unpaved. Bobby was up to the challenge for Langhorne Speedway's September 13 USAC stock car race, driving with the front-runners from the start. Bobby fell to fifth when he pitted to have a loose hood tightened, and then made a strong run back to finish second. Bob piloted a Zecol-Lubaid '64 Ford in the grueling 250-mile contest. Driving a Nichels Dodge, A. J. Foyt won at a record pace, and defending champion Don White took third.

On September 18, yellow-flag issues were part of the agenda for the USAC board of directors. The board reduced Parnelli Jones's fine for his August 28 yellow-flag infraction to $600, matching Rodger Ward's fine for the same violation in the same race. And in a decision that affected all drivers, the USAC set forth its revised yellow-flag rule, which called for cars to bunch up under the yellow. This replaced the long-established rule for cars to slow and remain the same relative distance behind the car ahead or behind. The board maintained that the old yellow-flag rule was unenforceable, and was creating an unsafe situation for track workers responding to crashed cars. In the weeks to come, the new yellow-flag rule would prove to be unpopular with drivers and fans alike.

Off the track, Bobby's family enjoyed news in a lighter vein. In mid-September, his father George was named technical adviser for a Warner Brothers movie, *The Great Race*, which had gone into production earlier in the summer. Directed by Blake Edwards and starring Jack Lemmon, Natalie Wood, and Tony Curtis, the comedic, slapstick film was very loosely based on the New York–to–Paris race of 1908. The movie was released in July 1965.

Chapter 93
"It's Going to Be Rough and Dirty" (1964)

Mother Nature forced a postponement of the September 19 Hoosier 100 USAC championship race, despite heroic efforts by race fans and track crews alike. After heavy rainfall for days before the event, the clay surface of the Indiana State Fair venue was more of a bog than a track. After working for hours to get the slick, rut-lined circuit in shape, officials appealed to the twenty-five thousand assembled fans for help. Soon, as many as two hundred passenger cars and trucks were taking turns circling the track with the road graders and tractors in an attempt to pack down the muddy, bumpy surface so it could be traveled at speed by the racers.

Even these hours of teamwork failed to improve the treacherous conditions sufficiently, as the drivers discovered when they tried a few slow practice laps. Race officials then conferenced with the

almost thirty drivers, and only A. J. Foyt and Bobby Unser voted to race. Bobby Marshman was firmly against running under the unsafe circumstances, and was supported by Rodger Ward, Len Sutton, Bob Harkey, Bud Tingelstad, and others. Legendary driver Tommy Hinnershitz, who was on hand as chief mechanic on Dee Jones's Windmill Truckers Special, said the surface would be brutal on cars. "Going in and out of those holes would be as tough on the drive lines as anything," he told Dave Overpeck for the *Indianapolis Star*, adding, "About the only thing that would get a worse beating is the driver." Safety concerns prevailed and the race was called off late in the day and rescheduled for the following week.

A highlight of the gloomy Saturday was an unexpected visit from Jim Hurtubise, who was on furlough from Brooke Army Burn Center. He was still in pain, the media reported, especially in his hands, and was unable to reach out to the many handshakes offered. Fans and drivers were thrilled to see him. "Herc's hands are in bad shape," was the concerned word that quickly spread around. (Herc was the abbreviated form of Hurtubise's nickname, Hercules.) Veteran mechanic Herb Porter kidded him, "Hey, you loafer. Come on over here and set this chassis up for me so we'll run fast today." Jim's brother Pete told well-wishers how determined Jim was to be ready for the next 500, saying, "If work and guts can get the job done, he'll be there." Hurtubise spent much of his time with Bobby, and the two men were featured in conversation in a *Star* photo.

The next day's race was in Wisconsin. The Tony Bettenhausen 250 ran on schedule on the Milwaukee Mile's paved oval, but proved frustrating to Bobby nonetheless. In the September 20 USAC stock car race, he was on lap 237 of the 250-lap contest when the engine seized on his Regeth

Ford, putting him out. He finished eleventh after starting eighteenth. Parnelli Jones was first and Rodger Ward second, both in Stroppe Mercury chariots.

For September's final contests, travel between tracks was once again a challenge unto itself. Prudent as the Hoosier 100 postponement was, drivers now faced two back-to-back championship races in one weekend: Saturday, September 26, in Indiana, and Sunday, September 27, in New Jersey.

The Indiana Fairgrounds dirt oval was still rough and slick on September 26, but the rescheduled Hoosier 100 USAC championship race was on. Bobby started second in the Hopkins Offy and took the initial race lead, until he was passed by Foyt on lap 7. But Bobby kept the pressure on A. J., never falling more than a few seconds behind—until a broken torsion bar put Bobby out after completing forty-five laps. He had only been in the pits for a few minutes when Len Sutton pitted in the Enterprise Machine Flynn-Offy after being hit in the teeth by a hard clump of dirt. Bobby took over for Sutton and brought the car home in eighth position. Foyt won in style, claiming his third victory in the Hoosier 100, and setting a new record of twenty-six races for the number of all-time championship victories.

The *Indianapolis Star*'s George Moore described the Indiana Fairgrounds track as "a jumble of potholes" on September 26, and reported on a string of car mishaps in addition to Bobby's broken torsion bar. Moore wrote that Bob Harkey "had the driveshaft let go from bouncing in and out of holes." He also described the woes of several other drivers, including Joe Leonard, who had a rod come out of the side of his engine; Johnny Rutherford, who lost the clutch on his racer; and Gordon Johncock, who had his oil tank knocked off.

Moore added, "Foyt said just before the start, 'It's going to be rough and dirty.' And it was."

After an overnight trek, Bobby qualified third for the Trenton USAC championship race on September 27. Driving the Hopkins Lotus 29 in the 200-mile race, he battled for second place with

A. J. Foyt and Jim McElreath before spinning on lap 32. Bobby recovered from the spin, but ignition problems ultimately put him out after 108 laps, for a sixteenth-place finish. Parnelli Jones was the winner, in his new Lotus 34. Jim Clark had reclaimed the other Lotus 34 for the Trenton run, and so A. J. was back in his roadster. Mechanical problems put the two aces out before the halfway mark, A. J. with clutch problems after ninety laps, and Clark with a broken halfshaft after ninety-six laps.

The USAC's new yellow-flag rule was in effect for the Milwaukee Mile race, as well as the Indiana and Trenton championship races. The regulation was already unpopular, with the *Star*'s Dave Overpeck dubbing it "a real crock," with "glaring weaknesses." After the Milwaukee race, Paul R. Harbaugh of the

Elwood, Indiana, *Call-Leader* described some questionable jockeying for position under the changed protocol, and commented, "It is hard to see how this new rule adds any safety, and it surely isn't fair to the leader." And George Moore noted in the *Star* that at the Hoosier 100, the new regulation "not only had pit crews complaining but had the fans jeering every time the yellow flag was displayed."

Chapter 94
162.3

As the fall progressed, Bobby blazed through a road race, a midget race, and a champ-car race in October, and also pushed the pedal to one news-breaking speed record after another during test runs.

Mid-America Raceways in Wentzville, Missouri, held its first stock car competition on the 2.75-mile road course on October 4. It was also Bobby's single road course appearance. The USAC race was a 200-miler, with a field of thirty-two competing before twenty-five thousand fans. Pre-race predictions named Bobby as a top contender, and he was—at least until car troubles plagued his progress. John Hillyer described the action in the *St. Louis Post-Dispatch*: "Bobby Marshman began as though he intended to give Jones a contest, but he encountered a broken wheel cylinder on the fourteenth lap and went off the course, into a field and onto some rocks. He solicited help from some spectators, and returned to action, but was unable to get back into contention." Bobby finished fourteenth in a Zecol-Lubaid Ford after starting fifth. Parnelli Jones was the victor in a Mercury.

The Hut-100 at the Terre Haute Action Track on October 11 was the last USAC open-cockpit event in the Midwest for 1964. Bobby started eighth in the 100-lap midget race on the half-mile dirt oval, and finished seventh. Bob Tattersall won after leading the field of Offy midgets most of the fifty miles. Fans and friends were delighted to see Jim Hurtubise driving the pace car for this Vigo County Fairgrounds race.

The memory of the Speedway crash in May remained fresh in the minds of the racing community, and safety debates continued through the fall. Proposals for changes covered a range of possibilities, including fuel limits and speed limits.

Nevertheless, test drives were ongoing, and sometimes harrowing. On October 1, Jim McElreath suffered serious injuries during a Firestone test at the Speedway. He was severely burned on his left hand and arm when he hit the outside wall in turn one in his rear-engine Zink-Urschel Offy. The impact tore off the left rear wheel and ruptured the fuel tank into a fiery explosion. McElreath managed to get out of the car and roll down the track to extinguish the flames but was hospitalized for burn injuries. The damaged car had been built by Jack Brabham, and raced by Brabham in May.

Bobby continued to participate in tire testing, and he scored some remarkable results. At the Speedway in mid-October, he set a new high mark. He was testing for Goodyear when he turned a lap at 161.4 mph, a new unofficial record for the track, besting his own speed of 161.1 mph just the day before, and his 160-mph record in May. Nor did his speed display stop at one or two quick turns. Bob proved his consistency and control by running five laps over 161 mph. And, on his final run, he calmly ran eight laps at an average of 160.8 mph. In reports from the *Indianapolis Star* as well as from the Associated Press, it was noted that Bobby was testing in the Lotus 34 that Dan Gurney piloted at the Indy 500 and Parnelli Jones drove to victory at Trenton.

All this in the midst of outcries for slower speeds on the track. George Moore of the *Star* reported that after setting the new record, "The Pottstown, Pa., chauffeur said the chassis felt secure at all times, and the job of tire testing didn't pay enough to get all out of shape."

In the same article, Moore noted that there was only one kind of car going 161 mph, and it was the Lotus, adding that "Marshman attributed this to the fact that the Lotus people had more experience with the chassis than the American builders, but feels this will change with new equipment constantly being built."

Back in competition on October 25, Bobby ran what several sportswriters concurred was a terrific race at the Sacramento Golden State 100. A. J. Foyt captured first place on the one-mile dirt oval in his Sheraton-Thompson Special, continuing his domination of the 1964 championship circuit by winning his tenth of the twelve national races to date. But Bobby's second-place finish in the Hopkins Special was a highlight of the 100-lap race, in front of a record 15,000-plus crowd at the California State Fairgrounds. As Ronnie Allyn wrote in *Illustrated Speedway News*, "The best battle of the day was for second place, with Bobby Marshman taking the number two spot from Rodger Ward on the forty-seventh lap and holding off the challenges of Ward and Don Branson for the rest of the race. Branson got by his teammate Ward on the eighty-third round as he made the pass in the south turn, but try as he may he couldn't pass Marshman." Bobby held his second-place position "by a matter of yards," reported UPI, beating out third-place Branson in his Wynn's Friction Proofing Watson-Offy, and Ward in fourth in the Kaiser Aluminum Special.

With the newsprint barely dry over Bobby's record-breaking lap time in Goodyear tests in the middle of the month, he returned to the Brickyard two weeks later and once more topped his own achievement. Bob was back at the Speedway on October 30 by special request from Firestone. The company hadn't planned to run more autumn tire tests, but was responding to the publicity generated by Bobby's unofficial record speed for Goodyear. Bobby delivered the goods on behalf of Firestone, upping the unofficial track record yet again, this time to 162.3 mph, piloting the Lotus 29. The *Star* captured the enthusiasm of the day in a gag photo staged by Bobby and Firestone manager of tire development Jim Thiese to humorously show how hard Bobby was applying the throttle to reach these ever-increasing speeds. In the photo, Bobby's shoe appears to be bursting through the nose of the Lotus as Thiese holds up an oversized blackboard reading "Bobby: 62—3" (shorthand for 162.3 mph, Bobby's record-breaking speed). In addition to setting the new bar, Bobby averaged 161.1 mph for nine laps in the Firestone tests.

At the Fort Stockton track in early November, Bobby poured on still more speed. On November 6, the Associated Press reported: "Indianapolis speedster Bobby Marshman drove his Lotus-Ford championship car around the 7.7-mile track here at 195.100 mph in a practice run. If winds calm, Marshman may attempt to break the unlimited closed-course record of 196.69 mph, which is held by the late Ab Jenkins in the Mormon Meteor." AP later confirmed that Bobby "set a world closed-course record of 196.964 miles an hour in his Lotus-Ford at Fort Stockton, Tex."

Chapter 95
Last of All, Phoenix

Phoenix International Raceway was the last stop on the Championship Trail for 1964, with the Bobby Ball National Championship Classic on November 22. PIR billed itself as "the Indianapolis of the West," and the 200-mile event promised the twenty thousand spectators another exciting battle between front- and rear-engine racers on the new D-shaped track.

Two days before the race, about a dozen drivers were tuning up at the Arizona track. Bobby was driving the Hopkins Lotus 29 and Parnelli Jones was piloting the Lotus 34, Clark's Indy 500 pole-winner that J. C. Agajanian had recently purchased from Ford.

A. J. Foyt was also there, but ran into trouble when he bounced his rear-engine Halibrand-Offy off the wall, shearing the right front wheel and causing extensive damage to the front suspension.

Late that day, crew chief George Bignotti took the car to Ted Halibrand's Los Angeles shop, where it had been built, and immediately began repairs. A. J.'s car was hustled back to Phoenix Saturday night, a round-trip of close to 750 miles.

But on race day, it was not A. J. in his resuscitated Halibrand who claimed victory, but fellow Texan Lloyd Ruby in another rear-engine Halibrand-Offy, the Bill Forbes Special. In his win, Ruby averaged 107.736 mph on the paved one-mile race course.

A. J. and Parnelli started the day in glory, lapping the entire field by their thirtieth go-round. However, after 54 laps Foyt spun and was out with a broken gear lever, and after 139 laps leader Jones went out with a leaking fuel injection line. Ruby had been running third with Bobby hounding him, and they were now running close in a 1-2 contest. On lap 160, Bobby's threat to Ruby collapsed, along with his left rear suspension, putting Bobby and the Pure Firebird Special out of the race.

In a race marred by spins and mechanical failures, eleven drivers finished from the starting field of twenty-five. Bobby started tenth and finished thirteenth.

Prolific author and motorsports historian Joe Scalzo was at the Phoenix race. He recalled that after Bobby's car broke and put him on the sidelines, Bobby got out of it very slowly. "And then I saw him walk slowly to the rear and give it a kick," Scalzo said. It was yet another frustrating end to an exciting and competitive run.

Looking back, it was a year of disappointments, but it was also a year of accomplishment.

No one could have known that the November 22 Phoenix championship run would be Bobby's last race.

Chapter 96
Bare November Days (1964)

After the final championship race of the 1964 season, Bobby stayed on in Phoenix to perform test drives. Janet and Robbie were back home in Fagleysville for the winter.

The Arizona test program was held up for two days by rain and blustery conditions, preventing Bobby from getting home to Pennsylvania, where he had planned to spend Thanksgiving with his extended family. This last-minute change was particularly disappointing because Bobby's grandmother, with whom he was especially close, was hosting the holiday dinner, and the family felt it might be her last year to do so. Bob stayed in Arizona to honor his work commitment.

On November 27, the day after Thanksgiving, Bobby and the rest of the test crew went to work at Phoenix International Raceway. The effort was primarily an engine testing session for Ford Motor Company.

A routine test day suddenly turned tragic. At 3:45 p.m., on the eighteenth lap of a twenty-lap run, Bobby was driving the Lotus 29 at approximately 148 mph when his car went almost straight into a

GILMORE GRAND PRIX CAPTURED BY JONES

By RONNIE ALLYN

LOS ANGELES, Calif., Nov. 26th.—1963 Indianapolis winner Parnelli Jones went wire-to-wire to score a record breaking victory in the 30th anniversary, 150-lap Gilmore Grand Prix USAC Midget race at Ascot Park, before some ,000 fans Thursday night driving the Agajanian-Bowes eal Fast Offy owned by Marv Edwards to victory on the -mile dirt track.

Jones made a comeback from a bad luck of the last two years o score his first win in the 30-year-old Grand Prix Last year ones was leading by a long mar-in, when his engine went sour on he 113th lap and Mel Kenyon went ast and on to victory.

Jones was out to break his rand Prix jinx as he set the ight's fastest qualifying time at 22.70, then went on to lap the field in the 150-lap feature setting a new track record of 57:06.30 to erase A. J. Foyt's 1961 mark of 5:41.56 in a race that saw the green wave from flag to flag.

Finishing second was Don Horvath in the Caruthers Offy, one lap behind Jones. Third was newly crowned National Midget driv-

(PLEASE TURN TO PAGE 14)

FOR PLAYMATES?—Playboy bunnies (left to right) Sandy, Pat and Tina hop into a French Peugeot, which was isplayed in front of the chic Manhattan club, as part of ts October French Festival. This was one of a series of monthly festivals sponsored by the Playboy Club, in which t is honoring different countries of the world. Such recog-ition may make Peugeot, long the car of the businessman, he favorite of the outdoor or indoor sportsman.

Marshman Injured in Tire Test

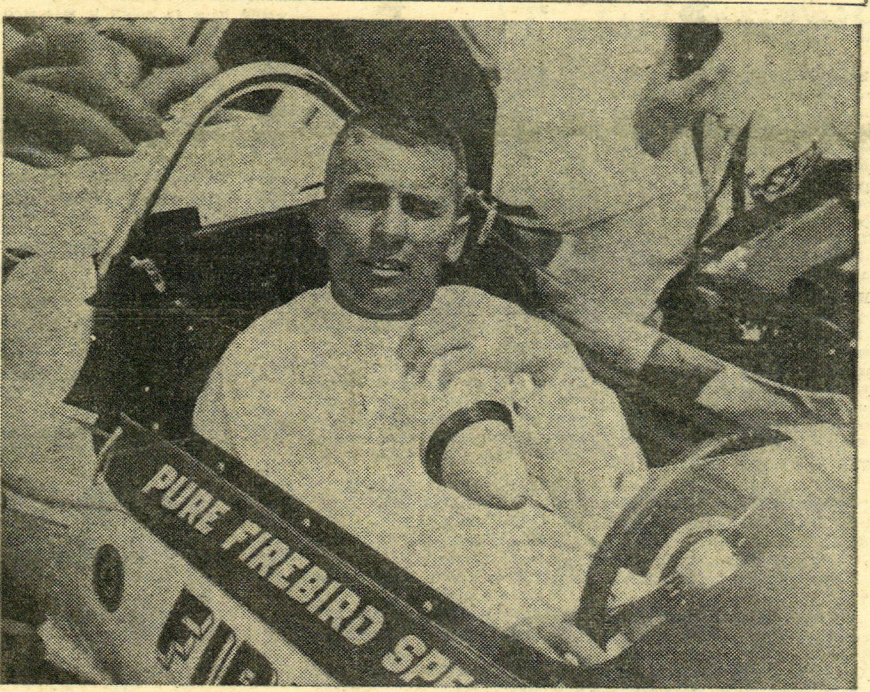

Bobby Marshman is shown receiving instructions in the Lotus-Ford Special, prior to his accident at the Phoenix, Ariz., Speedway.

PHOENIX, Ariz.—Veteran racer Bobby Marshman of Pottstown, Pa., suffered critical burns Friday when his Lotus Ford crashed into a wall at Phoenix International Raceway during a tire test.

A spokesman at the track said the 28-year-old racer, a veteran of the Indianapolis 500, had just turned a lap at more than 115 miles per hour when he lost control of the car.

It slammed into the west retaining wall of the track and burst into flames. Marshman was sprayed with flaming gasoline. He climbed out of the racer without help and firefighters covered him with foam.

The injured driver turned to his chief mechanic, Jack Buckley of Los Angeles, and said, "Jack, get me to the hospital quick. I'm burning all over."

Marshman was rushed to Good Samari-tan Hospital. Later he was flown to the Ft. Sam Houston Hospital at San Antonio, Texas.

Latest report has it that Bobby suffered 90% burns with 58% being third degree. He is being fed liquids through the mouth. His condition is listed as critical.

Officials said the Lotus Ford he drove at the Indy race this year was destroyed. The heat not only melted the car but burned through part of the concrete retaining wall.

Marshman finished 13th in the recent annual 200-mile Bobby Ball Memorial race at the Phoenix Speedway.

Marshman has had nothing but ill luck in the car in which he led this year's 500 miler until the oil plug was ripped out, when he went too low on a turn. At Mil-waukee he crashed the car during practice, but walked away.

retaining wall on his entrance to turn three. Bobby had just completed a test lap at a 115-mph average.

Witnesses told *Indianapolis Star* reporters that just before the crash "there was a loud roar as though something had gone wrong with the car." And according to the Collegeville, Pennsylvania, *Independent and Montgomery Transcript*, mechanics on the track said that the car's engine "changed tune" on the turn and that something then "locked." Some observers described the change in engine noise as "a breaking sound." Others, including chief mechanic Jack Beckley, said that the car was already on fire before it crashed. After it hit the wall, the car skidded two hundred feet before it stopped and exploded into an inferno, setting nearby guardrail posts and grass on fire.

Early reports said that Bobby stepped out of the car, but it was later confirmed that he was trapped in the flaming cockpit for approximately sixty seconds, and then rescued by firemen on duty who were wearing asbestos suits. Lloyd Ruby also helped Bobby from the flames, reported Forrest R. Kyle in the *Decatur Daily Review*.

One fireman pulled Bobby out of the car while the other sprayed chemical extinguisher on the fire. They also covered Bobby in foam. The firemen then used up the rest of their foam to put out the fire, only to have it start anew, virtually destroying the test car, the Lotus 29. (Some accounts have Bobby driving a Lotus 34 in the Phoenix test crash, but this is unlikely, since the test car was demolished, and the continuing history of the three 34s is well documented: Two Lotus 34s ran in the 1965 Indy 500; the third Lotus 34 is on record as "not rebuilt" after its return to Cheshunt following Walt Hansgen's August 1964 accident.)

Newspaper reports the following day recounted Bobby's words when he emerged from the car: To Beckley, he said, "Jack, get me to a hospital, quick. I'm burning all over."

Bobby was rushed to Good Samaritan Hospital in Phoenix, reportedly in the back of a pickup truck. He was conscious, and remained so throughout his ordeal. He was listed in extremely critical condition, suffering second- and third-degree burns to 85 to 90 percent of his body.

Beckley called Janet, who was at home, and she immediately made arrangements to fly to Phoenix, leaving Robbie in the care of her sister, Kay Scheffey. Kay's husband Donald accompanied Janet and her mother, Alice Fairlie, to Arizona. Bob's best friend, Jay Miller, arrived soon after, Janet recalled.

Efforts quickly began to have Bobby transferred from Phoenix to the Brooke Army Burn Center in San Antonio, widely considered to be the top burn center in the world. Ford executives appealed to US Secretary of Defense Robert McNamara, a former president of Ford Motor Company, to intercede on behalf of Bobby; moving him to the renowned military facility was complicated, since Bobby was not a veteran. At the same time, Richard Schweiker, congressman for the thirteenth congressional district, encompassing Bobby's home county of Montgomery, became involved, helping to orchestrate the move. On the night following the accident, Bobby was airlifted from Phoenix to the San Antonio burn center.

The next day, Janet, her mother, her brother-in-law, and Miller all flew to San Antonio.

"The first night or two my mother and I stayed with Janey and Jim Hurtubise," Janet recounted.

"Jim was still receiving treatment at Brooke because of his severe burns from the June race in Milwaukee." The house where they all stayed belonged to another USAC driver, Ebb Rose.

Bobby's spirits improved after Janet arrived, and he was able to talk with her. "My mother and I moved to a room in the Army barracks at Fort Sam Houston, next to the hospital," Janet added. "It was just a room to sleep in and put your clothes, but it put us right there, close to Bob."

Bobby's father George was away from home on business when he received word, and first flew to Phoenix on Saturday, and then on to San Antonio on Sunday. Bobby's mother Evelyn followed on Tuesday. According to the *Pottstown Mercury*'s Warren Howard, she had been advised by doctors "not to get her hopes up." Bobby's sister LaRone Marshman Innes told Howard, "But we can still hope, anyway, and pray."

As November bled into December, Bobby remained in critical condition in the intensive care unit of the Brooke Center. In addition to family members, a few close friends were also in San Antonio to support Bob and Janet. Jane Hurtubise stayed by Janet's side during the ordeal. (It was Bobby who had ridden in the ambulance to the hospital with her husband Jim after his Wisconsin crash, encouraging and supporting him.) As recounted by Bob Gates in his book *Herk Hurtubise*, Jane Hurtubise later said, "It was just awful. It was terrible how badly Bobby was burned."

Concern for Bobby's recovery was widespread, and other friends were in constant touch by phone. "Jack Beckley called me every day about Bobby," recalled longtime friend Bill Marvel. "We were like a family, all of us." The Marshmans also received an outpouring of care and support in telegrams and phone calls to Yerkes. And fans everywhere followed Bobby's progress in daily newspaper reports across the country.

Bobby remained mentally alert throughout his treatment. LaRone later told racing historian Brian Brown that Bobby talked about his situation with their father: Bobby told George he gave himself one week to make it.

Chapter 97
December 3, 1964

Bobby died on Thursday, December 3, six days after his accident at the Phoenix International Raceway track. Janet was at his side, as were his parents. Bobby was twenty-eight years old.

The sad news was reported across the country. Heartfelt articles and commentaries soon followed. The racing community lamented the loss of this fine young driver, with his many outstanding performances and his great promise. In a wide variety of voices and outlets, certain themes were constant: Bobby was liked and respected by all who knew him, admired as a fierce competitor on the track, and esteemed as a gentleman both on and off the track.

Early the next week, the shared grief was made visible. Over 650 mourners made their way to

Trappe, Pennsylvania, to pay their final respects to Bobby Marshman. Eulogies were given during Monday evening calling hours at the Holcombe Funeral Home.

Bobby's funeral service was held on Tuesday, December 8, in Augustus Lutheran Church in Trappe, the same church where Bob and Janet had been married. Reverend John McConomy, who had presided at their wedding five years earlier, officiated, along with Reverend Richard Wolfe. The church overflowed with the bereaved.

The racing community was present in force to honor one of their best. Bobby's former chief mechanics Jack Beckley and Joe Langley were there, along with car owner Lindsey Hopkins. Drivers who came included Roger McCluskey, Bob Cleberg, Ernie McCoy, Red Riegel, Bob Harkey, Dutch Schaefer, Mario Andretti, Carl Miller, Art Malone, Wayne Doerstler, Jack Turner, Mike Magill, and Tommy Hinnershitz. USAC officials present included Tom Binford, Tommy Nicholson, and Henry Banks. In addition to Hopkins, car owners attending included John Wergland, Harry Hespell, Dick Miller, George H. Hudick, Jake Vargo, Bruce Homeyer, Stan Frankenfield, Doug Stearly, and Philip Caruso. Corporate executives present included Dave Evans, Leo Beebe, and Jacques Passino of Ford; Firestone's Bill McCrary; Goodyear's John Laux; and Pure Oil's Dick Dolan. The *New York Herald Tribune*'s Leo Levine and *Car and Driver*'s David E. Davis Jr. were also there. It is impossible to name all who came to say good-bye.

Bobby's pallbearers were close friends and relatives: Bill Reiff, Jay Miller, Richard Heist, Donald Scheffey, Laverne Miller, Charles Innes, George Horrocks, and Gus Gaugler. The interment was to be in the Garden of Memories in the nearby town of Limerick.

The solemn funeral procession of 167 cars stretched all the way from the church in Trappe to Bobby's gravesite in Limerick, a distance of approximately three miles. His family had requested that friends not send flowers, but instead send contributions to the Johnny White Fund. Memorial gifts were sent on behalf of Bobby's fellow driver, but so were flowers sent for Bobby. There were 247 floral pieces at the cemetery. The flowers surrounded Bobby's gravesite and lined the entire driveway of the Limerick Garden of Memories almost to the gate.

Bobby's bronze casket was adorned with a large bouquet and encircled with a ring of red roses. The burial site where he was laid to rest was not far from Bobby's boyhood home in Yerkes.

The graveside service was brief, and the sense of loss was palpable. Cars and mourners continued to arrive even as the final words were spoken, and one by one, hundreds of men and women filed by Bobby's grave to make their last good-byes.

—UPI-Courier-Post Telefax

GRIEVING FAMILY and friends attend funeral services for race driver Bobby Marshman. His wife is escorted to the grave by friends. About 400 mourners paid last respects at services in Limerick, Pa.

ABOVE: The Marshman family grieves for Bobby at his funeral in Limerick, Pennsylvania. (RMA/CHERNOKAL)

Chapter 98
Questions and Speculation

From the moment Bobby's fatal accident happened, there was speculation about the cause.

Immediately after the crash, the *Indianapolis Star* reported that Ford's test chief Joseph Miller discounted the possibilities of an engine "blow" or a stuck throttle as the root problem. Despite Miller's position, many in the industry believed early on that a stuck throttle was the culprit, and this explanation continues to be the consensus of race insiders.

In *Team Lotus*, Lotus competitions manager Andrew Ferguson wrote that Bobby's accident was "caused reputedly by an engine intake instrumentation probe falling into an induction trumpet and jamming the throttle wide open." Danny Jones, a Ford engineer who was present at the Phoenix test, used almost identical language in a 1986 conversation with Lotus expert Walter Goodwin, owner of Racecar Restorations in Indianapolis. Jones explained to Goodwin that Bobby's accident happened when the airflow intake probe test instrument came loose and jammed the throttle open.

In the spring after the accident, the *Star*'s Dave Overpeck wrote that the throttle linkage was blamed for Bobby's death and other recent driver fatalities, noting repeated failures of cable-type throttle linkages used in rear-engine cars, and urging a USAC ban on them in the interests of

driver safety. In a 2014 interview, motorsports journalist and Marshman family friend Bill Marvel said he believed "a rock got into the throttle housing." Rocks and dirt were reported on the track that day because of the rainy, windy conditions preceding the tests.

Four days after Bobby's accident, in Philadelphia's *Evening Bulletin*, Sandy Grady reported this conversation: " 'What happened, Dad?' Marshman said through a throat tube when he first saw his father, George. 'We don't know, Bobby,' said George Marshman. 'We hoped you could help us.' 'I don't know either,' said Bobby. 'It was so fast.' "

In retrospect, a review of the evidence points to the stuck throttle as the cause of the tragedy. But whatever the core problem, the car suddenly failed to respond to the driver.

There was no speculation about what

happened after the car hit the wall: The collision's ensuing fire was traced to the car's center-mounted front fuel tank. As George Moore and Dave Overbeck wrote in the *Star*, the right front wheel of Bobby's car smashed into the side fuel tank, squeezing the gasoline out through the center tank in a hydraulic action and spraying the fuel all over him. On December 10, a week after Bobby's death, the USAC banned front fuel tanks on the Speedway.

However the accident came to be, it cost Bobby his life.

It is not surprising, then, that at the time of Bobby's death and in the years since, there has been keen interest in whether or not he was wearing protective clothing during his test run that fatal day. There are conflicting newspaper accounts on this detail, with opposing reports even in the same paper: On November 28, the day after the accident, the *Indianapolis Star*'s Special Report on Bobby's accident stated: "Marshman . . . was wearing a flame-resistant uniform"; on December 4, the day after Bobby's death, without any reference to their earlier story, the *Star* reported, "Marshman was not wearing the protective clothing or fireproof boots worn in a race." As for the wire services, in their initial reports, the Associated Press and United Press International did not address the question of what Bobby was wearing. After his death, UPI reported: "Because it was a test run, Marshman had decided to skip the usual fireproof driver's suit and boots required in races." Although no source was cited for this detail, the UPI story ran in newspapers across the country, and likely spread and solidified the belief that Bobby was not wearing protective clothing in his fatal Phoenix test drive.

Over the years, many commentators have repeated the era's newspaper accounts that Bobby was not wearing a fireproof suit. However, the question deserves closer attention, if only to note that many reported statements about Bobby's fatal accident were conjecture or opinion, rather than verified facts. For example, rumors persist, such as an anecdote that Bobby had changed out of his race uniform before his accident, because he thought testing was over for the day.

At the same time, the belief that Bobby was in fact wearing protective clothing also persists, and is firmly held by many in the racing community. In print and in interviews, those who knew Bobby professionally and personally have been adamant that he would have been wearing his fireproof driver's suit that day, as a matter of habit. They cite his extreme safety-conscious approach to driving, as well as his professionalism and his healthy concern about the hazards of fire in the cockpit.

"There is no question Bob was wearing a fireproof suit [in the Phoenix test]," Janet stated. "Bob wouldn't have raced or tested without a treated uniform. That's the way he was. Bob was safety-conscious from a young age."

"I know my dad said [Bobby] was in his racing suit and that the fire went up under his pant leg," said Bobby's sister LaRone Marshman Innes. "Knowing Bob, I think he would have had it on. Fire was a big concern of his."

Longtime friend Bill Reiff said, "I always have to come back and think of how we talked a lot [about fire]. We talked about Hurtubise getting burned. Bobby said, 'You know, you never climb into a race car without having used all the available safety equipment available to you.' So that would lead me to believe that he wouldn't have been dumb enough to go in his street clothes." As Reiff was suggesting, "dumb" was not the modus operandi of the man sportswriters called "the thinking man's driver."

Motorsports historian and author Joe Scalzo also shed light on the question. Scalzo, a former motorcycle racer and a contemporary of Bobby's, said it is very unlikely that Bobby was not wearing his driver's suit at the time of the accident. "He was a professional," Scalzo said. "He would not have done that."

A week after Bobby's death, Warren Howard of the *Pottstown Mercury* wrote that Bobby "wore a suit that was supposed to be fireproof. But no woven fabric has yet been developed that will shed fluid," adding that Bobby was "a careful driver who never took unnecessary risks." In a 2014 interview, Bill Marvel said: "I would be greatly surprised if Bobby did not have his uniform on at the time of the accident. Those uniforms back then were not so great in fire protection."

These comments—by Howard in 1964 and by Marvel fifty years later—remind us of a terrible, but indisputable, reality: There was no racing suit available at that time that could have withstood the intense gasoline fire in Bobby's cockpit that day. At best, they were fire-resistant, but they were not fireproof. No matter what Bobby was wearing on November 27, there was no clothing capable of protecting him from a full minute of engulfment in flames.

As with so many racing fatalities, there are aspects of Bobby's accident that will likely never be known for certain. What he wore, or did not wear, is one. But a judicious opinion can be reached by remembering Bobby's work habits and his day-in, day-out approach to his sport. He was a thoughtful professional, a responsible and reliable driver, a devoted husband and father of a young son, and not a man to make light of the risks he faced on every track, in whatever capacity. It seems inconceivable that he was not wearing protective clothing on that final test day. It would have been routine for him to do so.

Nevertheless, speculation is natural and is bound to continue, given Bobby's prominence then and now. In a sense, the inquiry is a testament to the admiration and respect Bobby Marshman earned in his life, and which continue to be in place long after his untimely death. And perhaps there is a deeper question behind the surface question. We ask what he was wearing, but it might be that what we really wonder is: Why did we have to lose him? Undoubtedly, none who admired him will ever stop asking that aching question, whatever form it takes.

Chapter 99
"Tremendous Stature Among Men"

Bobby Marshman was notable for his tremendous popular appeal. He embodied fine personal traits that separated him, in many aspects, from the then-prevalent characterization of oval drivers. Clean-cut, polite, and quietly dedicated, he was credited with improving the sport through his exemplary personal conduct and devotion.

At the same time, Bobby was enormously well-liked and admired by his peers. As John T. Cathers wrote in the Allentown, Pennsylvania, *Evening Chronicle*, "Throughout the pits he was everyone's pal. Racing people liked Bobby Marshman. And he liked them."

In the days and weeks following Bobby's death, tributes to the young man poured forth in papers across the country. And tributes have continued in the years and decades since, in magazines, newspapers, books on racing history, in awards, in race events, and, more recently, in online forums. The heartfelt homages are too numerous to mention individually, but a few can speak for the many, and provide a representative chorus of affection and admiration.

Jim Moffat in *Illustrated Speedsport News* wrote of Bob, "Never was a kindlier, considerate unassuming young man encountered. He was truly a man among men." *Time* magazine's obituary called Bobby a "cool, articulate racing driver." Bill Marvel wrote in *National Speed Sport News*, "as one person who called this evening said, '[Bobby's] helmet size was the same ever since I had met him.' Bobby was a true sportsman . . . He loved to race and always thought of what was best for racing."

Photographer and columnist Walter T. Chernokal said in *Illustrated Speedway News* that although Bob had not achieved all his dreams on the racetrack, "Success was his in a big, big way as he achieved tremendous stature among men with his humble and generous heart which was first to help any fellow man in need."

In Allentown's *Evening Chronicle*, John Cathers added, "Marshman's demeanor never disclosed the inner courage of the man. . . . Bobby Marshman stood out from the pack." These sentiments were echoed by Red McCarthy in the *Norristown Times Herald*: "From the men in the pits, the colleagues in the cockpit, the wealthy racing owners, and the mighty corporations he represented in their tests for automobile improvements, each will tell you Bobby Marshman had all the essentials plus."

The day before Bobby's funeral service and burial, George Moore told *Indianapolis Star* readers: "Bobby Marshman was a young gentleman from Pennsylvania who spent the best years of his life doing what he wanted to do most. This was driving a race car faster and better than anyone else." Moore went on to say that Bobby "was head and shoulders above the run of the mill. . . . He simply had a quiet belief in his own capabilities."

Nearly thirty-five years later another exceptional driver and contemporary of Bob's, Dan Gurney, added a recollection. In a 1998 response to racing historian Brian Brown, Gurney wrote, "At a time when there were major revolutionary changes in Champ Car [Indy Car] racing, Bobby Marshman was a young, up-and-coming, very talented example of a graduate of the old school. He had honed his skills on the traditional learning ladder of American oval track racing and had a very promising career ahead of him."

In his book *Ford: The Dust and the Glory*, Leo Levine called Bobby one of the "Indianapolis heroes of the old school."

In a 2015 interview, three-time Indy 500 winner Bobby Unser told J. C. Argetsinger that Bobby Marshman had "a love of the sport—for him, it was not about getting rich." Unser reflected that both Bobby and Parnelli Jones were unusual in that they were both "born race drivers." Unser went on to say, "Bobby had a hell of a feel for race cars and was just hitting the peak—he was a potential three- or four-time winner of the 500, but died too soon."

Just over a month after Bobby's death, at the January 9, 1965 URC banquet, the first Bobby Marshman Memorial Award was presented to Earl Halaquist, the 1964 URC champion. Later in the month, Bobby was posthumously inducted into the Hoosier Auto Racing Fans (HARF) Hall of Fame at the group's January 17 banquet. In June 1965, the first Bobby Marshman Memorial race was held at Hatfield Speedway, a fifty-lap ARDC championship race for midget drivers, many of whom Bobby had raced with. The winner the first year was Red Riegel. The race was organized by Bobby's father, George, on the track that Bobby helped to build.

The day after Bobby died, Warren Howard of the *Pottstown Mercury* spoke for many when he wrote, "I weep because he is gone, and I knew him for too short a time. Neither I, nor the rest of the racing enthusiasts, will ever see him drive again."

Bobby loved life and he loved racing. He was a young man doing his sport and bringing something special to it. When he died, Bobby was right on the cusp of achieving the full measure of his greatness as a driver.

In many ways, Bobby's story is the story of fellow drivers from his time, also doing the sport they loved, and doing it well—even with care, despite their daring maneuvers in a dangerous endeavor. When we think of him, we think of the best in all of them.

But the story is also Bobby's story alone. A boy from small-town Pennsylvania, imbued with the joys of fast cars throughout his childhood, he grew up to display prodigious talent on the track, and a spirit of dedication, fun, and compassion in all he did. Racing was not only a profession for Bobby: it was an essential part of who he was. He was a fine man and a fine driver.

It is Bobby Marshman we remember here, a young man now forever, who in his short life strove, and soared, and is sorely missed.

Epilogue

have wanted to write this book since 1964 when I was a private first class in Okinawa, listening to radio broadcasts of the Indy 500.

I had always listened to the Indy 500 races at home with my father, Cameron Argetsinger, and I had been aware of Bobby Marshman. I remember when he was named Co–Rookie of the Year in 1961; he went from thirty-third place to finish ahead of Parnelli, who had been getting so much publicity. I knew who Bobby was—he was one of the top guys.

But early in 1964, I had been reading about starting times in *Stars and Stripes*, and I was fascinated by Bobby's great speed and dominance over the greatest drivers in the world. I followed him the whole month prior to the race, and I heard the broadcast of the race itself far from home. I was also aware that a great change had come upon American oval racing, in part with the advent of drivers like Bobby Marshman. He made a tremendous impression on me, and that imprint has never left me.

The experience of researching and writing Bobby's Marshman's biography has been a gratifying one on many levels. Completing this book fulfills a long-held ambition to chronicle the life of one of my personal racing heroes. In addition, the research process introduced me to the incredible support of many men and women who also hold Bobby Marshman in the highest regard. I was the fortunate recipient of their interest, assistance, and enthusiasm, because they share my admiration and affection for the young man from Pennsylvannia. This universally positive response is a credit to Bobby Marshman as a person and as a driver.

When Bobby died, Janet lost a loving husband whose memory she will always cherish, and Robbie lost a loving father. LaRone and Elaine lost a brother who was never replaced in their love and affection,

ABOVE: A signed portrait of Bobby from the Racemaker Archive.

BELOW: Bobby proved himself one of the most talented drivers of his era. (RMA/BAIRD)

BELOW: Author Michael Argetsinger.

while his close friends lost an intimate who remained a modest and cheerful superstar to the end. The racing world lost a quiet leader who would have more rapidly brought about the changes that were developing in the sport.

I believe Marshman would have been one of the USAC drivers to go to Le Mans for Ford in 1966, and likely would have been a strong force for Ford in their road-racing program. I believe this because of Bobby's proven skill, and because of his youth and willingness to adapt to new challenges. I believe Bobby would have become one of the American and international stars of the 1970s. He was already known for the smoothness of his technique and relaxed speed.

Donald Davidson, renowned Indianapolis Motor Speedway historian, has told me how, "upon return to England, the Lotus mechanics dubbed Bobby as an 'American Jimmy,' referring to the world champion Jimmy Clark." Davidson has also said that "Bobby Marshman was Rick Mears before there was a Rick Mears." As Davidson suggests, these comparisons are the highest praise.

In his time, Bobby earned his own place as a driver to emulate. "Handles corners with the ease of a Bobby Marshman" and "in the clean-cut, all-American Bobby Marshman mold" are among the references to Bob that bestow high praise to any driver. And now, after talking to many who knew him, and reading the many contemporary accounts of his actions, as well as the many historical perspectives on his role in racing, I can attest that Bobby Marshman was a man esteemed both on and off the track. Time has not diminished this respect.

I am gratified to have had the chance to share a measure of Bobby Marshman's story.

—Michael Reynolds Argetsinger

Bobby Marshman's racing record, 1955-1964

Racemaker Press is indebted to Michael Argetsinger's rigorous research and to both UltimateRacingHistory.com and ChampCarStats.com in providing the framework for this compilation of Bobby's racing record over the ten years of his career. Racemaker's remarkable archive of newspapers, magazines and photos was also an invaluable tool in completing the details of this listing.

1955

May 15	Reading, PA	URC sprint cars	#99 Marshman-Ford	DNF, spun
June 18	Middletown, NY	URC sprint cars	#99 Marshman-Ford	finished 4th
July 4	Altamont, NY	URC sprint cars	#99 Marshman-Ford	started 3rd, finished feature
Aug 20	Hamburg, NY	URC sprint cars	#99 Marshman-Ford	finished 11th in semi-final
Sep 4	Nazareth, PA	URC sprint cars	#99 Marshman-Ford	qualified for feature, spun
Sep 24	Shelby, NC	URC sprint cars	#99 Marshman-Ford	won heat, DNF in feature, engine
Oct 9	Langhorne, PA	URC sprint cars	#99 Marshman-Ford	6th in heat
Oct 14	Winston-Salem, NC	URC sprint cars	#99 Marshman-Ford	spun
Oct 15	Winston-Salem, NC	URC sprint cars	#99 Marshman-Ford	DNF
Oct 22	Raleigh, NC	URC sprint cars	#99 Marshman-Ford	3rd in heat, 3rd in feature

10th in URC points, URC rookie of the year

1956

Feb 5	West Palm Beach, FL	USAC sprint cars	#99 Marshman-Ford	started 13th, DNF
Feb 12	Jacksonville, FL	USAC sprint cars	#99 Marshman-Ford	qualified and finished feature
May 20	Nazareth, PA	URC sprint cars	#99 Marshman-Ford	started 7th, finished 5th
June 3	Williams Grove, PA	URC sprint cars	#99 Marshman-Ford	accident in qualifying heat
June 30	Middletown, NY	URC sprint cars	#99 Marshman-Ford	accident
July 1	Flemington, NJ	URC sprint cars	#99 Marshman-Ford	3rd in heat
July 4	Fonda, NY	URC sprint cars	#99 Marshman-Ford	4th in heat
July 29	Marlboro, MD	URC sprint cars	#99 Marshman-Ford	3rd in heat
Aug 18	Flemington, NJ	URC sprint cars	#99 Marshman-Ford	finished feature out of points
Aug 25	Hamburg, NY	URC sprint cars	#99 Marshman-Ford	4th in heat, 7th in feature
Sep 1	Essex Junction, VT	URC sprint cars	#99 Marshman-Ford	finished feature out of points
Sep 3	Flemington, NJ	URC sprint cars	#99 Marshman-Ford	5th in feature
Sep 22	Shelby, NC	URC sprint cars	#8 Ellis Bros-Dodge	2nd in heat, 6th in feature
Sep 29	Richmond, VA	URC sprint cars	#99 Marshman-Ford	4th in heat, 8th in feature
Oct 8	Langhorne, PA	URC sprint cars	#99 Marshman-Ford	engine failure
Oct 20	Raleigh, NC	URC sprint cars	#8 Ellis Bros-Dodge	started 9th, finished 5th

8th in URC points

May 26	Williams Grove, PA	URC sprint cars	#8 Ellis Bros-Dodge	won qualifying heat
May 30	Hatfield, PA	URC sprint cars	#8 Ellis Bros-Dodge	2nd in heat, 4th in feature
May 31	Nazareth, PA	URC sprint cars	#8 Ellis Bros-Dodge	5th in feature
June 1	Manassas, VA	URC sprint cars	#8 Ellis Bros-Dodge	won heat, 3rd in feature
June 21	Old Bridge, VA	URC sprint cars	#8 Ellis Bros-Dodge	won heat, won feature (first major win)
June 22	Middletown, NY	URC sprint cars	#8 Ellis Bros-Dodge	won heat
July 4	Fonda, NY	URC sprint cars	#8 Ellis Bros-Dodge	won heat, 4th in feature
July 5	Nazareth, PA	URC sprint cars	#8 Ellis Bros-Dodge	3rd in heat, 4th in feature
July 12	Rochester, NY	URC sprint cars	#8 Ellis Bros-Dodge	3rd in heat, 3rd in feature
July 13	Buffalo, NY	URC sprint cars	#8 Ellis Bros-Dodge	4th in feature
July 20	Manassas, VA	URC sprint cars	#8 Ellis Bros-Dodge	won heat, 3rd in feature (took URC points lead)
Aug 2	Rochester, NY	URC sprint cars	#8 Ellis Bros-Dodge	won heat, 2nd in feature
Aug 4	Owego, NY	URC sprint cars	#8 Ellis Bros-Dodge	2nd in feature
Aug 10	Bedford, NY	URC sprint cars	#8 Ellis Bros- Dodge	2nd in heat, 4th in feature
Aug 31	Essex Junction, VT	URC sprint cars	#8 Ellis Bros-Dodge	won heat, 3rd in feature
Sep 1	Flemington, NJ	URC sprint cars	#8 Ellis Bros-Dodge	won heat, 6th in feature
Sep 1	Nazareth, PA	URC sprint cars	#8 Ellis Bros-Dodge	3rd in heat, 7th in feature
Sep 2	Flemington, NJ	URC sprint cars	#8 Ellis Bros-Dodge	4th in feature
Sep 20	Springfield, MA	URC sprint cars	#8 Ellis Bros-Dodge	finished feature out of points
Sep 28	Richmond, VA	URC sprint cars	#8 Ellis Bros-Dodge	DNF, engine
Nov 19	Raleigh, NC	URC sprint cars	#8 Ellis Bros-Dodge	won consolation race, 6th in feature
Nov 20	Waynesboro, VA	URC sprint cars	#8 Ellis Bros-Dodge	spun

2nd in URC points to Bert Brooks

May 17	Hatfield, PA	ARDC midgets	#7 Harry Hespell-Offy	finished out of top ten
May 30	Williams Grove, PA	ARDC midgets	#7 Hespell-Offy	4th in heat, 8th in feature
May 30	Sanatoga, PA	ATQMRA three-quarter midgets	Jack Dowie-Triumph	won feature
May 31	Hatfield, PA	ARDC midgets	#7 Hespell-Offy	3rd in feature
June 6	Middletown, NY	ARDC midgets	#7 Hespell-Offy	3rd in heat, 14th in feature
June 8	Sanatoga, PA	ATQMRA three-quarter midgets	#20 Dowie-Triumph	2nd in feature
June 14	Hatfield, PA	ARDC midgets	#7 Hespell-Offy	3rd in consolation race, out of top ten in feature
June 29	Langhorne, PA	ARDC midgets	#7 Hespell-Offy	started 8th, finished out of top ten
Aug 3	Trenton, NJ	ARDC midgets	#7 Hespell-Offy	won feature at record speed, 104.706 mph
Aug 9	Middletown, NY	ARDC midgets	#7 Hespell-Offy	5th in feature
Aug 16	Seekonk, MA	ARDC midgets	#7 Hespell-Offy	finished out of top ten
Aug 29	Freeport, NY	ARDC midgets	#7 Hespell-Offy	4th in heat
Sep 6	Hatfield, PA	ARDC midgets	#7 Hespell-Offy	won feature
Sep 19	Freeport, NY	ARDC midgets	#7 Hespell-Offy	5th in heat, 2nd in consolation race
Sep 20	Hatfield, PA	ARDC midgets	#7 Hespell-Offy	finished out of points
Oct 5	Trenton, NJ	ARDC midgets	#7 Hespell-Offy	5th in 100-mile feature
Oct 11	Bloomsburg, PA	ARDC midgets	#7 Hespell-Offy	won heat, 3rd in feature

3rd in ARDC points, named ARDC's 'Most Improved Driver'

Exhausted after a tough 100-mile race on the dirt.

May 1	Hatfield, PA	ARDC midgets	#7 Hespell-Offy	3rd in heat, 4th in feature
May 3	Menands, NY	ARDC midgets	#7 Hespell-Offy	won semi, did not place in feature
May 8	Hatfield, PA	ARDC midgets	#7 Hespell-Offy	4th in feature
May 9	Manassas, VA	ARDC midgets	#7 Hespell-Offy	did not place in feature
May 10	Richmond, VA	ARDC midgets	#7 Hespell-Offy	5th in feature
May 30	Roanoke, VA	ARDC midegts	#7 Hespell-Offy	2nd in heat, 2nd in feature
June 7	Danbury, CT	ARDC midgets	#7 Hespell-Offy	started 2nd, won heat, semi and feature
June 7	Old Bridge, NJ	ARDC midgets	#7 Hespell-Offy	won heat, 7th in feature
June 26	Hatfield, PA	ARDC midgets	#7 Hespell-Offy	won heat, did not place in feature
June 27	Belmar, NJ	ARDC midgets	#7 Hespell-Offy	4th in heat, did not place in feature
June 28	Heidelberg, PA	ARDC midgets	#7 Hespell-Offy	won heat and feature
July 5	Williams Grove, PA	ARDC midgets	#7 Hespell-Offy	5th in feature
July 18	Hatfield, PA	ARDC midgets	#7 Hespell-Offy	3rd in feature
July 24	Hatfield, PA	ARDC midgets	#7 Hespell-Offy	3rd in feature
July 26	Trenton, NJ	ARDC midgets	#7 Hespell-Offy	2nd in feature
Aug 23	Trenton, NJ	ARDC midgets	#7 Hespell-Offy	DNF
Sep 5	Flemington, NJ	ARDC midgets	#7 Hespell-Offy	won heat, 4th in feature
Sep 11	Hatfield, PA	ARDC midgets	#7 Hespell-Offy	DNF, accident
Sep 19	Reading, PA	ARDC midgets	#7 Hespell-Offy	3rd in heat, 3rd in feature
Sep 20	Trenton, NJ	ARDC midgets	#7 Hespell-Offy	DNF, mechanical
Sep 24	Springfield, MA	ARDC midgets	#7 Hespell-Offy	2nd in feature
Sep 26	Richmond, VA	URC sprint cars	#8 Ellis Bros-Dodge	won heat and feature
Oct 11	Williams Grove, PA	USAC sprint cars	Mike Caruso-Offy	won consolation race, 8th in feature
Dec 13	Hempstead, NY	ATQMRA three-quarter midgets	#2 Jack Dowie-Triumph	2nd in semi, 11th in feature
Dec 27	Hempstead, NY	ATQMRA three-quarter midgets	#2 Dowie-Triumph	2nd in consolation race, 3rd in feature

5th in ARDC points, named ARDC's 'Most Improved Driver'

1960

Jan 3	Hempstead, NY	ATQMRA three-quarter midgets	#2 Dowie-Triumph	2nd in heat, 2nd in semi, won feature
Jan 9	Teaneck, NJ	ATQMRA three-quarter midgets	#2 Dowie-Triumph	4th in feature
Jan 10	Hempstead, NY	ATQMRA three-quarter midgets	#2 Dowie-Triumph	2nd in feature
Jan 16	Teaneck, NJ	ATQMRA three-quarter midgets	#2 Dowie-Triumph	won heat, 4th in feature
Jan 17	Hempstead, NY	ATQMRA three-quarter midgets	#2 Dowie-Triumph	won heat, 2nd in feature
Jan 23	Teaneck, NJ	ATQMRA three-quarter midgets	#2 Dowie-Triumph	2nd in heat, won semi, 10th in feature
Jan 24	Hempstead, NY	ATQMRA three-quarter midgets	#2 Dowie-Triumph	5th in feature
Jan 30	Teaneck, NJ	ATQMRA three-quarter midgets	#2 Dowie-Triumph	3rd in semi, 2nd in feature
Jan 31	Hempstead, NY	ATQMRA three-quarter midgets	#2 Dowie-Triumph	won heat, 3rd in feature
Feb 20	Teaneck, NJ	ATQMRA three-quarter midgets	#2 Dowie-Triumph	DNF, accident
Feb 21	Hempstead, NY	ATQMRA three-quarter midgets	#2 Dowie-Triumph	2nd in feature
Feb 27	Teaneck, NJ	ATQMRA three-quarter midgets	#2 Dowie-Triumph	2nd in heat
Mar 5	Teaneck, NJ	ATQMRA three-quarter midgets	#2 Dowie-Triumph	6th in feature
Apr 10	Houston, TX	USAC midgets	#4 Hespell-Offy	DNF
Apr 17	Reading, PA	USAC sprint cars	#52 Frankie Calandrillo Cal-Offy	3rd in consi, DNS feature, mechanical
May 6	Hatfield, PA	ARDC midgets	#4 Hespell-Offy	3rd in heat, 8th in feature
May 15	Williams Grove, PA	ARDC midgets	#4 Hespell-Offy	won heat, 3rd in feature
June 3	Freeport, NY	ARDC midgets	#4 Hespell-Offy	2nd in feature
June 4	Danbury, CT	ARDC midgets	#4 Hespell-Offy	DNF, accident
June 5	Hatfield, PA	ARDC midgets	#4 Hespell-Offy	3rd in heart, 8th in feature
June 11	Manassas, VA	ARDC midgets	#4 Hespell-Offy	3rd in feature
June 25	Danbury, CT	ARDC midgets	#4 Hespell-Offy	3rd in heat
June 26	Reading, PA	ARDC midgets	#4 Hespell-Offy	2nd in heat
July 3	Williams Grove, PA	ARDC midgets	#4 Hespell-Offy	DNQ, engine trouble
July 4	York, PA	ARDC midgets	#4 Hespell-Offy	3rd in consi, DNF accident in feature
July 7	Danbury, CT	ARDC midgets	#4 Hespell-Offy	won heat
July 24	Trenton NJ	ARDC midgets	#19 Bill Homeyer/Konstant Hot-Offy	won 300-mile feature
Aug 6	Danbury, CT	ARDC midgets	#19 Homeyer/Constant Hot-Offy	2nd in heat, 4th in semi
Aug 11	Freeport, NY	ARDC midgets	#19 Homeyer/Konstant Hot-Offy	3rd in semi
Aug 13	Hamburg, NY	ARDC midgets	#19 Homeyer/Konstant Hot-Offy	3rd in heat, 9th in feature
Aug 14	Hatfield, PA	ARDC midgets	#19 Homeyer/Konstant Hot-Offy	3rd in feature
Aug 27	Milwaukee, WI	USAC midgets	#19 Homeyer/Konstant Hot-Offy	8th in feature
Sep 13	Reading, PA	ARDC midgets	#19 Homeyer/Konstant Hot-Offy	2nd in heat, 9th in feature
Sep 14	Marlboro, MD	ARDC sprint cars	#19 Homeyer/Konstant Hot-Offy	won heat, 7th in feature, DNF accident in second feature
Sep 24	Allentown, PA	USAC sprint cars	#59 Ray Brady/Kurtis-Offy	6th in semi
Sep 25	Trenton, NJ	USAC championship	#59 Ray Brady/Kurtis-Offy	DNQ
Oct 1	Bloomsburg, PA	ARDC midgets	#19 Homeyer/Konstant Hot-Offy	won heat, 4th in feature
Oct 2	Old Bridge, NJ	ARDC midgets	#19 Homeyer/Konstant Hot-Offy	4th in feature
Nov 5	Commack, NY	ATQMRA three-quarter midgets	#2 Dowie-Triumph	4th in heat, 2nd in semi, 11th in feature

3rd in ATQMRA points, 9th in ARDC points

Bobby battles wheel to wheel with race winner Don Branson at the Trenton 200 in September. (RMA/CHERNOKAL)

1961

Jan 7	Teaneck, NJ	ATQMRA three-quarter-midgets	#63 Norm Smizer-Offy	3rd in heat, 3rd in semi, DNF in feature
Jan 14	Teaneck, NJ	ATQMRA three-quarter midgets	#63 Smizer-Offy	3rd in feature
Jan 21	Teaneck, NJ	ATQMRA three-quarter midgets	#63 Smizer-Offy	3rd in heat, 2nd in semi, 3rd in feature
Jan 28	Teaneck, NJ	ATQMRA three-quarter midgets	#63 Smizer-Offy	6th in heat, won semi
Feb 18	Teaneck, NJ	ATQMRA three-quarter midgets	#2 Dowie-Triumph	7th in semi, DNF in feature, mechanical
Feb 25	Teaneck, NJ	ATQMRA three-quarter midgets	#2 Dowie-Triumph	DNF in feature
Mar 4	Teaneck, NJ	ATQMRA three-quarter midgets	#2 Dowie-Triumph	3rd in feature
Mar 11	Teaneck, NJ	ATQMRA three-quarter midgets	#2 Dowie-Triumph	DNF in semi, mechanical
Mar 18	Teaneck, NJ	ATQMRA three-quarter midgets	#2 Dowie-Triumph	won consi, DNF in feature
Mar 26	Reading, PA	USAC sprint cars	#93 Howard Iddings/Meyer-Offy	started 3rd, finished 12th, engine trouble
Apr 9	Trenton, NJ	USAC championship	#93 Iddings/Meyer-Offy	started 20th, DNF accident, brake failure. USAC championship debut
Apr 30	Langhorne, PA	ARDC/USAC midgets	#9 Homeyer/Konstant Hot-Offy	started 2nd, finished 2nd
May 30	Indianapolis 500	USAC championship	#31 Eph Hoover Motor Express/ Epperly-Offy	started 33rd, finished 7th, co-rookie of the year with Parnelli Jones
June 4	Milwaukee, WI	USAC championship	#31 Hoover/Epperly-Offy	started 12th, DNF, engine
June 10	Hatfield, PA	ARDC midgets	#9 Homeyer/Konstant Hot-Offy	3rd in heat, DNF in feature, mechanical
June 11	Terre Haute, IN	USAC sprint cars	#93 Iddings/Meyer-Offy	DNQ
June 18	Langhorne, PA	USAC sprint cars	#44 Wally Meskowski/ Meskowski-Offy	started 5th, DNF, eye injury
July 2	Trenton, NJ	USAC/ARDC midgets	#9 Homeyer/Konstant Hot-Offy	started 6th
July 14	Old Bridge, NJ	ARDC midgets	#9 Homeyer/Konstant Hot-Offy	won heat and feature
July 30	Indianapolis Raceway Park	USAC sprint cars	#93 Iddings/Meyer-Offy	DNQ
Aug 12	Milwaukee, WI	USAC midgets	#9 Homeyer/Konstant Hot-Offy	started 8th, finished 4th
Aug 13	Terre Haute, IN	USAC sprint cars	#44 Meskowski/Meskowski-Offy	started 11th, finished 8th
Aug 20	Milwaukee, WI	USAC championship	#31 Hoover/Epperly-Offy	started 20th, DNF, mechanical
Aug 21	Springfield, IL	USAC championship	#44 Meskowski/Meskowski-Offy	started 8th, finished 9th
Aug 27	Langhorne, PA	USAC sprint car	#44 Meskowski/Meskowski-Offy	started 3rd, DNF, accident
Aug 27	Langhorne, PA	USAC sprint car	#44 Meskowski/Meskowski-Offy	started 13th, finished 3rd
Sep 2	DuQuoin, IL	USAC sprint car	#44 Meskowski/Meskowski-Offy	started 8th, finished 6th
Sep 4	DuQuoin, IL	USAC championship	#44 Meskowski/Meskowski-Offy	started 10th, finished 8th
Sep 8	Lancaster, NY	USAC sprint car	#44 Meskowski/Meskowski-Offy	started 10th, finished 4th
Sep 9	Syracuse, NY	USAC championship	#44 Meskowski/Meskowski-Offy	started 10th, finished 7th
Sep 10	New Bremen, OH	USAC sprint car	#44 Meskowski/Meskowski-Offy	started 6th, DNF, mechanical
Sep 16	Indiana State Fairgrounds	USAC championship	#44 Meskowski/Meskowski-Offy	started 2nd, finished 2nd
Sep 17	Trenton, NJ	ARDC midgets	#19 Homeyer/Konstant Hot-Offy	started 2nd, won
Sep 24	Trenton, NJ	USAC championship	#44 Meskowski/Meskowski-Offy	started 5th, DNF, engine
Sep 24	Trenton, NJ	USAC championship	relieved Johnny Boyd in #21 Leader Card/Watson-Offy	DNF, spun
Sep 30	Bloomsburg, PA	ARDC midgets	#22 Berks-Offy	won consi, 4th in feature
Sep 31	Nazareth, PA	ARDC midgets	#22 Berks-Offy	2nd in heat, engine trouble, took over #3 Bennett Bros-Offy, 3rd in feature
Oct 8	Williams Grove, PA	USAC sprint car	#44 Meskowski/Meskowski-Offy	DNQ, clutch failure

Oct 21	Ascot, CA	USAC midgets	#5 Algon-Offy	started 16th, DNF, clutch
Oct 29	Sacramento, CA	USAC championship	#44 Meskowski/Meskowski-Offy	started 13th, finished 3rd
Nov 4	Orange Show, CA	USAC midgets	#20 Ward-Offy	DNQ
Nov 11	Ascot, CA	USAC sprint cars	#5 Conze-Offy	DNQ
Nov 19	Phoenix, AZ	USAC championship	#44 Meskowski/Meskowski-Offy	started 12th, finished 11th, relieved by Jim Hurtubise

3rd in ATQMRA points, 8th in USAC championship points

1962

Mar 25	Reading, PA	USAC sprint cars	#8 Meskowski/Meskowski-Offy	started 5th, finished 4th
Apr 8	Trenton, NJ	USAC championship	#8 Meskowski/Meskowski-Offy	started 10th, finished 10th
Apr 22	Eldora, OH	USAC sprint car	#8 Meskowski/Meskowski-Offy	started 5th, DNF
May 30	Indianapolis 500	USAC championship	#54 Bryant Heating & Cooling/Epperly-Offy	started 3rd, finished 5th
June 3	Trenton, NJ	ARDC midgets	#9 Homeyer/Konstant Hot-Offy	started 2nd, DNF engine
June 10	Milwaukee, WI	USAC championship consolation race	#8 Meskowski/Meskowski-Offy	started 12th, finished 2nd
June 10	Milwaukee, WI	USAC championship	#8 Meskowski/Meskowski-Offy	started 21st, finished 12th
June 30	Williams Grove, PA	USAC sprint car	#1/Harlan Fike-Chevy	DNQ accident in consi
July 1	Langhorne, PA	USAC championship	#8 Meskowski/Meskowski-Offy	started 5th, finished 5th
July 22	Trenton, NJ	USAC championship	#8 Meskowski/Meskowski-Offy	started 16th, DNF, engine
Aug 11	Hatfield, PA	ARDC/USAC midgets	#9 Homeyer/Konstant Hot-Offy	finished 2nd
Aug 12	Owego, NY	ARDC midgets	#9 Homeyer/Konstant-Hot-Offy	5th in heat, DNF in feature, fuel injection
Aug 18	Springfield, IL	USAC championship	#14 Ansted-Murphy/Thompson Rotary Meskowski-Offy	started 10th, finished 4th
Aug 19	Milwaukee, WI	USAC championship	#14 Ansted-Murphy/Thompson Rotary Trevis-Offy	started 1st, finished 3rd
Aug 26	Langhorne, PA	USAC championship	#14 Ansted-Murphy/Thompson Rotary Meskowski-Offy	started 7th, finished 9th relieved by Elmer George
Sep 8	Syracuse, NY	USAC championship	#14 Ansted-Murphy/Thompson Rotary Meskowski-Offy	started 7th, DNF, shift lever
Sep 15	Indiana State Fairgrounds	USAC championship	#14 Ansted-Murphy/Thompson Rotary Meskowski-Offy	started 8th, finished 6th
Sep 16	Trenton, NJ	ARDC/USAC midgets	#7 Homeyer Konstant Hot-Offy	started 5th, won 100-lap feature
Sep 23	Trenton, NJ	USAC championship	#14 Ansted-Murphy/Thompson Rotary Meskowski-Offy	started 14th, finished 3rd
Oct 7	Terre Haute, IN	USAC midget	#5 Ralph Wilke/Leader Card-Offy	started 20th, DNF, broken shock
Oct 14	Williams Grove	USAC sprint cars	#21 HOW-Chevy	started 9th, finished 15th
Oct 28	Sacramento, CA	USAC championship	#1 Lindsey Hopkins/Kuzma-Offy	started 5th, DNF, accident
Nov 3	Ascot, CA	USAC sprint car	#5 Colvin-Chevy	started 15th, finished 8th
Nov 10	Ascot, CA	USAC sprint car	#5 Colvin-Chevy	started 19th, DNF, throttle
Nov 18	Phoenix, AZ	USAC championship	#1 Lindsey Hopkins/Kuzma-Offy	started 4th, won, first USAC championship victory

5th in USAC championship points

Bobby made his first attempt to qualify for a USAC Championship race at Trenton in September, 1960, aboard Ray Brady's Kurtis 400, but failed to make the field. (MARSHMAN FAMILY COLLECTION)

Mar 24	Reading, PA	USAC sprint car	#8 KEY-Chevy	started 9th, finished 7th
Mar 31	Williams Grove, PA	USAC sprint car	#8 KEY-Chevy	DNQ for feature
Apr 7	Langhorne, PA	USAC sprint car	#8 KEY-Chevy	started 8th, finished 3rd
Apr 7	Langhorne, PA	USAC sprint car	#8 KEY-Chevy	started 3rd, finished 4th
Apr 21	Trenton, NJ	USAC championship	#5 Hopkins/Kuzma-Offy	started 7th, finished 6th
Apr 28	New Bremen, OH	USAC sprint car	#8 KEY-Chevy	started 4th, finished 3rd
May 30	Indianapolis 500	USAC championship	#5 Hopkins/Epperly-Offy	started 7th, DNF, rear end
June 2	New Bremen, OH	USAC sprint car	#9 Meskowski/Meskowski-Offy	started 3rd, DNF, accident
June 9	Milwaukee, WI	USAC championship	#5 Hopkins/Epperly-Offy	started 9th, finished 7th
June 16	Terre Haute, IN	USAC sprint car	#9 Meskowski/Meskowski-Offy	DNQ, broken piston
June 23	Langhorne, PA	USAC championship	#5 Hopkins/Kuzma-Offy	started 6th, finished 5th, relieved by Don Branson
June 28	Columbus, IN	USAC midgets	#5 Wilke/Leader Card-Offy	started 2nd, finished 5th
June 30	Indianapolis Raceway Park	USAC sprint car	#9 Meskowski/Meskowski-Offy	DNQ, broken crankshaft
July 7	Williams Grove, PA	USAC sprint car	#9 Meskowski/Meskowski-Offy	started 10th, finished 3rd
July 26	Hatfield, PA	USAC sprint car	#9 Meskowski/Meskowski-Offy	started 4th, finished 2nd
July 28	Trenton, NJ	USAC championship	#5 Hopkins/Epperly-Offy	started 16th, DNF, piston
Aug 2	Columbus, IN	USAC midgets	Harry Turner-Offy	started 2nd, won, led flag to flag
Aug 4	Salem, IN	USAC sprint car	#9 Meskowski/Meskowski-Chevy	started 3rd, finished 3rd
Aug 11	Terre Haute, IN	USAC sprint car	#9 Meskowski/Meskowksi-Chevy	started 7th, won
Aug 17	Springfield, IL	USAC championship	#5 Hopkins/Kuzma-Offy	started 3rd, DNF, magneto
Aug 18	Milwaukee, WI	USAC championship	#5 Hopkins/Epperly-Offy	started 12th, DNF, differential
Aug 25	New Bremen, OH	USAC sprint car	#9 Meskowski/Meskowski-Chevy	started 4th, finished 2nd
Aug 31	DuQuoin, IL	USAC sprint car	#5 Hopkins/Kuzma-Offy	started 2nd, finished 2nd
Sep 1	Kansas City, KS	USAC sprint car	#9 Meskowski/Meskowski-Chevy	DNQ, arm injury in heat
Sep 2	DuQuoin, IL	USAC championship	#5 Hopkins/Kuzma-Offy	started 8th, finished 4th
Sep 14	Indiana State Fairgrounds	USAC championship	#5 Hopkins/Kuzma-Offy	DNQ, piston
Sep 15	Reading, PA	USAC sprint car	#9 Meskowski/Meskowski-Chevy	qualified 3rd, did not start
Sep 21	Allentown, PA	USAC sprint car	#9 Meskowski/Meskowski-Chevy	started 12th, finished 11th
Sep 22	Trenton, NJ	USAC championship	#5 Hopkins/Epperly-Offy	started 9th, DNF, throttle linkage
Oct 5	Williams Grove, PA	USAC sprint car	#9 Meskowski/Meskowski-Chevy	DNQ
Oct 6	Terre Haute, IN	USAC midgets	Nowicki-Offy	accident, drove Kenyon-Offy in feature, finished 9th
Oct 27	Sacramento, CA	USAC championship	#5 Hopkins/Kuzma-Offy	started 3rd, DNF, piston
Nov 17	Phoenix, AZ	USAC championship	#5 Hopkins/Kuzma-Offy	started 3rd, DNF, mechanical

15th in USAC championship points

1964

Feb 8	Daytona, FL	NASCAR Grand National	#06 Holman-Moody Ford	started 7th, finished 6th
Feb 21	Daytona, FL	NASCAR Grand National	#06 Holman-Moody Ford	started 7th, finished 8th
Feb 23	Daytona 500	NASCAR Grand National	#06 Holman-Moody Ford	started 16th, DNF, overheating
Mar 22	Phoenix, AZ	USAC championship	#17 Hopkins/Epperly-Offy	started 13th, finished 7th
Mar 29	Reading, PA	USAC sprint car	#5 McDermott-Chevy	started 10th, DNF, accident
Apr 5	Eldora, OH	USAC sprint car	#5 McDermott-Chevy	started 4th, finished 2nd
Apr 12	Williams Grove, PA	USAC sprint car	#5 McDermott-Chevy	DNQ
Apr 19	Trenton, NJ	USAC championship	#17 Hopkins/Epperly-Offy	started 5th, finished 3rd
Apr 26	Langhorne, PA	USAC stock car	#06 Ford	started 8th, DNF
May 3	Indianapolis Raceway Park	USAC stock car	#48 Rudy Hoerr Ford	finished 11th
May 30	Indianapolis 500	USAC championship	#51 Hopkins/Lotus-Ford	started 2nd, DNF, oil plug, led 33 laps
June 7	Milwaukee, WI	USAC championship	#17 Hopkins/Epperly-Offy	started 18th, DNF, engine
June 14	Terre Haute, IN	USAC sprint car	#1 Meskowski-Chevy	started 4th, finished 3rd
June 21	Langhorne, PA	USAC championship	#17 Hopkins/Kuzma-Offy	started 5th, finished 3rd
July 5	Eldora, OH	USAC sprint car	Clyde Gutzwiller-Chevy	DNQ
July 12	Milwaukee, WI	USAC stock car	#2 Vanda Hurst Ford	DNF, accident
July 18	Williams Grove, PA	USAC sprint car	Walter Beletsky-Offy	DNQ
July 19	Trenton, NJ	USAC championship	#51 Hopkins/Lotus-Ford	started 3rd, DNF, radius rod. Relieved Rodger Ward in #2 Wilke/Watson-Ford, DNF, out of fuel
July 20	Hatfield, PA	USAC sprint car	#9 Meskowski-Chevy	started 4th, finished 2nd
Aug 15	Allentown, PA	USAC sprint car	#9 Meskowski-Chevy	started 7th, finished 6th
Aug 16	Milwaukee, WI	USAC stock car	#2 Hurst Ford	started 9th, DNF, accident
Aug 20	Milwaukee, WI	USAC stock car	#2 Hurst Ford	started 8th, DNF, engine
Aug 22	Springfield, IL	USAC championship	#17 Hopkins/Kuzma-Offy	started 2nd, finished 2nd
Aug 23	Milwaukee, WI	USAC championship	#51 Hopkins/Lotus-Ford	started 7th, DNF, engine
Aug 29	Eldora, OH	USAC midgets	#4 Wilke/Leader Card-Offy	started 2nd, won
Aug 30	Springfield, IL	USAC stock car	#2 Hurst Ford	started 3rd, won
Sep 5	DuQuoin, IL	USAC midgets	#65 Mataka Bros-Offy	started 5th, finished 10th
Sep 6	DuQuoin, IL	USAC stock car	#2 Hurst Ford	started 5th, finished 3rd
Sep 7	DuQuoin, IL	USAC championship	#17 Hopkins/Kuzma-Offy	started 4th, finished 2nd
Sep 9	Indiana State Fairgrounds	USAC stock car	#2 Hurst Ford	started 1st, finished 3rd
Sep 13	Langhorne, PA	USAC stock car	#2 Zecol-Lubaid Ford	started 6th, finished 2nd
Sep 20	Milwaukee, WI	USAC stock car	Roger Regeth Ford	started 18th, DNF, engine
Sep 26	Indiana State Fairgrounds	USAC championship	#17 Hopkins/Kuzma-Offy	started 2nd, DNF, torsion bar. Drove relief for Len Sutton in Walter Flynn's Flynn-Offy, finished 8th
Sep 27	Trenton, NJ	USAC championship	#51 Hopkins/Lotus-Ford	started 3rd, DNF, ignition
Oct 4	Wentzville, MO	USAC stock car	Zecol-Lubaid Ford	started 5th, finished 14th after accident
Oct 11	Terre Haute, IN	USAC midget	#4 Wilke/Leader Card-Offy	started 8th, finished 7th
Oct 25	Sacramento, CA	USAC championship	#17 Hopkins/Kuzma-Offy	started 6th, finished 2nd
Nov 22	Phoenix, AZ	USAC championship	#51 Hopkins/Lotus-Ford	started 10th, DNF, suspension

7th in USAC championship points

In a good mood ready for some practice laps at Indianapolis in 1964 with the Pure Oil Lotus-Ford.